THE PSYCHOLOGY OF
CONCENTRATION IN SPORT
PERFORMERS

The Psychology of Concentration in Sport Performers
A Cognitive Analysis

Aidan P. Moran
Department of Psychology
University College, Dublin
The National University of Ireland

Psychology Press
Taylor & Francis Group

HOVE AND NEW YORK

Published in 1996 by Psychology Press Ltd
27 Church Road, Hove, East Sussex, BN3 2FA

http://www.psypress.co.uk

Reprinted 2004 and 2006

Psychology Press Ltd, Publishers
27 Church Road, Hove, East Sussex, BN3 2FA
270 Madison Avenue, New York NY10016

Psychology Press is part of the Taylor & Francis Group, an informa business

British Library Cataloguing in Publication Data
A catalogue record for this book is available from the British Library

ISBN10: 0-86377-444-X (Pbk)
ISBN13: 978-0-86377-444-7 (Pbk)

Cover design by Peter Richards
Cover photograph by Helene Rogers, TRIP Photographic Library
Printed and bound in the UK by TJ International Ltd, Padstow, Cornwall
This publication has been produced with paper manufactured to strict
environmental standards and with pulp derived from sustainable forests.

To my mother, Nora Moran, who
showed me through her love and support
that

"Ní neart go cur le chéile"
("Unity is strength")

Contents

Preface xi
Acknowledgements xv

Section One: Cognitive sport psychology 1

1. **Cognition, psychology and sport: Mental factors in athletic performance 3**

   Introduction 3
   Cognitive processes in athletes 4
   Cognition, cognitive psychology and cognitive science 6
   Influence of cognitive psychology on sport psychology 12
   Expertise in sport performers: Hardware or software? 23
   A challenge to cognition in sport: Direct perception theory 27
   Can cognitive psychology benefit from research in sport? 32
   Summary 35

2. **Understanding attention: The psychology of concentration 37**

Introduction 37
What is attention? Nature, characteristics and
   metaphors 39
A brief history of research on attention 43
Types of attention 46
Theories of attention 52
Attention as a skill 57
Summary 62

Section 2: Concentration in Sport 65

3. **Concentration in sport performance 67**

Introduction 68
Nature and importance of "concentration"
   in sport 70
Research on concentration in sport 77
Selective attention in athletes 78
Divided attention in athletes 86
Implications of research on concentration
   in sport 91
Summary 97

4. **Losing concentration in sport: External and internal distractions 101**

Introduction 102
What is "distraction"? 103
Why does the mind tend to wander? 105
General effects of distractors 107
Distractions in sport: Internal and external 109
External distractions 110
Internal distractions: How mental factors affect
   concentration 121
Summary 130

5. **Measuring attentional processes in athletes: From brain states to individual differences 133**

Introduction 133
Psychophysiological measurement techniques 134
Measuring attention experimentally: The
    dual-task paradigm 140
Measuring attention through self-report
    procedures 141
Nideffer's theory of attentional styles 142
Attentional processes in marathon runners 150
Attentional sub-scales in psychological skills
    inventories 158
Summary 161

Section 3: Concentration Techniques 165

6. **Improving concentration in sport, I: Assumptions, exercise and techniques 167**

Introduction 168
Assumptions of mental skills training
    programmes 169
Concentration exercises and techniques 170
Goal-setting as a concentration strategy 174
Pre-performance routines as concentration
    strategies 176
Arousal-control as a concentration technique 183
Arousal enhancement strategies as concentration
    techniques 192
Instructional self-talk as a concentration
    technique 194
Efficacy of attentional skills training
    programmes 198
Summary 199

7. **Improving concentration in sport, II: Mental practice 201**

Introduction 202
What is "mental practice"? 203

History of research on mental practice 204
Does mental practice work? Claims and
   evidence 206
Efficacy of mental practice: Conclusions and
   cautions 212
Theories of mental practice effects 217
Mental practice and attention 225
Mental practice as a concentration technique 229
Summary 230

Section 4: Integration 233

8. **Concentration in sport performers: Implications and new
    directions 235**

Introduction 235
Benefits of research on concentration in sport
   performers 236
New directions in the field 243
Summary 261

References 263

Author Index 297

Subject Index 310

Preface

The capacity to concentrate effectively is widely regarded as a vital pre-requisite of successful performance in all sports. For example, interviews with top-class "sport performers" (a term I shall use interchangeably with "athletes") reveal the importance to competitors of being mentally ready for, and "focused" on, the specific challenges posed by forthcoming encounters (see Chapter 3). Indeed, the word "focused" is often used synonymously with "concentration" to designate a state of effortless absorption which usually accompanies moments of sporting excellence. This state of mind is desirable because, as coaches and sport psychologists remind us, no amount of technical talent or physical fitness can compensate for a propensity to be easily distracted in sport situations. Although anecdotal in nature, these observations illuminate the importance to athletes of paying attention to the sporting task at hand while disregarding irrelevant stimulation. Surprisingly, however, nobody has yet published an academic book devoted exclusively to this skill of concentration in sport performers. In attempting to fill this gap in the literature, I set out to obtain research-based answers to a number of key questions in this field. For example, what exactly is "concentration"? Why do athletes often "lose" it, paradoxically, at the very time they need it most? Can it be measured and improved? If so, how? More generally, what does research on athletes' attentional processes reveal to us about how the mind works? Unfortunately, until now, these questions have remained unanswered due to two main problems - the atheoretical nature of research in sport psychology and the reluctance of cognitive psychologists to explore how the mind works under the real-life pressures and distractions that pervade the domain of sport. I propose to overcome these difficulties by analysing the attentional processes of athletes from a cognitive perspective (hence the phrase "cognitive analysis" in the sub-title of this book).

This monograph is intended as a reference source for anyone (particularly, upper-level students and post-graduate researchers in sport psychology, sport science and cognitive psychology) who is intrigued by the cognitive processes of athletes or the "mental side" of sport. In particular, I hope to convince you that exploration of this relatively uncharted realm is rewarding for both theoretical and practical reasons. For example, at a theoretical level, the study of mental processes (such as attention) in athletes may give cognitive psychologists a new testing ground for research on such important topics as how emotional factors (e.g. anxiety) affect skilled performance. In other words, sport offers an exciting new domain for the sub-discipline of applied cognitive psychology. At a practical level, research on the efficacy of various concentration techniques in sport will help to establish psychological guidelines for athletes and coaches on how to optimise preparation for competitive performance. My assumption here is that intervention programmes in applied sport psychology should, ideally, be based on sound empirical principles rather than on intuitive speculation. In summary, just as the construct of attention links thought and action, research on the topic of concentration in athletes allows us to build a bridge between cognitive theory and applied sport psychology. Throughout this book, therefore, I shall argue that the benefits of increased collaboration between cognitive and sport psychology are mutual. Intellectual "traffic" will flow in both directions across this new bridge built by the scientific study of concentration in sport performers.

In retrospect, two specific issues prompted me to write this book. First, as a cognitive psychologist, I was puzzled by the failure of textbooks on cognition to refer to any aspect of athletic behaviour or sporting experience in their coverage of the relationship between attention and skilled performance. I found this omission disconcerting because attention is a psychological construct that refers explicitly to the relationship between mental effort and physical action—and sport offers an ideal opportunity to investigate this relationship. However, the attentional research that is typically covered in cognitive textbooks is derived mainly from laboratory-based experimental paradigms which tend to ignore "internal" influences (i.e. potential distractions arising from unhelpful thoughts or emotions) on skilled performance. In short, cognitive psychology appears to have neglected important cognitive substrates of athletic performance. I encountered my second disappointment when, as Official Psychologist to the Irish Olympic Squad, I reviewed the popular literature in sport psychology on concentration training for athletes. Briefly, few authors in this field provided any theoretical justification or empirical evidence to support the claims which they promulgated about the nature and "trainability" of concentration skills. At the very least, this oversight indicated that their advice in this domain was somewhat premature. In combination, these twin disappointments encouraged me to write a monograph which would attempt to provide a scholarly yet accessible analysis of concentration processes in athletes.

This book is divided into four sections. Section 1 (Chapters 1 and 2) is devoted to the topic of "Cognitive Sport Psychology". In it, I trace the intellectual and historical background to the study of mental factors in athletic performance (Chapter 1) and summarise briefly what is known by cognitive psychologists about the construct of attention (Chapter 2). Although Chapter 1 deals mainly with how cognitive psychological principles have influenced sport scientists' theories of skill learning and athletic expertise, some influences in the reverse direction are also examined. Specifically, this chapter concludes with the possibility that research on mental aspects of sport may enhance cognitive psychological theories. I return to this theme in Chapter 8. Section 2 (Chapters 3-5) addresses the theme of "Concentration in Sport". Thus Chapter 3 presents a review of psychological research on the concentration processes of athletes. This chapter focuses particularly on such topics as selective and divided attentional skills in sport performers. It concludes by highlighting some theoretical implications of this research (e.g. the idea that attention may be regarded as a skill that can be improved). Chapter 4 is devoted to an analysis of why athletes often "lose" their concentration in competitive settings. Following a theoretical discussion of why the mind tends to "wander" at all, I explore a variety of "external" (i.e. environmental) and "internal" (i.e. subjective) factors which may distract athletes from their intended thoughts or actions. In Chapter 5, I consider the issue of how attentional processes in athletes can be assessed empirically. In particular, I evaluate a variety of measures of concentration that are derived from psychophysiological, experimental and self-report paradigms. Special consideration is devoted to paper-and-pencil tests of concentration processes. In addition, as a case-study, this chapter examines the strengths and limitations of the attentional strategies used by athletes in endurance-events (e.g. marathon runners). Section 3 of the book (Chapters 6 and 7) is entitled "Concentration Techniques" and provides a critical review of the efficacy of a range of psychological exercises and techniques which are alleged by sport psychologists to improve concentration skills in athletes. Among the putative concentration strategies examined here are goal-setting, pre-performance routines, arousal-control techniques, cue-words (a form of instructional self-talk) and mental practice (or "visualisation"). The final section of the book, called "Integration", outlines some recurrent themes and potential new directions in research on concentration in athletes. In an effort to make the material more accessible to non-specialist readers, I include in these chapters a variety of anecdotes and examples from the world of sport. Wherever possible, precise reference sources are indicated for this material.

Acknowledgements

Most of the research for this book was conducted while I held a Fulbright Scholarship to visit the following institutions in the United States: the US Olympic Training Centre (USOC; Colorado Springs), the University of Florida (Gainesville) and the Cognitive Science Institute of the State University of New York (SUNY) in Buffalo. I am deeply indebted to the Fulbright Commission for this award and also to Dr. Sean McCann (USOC), Dr. Shane Murphy (formerly USOC), Dr. Roger Whitehead (University of Colorado, Denver) and Prof. Robert Singer (University of Florida) for their generous advice, support and encouragement throughout my visit. Other staff in the University of Florida who helped me enormously were Drs. Pat and Mary Bird, Prof. Paula Welch and Ms. Diane Williams. I am also very grateful to University College, Dublin (UCD), and to my colleagues and friends, Prof. Ciaran Benson (Dept. of Psychology) and Dr. Fergus D'Arcy (Dean of Faculty of Arts) for supporting my request for sabbatical leave to conduct the research for this book. Furthermore, I wish to acknowledge the invaluable financial support which I received for this project from the President's Award (UCD) and from the Revenue Committee of the Faculty of Arts. The editorial support of Mr. Michael Forster and Ms. Jane Charman (both of Psychology Press), the continuous encouragement provided by my colleagues and friends, Prof. Bill Mikulas (University of West Florida) and Prof. Brian Mullen (Syracuse University, New York), the meticulous research assistance of Ms. Karen Lyons and the technical advice of Mr. John Conboy are also recorded with sincere gratitude. Next, I wish to express my gratitude to Dr. John Kremer (The Queen's University of Belfast), Dr. Deirdre Scully (University of Ulster, Jordanstown) and to various anonymous reviewers for their constructive criticism and suggestions. Finally, I wish to thank my mother, Nora, my brothers, Ciaran and Dermot, my sister, Patricia, and my friends (especially, Aine, Aisling, Brendan (Prof), Brendan and Neil) for their enthusiastic support for my work at all times.

SECTION ONE

Cognitive sport psychology

Recent years have witnessed increasing interest among athletes, coaches and psychologists in mental aspects of sport performance (e.g. the use of "visualisation" or "mental practice" to enhance skilled actions). In this section (which comprises Chapters 1 and 2), I shall explore the background to and implications of this movement known as "cognitive sport psychology", or the scientific study of cognitive processes in athletes. To begin with, in Chapter 1, I shall explain how the information processing paradigm of cognitive psychology has influenced the theoretical models used by contemporary sport scientists to understand such topics as skill-representation (discussed briefly) and athletic expertise (treated to a more detailed analysis). The challenge which "direct perception" theory offers to the hegemony of this paradigm will then be reviewed. In the final part of this chapter, I address a recurrent theme of this book by sketching some possible ways in which cognitive theory can benefit from research in the domain of sport.

One of the most important topics in cognitive sport psychology is the study of how athletes manage to concentrate on the sporting task at hand while ignoring a profusion of distractions. In order to understand this remarkable skill, we need to explore the way in which our mental "focusing" system works. Therefore Chapter 2 is devoted to a review of the psychology of "attention" or the capacity to focus mental effort on sensory or mental events. It includes coverage of such topics as the nature, characteristics and types of attentional processes as well as analysis of the main theoretical models that have been developed in this field. It concludes with the idea that attention may be viewed as a skill which is enhanced through practice.

CHAPTER ONE

Cognition, psychology and sport: Mental factors in athletic performance

"The mind is sport sciences' last frontier"

(Straub, 1978, p. 1)

INTRODUCTION

Competitive sport provides psychologists with many fascinating opportunities to explore the success with which people can control their own mental processes in the face of adversity. Indeed, some psychologists (e.g. Kirschenbaum, 1984) claim that competitive sport is almost *entirely* an exercise in cognitive and behavioural "self-regulation". To illustrate contrasting aspects of this psychological skill, consider two sporting incidents which captured popular imagination around the world in January 1995. The first incident occurred during the quarter-final match of the Australian Open Tennis Championship in Melbourne between the tournament favourite, Pete Sampras, and his main rival, Jim Courier. In the fifth set of this four-hour match, Sampras suddenly broke down in tears after he had learned that his coach, Tim Gullikson, had suffered a suspected brain tumour. Although such concern for the health of one's coach is understandable, what surprised many observers was that Sampras' distress did not appear to hinder his performance on court. In fact, statistics reveal that he conceded only *two points* on his serve for the remainder of the fifth set even though he wept

3

repeatedly during rallies and at the "change-overs" between games. This remarkable disjunction between emotion and behaviour illustrates not only the "automaticity" (see Chapter 2) of Sampras' tennis skills, but also the fact that athletes must learn to suppress *self*-generated (or "internal") distractions in order to perform successfully (see also Chapter 4). But what happens if sport performers lose their mental discipline? This possibility leads us to our second vignette. The incident in this case concerned the brilliant but volatile soccer player, Eric Cantona (of Manchester United and France). Following a "sending off" offence in a league match, Cantona reacted to a taunt from a spectator by leaping over the crowd barrier and launching a "kung fu" kick at him. As a result of this bizarre loss of control, the player was fined by his club, banned by the English Football Association for the rest of the season and required to perform a period of "community service" as restitution for his offence. Clearly, this unprecedented incident reveals a lamentable lack of self-regulation in an otherwise gifted athlete. It also illuminates the wisdom of Straub's (1978) observation that the mind of the athlete is the last frontier for research in sport science.

These dramatic incidents involving two of the world's greatest athletes raise the two important questions that underlie this book. What factors (including thoughts and emotions) serve to distract us from our intended actions? Perhaps more importantly, how can we learn to ignore these distractions and improve our concentration? It is interest- ing to note that questions of this nature are currently receiving research attention, outside the sphere of sport, in the emerging fields of "mental control" (Wegner & Pennebaker, 1993) and "self-regulation" (Karoly, 1993). In these domains, psychologists are beginning to examine people's mundane struggle to regulate their thoughts and emotions in everyday life. The activities in question here involve attempts to "suppress a thought, concentrate on a sensation, inhibit an emotion, stir up a desire, squelch a craving, or otherwise exert an influence on their own mental states" (Wegner & Pennebaker, 1993). Clearly, if paying attention is viewed as an effort to exert control over what we perceive and do, then the study of concentration in athletes offers a potentially fruitful new avenue for the study of how the mind works.

COGNITIVE PROCESSES IN ATHLETES

Over the past decade, there has been a rapid growth of interest in the mental processes of competitive athletes. This interest is reflected in the upsurge of cognitive research in sport psychology (see overview by Abernethy, 1994b) and in the proliferation of applied "mental skills" training programmes for sport performers (see Chapter 6). Furthermore, an increasing awareness of the "mental side" of sport is evident from interviews with many professional athletes. For example, Alan Kelly, the Sheffield United soccer goalkeeper, explained after his competitive debut for the Republic of Ireland in 1994 that he "didn't have a lot to do in that game but when I came off I was drenched with sweat as much as rain. And that was all down to concentration. Packie (Bonner) had warned me about this beforehand: It's one of the biggest differences when you jump up from league to international football" (Mackey, 1994, p. 38). Clearly, this performer understood that the transition from club-level to international-level sporting competition is accompanied by increased *mental* as well as physical effort. The exertion of this type of mental effort is known as "concentration" (see Chapter 2). The importance of mental factors in sport was also underlined by Mike Marsh, the American champion sprinter, who claimed that the ability to win comes "90% from the mind and 10% from the body" (Chadband, 1995). Taken together, these remarks underline the importance of effective psychological preparation for athletes. Therefore, perhaps Loehr (1989) was more perceptive than Straub (1978) when he observed that "the area of *mental training* is the last frontier of sport research" (italics mine). Clearly, one reason for the popularity of such training is that in competitive sport, where hundredths of a second may separate winners from the rest, "the extra edge which proper mental preparation can give an athlete is a precious and much sought-after commodity" (Murphy, 1990). Of course, another appeal of mental training is that it offers athletes a desirable alternative to the illegal use of certain "banned" drugs (e.g. steroids and "beta-blockers") which are alleged to enhance performance.

Given the importance of mental preparation for optimal sporting performance, it is not really surprising that the study of cognitive processes in athletes is now a "hot topic" in sport science. To illustrate, over the past few years, sport psychologists have conducted research on such "cognitive" areas as attention (Abernethy, 1993), memory (Smyth & Pendleton, 1994), perception (Garland & Barry, 1991), mental imagery (Murphy, 1994), attributional processes (Hanrahan, 1995) and decision making (Tenenbaum & Bar-Eli, 1993). In addition, special issues of the *International Journal of Sport Psychology* have been devoted recently to such cognitive themes as "Information Processing and Decision Making in Sport" (Ripoll, 1991) and to "Expert-Novice Differences in Sport" (Abernethy, 1994b). It is regrettable that this research is rarely cited by contemporary cognitive psychologists (e.g. Hampson & Morris, 1996). Perhaps these researchers view sport solely as a leisure activity and are unaware either of its mental aspects or its potential value as a testing ground for cognitive theories. In this regard, I shall argue that the study of attention in sport performers enables us to investigate the relationship between cognition and action—a topic that has been neglected somewhat by cognitive science. Support for my proposal comes from theorists such as Adams (1987) who criticised cognitive research for being "preoccupied with disembodied perceptions and higher processes, and indifferently concerned with translating perceptions and higher processes into 'action'" (p. 66). As we shall see in Chapter 2, attention is the bridge between cognition and action. Therefore, the study of attentional processes in athletes helps us to establish a link between cognitive psychology and sport psychology.

The purpose of this chapter is to forge an alliance between cognitive and sport psychology. It is organised as follows. To begin with, I shall explain the terms "cognition", "cognitive psychology" and "cognitive science". Then, I shall outline some influences of cognitive theory and research on contemporary sport psychology. Next, I shall examine the challenge which "direct perception" theory (or the "dynamical systems" approach; see review in Clark, 1995) poses to cognitive accounts of motor skill learning. Finally, I shall consider some benefits to cognitive psychology that arise from research on performance in sport.

COGNITION, COGNITIVE PSYCHOLOGY AND COGNITIVE SCIENCE

So far, I have used the terms "cognition" and "cognitive psychology" somewhat loosely. A more precise analysis is now required. The term "cognition" (from the Latin "*cognoscere*", to know) refers to the activity or process of "knowing" (Wood, 1983) or to the tasks of gathering and making use of knowledge (Gellatly, 1986). In contemporary usage, "cognition" has been used as a synonym for "mental activity" (Matlin, 1994), thinking (Anderson, 1995b) or "information processing" (Lachman, Lachman, & Butterfield, 1979). For our purposes, therefore, "cognition" refers to any mental activity which is involved in obtaining, storing or using knowledge (including skilled behaviour).

According to Aristotle, our "knowing" capacities (e.g. problem solving) may be distinguished from our "affective" (feeling) and "conative" (willing) activities. This tri-partite view of the mind was also endorsed by the "faculty" psychologists of the 18th century (Hilgard, 1980). For these theorists, the mind contained three faculties: "cognition" (knowing), "conation" (voluntary or intentional activity) and "affect" (emotion). However, since the adoption of the "information processing" paradigm in the 1960s, modern psychologists have focused almost exclusively on cognitive processes, thereby neglecting other aspects of mental life. This oversight means that researchers who investigate cognition "tend to avoid the topics of motivation and emotion" (Eysenck, 1993). Unfortunately, this neglect of non-cognitive factors has led to a rather sterile and constrained approach to understanding how the mind works. For example, Claxton (1980) caricatured contemporary cognitive research by arguing that its typical subject "does not feel hungry or tired or inquisitive; it does not think extraneous thoughts or try to understand what is going on. It is, in short, a computer". Happily, many psychologists now acknowledge this criticism—and see the study of attention as the ideal means of uniting "hot" and "cold" mental processes. H.A. Simon, the pioneering cognitive scientist, admitted recently that "we need to reconnect cognition with affect and motivation, probably via the mechanisms that determine the focus of attention" (Simon, 1995). Interestingly, this idea has been investigated in clinical psychology where Mathews (1993) has reviewed evidence which indicates that emotional states (e.g. anxiety) influence the manner in which attentional resources are allocated within the cognitive system. I shall return to this idea in Chapter 3 and in Chapter 8.

If "cognition" means "knowledge seeking", then "cognitive psychology" is the scientific study of this human activity. More generally, this term refers to a modern branch of the discipline of psychology which seeks to obtain empirical answers to the venerable question of how the mind works (Casey & Moran, 1989). Specifically, it may be defined as the scientific study of mental activity or human information processing. Therefore, cognitive psychologists are concerned with explaining the "internal" processes by which people acquire, store and use their knowledge (including skills or "procedural" knowledge) in everyday life (Neisser, 1967). These internal processes are the means by which current stimulus input is combined with past experience. The subject matter of cognitive psychology, therefore, comprises such "knowledge-seeking" processes as attention, memory, problem solving, concept formation and decision making. Although psychological interest in such mental phenomena is at least a century old (e.g. James, 1890, defined psychology as the "science of mental life"), the formal birth of modern cognitive psychology is often traced to a specific date: 11th September, 1956. At this time, the world's first conference on cognition was held at the Massachusetts Institute of Technology.

The term "cognitive science" has become increasingly popular in recent years. Although this term has acquired many meanings (see Estes, 1991), it can be defined most generally as an inter-disciplinary movement that is concerned with the study of human intelligence in all of its forms (Osherson & Lasnik, 1990). This movement comprises cognitive psychology, neuroscience, artificial intelligence, anthropology, linguistics and philosophy. One of its central tenets is the proposition that the mind is a computational system with three major components (McShane, Dockerell, & Wells, 1992): "cognitive architecture" (i.e. the fixed structure of the cognitive system), "mental representations" (i.e. different formats for the storage of knowledge) and "cognitive processes" (which manipulate these representations). In general, cognitive scientists are concerned with such issues as the nature, development and use of knowledge (Matlin, 1994). They tend to investigate these topics using "computational modelling" techniques whereby working models of human cognitive processes are tested using computer simulations (Eysenck & Keane, 1995). Although they are strongly interested in the mental representation of knowledge, cognitive scientists are less concerned with the behavioural consequences of cognition than are cognitive psychologists.

For many commentators (e.g. Gardner, 1985), the rise of cognitive psychology and cognitive science is acclaimed as a *revolution* in 20th century psychology: revolution which was hastened by three key developments between 1940 and 1960. First, Chomsky (1959) demonstrated logically that Behaviourism, the dominant paradigm in psychology between the 1920s and the 1950s, was inadequate for the task of explaining how people understand and acquire one of our most important cognitive attributes—language. Second, the development of "communication theory" (Shannon & Weaver, 1949) raised the idea that people may be regarded as "channels" through which information "flows". Third, the advent of digital computers provided psychologists with the metaphor of the mind as a general-purpose, computational system (see Casey & Moran, 1989). The essence of this view is the notion that thinking is a form of "computation" in which knowledge is manipulated symbolically according to formal rules or "programs". Neisser (1967) proposed that the task of exploring human cognition is analogous to "trying to understand how a computer has been programmed". In combination, these influences heralded the symbolic "information processing" approach to cognition which was to become the standard paradigm in cognitive psychology (see Lachman, Lachman, & Butterfield, 1979 for details) until the advent of "connectionism" (discussed later).

Briefly, the central tenet of the information processing paradigm is the view that the mind is a representational system. It does not store knowledge or experiences directly. Instead, it stores *symbolic* representations of these phenomena. Through cognitive activity, the mind actively transforms these symbolic representations over time (i.e.

during the period between stimulus detection and response execution) through "thinking". In short "thinking" involves the manipulation of internal representations of the external world. Therefore, all cognitive processes (e.g. memory) may be regarded as a series of hypothetical stages during which unique transformations are performed on incoming sensory information (Solso, 1995). To illustrate, in order to remember the name of someone to whom one is introduced at a party, one must "encode" the name in working memory (e.g. by repeating it aloud—an acoustic representation), "store" it in some meaningful format in long-term memory (e.g. by labelling a mental image with the appropriate name) and be able to "retrieve" it later using some recall cue (e.g. the person's face). In this way, the symbolic representation of the person's name has been transformed through a sequence of stages from a sound, to an image and, finally, to a verbal response elicited by a social cue (e.g. when someone else joins the conversation, one is expected to introduce one's new acquaintance to them). Of course, such "stage analyses" of cognitive processes are not the only way of exploring mental life. As an alternative, we could explore cognitive processes in terms of the different types of *knowledge* which they require. For example, we can distinguish between people's knowledge of general facts and rules ("semantic knowledge"), specific personal experiences ("episodic knowledge") and non-verbal skills ("procedural knowledge"). These three types of knowledge interact continuously in daily life. Consider the activity of playing a game of tennis with a friend. Successful play demands all three types of knowledge at different times. For example, in order to play tennis properly, one must be able to understand the rules of the game (semantic knowledge), keep track of the score (episodic knowledge) and, of course, hit the ball over the net (procedural knowledge). This example shows that cognitive psychology is concerned with analysis of the knowledge base of many everyday processes.

Theoretically, the information processing approach to cognition is based on at least five key assumptions (Best, 1995; Eysenck, 1993). First, as I indicated earlier, knowledge is held to be represented symbolically and processed by the mind in a series of cognitive systems (e.g. attention, memory). Second, these processing systems transform information in various ways (e.g. the symbol "a" on a sheet of paper is repeated subvocally in working memory as the sound "ay" before it is processed further). Third, cognitive processes are assumed to take time. Accordingly, inferences about mental organisation may be drawn from the comparative duration of various information processing activities (the "mental chronometry" assumption; Haberlandt, 1994). Fourth, the objective of cognitive research is to specify the structures and processes that underlie cognitive performance. As Barber (1988) proposed, information processing psychologists investigate mental activities "in terms of component processes and procedures". Finally, certain parallels are held to exist between the minds of people and the information processing activities of computers (both computers and minds can store information symbolically). In summary, the information processing approach to the mind provides an abstract, serial (step-by-step) analysis of cognitive processes. This approach has become known as the "symbolic approach" to human cognition (Eysenck & Keane, 1995). However, although it has been the predominant approach in cognitive psychology, the symbolic approach has been challenged over the last decade by an alternative view of the mind called "connectionism", "parallel distributed processing" (PDP) (McClelland, Rumelhart, & The PDP Research Group, 1986; Rumelhart, McClelland, & The PDP Research Group, 1986) or the "neural network" approach to cognition. This paradigm, which reflects a different computational modelling approach from its symbolic precursor, examines the behaviour of systems comprising inter-connected sets of simple processing units.

To simplify, PDP approaches suggest that the *brain*, rather than the digital computer, offers the most fruitful model of the mind (Rumelhart & Todd, 1993). In particular, connectionists argue that the mind is best understood as a dynamic collection of inter-connected neural units. These networks are held to comprise a vast number of simple processing units (each of which has a current state of "activation") linked together by a set of connections (each of which has a current strength or "weight"). One set of units is assigned the role of receiving inputs from the external world. The activation levels of these "input units" are influenced by external stimuli. Other sets of units reflect the "output" of the neural system. The activation of these units is determined more by "internal" processes. Interestingly, however, there is no reference to any symbolic knowledge base in this system. Instead, processing is held to involve a series of cycles. During these cycles, the neural units take on new states of activation as a function of their own prior activations, the activations of units to which they are connected and the weights (excitatory or inhibitory) of the inter-connecting links (Holyoak & Spellman, 1993).

In order to appreciate the general thrust of the parallel distributed processing paradigm, consider the key terms "parallel" and "distributed". Briefly, connectionists reject the "serial processing" hypothesis of traditional symbolic theory—the proposition that cognitive processes occur "one step at a time", just like the operations of a digital computer. This rejection is based on mounting evidence that many everyday mental activities occur so rapidly that they cannot be explained parsimoniously as the aggregate of a sequence of processing stages. For example, it has proved impossible for serial computers to simulate the human ability to recognise a face in only about 250–350 milliseconds (Haberlandt, 1994). This finding suggests that many of our cognitive activities are "parallel" rather than "serial" in nature. In addition, PDP models challenge the assumption from digital computer technology that knowledge is stored in some specific "address" in the mind. In connectionist models, knowledge is distributed across sets of units rather than stored in some central "executive" location. Clearly, this idea conflicts with the classical symbolic approach which claims that knowledge is encoded in a "production rule" (discussed later) which is represented centrally in the mind. The PDP approach also reflects a shift from theories that are "rich in process but short on knowledge to theories that are rich in knowledge but short in process" (Lohman, 1989).

In passing, however, it should be noted that although the symbolic and connectionist approaches to the mind are often presented as antagonistic perspectives, they may in fact be *complementary* because they operate at different conceptual levels. For example, Baddeley (1989) suggested that whereas symbol processing approaches to cognition are concerned largely with "cognitively penetrable" processes (i.e. those which are accessible to introspection and control, such as the direction of one's gaze), connectionism is attracted to "cognitively impenetrable" processes (which are neither consciously accessible nor modifiable, e.g. facial recognition). A similar distinction is made by Holyoak & Spellman (1993) who suggest that the symbolic and connectionist approaches to cognition correspond roughly to two different historical perspectives on thinking—the information processing and Gestalt paradigms. To explain, information processing researchers (e.g. Newell & Simon, 1972) were concerned with the mental rules and strategies by which people solved "well-defined" problems (i.e. ones which had a clear starting point and goal state). Conversely, Gestalt researchers (e.g. Duncker, 1945) were attracted to "ill-defined" problems which required parallel integration of knowledge from different domains.

So far, connectionist approaches to cognition have had relatively little impact on sport psychology. This is surprising in view of the fact that PDP models seem to be especially useful for the study of learning effects —a characteristic which should appeal to sport psychology researchers. For present purposes, it exceeds the scope of this chapter to provide further explanation of the PDP paradigm. Such information is readily available in Rumelhart & Todd (1993) and Quinlan (1991). However, there is at least one sport psychological topic, namely "contextual interference" (Shea & Morgan, 1979) which has attracted some interest recently from connectionists. I shall return to this issue briefly later in this chapter. But let us now consider two more pressing questions—what is sport psychology and how has it been influenced by cognitive approaches to the mind?

INFLUENCE OF COGNITIVE PSYCHOLOGY ON SPORT PSYCHOLOGY

For many theorists, "sport psychology" is a branch of applied psychology which involves the application of the principles and findings of psychology to sport settings (Cox, 1994). These sport settings comprise situations in which people compete against each other, usually through the medium of physical action, according to certain rules which result in one of the competitors being declared a winner (Allard & Starkes, 1991). This theme of becoming a winner has preoccupied many sport psychologists under the guise of "performance enhancement" (Hoberman, 1992).

Although sport psychology may appear to be a recent development, research on mental aspects of athletic performance is almost as old as psychology itself. For example, a century ago, Triplett (1898) discovered that cyclists tended to perform faster when competing against each other than when racing against the clock. He attributed this result to the capacity of an opponent to "liberate latent energy not ordinarily available". This research led to the discovery of the "social facilitation" principle in experimental social psychology. Briefly, this principle asserts that the mere presence of someone else (whether a fellow competitor or a spectator) tends to facilitate one's performance of simple or well-learned skills whereas it tends to impair the performance of skills that are either complex or poorly learned (see Guerin, 1993). Similarly, in the early part of this century, Judd (1908), Swift (1910) and Lashley (1915) conducted research on the determinants of such sport skills as ball-tossing and archery. However, despite such pioneering research, sport psychology did not emerge as an independent discipline until the 1960s (see Williams & Straub, 1993, for a brief review of the evolution of this discipline). This decade is important for two reasons. First, it witnessed the organisation of the first major conferences and professional societies in sport psychology (see review by Cox, Qiu, & Liu, 1993). In addition, it saw the emergence of a new approach to the study of the mind. This approach, which I mentioned earlier as the "information processing" paradigm (Neisser, 1967) soon became the standard approach in cognitive psychology. And as we shall see, this approach has influenced sport psychology significantly.

Given this confluence of the formal birth of sport psychology and the emergence of the cognitive paradigm, it is not surprising that research on athletes has been influenced significantly by cognitive theories (Singer, 1992; Zani & Rossi, 1991). This cognitive influence is reflected not only in the growing popularity of topics concerned with "athletes' thoughts and images" (Williams & Straub, 1993) but also in the emergence of such topics as "mental practice" (or the symbolic rehearsal of sport skills; see also Chapter 7). But we must be careful about our use of the term "cognitive" in sport psychology because it has been employed rather loosely in this discipline (as noted by Kremer & Scully, 1994). For example, McLean (1986) discussed such factors as "confidence" among athletes in his analysis of cognitive constructs in sport psychology. Unfortunately, this "lay" term is rather imprecise and is not found in the subject indices of any modern textbook of cognitive psychology. In view of these concerns, I shall restrict my analysis of "cognitive" themes in sport research to ideas which emphasise some form of "central" mental representation of athletic knowledge in performers. Using this criterion, I have identified a central theme in modern sport psychology. This theme, which stresses the role of knowledge representation in athletes' minds, has two components. First, sport skills are held to be "compiled" in athletes' long-term memories as an abstract "knowledge base". Second, it is believed that expertise in athletic performance is attributable more to aspects of this knowledge base (e.g. anticipatory strategies) than to any physical characteristics of the performer (Abernethy, Neal, & Koning, 1994). In other words, expert athletes appear to have a distinct "cognitive advantage" (Allard & Burnett, 1985) over less proficient counterparts. Let us now consider each of these propositions in more detail.

Skill representation: From schemata to production systems

Skilled performance involves the fluent and rapid production of complex movement sequences. But how are these sequences organised in the mind of the performer? In the Behaviourist era, skills were regarded as simple action-strings which were chained together by association. However, this theory was challenged by cognitive researchers who pointed out that theories based on associative-chaining cannot explain certain kinds of fast serial behaviour. For example, expert pianists can produce 20–30 successive note events per second (approximately one every 40 milliseconds) with each hand—a rate which is so fast that it precludes the possibility that feedback from one movement could affect the planning of its successor (Palmer & van de Sande, 1995). Based on such findings, most cognitive psychologists now believe that skills are represented "vertically", rather than "horizontally", in the mind (Reed, Montgomery, Palmer, & Pittenger, 1995). Perhaps the two most important "vertical" representational constructs are "schemas" (or perhaps more correctly, "schemata"; Bartlett, 1932; Schmidt, 1975) and "production systems" (Anderson, 1983; Anderson, 1995a). Before exploring these constructs, I should specify what the term "skill" means.

At first glance, a "skill" may be regarded as some aspect of performance that does not depend solely on one's innate capacities but which develops as a result of training or practice. However, it would be inaccurate to suggest that skills are simply synonymous with "learned behaviour". Such a definition omits two essential criteria of skills: economy and efficiency (Welford & Bourne, 1976). Taking account of these criteria, a "skill" may be said to represent a strategy for dealing with a specific task demand. In other words, it is essentially a form of *problem solving*. Thus Annett (1991) proposed that a "skill" is a piece of behaviour which is goal-directed, organised and acquired through training and practice rather than through innate factors. More generally, he uses the term "skill" to designate a behavioural solution to a behavioural problem. From this perspective, skilled performance, regardless of whether it involves passing a ball, driving a car or playing a game of chess, confronts people with a problem-solving situation which requires the usage of certain kinds of knowledge in order to achieve a specific goal.

Other theorists agree that skilled behaviour is rooted in problem solving. For example, Anderson (1995a) suggests that the "problem" for which skills are a solution is that of translating an intention into an autonomous action. It is precisely this focus on intentions which reveals the influence of cognitive theory on motor learning research. As Allard & Burnett (1985) concluded, "if intentions are the guiding elements for the motor system, the importance of cognition to sport skill becomes more apparent". However, we must be careful not to accept too readily Anderson's claim that skill learning is nothing more than the conversion of declarative or factual knowledge (i.e. what we can report or describe, "knowing that") into procedural knowledge ("knowing how" —knowledge which we manifest through what we do). After all, as Berry & Broadbent (1984) pointed out, we cannot describe all that we can do and, conversely, we cannot do all that we can describe. If skills are indeed a form of problem-solving behaviour, then how is the procedural knowledge on which they are based represented in people's minds? This concern with the "knowledge base" of sport skills reflects the dominance of the information processing tradition in sport psychology.

In the last century, during the associationist reign, motor (including sport) skills were regarded as "habits" that had been learned through "response chains" (see historical review by Adams, 1990). In particular, theorists like Bain (1868) proposed that the response-produced stimuli that occur as a result of a movement segment become associated with contiguous movements through a mechanism called "habit connection". Unfortunately, this approach quickly encountered a major theoretical difficulty. How can we store all of the unique habits that are associated with all conceivable movements?

In an effort to resolve this classical "storage problem" (Adams, 1990), cognitive theories replaced behaviourist approaches to skill learning by postulating central mental representation of skills (Masson, 1990). The most influential of these representational constructs are "schemata" (Bartlett, 1932; Schmidt, 1975) and "production systems" (Anderson, 1983)—both of which will be discussed later. Briefly, these constructs try to solve the storage problem by suggesting that the mind represents *generic* movements, rather than unique "habits". For example, experienced tennis players may store a schema of a "typical" serve, filling in the particular details of specific strokes (e.g. slice, top-spin) as the occasion demands. In other words, schemata have "slots" which may be filled with different values depending on contextual factors (Rumelhart & Norman, 1983). Likewise, such players may use highly practised "IF-THEN" rules called "productions" to decide what shots to play in certain situations. For example, most experienced tennis players know that "cross-court" shots should be returned cross-court rather than "down the line". Incidentally, a production may be regarded as a procedural unit of knowledge. Let us now consider schemata and production systems in more detail.

Although many definitions of "schema" exist (see Eysenck & Keane, 1995), a standard view of this construct is that it is a mental representation which encapsulates our knowledge (including skills) about some recurrent object, event or action. Therefore, "schemata" (plural of schema) are abstract, generic memory representations which contain generalised sets of rules or procedures that act as plans for future actions. Although "schematic" motor behaviour shares certain characteristics with other intentional cognitive activities (e.g. planning a journey), it differs in at least two important ways (Wright, 1990). First, the execution of a motor program results in overt physical activity. This is not always the case with other cognitive plans (e.g. writing a book!). Second, due to their automatic character, schematic actions are inaccessible to conscious introspection (and hence may be called "cognitively impenetrable" processes). Again, this is rarely the case with other forms of planned behaviour.

Introduced early in this century (Head, 1920), the Greek term "schema" is most often associated with Bartlett (1932) who defined it as "an active organisation of past reactions or past experiences, which must always be supposed to be operating in any well-adapted organic response". This term was invoked to explain the fact that when people try to remember stories that they have heard, they tend to introduce certain distortions and rationalisations which reflect their prior knowledge about the material in question. According to Bartlett (1932), these distortions indicate that people re-construct their memories in accordance with what they already know or believe. In other words, when we try to recall things, we re-build our memories in the light of current "schematic" knowledge. Furthermore, Bartlett (1932) believed that schemata govern procedural (i.e. skilled) as well as declarative knowledge. For example, he suggested that when people play a shot in tennis or cricket, "the stroke is literally manufactured out of the living visual and postural 'schemata' of the moment and their interrelationships". In general, therefore, a tennis player does not have to learn a different habit for all possible serves but instead must acquire a few basic schemata that can be tailored to meet the requirements of different circumstances. In other words, all skills are knowledge intensive (see also Anderson, 1995a).

Inspired by the ideas of Bartlett (1932), modern motor learning theorists (e.g. Schmidt, 1975) postulate that the repeated practice of a specific movement pattern (e.g. typing a string of letters, serving a tennis ball) creates a generic mental representation known as a "schema" or "motor program" (note the explicit use of a computational metaphor here). In simple terms, this program is a pre-packaged sequence of actions (Anderson, 1995a). For example, observe how a skilled touch-typist behaves when typing the word "the". While using the left index finger to type the letter "t", the right index finger is "programmed" to go to the letter "h". These two actions are almost simultaneous. Conversely, a novice typist will execute the keystrokes for the letters "t" and "h" in separate movements. There will be a time-lag as the typist waits to receive feedback from one action before commencing the next keystroke. Interestingly, high-speed film evidence shows that skilled typists look well ahead of the text they are typing at a particular moment (Ericsson & Charness, 1994). The motor program, therefore, serves as a repository of the procedural knowledge that underlies fluent, skilful activity. Accordingly, a "schema" is the bridge between the processes of planning and control. But how exactly is this bridge formed?

In the opinion of Schmidt (1988), the learner develops two representations of the skill in question. The first representation is the "recall" schema which is the motor program itself (i.e. the pre-packaged action sequence). But the second representation, called the "recognition" schema, stores the anticipated outcome of the action. Crucially, Schmidt believes that the recall memory is improved by comparing the action produced with an internal standard (in the recognition memory) of what the action should be like. Therefore, the motor program may be adjusted or "tuned" for different circumstances through cognitive intervention. As Anderson (1995a) puts it, "we learn what the appropriate execution of a motor program is like and use this knowledge to correct this program". According to Schmidt (1975), therefore, a person learning a sport skill stores four aspects of the movement involved in their recall schema: (i) the initial conditions, (ii) the parameters assigned to a generalised motor program (e.g. force, speed), (iii) the knowledge of results provided by the environment following the action, and (iv) the sensory consequences of the action. These data are stored temporarily while the learner extracts from them various sets of relationships. Thus the recall schema comprises the stored relationships between the initial conditions, movement parameters and the outcome of the response. To illustrate, Schmidt (1988) used the example of throwing objects. He suggested that people can learn to throw a ball a novel distance by extrapolating from the forces needed to achieve lesser distances in training. The fact that such extrapolation is usually successful suggests that we have the capacity to abstract generalised relationships from stored experiences.

"Schemata", however, are not the only psychological constructs used to explain how skilled behaviour is represented mentally. The theory of "production systems" (Anderson, 1983) was also developed for this purpose. According to this theory, procedural knowledge (which underlies cognitive and motor skills) is stored in long-term memory in the form of abstract units called "condition-action" (or IF-THEN) rules. Each of these rules is called a "production" and specifies the exact conditions which must be satisfied for a given action to be executed. Productions are triggered by the contents of working memory which are determined largely by one's current attentional focus. Put simply, when a specific situation is recognised, an action is triggered automatically. For example, drivers must learn the production that "IF you are driving along a road, and you encounter a red traffic light, THEN you must prepare to stop". Accordingly, the IF clause of a production rule specifies a state of affairs or situation in working memory and the THEN clause activates the appropriate action from long-term procedural memory. By this theory, skill learning is synonymous with "proceduralisation" or the acquisition of production rules (Anderson, 1983; Anderson, 1995a). Expressed differently, skill learning takes place when declarative knowledge becomes represented as a series of "conditions" (IF statements) which are linked to action selection (THEN-statements) and then to actions (DO statements). In Anderson's model, productions change with experience. For example, "composition" occurs when sequences of production which occur together reliably become integrated into higher-order productions. For example, in order to become a proficient serve-and-volley player in tennis, one must "compile" a skill sequence which involves serving, moving into the net, anticipating an opponent's return of serve, and volleying deeply.

According to Anderson (1995a), thousands of production rules underlie any complex skill. For example, consider chess. Although the rules of this two-person game are simple enough to be learned by children, skilled chess play requires years of study and practice. But what specific factors account for expertise in this domain? At first glance, it might be expected that chess experts would have better memories for chess than would relative novices. But Chase & Simon (1973) found that this recall advantage depended on the experts' pattern-recognition abilities. Chess experts did not differ from novices in the *absolute number* of chess patterns or "chunks" recalled (which was usually in line with gross working memory capacity, estimated at between 5 and 9 units). But significant differences were evident in the *composition* of these units. Whereas novices tended to recall chess pieces as individual units, experts recalled them in meaningful clusters. This finding suggests that chess experts have access to a vast array of stored meaningful chess-game patterns in their long-term memory. Indeed, Chase & Simon (1973) estimated that these chess experts have stored at least 50,000 chess patterns (or IF-THEN "productions") in their long-term memories. If this sounds like an extravagant claim, remember that the vocabulary size of an average university - educated person is estimated to be between 50,000 and 100,000 words (Kahney, 1993). In the light of this discovery, the pattern recognition "vocabulary" of chess experts is not unusually large. As Kahney (1993) remarked, the difference between the pattern recognition abilities of expert and novice chess players is analogous to the difference between the word recognition abilities of university-educated readers and the recognition of individual letters by novice readers. Chess masters have learned to "read" chess patterns fluently whereas novices are merely struggling with the "letters" of the game. But how is this production-rule "vocabulary" acquired? Clearly, the acquisition of these production rules occurs as a result of prolonged practice. Therefore, researchers like Hayes (1985) propose that it takes at least 10 years of intensive experience to become an expert in any domain. But experience alone is rarely sufficient to develop expertise. Learners must work systematically in order to improve their performance. Therefore, according to Ericsson, Krampe, & Tesch-Romer (1993) and Ericsson & Charness (1994), expert performance in any domain is almost entirely due to "deliberate practice" (or the intentional effort to enhance one's performance). Controversially, these authors suggest that innate talent contributes only minimally to the development of expertise. This conclusion about the dramatic power of practice appears to be somewhat exaggerated, however. Anderson (1995a) offers the more cautious opinion that extensive practice is a necessary, but *not sufficient*, condition for developing skilled performance in any field.

Before I conclude this section, I should mention a finding in skill learning research which has attracted special attention from cognitive theories. This area of research concerns the "contextual interference" effect (Shea & Morgan, 1979). This phenomenon refers to a finding which occurs when people are required to learn certain response patterns under different conditions of practice trials. When the practice trails are presented in a "blocked" order (i.e. when the practice trials for a given pattern are performed consecutively), superior training performance occurs. But surprisingly, when a random order of practice trails is used (i.e. when practice of the patterns is undertaken in an unsystematic order), superior *retention* of the skill occurs. Therefore, the "contextual interference" effect refers to the discovery that "blocked" practice produces better acquisition of motor skills than does "random" practice but poorer long-term (and transfer) learning. In other words, more learning occurs when random practice conditions are employed despite the fact that actual performance at the time of acquisition may not be as good as when practice is undertaken using "blocked" conditions.

What psychological theories could explain this counter-intuitive effect? At least two cognitive theories of contextual interference have been postulated (Gabriele, Hall, & Lee, 1989). To begin with, Shea & Morgan (1979) proposed that when several tasks are present in the learner's working memory at the same time, they have to use "elaborative" processing strategies to keep these tasks distinct. This effortful processing is held to enhance the memory representations of these tasks, thereby improving skill retention. More recently, Lee & Magill (1983) speculated that when learners practise a task on trial one but do not repeat it until several trials later, there may be some forgetting of the "action-plan" for the task. Therefore, learners are forced to generate more "solutions" as a result of random rather than blocked practice, thereby improving retrieval. In summary, traditional explanations of "contextual interference" effects have been couched largely in symbolic information processing terms. Within the past few years, however, an alternative model of this phenomenon has been proposed. This model is based on the connectionist approach to cognition (explained earlier in this chapter). Briefly, Masson (1990) developed a neural network model in which knowledge about how to perform a variant of a task is represented as pairs of input-output patterns. When training involves blocked presentation, the connectionist system works with a relatively small set of training patterns in each block. Hence, appropriate connection weights are established fairly quickly. In the random practice condition, however, the system is faced with the entire collection of input-output patterns throughout training and it must develop a set of weights that is capable of simultaneously representing this larger set. As the number of patterns that must be mastered is larger and more variable this time, the random condition should produce slower learning. But during a retention test in which each variant is tested in turn, blocked training should be at a disadvantage. The problem for the blocked condition is that the set of weights established by the end of the training is most appropriate only for the most recently learned task variant. But when the system is trained in the random practice condition, it is prepared to deal with any variant used during training. Therefore, in the random condition, the weights are developed to deal with the entire collection of input-output patterns. Having taken this brief "detour" into connectionism, let us now return to the second cognitive theme in sport psychology—namely, the idea that athletic expertise is "knowledge driven".

Expertise

Earlier, I explained that the computational metaphor of mind (see Casey & Moran, 1989) lies at the heart of modern cognitive psychology. This metaphor suggests that the task of understanding how the mind works is analogous to that of determining how a computer has been programmed (Neisser, 1967). In other words, cognitive processes are interpreted as the "software" run by the brain, which is viewed as the "hardware" of the information processing system. This metaphor is also invoked frequently by sport psychologists in attempting to understand the origins of athletic expertise. In general, these theorists are trying to evaluate the relative contributions of physical ("hardware") and mental ("software") processes to the development of proficiency in sport performance. Before reviewing their progress on this issue, however, we need to explain briefly why psychologists are interested in expert-novice differences in any domain.

Expertise, or the growth of special knowledge and skills through experience (Klein, 1992), is currently a "hot topic" in cognitive psychology (Ericsson & Lehmann, 1996). In general, interest in this topic is motivated simply by an age-old desire to understand the characteristics which differentiate outstanding performers in any field from those who are less proficient in it. Since the pioneering studies of De Groot (1965; 1966) on chess grand-masters, a considerable amount of research has accumulated on the cognitive mechanisms which are alleged to underlie expert-novice differences in various domains (e.g. chess, Reynolds, 1982; bridge, Charness, 1979; computer programming, Soloway, Adelson, & Ehrlich, 1988). Not surprisingly, the term "expert" has been used to refer to a wide variety of knowledge and behaviour (Cooke, 1992). Sometimes, the possession of specialist knowledge in a particular domain is regarded as the hallmark of expertise. On other occasions, expertise is associated with unusually skilled performance on a given task (e.g. piano tuning). Overall, perhaps the only consensus is that expertise depends on lengthy experience and specialised training in a given field. But what exactly does the term "expert" mean? Several humorous definitions have been proposed (Salthouse, 1991). For example, an expert may be anyone carrying a brief case who is more than 50 miles from home. Alternatively, an expert could be someone who knows more and more about less and less—until eventually, they know everything about nothing! But although these definitions are entertaining, they are of no scientific value. So, for researchers, the term "expert" is usually reserved for someone who has attained a high level of proficiency or performance in some domain as a result of a number of years of experience in it (Foley & Hart, 1992). More precisely, the term "expert" refers to "the possession of a large body of knowledge and procedural skill" (Chi, Glaser, & Rees, 1982). Unfortunately, little consensus exists among researchers as to either the nature of this "expert" knowledge, the duration of "experience" or the quantity of skill required for top-level performance in a given cognitive domain. For example, Chase & Simon (1973) proposed that chess masters should have amassed 10,000–20,000 hours of experience in examining chess board configurations before they could be regarded as "experts". On the basis of such estimates, these authors subscribe to the "ten year" criterion of expertise (see Hayes, 1985): It takes at least ten years of sustained practice in order to achieve world-class proficiency in a given skill. But Cooke (1992) points out that the relationship between "hours of experience" and expertise in some domains (e.g. chess performance) is not linear. Thus some chess players fail to progress in either performance level or ranking despite gaining increased experience of this game. This problem of establishing objective criteria for expertise is also apparent in sport. For example, Thomas & Thomas (1994) point out that three components of athletic expertise—namely, knowledge, skill and game performance—may not overlap. For example, a person may know a great deal about a sport (expert declarative knowledge) but be unable to execute specific sport skills. Therefore, these authors recommend that multiple criteria should be used when defining sporting expertise. In view of these problems of definition, Ericsson & Charness (1994) propose that the more objective term "expert performance" should replace the rather diffuse construct of "expertise". These researchers define "expert performance" as "consistently superior performance on a specified set of representative tasks for the domain" in question. This approach suggests that the hallmark of expertise is the capacity to reproduce reliably a high standard of proficiency in a given domain. Fortunately, the standardised conditions of most competitions in sport facilitates the objective identification of expert performance in the athletic domain.

In general, at least four consistent findings may be identified from research on expert-novice differences in different domains (Bedard & Chi, 1992). First, and most obviously, experts possess a greater amount of declarative knowledge about their domain than do novices. Second, this knowledge is more detailed and better organised in the minds of experts than in those of relative novices. Third, on the basis of a richer knowledge base, and a more extensive repertoire of automated skills, experts perform better (usually faster and more accurately) than novices on tasks related to their specialist field. Finally, the skill of experts tends to be domain-specific: Little of their specialist knowledge appears to transfer to other fields. But how well do these principles of expertise apply to the domain of sport or movement skills? Two intriguing differences exist between sport and the more "cognitive" domains (e.g. chess, computer programming) in which expert-novice differences have been studied (Thomas & Thomas, 1994). First, many sport skills are performed under severe time constraints. For example, a tennis player in a doubles match has to make rapid decisions about where to direct an interception volley. Conversely, the speed at which decisions are made in writing computer programs is not usually regarded as an essential quality of successful performance. In addition, sport skills require both declarative (knowing what to do) and procedural (knowing how to do it) types of knowledge. But as Thomas & Thomas (1994) indicated, it is possible for people in sport to know what to do in a certain situation yet be unable to execute a given movement. As they say, "a player can have an expert knowledge base and yet be inept as a performer". This is not usually the case in more "cognitive" domains like computer programming. Here, "knowing" and "doing" are usually synonymous.

EXPERTISE IN SPORT PERFORMERS:
HARDWARE OR SOFTWARE?

Intuitively, it seems plausible that expert performers in sport should be distinguishable from relative novices in anatomical and physiological characteristics (e.g. musculature, aerobic activity) and/or in psychomotor abilities (e.g. reaction time, visual acuity). By this assumption, athletic expertise is attributable to some prototypical constellation of physiological attributes (e.g. a "superior" nervous system) and perceptual-motor skills (e.g. dynamic visual acuity). At first glance, this theory is compelling because sport commentators and analysts refer regularly to overt signs of athletic excellence. For example, in tennis, coaches admire the possession of "quick hands" or "foot speed" in serve-and-volley players (Starkes, Allard, Lindley, & O'Reilly, 1994). Conversely, even to an untutored eye, the actions of many sporting novices appear to be ungainly, poorly co-ordinated and badly timed. In short, they reflect a state of "skeletomuscular anarchy" (Davids, Handford, & Williams, 1994).

Unfortunately, the "physical" theory of athletic expertise has received little empirical support from researchers. In other words, there is little evidence that athletic expertise is determined by the possession of distinctive "hardware" characteristics (Garland & Barry, 1991). In fact, it has been found repeatedly that neither physical characteristics nor perceptual-motor factors discriminate reliably between the performances of expert and novice athletes. Moreover, a growing body of evidence suggests that "knowledge base" factors (or "software" processes) may account for performance differences between expert and novice athletes in a variety of sports (Allard, 1982; Allard, Graham, & Paarsalu, 1980; Starkes & Deakin, 1984). For example, contrast the way in which a tennis expert and a beginning player might respond to the same pattern of play in a match (McPherson & Thomas, 1989). If a "short" (i.e. mid-court) ball is played to a proficient tennis player, they will probably respond with an attacking drive "down the line" followed by an approach to the net in order to volley the anticipated return shot from the opponent. But under similar circumstances, a novice player will probably concentrate only on returning the ball, before running back to the baseline in order to take up a defensive position for the next shot. Clearly, in this example, the expert player displays awareness of the knowledge that when one hits a deep approach shot in tennis, one should move to the net in the direction of the shot in order to bisect the opponent's angle of return. Accordingly, whereas the expert player anticipates the next shot in a tennis rally, the novice performer is preoccupied with the more basic problem of keeping the ball in play. In summary, expert athletes seem to be better at perceiving patterns among task-relevant cues than are relative novices (Garland & Barry, 1991). In this way, expert athletes are distinguished from novices mainly by the possession of strategies that enable them to "organise, interpret and utilise the information their sport provides to them" (Abernethy, Neal, & Koning, 1994). In general, therefore, expertise seems to be mediated by a set of production rules which are triggered by a skill in pattern recognition. Indeed, pattern recognition has been proposed as the interface between working memory and procedural memory (Anderson, 1983). Put differently, actions are activated when the content of working memory is matched against the "condition" parts of the production rules stored in declarative memory (Newell & Simon, 1972, proposed that patterns constitute the "IF" part of the production rule). Furthermore, as people become more proficient in any field, they learn new production rules which re-organise their knowledge base (Anderson, 1995a). Therefore, experts in any field seem to have developed a larger, and more extensively cross-referenced, system of production rules for their specialist domain than do relative novices. As I explained earlier, the size of this database of productions in chess experts was estimated by Simon & Gilmartin (1973) at around 50,000 "chunks" of information (or pattern-action rules). Unfortunately, no corresponding estimate for the size of the production rule "vocabulary" of sport experts has yet been offered.

Superficially, the theory of production rules seems very similar to that of "stimulus-response" (S-R) bonds. Thus a "condition" may be regarded as equivalent to a "stimulus" which elicits an observable action or response. But closer analysis shows that there is one major difference between the production rules of cognitive psychology and the S-R bonds of classical behaviourism. Specifically, Simon (1992) claimed that while the stimuli of behaviourism were confined to the environment, "the conditions that have to be satisfied to trigger the action of a production may (but need not be) symbol structures held in memory". In other words, production rules can implement either "externally" or "internally" located actions.

One of the most influential theories of expertise is the "recognition-association" model of chess mastery proposed by Chase & Simon (1973). Briefly, this theory holds that a chess position is "recognised" by an expert in terms of groups of two or three chess pieces corresponding to familiar chunks (i.e. patterns stored in long-term memory). These chunks are each "associated" with plausible moves. Skilful players can "see" the best moves by recognising patterns that trigger certain strategic actions. In short, chess expertise is attributed to pattern-recognition skills. Applying this "recognition-association" theory to sport performance, it seems plausible that expert athletes should also have a larger vocabulary of "recognisable configurations" (Chase & Simon, 1973) than do relative novices. Therefore, proficiency in pattern recognition should give top athletes a distinct "cognitive advantage" over beginners in their chosen sport (Allard & Starkes, 1991; Starkes & Allard, 1993). Indeed, Simon (1992) suggested that pattern recognition processes underlie expertise in any domain. As he put it, "intuition is nothing more and nothing less than recognition". Let us now consider some sporting examples of this cognitive superiority of experts.

To begin with, research indicates that, contrary to popular belief, top professional tennis players do *not* watch the ball approaching them as they prepare to return a serve because it is virtually impossible for someone to "track" a ball travelling at speeds of up to 130 miles per hour (Abernethy, 1991). Instead, evidence from laboratory simulations of high-speed sporting encounters indicates that top tennis players tend to use *advance cues* from the server's racquet and ball-toss in order to make accurate predictions about the likely flight and destination of the ball. This capacity to extrapolate from "advance cues" appears to be a distinctive characteristic of expert athletes. For example, Abernethy & Russell (1987) found that expert squash players based their predictions about ball-flight on early signals from opponents' movements (e.g. from both the position of the racquet and the racquet arm) when watching film simulations of squash matches. However, squash beginners tended to adopt a more constrained visual search process, looking only at those cues that were yielded by the racquet itself. Findings of this nature suggest that expert athletes have access to a large repertoire of "recognisable configurations" (Chase & Simon, 1973) in their sporting domain. These patterns are responsible for triggering appropriate actions quickly and efficiently. This cognitive approach to expertise in sport is based on the idea that procedural knowledge is *enacted* through perceptual recognition. I shall return to this issue in Chapter 3 when considering selective attention in athletes.

The "cognitive advantage" of proficient athletes over relative beginners is confirmed by several other findings from research on expert-novice differences. For example, Abernethy, Neal, & Koning (1994) used protocol analysis to show that expert snooker players were more adept than novices in planning future shots. Also, Bedon & Howard (1992) found that expert karate practitioners were significantly superior to beginners in memorising various karate techniques. Apparently, the experts relied on "a storehouse of prior relevant knowledge gained through years of experience in seeing these techniques paired together". Similarly, Allard, Graham, & Paarsalu (1980) discovered that basketball players were more accurate in recalling the positions of players in "structured" game situations (e.g. when the point guard was about to initiate a move) than in "random" circumstances (e.g. when players were scrambling for a loose ball on court). This finding that experts have superior domain-relevant recall skills to novices is remarkably robust across different sporting domains and has been called the "skill-by-structure interaction" (Allard & Starkes, 1991). Put simply, if the sporting situation is random rather than structured, the "cognitive advantage" of experts over beginners usually disappears. For example, Borgeaud & Abernethy (1987) found that novice volleyball players were not significantly different from experts in their recall of dynamic volleyball sequences. In summary, researchers like Starkes & Allard (1993) propose that the experience accumulated by experts in sport (e.g. from detection of advance cues from opponents in competitive settings) is organised (e.g. through a network of production rules) in an extensive knowledge base which facilitates rapid inferences about what actions follow what perceptions.

So far, I have explained why sport skills are believed to have a strong cognitive foundation or are "knowledge intensive" (Anderson, 1995a). We have also seen how cognitive influences on sport research are evident in the study of athletic expertise. As we discovered, the search for the distinctive attributes of highly proficient athletes has highlighted the importance of *cognitive* rather than physical factors. In other words, substantial research evidence suggests that athletic expertise is attributable more to the mind than to the body of the performer. This finding has been called the "cognitive advantage" (Garland & Barry, 1991) of expert athletes over novices. Having considered these two topics briefly, we can begin to appreciate the influence of cognitive theories on sport psychological research. But we must acknowledge that cognitive theories are not universally accepted by sport researchers. Therefore, before concluding this section, I shall sketch a challenge to the hegemony of "cognitivism" in sport psychology. This challenge is posed by proponents of natural physical approaches to psychology. Essentially, theorists adopting this paradigm (see review by Davids, Handford, & Williams, 1994) argue that human movement is controlled by *direct* links between perceptual and action systems (Turvey, 1994; Turvey & Kugler, 1984). Clearly, "direct" perception theories attack the mediating role of mental representations in information processing accounts of skilled behaviour. Extreme proponents of this view argue that constructs such as "mental representations" are unnecessary and misleading. I shall consider this approach in more detail below. In passing, similarities may be identified between two current paradigm clashes in psychology. Specifically, the disagreement between "symbolic" and connectionist researchers in cognitive psychology is paralleled by a somewhat less noisy clash between cognitive and ecological theorists in the field of motor learning. What is clear from these disputes is that cognitive approaches to the mind are changing rapidly. Therefore, it may be more accurate to speak of the *evolution* rather than the "revolution" (Baars, 1986) of cognitive theory.

A CHALLENGE TO COGNITION IN SPORT:
DIRECT PERCEPTION THEORY

Human motor skill learning is a remarkable achievement. For example, as Clark (1995) observed, we are born unable to transport ourselves physically and yet, in little more than a decade, some of us can learn to display astonishing athletic feats (e.g. performing complex triple-toe loop jumps in figure skating using only millimetre-wide skating blades). What theoretical mechanisms can explain such control of motor actions?

Since the 1960s, most explanations of movement co-ordination have used computational models and principles derived from the information processing paradigm in psychology (see Williams, Davids, Burwitz, & Williams, 1992, for an historical review). Briefly, a key assumption of this paradigm is the idea that centrally based cognitive representations (e.g. "production systems" and "schemata") are developed by the performer as generic solutions to specific motor problems. These representations are alleged to provide executive control over behaviour by issuing "commands" to muscles which initiate subsequent actions. For example, through practice, a golfer must learn to replicate a putting motion until it becomes a "programmed component" (Davids, Handford, & Williams, 1994) of his or her motor repertoire and can be performed automatically when required. In order to achieve this postulated central control of motor behaviour, three different levels of the information processing system are held to exist (Davids, Handford, & Williams, 1994): a level at which sensory input is received, an executive level at which symbolic transformation of this input is performed, and an effector level for the production of appropriate motor output. These three levels are alleged to interact continuously as central representations become transformed into actions using knowledge obtained from feedback loops.

Recently, however, this information processing perspective on motor control has been challenged by a rather different movement which has been called variously the "natural physical" approach (Davids, Handford, & Williams, 1994), "action perception" theory (McCullagh, Weiss, & Ross, 1989), the "emergent properties and dynamic systems" perspective (Clark, 1995; Kelso, 1995) or the "Bernstein revolution" (Thelen, 1995). In brief, this "natural physical" movement, which may be traced back to the work of such "ecological" theorists as Bernstein (1967) and Gibson (1979), attempts to explain goal-directed behaviour in terms of physical laws rather than through putative cognitive constructs (Summers & Ford, 1995). Specifically, this movement proposes that perceptual experience itself, rather than some hypothetical mental representation of it, provides perceivers with direct information about the world. For example, the speed of response of an expert table-tennis player may be due to his or her ability to pick up visual information directly (e.g. using a parameter called the "tau" index to plot time-to-contact information; Summers & Ford, 1995, explained below).

Using natural physical principles, researchers like Turvey (1994) criticise cognitive schematic theory of motor behaviour on the grounds that the number of variables to be represented in all but the simplest of actions would require an impossibly large storage capacity in the mind. In short, direct perception theorists argue that is implausible to suggest that "internal" representational constructs (e.g. schemata) serve as mediators between the output of the perceptual system and the input of the action system. For example, consider the apparently simple task of running to catch a ball thrown through the air. According to Lee (1976), the key problem for the runner is how to calculate the "time-to-ball-contact" information. Traditional information processing theories would explain this feat by postulating that the runner derives this information from central calculations involving such parameters as the speed of the ball and the distance to be traversed. But the direct perception approach suggests the simpler alternative that the runner relies on only one variable, namely, the rate of expansion of the retinal image of the ball. Specifically, the quicker this image expands, the shorter is the time to contact. The inverse of the rate of expansion of the retinal image is called "tau" (Lee, 1976). Ironically, therefore, cognitive theories of motor learning are now being assailed using the same "storage problem" argument that previously led to the demise of habit theories of skill learning (explained earlier in this chapter). The implications of this critique were expressed succinctly by Reed (1982): "Cognitive theories, with their Pandora's boxes of intervening variables, can no longer be accepted".

As an example of this ecological approach, consider a recent study by Savelsbergh & Bootsma (1994) on the issue of the determinants of expertise in hitting and catching in fast-ball sports. Briefly, these researchers tested the proposition, from natural physical theory, that perception and action act as a "coupled" unitary process. Using the expert-novice paradigm applied to table-tennis, these authors showed that the way in which beginners learned to play an attacking forehand drive shot did not seem to be related to the acquisition of a specific movement pattern (or centrally stored schema). Instead, an increase in the number of table-tennis balls directed correctly at a specific target was associated with a smaller scatter in the direction of travel of the bat at the moment of ball/bat contact. The authors concluded that this finding showed that "the learning process can be viewed as the establishment of a skill-specific perception-action coupling". Also, when catching balls, it was found that players made adjustments to the apertures of their hands. This finding suggested evidence of "finely attuned perception-action coupling" which appears to be based on time-to-contact information. Thus what was held to change with the development of expertise was not some central movement schema but rather the tuning of actions to specific visual information sources.

But if cognitive representations of skills are dismissed as irrelevant constructs, how can we account for motor learning? According to Turvey (1994) and his fellow "ecological" researchers, we should regard the *environment* as a storehouse of all the information which skilled performers require in order to control their behaviour effectively. Although space limitations preclude a detailed analysis of "natural physical" theories of motor learning, it is important to understand the basis of their challenge to cognitive models in this field. To do so, we need to consider some influential ideas proposed by the precursor of the "action perception" movement, the Russian physiologist Bernstein (whose work was published in originally in Russian in 1947 but translated into English in 1967). Bernstein (1967) identified the "degrees of freedom" problem as the central issue in motor learning. This problem concerns the fact that the number of muscles that have to be controlled by the performer in order to regulate a movement poses a massive computational problem for the brain. Given the enormous number of variables involved, it seems implausible that there is a one-to-one correspondence between the elements of action and their corresponding mental representations. Bernstein's solution to this computational problem was to suggest that groups of muscles and joints become "constrained" to act as autonomous functional units. These units are called "coordinative structures" (Bernstein, 1967). Therefore, by developing coordinative structures, the proficient performer can reduce the number of degrees of freedom necessitated by skilled action. For example, a coordinative structure for serving in tennis might involve the unitary action of hand, arm, shoulder and hip movements. This hypothesis of co-ordinated actions suggests that motor control can be achieved without recourse to central executive processes. Therefore, natural physical theorists (e.g. Turvey, 1994) propose that motor control is an "emergent property" of a self-organising system rather than a slave to some representational structure. One task facing these global muscular units is to encode functions which describe the complete time-course for a particular type of movement. Accordingly, these functions were thought to specify the dynamic characteristics of a whole class of movements. Hence, movements within a particular class were thought to be "tuned" by altering certain parameters of the stored functions.

Influenced by the ideas of Bernstein (1967), "natural physical" theories of motor learning are concerned primarily with exploring the problem of motor "co-ordination" (i.e. how the organisation of the control of motor movements occurs; Turvey, 1990). More precisely, this problem of co-ordination raise the question of how organisms master the many "degrees of freedom" involved in a particular movement (Turvey, 1990). The solution of this computational problem lies in the coupling of action and perception. Thus Turvey (1990) proposed that visual perception of environmental constraints during motion results in alterations ("tuning") of the coordinative structures involved. For example, imagine how it feels to step off the kerb of a street unexpectedly. The motor system tends to respond rather dramatically to a slight change in elevation between the kerb and the street. However, if one perceives the kerb before stepping off it, then a "tuning" of the movement pattern occurs automatically. In summary, whereas information processing theories claim that central representations underlie motor behaviour, natural physical theories take a different stance in emphasising the direct and inextricable link between action and perception.

The cornerstone of these theories is the proposition that motor actions are controlled by parameters that have been extracted directly from the environment (see Harvey, 1988). For example, imagine an observer who is approaching an object with some constant velocity. The rate of magnification of the optical texture of this object will give a measure of the time that remains before the observer will physically contact it. Research evidence suggests that people may be exploiting this temporal parameter to control their actions in various domains. Tasks used to explore this hypothesis include the control of braking by car drivers (Lee, 1976) and the control of gait by long-jumpers (Lee, Lishman, & Thomson, 1982). In general, therefore, "natural physical" theories seek to identify general physical principles that govern the behaviour of "movement systems", regardless of whether such systems belong to humans or animals (e.g. see research by Lee & Reddish, 1981, on the control of wing-folding by gannets as they dive into the sea). Accordingly, these theories assume that biological movement systems are "self-organising" (Turvey, 1994) and that people's movement behaviour is best explored by establishing its functional relationship with the dynamic natural environment in which it evolved.

The "ecological" flavour of this approach arises from the argument that it is not possible to study realistic functional relationships using traditional laboratory experiments. This is because research subjects in laboratories are largely inactive as they wait to make responses to pre-arranged stimuli. Indeed, traditional notions of central control of motor behaviour *assume* an inactive organism. Therefore, natural physical theories examine the "constraints on action" (Davids, Handford, & Williams, 1994, p. 501) which have evolved through interaction with natural environments. The argument here is that there is no need to postulate a central executive or representational system to explain motor behaviour. Instead, movements are regarded as "emergent properties" of the system as it interacts dynamically with its environment.

To what extent have natural physical theories replaced cognitive accounts of motor behaviour? According to Davids, Handford, & Williams (1994), the former theories are especially suitable for the explanation of actions which display a "tight fit" between action and perception (e.g. rhythmical or repetitive movements). However, it is far too early to determine if they have replaced cognitive models in this field. For example, "direct" action-perception theories cannot provide an adequate alternative for the role of memory and strategic planning in cognitive models of motor learning (ibid.). Indeed, direct perception theories are somewhat vague in explaining how perception-action links are acquired and retained.

In summary, just as symbolic and connectionist approaches to cognition may be viewed as complementary rather than as mutually exclusive (as proposed earlier in this chapter), so also may representational and action-perception theories of motor learning be reconciled simply because they operate at different levels of analysis. As Glencross (1992) suggested, "what we are talking about is a cognitively organised and constrained higher-order system integrated with a dynamically driven lower-order system interacting with the periphery". Accordingly, future research on motor skill learning should address the issue of how these two systems interact continuously.

In passing, it is interesting to speculate on what makes skilled behaviour so fascinating for psychologists. According to Viviani (1992), human skills are unique because they differ from non-biological movement patterns in their flexibility. Although they must satisfy certain physical principles for the generation of any movement, they are nevertheless quite variable. By analogy, there are as many different ways of achieving a given motor goal as there are different ways of expressing the same thought linguistically. For example, consider a comparison between the movement patterns displayed by two pianists playing the same piece (Viviani, 1992). If video recordings of these performers are superimposed on each other, considerable variability will be evident in the trunk and arm movements of the performers. But the two images will overlap significantly when it comes to what matters most—namely, the movement patterns of the fingertips. By contrast, imagine two robots playing the same piano piece. In this case, to satisfy computational constraints, the essential requirement of robot pianists is a *consistency* of movement. Thus if the video recordings of two robotic pianists were fused, movement overlap would occur everywhere. Therefore, human skills are paradoxically constrained yet flexible.

CAN COGNITIVE PSYCHOLOGY BENEFIT FROM RESEARCH IN SPORT?

So far, I have highlighted the influence of cognitive psychology on research in sport. In particular, I have tried to show how the study of mental aspects of sport performance has benefited considerably from the information processing tradition of cognitive psychology. In this final section, I shall reverse the thrust of this argument by exploring briefly how research on sport may extend theoretical and methodological horizons in cognitive psychology. I shall return to this theme in Chapter 8.

To begin with, a major proposition of this book is that sport offers a natural context for research on the relationship between cognition and action—a topic which has been neglected in contemporary cognitive psychology (despite William James' insight that "my thinking is first and last and always for the sake of my doing"; James, 1890). This neglect of cognition-action relationships has been acknowledged by several critics. For example, Heuer (1989) observed that "cognition is not a purpose in itself but rather has to serve action". Furthermore, Eysenck & Keane (1990) pointed out that whereas our cognitive processes serve as a means to an end (e.g. by leading to actions) in everyday life, "they function as ends in themselves" in research laboratories. By contrast, consider the topic of expertise in sport. This topic yields several benefits for cognitive psychologists, according to Abernethy (1994b). First, research on sport experts facilitates exploration of the effects of prolonged, naturalistic *practice* on motor skills "to a degree that cannot be matched by conventional laboratory-based studies of learning". This point is timely in view of the current controversy over the relative roles of innate talent and deliberate practice in skill mastery (Ericsson, Krampe, & Tesch-Romer, 1993; Ericsson & Charness, 1994). In addition, studies of people who are highly proficient in sport skills allow researchers to test the validity of theories of expertise that have been developed in other domains (e.g. chess). Here, researchers (e.g. Thomas & Thomas, 1994) have pointed out that expertise in sport is worth studying simply because it is different from other domains. Whereas time constraints are not usually a feature of performance in the domains of mathematics or music, for example, they exert considerable influence on proficiency in "open skill" sports. Thus to achieve success in "doubles", tennis players have to make decisions extremely rapidly.

To illustrate a promising new direction in the study of athletic expertise, consider a study by Russell & Salmela (1992). These authors attempted to elicit details of the meta-cognitive "knowledge base" which underlies expertise in cycling. In particular, these researchers were interested in finding out how an expert international cyclist perceived, and planned strategies for, typical problems which confronted him in competition. The relevance of this study for cognitive psychology is that it uses a combination of quantitative and qualitative techniques to tackle the "knowledge elicitation problem" (i.e. the difficulty of obtaining details of expert procedural knowledge which, by definition, is largely automated and hence inaccessible to conscious awareness). In the first stage of this single-case study, Russell & Salmela (1992) used a structured interview to identify a total of nineteen practical problems which confronted the expert cyclist during a typical competition. Then these problems or "sport task situations" (e.g. how to deal with distractions during a race) were used as stimuli in a card-sorting task in order to establish how the cyclist categorised domain-specific problems. This method is commonly employed in studies of expertise in order to explore the type of information (e.g. superficial or "deep" aspects of the problem) that experts and novices use to make categorisation decisions (Bedard & Chi, 1992). Finally, administration of a repertory grid (Kelly, 1955) allowed the researchers to identify the cyclist's "personal constructs" (i.e. his unique ways of perceiving the similarities and differences between the elements under analysis) about cycling tasks. The data from the repertory grid analysis were subsequently analysed using multi-dimensional scaling in order to examine the relationship between the cycling problems identified and the performance strategies advocated to tackle them. Overall, a cluster of four problem categories were identified. The first comprised minor setbacks encountered during the race (e.g. a puncture). The second consisted of physical difficulties experienced when cycling (e.g. fatigue or pain when challenging on a climb). The third category included dangerous situations (e.g. being jostled by opponents). The final cluster comprised strategic decisions required near the completion of the race to "push home" an advantage. In order to deal with these problems, the cyclist advocated a range of strategies varying from automation ("let your body go ... without thinking about it") to deliberate and "intense constant monitoring". Studies like this are valuable to cognitive psychology because they address the neglected issue of how procedural skills are used to tackle problem solving in real-world settings. A promising study in this field was conducted recently by Cote, Salmela, Trudel, Baria, & Russell (1995) on the technical knowledge possessed by expert gymnastics judges.

Another way in which sport-related research can help cognitive psychology is by enhancing the ecological validity of some of its methods. For example, traditional laboratory studies of attentional processes have been somewhat artificial because the tasks employed (e.g. "shadowing" auditory messages presented over headphones; see Chapter 2) are relatively brief and emotionally neutral for the performer. By contrast, complex skills (e.g. archery) that are performed in competitive contexts may take place over prolonged durations and may arouse significant emotional reactions from the performer. As Singer et al. (1991) pointed out, cognitive researchers have conducted few studies on "tasks that are repeatedly performed, requiring constant refocusing of attention, as is the case in such sports as archery, riflery, bowling and golf".

In conclusion, it is clear that cognitive psychology has had a significant influence on many current propositions in sport psychology (e.g. the idea that sport skills have a schematic "knowledge base"; Schmidt, 1975). But cognitive theory and research can also benefit from the study of certain topics (e.g. attention, expertise) in sport psychology. For example, Kremer & Scully (1994) observed that, traditionally, "cognitive psychology has tended to neglect social, motivational and emotional factors of cognition", while sport psychology has examined these topics in the attempt to develop effective performance enhancement strategies. Throughout this book, therefore, I shall argue that sport research can expand the scope of contemporary cognitive psychology. By examining mental aspects of sport performance, we can begin to explore how intentions become translated into skilled performance in real-life settings, where pressure and distractions are ubiquitous. Accordingly, I shall outline some specific ways in which cognitive research in sport may strengthen cognitive theory and, overall, I shall argue that the study of cognition in sport represents a new and exciting branch of applied cognitive psychology.

SUMMARY

Mental aspects of performance in sport have attracted increasing attention from athletes, coaches and psychologists in recent years. In exploring this relatively uncharted field, the present chapter illuminated the conceptual origins of cognitive sport psychology. For athletes and coaches, interest in the "mental side" of sport has been stimulated mainly by the belief that effective psychological preparation can provide performers with a practical and legal "winning edge" in competition. However, for research psychologists, the scientific appeal of athletic performance concerns the fact that it provides a dynamic, "real-world" environment in which to study the relationship between cognition and action. For example, the study of attentional processes in competitive athletes illuminates the extent to which "external" (e.g. noise) and "internal" (e.g. intrusive thoughts) distractions may combine to disrupt skilled behaviour. Similarly, the field of "mental practice" (or cognitive rehearsal of motor actions) facilitates investigation of how mental imagery affects subsequent performance. In general, therefore, the struggle by athletes to exert mental control over intended thoughts and actions suggests that competitive sport demands a considerable capacity for cognitive monitoring and behavioural self-regulation. Accordingly, in this chapter, I used the topic of cognitive processes in sport as a medium through which to explore the relationship between cognitive psychology and sport psychology.

Until recently, the information processing (or "symbolic") approach to the mind was the standard paradigm in cognitive psychology. I have shown how this paradigm has influenced the way in which contemporary sport science understands such topics as skill representation and athletic expertise. Specifically, according to information processing theory, skilled behaviour may be regarded as a form of problem solving in which the performer's goal is to translate an intention into a purposeful and autonomous action. This translation process requires an extensive knowledge base in the mind of the performer. In the cognitive approach, therefore, sport skills are believed to be "compiled" symbolically in long-term memory through hypothetical constructs such as "schemata" (Bartlett, Schmidt) and "production systems" (Anderson). Not surprisingly, these cognitive constructs feature prominently in attempts to understand expert-novice differences in athletes. For example, the procedural knowledge base of top athletes has been shown to be larger and more extensively cross-referenced than that possessed by relatively less proficient performers in that sport. This knowledge base difference gives experts a "cognitive advantage" over beginners in that sporting domain. Within the past few years, the hegemony of the symbolic approach to cognition, with its strong emphasis on the central control of behaviour, has been challenged by such movements as connectionism and direct perception theory. Although these rival approaches differ in many ways, they share a scepticism about the merit of postulating central executive processes and hierarchical models (i.e. conceptually driven or "top-down" approaches) to explain skill learning. For example, direct perception theorists argue that motor control may be an "emergent property" of the mind rather than a product of some hypothetical representational structure (e.g. a schema). Unfortunately, neither connectionism nor direct perception theory is sufficiently well established as yet to supplant the symbolic information processing tradition in cognitive sport psychology. It seems likely, however, that sport science, over the next decade, will witness considerable cross-fertilisation of ideas from these different theoretical paradigms.

CHAPTER TWO

Understanding attention: The psychology of concentration

"Everyone knows what attention is. It is the taking possession by the mind, in clear and vivid form, of one out of what seem several simultaneously possible objects or trains of thought. Focalisation, concentration of consciousness are of its essence. It implies withdrawal from some things in order to deal effectively with others"

(James, 1890, pp. 403–404).

INTRODUCTION

In Chapter 1, I examined the role of cognition in sport. Amid the welter of details presented, two ideas were especially important. I shall recapitulate these themes before outlining the purpose of the present chapter. The first idea concerned the fact that sport skills (like all forms of procedural knowledge) are believed to be compiled in long-term memory as a "knowledge-base" of abstract pattern-action relationships called "production rules" (Anderson, 1983). The quantity of these procedural rules is probably vast because even simple actions (like brushing one's teeth) have been shown to involve a large number of component processing units (Reed, Montgomery, Palmer, & Pittenger, 1995). As I explained, production rules are "if-then" statements which specify the conditions under which it is appropriate to take certain actions. The "if" part of the relationship indicates the circumstances under which the rule will apply while the "then" part stipulates the nature of the action to be taken. In this way, the content of our working memory (which reflects the current focus of our attention) serves as a cue for the execution of stored automatic skills or "productions". For example, when an expert tennis player receives a "short" ball from an opponent, they will attack it instantly. No controlled cognitive processing is required here because a production rule stating "if mid-court, then attack" has been triggered. Therefore, an offensive drive is produced intuitively. Of course, as Simon (1992) claimed, such intuitive performance is "nothing more or less than recognition". In other words, what seems like the spontaneous execution of a skill masks a rapid pattern recognition process in which the contents of working memory are matched against the conditions which activate relevant productions. This process of pattern recognition is enhanced by practice and instruction. The practice comes from repeated execution of basic technical skills and the instruction involves formal training in the recognition of sport-specific patterns. This insight leads us to a second important theme in Chapter 1. Specifically, the technical proficiency of expert athletes suggests that they have access to a large and highly cross-referenced "vocabulary" of domain-specific production rules. The possession of this knowledge gives experts a significant "cognitive advantage" (Starkes & Allard, 1993) over less competent performers in their specialist sporting domain. For example, they can anticipate the likely actions of opponents in their sport faster and more accurately than can less experienced counterparts (Abernethy, 1994b). In this way, expert athletes seem to make more efficient usage of their limited-capacity information processing system than do relative novices (Abernethy, 1993). This proposition is endorsed by Salthouse (1991) who observed that the essence of expert performance in any field is the fact that it appears to be less constrained by the limitations "that serve to restrict the performance of non experts". I shall develop this point further in Chapter 3. For the present, I wish to clarify the nature of the processing constraints with which all of us—including top athletes—have to contend. Therefore, the present chapter is concerned mainly with the following question: How does our attentional system place limits on what we can perceive and do at any given moment? I shall try to answer this question by exploring the nature and characteristics of our attentional system. This analysis serves as a necessary prelude to my study of concentration processes in athletes. Clearly, unless we examine how our attention system works in general, we cannot hope to understand such topics as the importance of concentration in sport (Chapter 3), or the reasons why the minds of athletes tend to wander during competition (Chapter 4) or even how to improve concentration skills (Chapters 6 and 7).

My plan is as follows. I shall begin by exploring the nature and characteristics of, and metaphors associated with, the construct of attention. Then, I shall summarise briefly the history of research in this field. Next, I shall examine selective and divided attentional processes as well as the phenomenon of "alertness". Then the principal theories and findings in research on attention will be reviewed. The final section will be devoted to consideration of a recurrent theme in this book, namely, the concept of attention as a skill.

WHAT IS ATTENTION?
NATURE, CHARACTERISTICS AND METAPHORS

For the past century, psychologists have used the term "attention" to refer to at least three different types of mental activities (Matlin, 1994; Posner & Boies, 1971). First, and most frequently, the construct of attention has been postulated to explain "concentration and its shifts" (Best, 1995). Theorists who adopt this perspective suggest that concentration, or our capacity to focus mental effort on some specific target, is a highly valued practical skill. For example, in school, pupils are exhorted to "pay attention" to key features of a lesson which they are being taught. Conversely, they are scolded for letting their minds wander during such lessons. Likewise, a student may try to "focus" on a book which they are reading for an examination while attempting to "block out" distracting noises coming from another room. In these educational examples, attention involves the "selective aspect of perception" (Kosslyn & Koenig, 1992). Theoretically, this capacity for attentional selectivity is thought to have evolved in order to protect us against the threat of "cognitive overload" (i.e. the experience of being overwhelmed by the profusion of environmental information available to us). According to this view, our experience would be "an utter chaos" (James, 1890) without selective attentional mechanisms.

The second meaning of the term "attention" concerns the fact that, under certain circumstances, we can spread our mental resources quite efficiently across several concurrent actions. Thus experienced car-drivers can easily hold a conversation with a passenger while they are motoring. Although apparently mundane, this feat is actually quite remarkable because it illustrates a mental "time-sharing" ability which develops as a result of extensive practice. Such an ability is known as "divided attention" (Eysenck & Keane, 1995). Interestingly, all mental "time-sharing" skills (whether found in driving or in sport) attest to the role of practice in helping people to overcome structural information processing constraints (Ericsson, Krampe, & Tesch-Romer, 1993). Accordingly, perhaps the only limits in our minds are those imposed by our *willingness* to engage in systematic practice of our skills (Best, 1995).

A third usage of the term "attention" is to denote a brief, and usually involuntary, state of alertness or "preparedness" for action. Put simply, a person who is aroused is attentive to the environment whereas a person who is drowsy is not as sensitive to it. Therefore, most psychologists agree with Posner & Petersen (1990) that a vital attentional function is the "ability to prepare and sustain alertness to process high priority signals". This state of alertness, which may be measured indirectly through such physiological indices as heart rate (see Chapter 5), is thought to be heavily dependent on the integrity of the right cerebral hemisphere. Furthermore, it is usually short-lived. For example, if you are roused from a pleasant slumber in a plane by the captain's voice saying "Attention, please! This is an emergency", you will display an immediate "startle" or "orienting" response (Posner, 1980). As one might expect, this seizure of attention (or "what is it?" reaction), is commonly elicited by stimuli that are novel or intense. Clearly, this finding makes evolutionary sense. It is biologically adaptive for us to possess a system which is tuned to attend involuntarily and briefly to any sudden changes that occur in environmental stimulation. After all, such changes may signal potential danger to us. But the orientation response is unlikely to be helpful to us when we need to pay prolonged attention to some important source of stimulation. Interestingly, this skill of "vigilance", or the capacity to maintain alertness over long durations, was one of the earliest topics explored by attention researchers (Parasuraman, 1984). The impetus for this research stemmed from the discovery of a "vigilance decrement" during World War II. Briefly, this decrement in target detection performance was noted when Subjects had to monitor displays for unpredictable signals occurring over time periods which ranged from 30 minutes to one hour (See, Howe, Warm, & Dember, 1995). In summary, I have shown that the construct of attention is multi-faceted. In particular, it involves at least three different psychological processes: selectivity of perception, regulation of concurrent actions and maintenance of alertness. As I shall explain in Chapter 5, attempts to measure attentional processes are usually based on "tracking" one or more of these three components of this construct.

As the construct of "attention" has at least three different meanings, it is not surprising that terminological confusion is widespread in this field. For example, as Summers & Ford (1995) pointed out, "the same labels are used to denote different aspects of attention (e.g. alertness) and different labels are used to denote the same aspect (e.g. narrow, focused, selective)". In spite of such semantic chaos, however, the exertion of mental effort has been regarded for over a century as a criterion feature of attention. To illustrate, James (1890) observed that "it takes effort" to maintain our concentration on something which has "caught our mental eye". Likewise, Solso (1995) defined attention as "the concentration of mental effort on sensory or mental events". Matlin (1994) refers to attention as a "concentration of mental activity". So, throughout this book, I shall use the term "concentration" to refer primarily to this "mental effort" aspect of attention.

Many metaphors of attention have been postulated by psychologists. Invariably, these metaphors have been visual in nature (although surprisingly, initial research in this field was conducted mainly on auditory attention). For example, visual selective attention has been likened variously to an "internal eyeball" (Skelton & Eriksen, 1976), the "mind's eye" (Jonides, 1980) and the zoom lens of a camera (Orlick, 1990). Interestingly, the "mind's eye" metaphor also occurs in Zen writings on attention. To illustrate, Herrigel (1953) proclaimed that "mastery in ink-painting is only attained when the hand, exercising perfect control over technique, executes what hovers before the mind's eye at the same moment as the mind begins to form it, without there being a hair's breadth between" (pp. 101–102).

Of the various metaphors of attention, the "spotlight" theory has been especially influential. According to this idea, concentration is "a spotlight that comes equipped with a variable lens" (Best, 1995). This metaphor probably comes from the anatomical discovery that visual perceptual acuity is governed by a small area in the foveal region of the eye. In the periphery of this region, visual perception is less clear. Therefore, visual perception resembles a spotlight. Thus targets in the foveal region are seen most clearly whereas those in the periphery are perceived less clearly (Eysenck & Keane, 1995). By analogy, attention resembles a beam of light with a variable focus which can be used selectively to explore different locations in space. A similar view is proposed by Bernstein, Roy, Srull, & Wickens (1994) who remarked that attention is like "a spotlight that illuminates different parts of the external environment or various mental processes". With regard to visual attention, this spotlight metaphor is often taken literally. Thus Eysenck (1992) suggested that although the location of a stimulus can be detected in peripheral vision, only stimulation within the central beam of the spotlight receives complete semantic processing. Interestingly, spotlight theorists acknowledges that the "beam" of our mental energy can be directed *inwards* as well as outwards. This phenomenon occurs when people become anxious or self-conscious (see also Chapter 4). An obvious implication of this idea is the notion that we can distract ourselves as well as being distracted by factors in the external world.

One of the earliest proponents of the spotlight metaphor was Hernandez-Peon (1964) who suggested that "attention may be compared to a beam of light in which the central brilliant part represents the focus surrounded by a less intense fringe. Only the items located in the focus of attention are distinctly perceived whereas we are less aware of the objects located in the fringe of attention" (p. 167). In other words, everything illuminated by the beam is perfectly clear whereas objects that fall outside the central beam are either blurred or not visible at all (Eysenck, 1993). Other theorists have expressed similar views: For example Philips (1988) likened attention to "a spotlight that accentuates the object on which it is focused. By contrast, all other objects outside the circle will appear unclear, distant, and possibly irrelevant" (p. 106). Similarly, Hilgard (1992) claimed that "the focus of attention shifts about, like a spotlight in the dark, permitting one facet at a time to be spotted and acted upon". Overall, there are three main aspects to the analogy between attention and a spotlight (Van der Heijden, 1992). First, just as light is necessary for vision, so also is attention required for information processing. Second, just as a spotlight illuminates only a portion of the world, so also is attention restricted to a limited domain. Finally, just as a beam is shone by a torch, so also are our attentional resources directed at the spatial position of objects. But there are problems with all mechanical metaphors of attention. To explain, consider what happens when we tape record a noisy lecture or a conversation in a crowded room. Usually, when we replay the tape, we are surprised to discover just how much noise (e.g. coughs) were present at the time. Unknown to ourselves, we managed to "filter out" distractions *while* we were listening. So, our attentional system is more sophisticated than a tape recorder because we have the capacity to exclude distractions at the same time as they occur. We do not have to edit our "mental" tape afterwards. In the same way, human concentration is far more flexible than a spotlight. Specifically, the *width* of our mental "beam" of concentration (i.e. its resolution or focus) can be changed. For example, it can be enlarged with *practice*. In other words, we can learn to "take in" or do more than one thing at a time as a result of systematic experience. To illustrate, over time, we can perform two demanding tasks simultaneously. Thus we can learn to talk while driving or to read while listening to the radio. In each of these cases, two skills which were initially challenging were rendered fast and effortless ("automatic") through practice. I shall return to this point later in the chapter.

Now that we have learned about the nature of attention, what role does it play in the cognitive system? Ever since the work of James (1890), it has been known that our attentional system plays a vital role in shaping our experience. In particular, it has three important functions in our lives (Zimbardo, 1992). First, as I explained above, it allows us to select sensory input from the world for further processing. This view is reflected in "filter" models of attention (e.g. Broadbent, 1958). Second, attention influences how we select appropriate responses for daily situations. By this theory, attention is valuable to us *not* only in limiting the amount of information which we can take in (filter theory) but rather, in limiting the number of *responses* which we can make at any time. This limitation in performing concurrent actions is clearly implicated in everyday life when we hear people complain that they "only have two hands!" Similarly, consider what might happen if you were jogging with a friend and suddenly asked them to multiply 47 by 29. You will probably find that you will need to stop or slow down in order to enable your friend to answer you. This shows that a vital task of our attention system is to "keep us from switching to a new task before the old one is successfully completed" (Zimbardo, 1992). But apart from regulating perception and action, the attention system mediates our awareness of the world. It yields a "gateway to consciousness". Thus of all the things which happen in our vicinity, "we actually become aware of only those on which we focus attention" (Zimbardo, 1992).

Before concluding this part of the chapter, I would like to comment briefly on a key "design feature" of the human attentional system. According to Allport (1989), concentration is a paradoxical system from an evolutionary perspective. To explain, our attention system appears to have evolved in order to satisfy two apparently conflicting constraints. On the one hand, in order to facilitate the learning of complex behavioural routines, the capacity to maintain our attentional focus over time is vital. But on the other hand, human attention must be sufficiently flexible to be capable of being diverted or overridden by changing circumstances—regardless of whether these originate externally (e.g. a threat from the environment) or internally (e.g. from a decision simply to change one's priorities). I shall return to this idea in Chapter 4 when exploring distractibility among athletes.

A BRIEF HISTORY OF RESEARCH ON ATTENTION

Although the history of research on attention is well documented (see Lachman, Lachman, & Butterfield, 1979), a brief summary may be helpful in this section. For over a century, attention has been regarded as a vital topic in the attempt to understand how the mind works. For example, Titchener (1908) proclaimed that psychology rests upon a three-fold foundation: "The doctrine of sensation and image, the elementary doctrine of feeling and the doctrine of attention". In order to explore attention empirically, the technique of "introspection" was used. This technique, which was regarded as a skill rather like wine-tasting, required highly trained observers to conduct a controlled search of the contents of their own minds before making a verbal report on what they found. For example, people might be asked to introspect on the mental experiences evoked for them by the word "table". Through the technique of introspection, Wundt (1907) hoped to unravel the mystery of how our ideas were bound together. Put differently, he used this method to "uncouple" the train of our thoughts.

Unfortunately, the paradigm of introspection soon encountered difficulties. In particular, it was discredited by Watson (1913) on the grounds that it is subjective, unreliable (e.g. a person's introspections tend to differ on different occasions) and unverifiable (since it proved impossible to arbitrate empirically between conflicting introspective reports about a given experience). As a result of these criticisms, introspection was abandoned as a research tool. Accordingly, attention became regarded as a "mentalistic" concept that was inimical to the prevailing Behaviourist philosophy. Not surprisingly, therefore, little research on concentration appears to have been conducted between 1920 and 1950. However, a challenge to this "received view" of the history of attentional research was offered by Lovie (1983). Briefly, by combing *Psychological Abstracts* meticulously, this historian shows that a considerable number of papers on attention were published during the allegedly barren years of this topic.

With the decline of "hard-line" Behaviourism in the 1950s, interest in mental topics was re-kindled. Accordingly, this era witnessed a strong resurgence of research interest in attention. This revival is attributable to several factors (Reddy, 1991). First, many radar operators during World War II experienced difficulties in sustaining concentration while awaiting the occurrence of infrequent but critical events (the problem of "vigilance" or sustained attention; see Parasuraman, 1984). This practical problem of maintaining vigilance highlighted the need for a new theory of concentration to replace traditional introspective accounts. Therefore, the 1950s heralded the arrival of applied, inter-disciplinary research on attention. More precisely, psychologists and engineers joined forces to explore practical issues surrounding human-machine interaction in military systems. This research quickly restored attention to its rightful place as an important problem in psychology. As Broadbent (1980) recalled: "It was only when applied psychologists were summoned to look at modern communication centres, and realised that there was nothing in the academic theory at the time to handle these problems, that attention had to be brought back into respectability" (p. 118). Second, technological advances like digital computers gave researchers a new way of thinking about the mind in information processing terms (i.e. as a communication channel). For example, researchers like Broadbent (1958) and Cherry (1953) proposed the analogy between the mind and a communication channel. The telephone, for example, takes the input of a human voice and transforms it into electrical signals which are relayed along the telephone line to be converted into a human voice signal at the receiver's end. Finally, the development of tape recorders allowed researchers to develop objective methods for the investigation of certain aspects of auditory attention (e.g. how people can concentrate on information presented to one ear while ignoring that presented to their other ear). Thus a prominent attention researcher in the 1950s, Moray (1969) claimed that "it is impossible to overestimate the importance of the tape recorder" in this field.

Historical scholars identify two main "waves" of theory-building on attention (Best, 1995). Although the first stage (i.e. between the 1950s and early 1970s) was dominated by the issue of how the attention system governs the selection of stimuli by limited-capacity perceptual channels, the second wave of studies (influenced by Kahneman, 1973) examined the cognitive resources that are required to perform concurrent actions. The first tradition explored attention primarily as a perceptual process and was concerned with selectivity of information processing. But the second tradition is concerned with attention as a form of mental "energy" which regulates our behaviour. Overall, therefore, research on "selective" attention gave way to studies of "divided" attention (see later in this chapter).

At first glance, the fact that the topic of attention has inspired a long and venerable research history suggests that considerable progress has been made in this field. However, a closer inspection of relevant literature indicates that at least three important issues remain unresolved. First, consider the issue of *internal* determinants of attention (see also Chapter 4). As Summers & Ford (1995) indicated, "internal attention, attention to cues that originate within the individual, has been largely neglected". This neglect is attributable mainly to methodological factors (Eysenck & Keane, 1995). In brief, it is easier to measure objectively external determinants of attentional processes than to assess the impact of putative "internal" phenomena (e.g. distracting thoughts or emotions). This neglect is rather disappointing because theorists like Posner (1980) clearly acknowledged the "aligning of attention with a source of sensory input or an internal semantic structure stored in memory". More generally, the reluctance of cognitive scientists to examine our internal world is unfortunate for both theoretical and practical reasons. Theoretically, in order to understand certain cognitive processes (e.g. memory), modern researchers have recognised the limitations of the assumption (e.g. Neisser, 1967) that information "flows" in only one direction in the mind (i.e. from the outside world inwards). For example, the multi-store model of memory (Atkinson & Shiffrin, 1968) has been revised recently in order to take account of this fact (Eysenck & Keane, 1995). In practical terms, the neglect of internal determinants of attention has been equally damaging. Specifically, it has led to a situation in which most cognitive psychologists today know little more about either the phenomenology or consequences of self-generated distractions than they did a century ago. Unfortunately, the study of "self-focused" attention has attracted relatively little interest from cognitive psychologists. Allied to this neglect of internal determinants of attention has been a marked reluctance among cognitive theorists to tackle the issue of individual differences in attentional processes. Perhaps the main problem in this case is that traditionally, experimental psychologists have adopted a *nomothetic* rather than an idiographic research strategy. To explain, by searching for general principles which explain how the mind works, cognitive researchers have neglected to investigate how people differ from each other in mental processes. As a result of this research strategy, individual differences have been interpreted by experimentalists as a source of error variance (Eysenck & Keane, 1995). I shall attempt to redress this neglect of individual differences in Chapter 5. A third criticism of laboratory-based research on attention concerns the fact that in most studies, it is the *experimenter* who tries to influence the focus of the subject's concentration through his or her instructions. As a result, according to Eysenck & Keane (1995), little is known about variables that "normally influence the focus of attention" such as the "unexpectedness" of stimuli.

TYPES OF ATTENTION

Let us now consider the two main types of attentional processes that have been identified by psychologists over the past century. "Selective" attention concerns the way in which we process some things while ignoring others and "divided" attention refers to the fact that, under certain circumstances, we can perform two or more simultaneous tasks equally well (Hampson & Morris, 1996). In addition to explaining these standard types of attention, I shall consider a third aspect of this construct (namely, alertness) because it offers important clues as to how concentration processes in athletes can be measured (see Chapter 5) and perhaps improved (see Chapter 6).

Selective attention

Research on selective (or "focused") attention examines the process by which we "select particular stimuli for awareness" (Pashler, 1994). Therefore, "selective" (or focused) attention refers to the process by which a person "selectively attends to some stimuli, or aspects of stimuli, in preference to others" (Kahneman, 1973). This preferential processing ability is essential to the performance of many skilled activities. For example, the complexity of instrument displays in modern jet fighters challenges pilots to pay attention to relevant visual information in the presence of an enormous number of distracting signals (Arthur et al., 1995). This emphasis on processing *relevant* features of the stimulus array is important as it reminds us that there are two aspects of selective attention: The ability to pinpoint one's attentional "beam" voluntarily and the ability to direct that beam at relevant parts of the stimulus array.

One of the earliest studies of selective attention was conducted by Cherry (1953) on the "cocktail party" phenomenon. This phenomenon refers to the common experience whereby someone, who is in a crowded room and apparently attending to a conversation with another individual, can somehow detect personally relevant information (e.g. the sound of their name) spoken in another part of the room. In other words, no matter how intensely we concentrate on a conversation, our attention can be "captured" by hearing our name spoken in an unattended sensory "channel". With the advent of research on this common experience, selectivity of processing has become the most frequently studied aspect of attention. Indeed, Wachtel (1967) went so far as to claim that "the study of attention is essentially the study of selectivity in perception and cognition".

A useful way of investigating how a particular mental system works is by studying what happens when we overload it deliberately (Pashler, 1994). This tactic was adopted by Broadbent (1958) who developed the "dichotic listening" task. In this procedure, two different auditory messages (e.g. two three-digit numbers) were presented simultaneously, via headphones, to both ears of the subjects. Participants were required to listen to both messages at the same time and repeat what they had heard. Using this task, Broadbent (1958) discovered that people paid attention to only one ear ("channel") at a time. Although some information was reported back from the "unattended ear", most of it was lost. Therefore, Broadbent (1958) concluded that a selective "filter" regulates the selectivity of our attention, processing messages according to such physical characteristics as the particular ear through which the information was received. All semantic processing was held to be carried out *after* the filter had selected the channel to which attention was to be paid. Treisman (1960) developed a modification of the "dichotic listening" task known as the "shadowing" procedure. In this task, people were equipped with headphones and required to respond to information presented to one ear while ignoring messages presented simultaneously to their other ear. For example, people might be asked to repeat aloud or "shadow" a message to their left ear such as *"One day, a little boy was playing on the road ..."* while hearing *"Two six five seven ... and a car came around the bend"* in their right ear. This research challenged the model of Broadbent (1958) because it found that people "swapped" channels in order to make sense of the auditory messages presented. For example, they reported back messages such as *"A little boy was playing on the road when a car came around the bend"*. The significance of this finding was immense as it showed that some semantic processing had in fact occurred in the unshadowed ear. Therefore, the meaning of the message must have been analysed *before* the filtering had taken place. But as theoretical interest changed from the perceptual aspects of attention to the action-control components of this construct (evident in Kahneman, 1973), the idea that attention refers to *concentration* of mental activity (or allocation of central resources) has gained prominence. This latter approach is associated with the concept of "divided" attention.

Divided attention
In daily life, we can observe that people often have trouble in performing two tasks equally well at the same time. The usual explanation for this phenomenon is that joint task performance consumes more of the attentional resources governed by the central executive of working memory (see Baddeley, 1986) than does single task performance. Indeed, it is assumed that performance of most tasks (e.g. driving a car) demands mental effort or "resources". These processing resources are thought to be limited. Therefore, when the joint "resource demands" of two tasks exceeds the available supply, time-sharing ability will drop (Wickens, 1984). For example, while driving, I often listen to the radio but when I face a potentially hazardous situation (e.g. trying to drive between two cars parked on opposite sides of a narrow road in heavy rain), I automatically turn off the radio so that I can "concentrate better". Similarly, drivers may stop conversing with passengers when the demands of driving are increased by poor visibility or heavy traffic. In other words, our performance suffers mainly because our attentional resources are thought to be limited, and because more mental effort

(concentration) is required in the "dual-task" condition than in single-task performance (see Pashler, 1994). In view of this phenomenon, "divided" or "distributed" attention refers to the mental process which governs our ability to perform two or more concurrent tasks efficiently. Sport provides countless examples of this skill. For instance, a basketball player must acquire the skill of looking for the best opportunities to attempt a shot or a pass while running with the ball (Gopher, 1992).

In general, research on divided attention is designed to explore the number and kinds of things a person can attend to at a given time. For example, we find it quite easy to walk while talking or to read while listening to music. But sometimes we experience problems in dividing our attention successfully. To illustrate, it is difficult to talk to someone while reading a book. In such situations, our mental "time-sharing" ability suffers (Wickens, 1984). It is this problem of establishing the limits of our time-sharing skills which attracts researchers in the field of divided attention. Specifically, they explore the *efficiency* with which we can attend to and perform simultaneous actions.

One of the most popular ways of exploring divided attention is through the "dual-task" paradigm (e.g. Posner & Boies, 1971). This paradigm attempts to measure the *spare mental capacity* of people while they are engaged in concurrent cognitive activities. In this procedure, Subjects are given a primary task (e.g. in sport, receiving a serve in volleyball; see Castiello & Umilta, 1988) and simultaneously required to monitor some intermittent secondary stimulus (e.g. by responding vocally whenever they hear an auditory tone). The assumption here is that the secondary "probe" demands some attentional capacity. Accordingly, the speed of responding to this probe is held to be inversely related to the momentary attention devoted to the primary task. In short, the secondary task is used to assess the amount of mental effort expended in performing the primary task. Clearly, the secondary task is assumed to function as a measure of the residual attentional resources (spare mental capacity) not required by the primary task. The attentional costs associated with dual-task performance can be estimated by subtracting single-task reaction time (RT) from dual-task RT and then dividing the difference by single-task mean RT. This proportional change in RT is usually the dependent variable in "dual-task" performance research (Marquie & Baracat, 1992).

Dual-task techniques assume that there is a limit to the performer's attentional capacity. Therefore, when a great deal of resources are consumed by the primary task, less capacity is available for the performance of the secondary task. So, differences between the peoples' performance on some baseline measure of the secondary task and their performance under experimental conditions are assumed to reflect the amount of "mental effort" expended on the primary task. One criticism of the dual-task procedure is that it is insensitive to speed-accuracy "trade-offs"—the fact that people may "swap" performance on one task so that they can improve performance on the concurrent companion task (Fisk, Derrick, & Schneider, 1986–1987). Thus "without a sensitive measure of primary task performance and some indication that primary task performance was held relatively constant to the single-task performance level, little meaningful information can be inferred from secondary-task performance" (p. 317).

A good example of the use of dual-task methodology in attentional research in sport comes from a study conducted by Goulet, Bard, & Fleury (1992). Briefly, these authors examined the relative attentional demands of the processes leading to anticipation of a serve in tennis. The primary task in this experiment consisted of identifying the type of service presented in a 16mm film and the secondary task required a manual response to an auditory probe. Three different experimental conditions were used. In the first situation, the probe was presented during the "ritual" stage of serve preparation. In the next condition, the probe appeared during the "preparatory" phase. Lastly, the probe was presented during the "execution" phase of the serve. Subjects were instructed to maintain their level of performance during single- and dual-task performance. Results showed that, as expected, the primary task performance of the expert group was superior to that of the novice group. But no differences were apparent between the groups in performance of the secondary task (i.e. probe reaction time). However, the probe reaction time was longer in the first condition (when presented during the "ritual" phase) than in either of the other conditions. This result suggests that the initiation of the perceptual part of the anticipation of a tennis serve is more demanding of attention than are the other component processes. Clearly, this paradigm is a potentially useful tool for exploring the mental resources required by different sport skills.

Alertness

As I explained earlier, attention has physiological as well as cognitive components. These components interact continuously. For example, according to Kahneman (1973), the amount of cognitive resources available in the central executive of the attention system at any moment is influenced by the arousal level of the person. Specifically, the more aroused the person is, the greater the attentional resources available to him or her. Therefore, being tired or otherwise under-aroused tends to restrict one's attentional capacity relative to states of heightened alertness. Therefore, we need to learn more about the biological substrates of the attention system.

At least three different neuroscientific techniques facilitate the exploration of the functional anatomy of human attention (see reviews by Posner & Carr, 1992; Posner & Petersen, 1990; and Posner & Rothbart, 1992). First, neuroimaging techniques involving positron emission tomography (also known as "PET-scanning") may be used to detect changes in blood flow in localised cerebral regions. To explain, every cell in the body needs energy to conduct its metabolic processes. In the brain, neurons obtain this energy from glucose which is available from the bloodstream. In the PET scan, a patient is injected with a mixture of glucose and a non-toxic radioactive tracer compound. The blood absorbs this mixture and transports it to the brain. In minutes, while on its way to various brain sites, this mixture emits positively charged particles called "positrons" (hence the term "positron emission tomography"). These positrons, in turn, give rise to gamma radiation that can be measured and photographed. These measurements of changes in blood flow are then used to indicate the extent of cognitive activity occurring in the brain region under investigation. In this way, PET blood-flow mapping techniques provide multiple pictures of the brain "at work". Clearly, the assumption here is that changes occur in the metabolic requirements of specific brain regions that are involved in cognitive activity. Therefore, increased blood flow in certain cortical regions is held to be associated with greater cognitive processing in these locations. Second, electrical activity recorded from scalp electrodes can provide details of "event related potentials" (ERP) in the brain (see also Chapter 5). These potentials represent the average of electroencephalogram (EEG) waves recorded over a large (e.g. up to 100) number of trials (Haberlandt, 1994). The ERP data are useful because they yield a continuous temporal record of what is happening electrically in the brain as the person engages in specific cognitive activities. Finally, clinical case studies are being used increasingly to explore localisation of cognitive functions in the brain. Specifically, the study of task performance by people suffering from various pathologies of attention (e.g. as a result of localised lesions in the brain) may shed light on how the different components of the attention system are organised. For example, people who have lesions in the posterior parietal lobe often experience difficulty in disengaging their attention from a given location (Posner & Petersen, 1990). This result suggests that the parietal lobe controls the ability to shift attention away from its present focus. Conversely, people who have suffered damage to the thalamus may have trouble in engaging attention. Taken together, these findings suggest that our attention system does not have a single neural "control centre" in the brain. Instead, it is monitored by a network of anatomical areas (Posner & Petersen, 1990). But what are these areas?

According to Posner & Rothbart (1992), there are three important systems in the brain which regulate attentional processes. These are the "posterior network" (which involves some portions of the parietal cortex, associated thalamic areas such as the pulvinar nucleus, and parts of the mid brain's superior colliculus), the "anterior network" (which includes areas of the mid pre-frontal cortex) and the "vigilance system" (which involves the right lateral mid frontal cortex). The posterior attention network is involved in directing attention to different spatial locations (e.g. when looking for a target item in a visual search task). Damage to this region appears to produce a deficit in one's ability to disengage or shift one's visual attention. The anterior attention network appears to underlie our ability to attend to cognitive operations such as semantic processing. As I mentioned previously, alertness seems to be associated mainly with the right cerebral hemisphere (which is associated also with regulation of heart rate). In particular, the right lateral mid frontal cortex seems to be especially active during auditory vigilance tasks (Posner & Rothbart, 1992). Another brain process that is implicated in the control of alertness is the norepinephrine (NE) system. Therefore, NE pathways provide the physiological basis for maintaining alertness. In summary, there are a number of brain structures involved in mediating visual attentional processes (Kosslyn, 1994). These areas include the parietal lobes, the frontal eye fields, the superior colliculus, the anterior cingulate, and the pulvinar nucleus of the thalamus (which has long been considered as a "switching station" by attention researchers). However, in view of the fact that attention is a multi-faceted construct, it would be wrong to expect that any single brain region could serve as our "attentional centre". I shall return to this topic in Chapter 5 when I examine how concentration skills in athletes can be measured.

THEORIES OF ATTENTION

At least two classes of attentional theories can be identified: "Bottleneck" models and capacity theories (Hampson & Morris, 1996). These approaches may be characterised as follows.

Filter models of attention

Early theories of attention assumed two propositions (Hirst, 1986): First, the human information processing system is thought to have a fixed capacity. Thus Garner (1974) remarked that "the human organism exists in an environment containing many different sources of information ... and the amount of information available for processing is always much greater than the limited capacity" (pp. 23–24). Also, according to Broadbent (1971), "selection takes place in order to protect a mechanism of limited capacity" (cited in Allport, 1989). The attention system had evolved, it was argued, to protect the mind from informational overload. Second, this limitation is best understood as a "bottleneck" or filter in the system.

On the basis of these assumptions, researchers in the 1950s examined the mechanisms by which selective attention was achieved. The traditional views (e.g. Broadbent, 1958; Treisman, 1964) invoked some sort of hypothetical filtering mechanism, like a "bottleneck" or an attenuator, which restricted the flow of information through the processing system. For example, Broadbent (1958) referred to a "filter at the entrance of the nervous system which will pass some classes of stimuli but not others". The filter was thought to operate in the nervous system between the time that sensory information was registered and the time it was subsequently analysed by the perceptual system. It was held to let through stimuli which are intense, novel, changing or unexpected (Zimbardo, 1992). Furthermore, Broadbent (1958) proposed that filtering is an "all-or-none" process. For example, participants in shadowing tasks were assumed to be incapable of understanding material presented to the unattended channel. But it soon emerged that, just as in the case of the "cocktail party" phenomenon, the attentional filter does not block out unattended messages completely: It merely attenuates them (or turns down their "volume"). Items which contain some special significance (e.g. the sound of one's name) bypass the filter. Therefore, it was concluded that the processing of highly familiar and relevant words was automatic or involuntary (Kinchla, 1992).

"Filter theories" are theories which explored the location and characteristics of this processing "bottleneck" of attention. Indeed, Kahneman (1973) claimed that the study of selective attention was really the search for the bottleneck in the information processing system. Unfortunately, subsequent research failed to locate a structural bottleneck in a fixed location anywhere in this system. Two questions preoccupied filter theorists. First, at what stage was the information filtered out of the mind? Put differently, was selection of information based on stimulus characteristics ("early selection" approach) or was it based on semantic features as well ("late selection")? The first attentional models (e.g. Broadbent) adopted the former view—by proposing that the filtering of stimulation occurred early in the process of perception. However, subsequent research (e.g. by Deutsch & Deutsch, 1963) suggested that the bottleneck occurred later in the information processing process—as a filter for the selection of appropriate *actions*. Indeed, a third theoretical position on this debate (e.g. by Norman, 1968) postulated a *moving* bottleneck! A second question also preoccupied attention researchers in the 1950s. What happened to the "non-shadowed" or unattended message in the filtering process?

Unfortunately, no conclusive answers were found to these questions. In fact, serious doubts were raised about the plausibility of filter models. First, Neisser (1976) showed that there was no evidence of any physiological limit on the amount of information that can be attended to at once. Indeed, the brain routinely conducts an immense amount of parallel processing in controlling such mundane activities as standing upright (e.g. integrating perceptual information from visual, vestibular and proprioceptive sources). Second, in dichotic listening tasks, people sometimes reported detecting meaningful phrases (e.g. their names) inserted into the message presented to the unattended ear. Overall, one of the biggest problems faced by filter models was that there seemed to be no obvious location in the information processing system in which a definite structural limitation could be identified. Furthermore, as explained above, selective attention has been studied traditionally by presenting people with competing auditory messages and drawing conclusions from what they could, or could not, report afterwards. But this approach has been criticised by Neisser (1976) on the grounds of excessive passivity. To explain, he claimed that "shadowing" experiments deal more with what is *done to people* rather than with how people direct their own attention. In this regard, recent research by Logan (1995) has explored the process by which people use linguistic cues (e.g. "below") to direct their visual attention to different spatial locations. Neisser's research, however, indicates that people's concentration in real life is far more active than had been assumed by Broadbent's models. In short, people usually choose the information they want to attend to and this process is governed by expectations which are not typically elicited by the tasks studied in laboratory research. In summary, the bottleneck metaphor of attention was largely discarded in the 1970s (Hirst, 1986) but the assumption of a finite capacity in our information processing system endured. Indeed, this assumption also underlies "capacity" theories in this field.

Capacity models of attention

Capacity models of attention (e.g. Kahneman, 1973) arose from the study of divided attention. Instead of viewing attention as a mechanical operation (i.e. the product of a filtering system; see Broadbent, 1958), capacity theorists speculated that the construct is best understood as a form of "fuel" or energy that may be allocated strategically between different tasks in accordance with the person's expectations and current priorities. Indeed, this *economic* metaphor of attention fits in neatly with many of our everyday experiences. For example, note how often we use such terms as *"paying"* attention to something or *"investing"* mental effort in it.

In general, capacity theories of attention have explored people's ability to do two or more things at once. In the laboratory, this skill can be studied by giving people two or more simultaneous tasks and asking them to perform each of them as well as possible. Success here involves dividing one's concentration between the performance of two or more concurrent activities (e.g. reading the paper while listening to the news on the radio). Another example of capacity theory comes from the everyday experience of driving a car. To explain, consider how easy it is to drive a car around one's own locality—especially in good weather or lighting conditions. Here, your driving skill is so automatic that you can probably do several things at the same time—like listening to the radio, talking to a passenger and planning your day. In this situation, you are easily able to divide your attention between concurrent activities. But note what usually happens when you are driving an unfamiliar car, in a strange neighbourhood in poor weather conditions or in darkness. Here, you will have little spare attentional capacity as all of your "mental effort" will be devoted to safe driving.

The preceding examples raise the question of how many things we can do at any one time. According to James (1890), the answer is "not easily more than one (thing), unless the processes are very habitual; but then two, or even three, without very much oscillation of attention". Indeed, research shows that people are capable of some extraordinary feats of divided attention. For example, skilled pianists can play written musical scores while shadowing verbal messages (Allport, Antonis, & Reynolds, 1972). Less dramatically, people's ability to divide their attention effectively depends on two key factors (Eysenck & Keane, 1995): (i) the amount of practice or experience gained by the person in performing the tasks simultaneously; (ii) whether or not the tasks to be performed use different senses. These factors were expanded by Hirst (1986) who identified four general techniques used by people to divide their attention successfully: (i) co-ordinating two tasks into a single higher-order task. For example, when putting on a coat, people are doing several things at the same time—such as moving their arms, swinging their torsos and lowering one shoulder; (ii) practising one task until it is automatic and then combining it with a second task; (iii) learning to keep competing tasks insulated from each other (as there is strong evidence that less interference occurs between tasks when they have different stimulus characteristics than when they share the same features); (iv) finding processing time in one task to share with another task. Unfortunately, the skill of dividing one's attention successfully appears to be task-specific (Hirst, 1986). Thus a person who can play the piano while talking cannot necessarily type while talking and vice versa. Likewise, people have difficulty in performing two actions which use the same sensory system. For example, notice how difficult it is to whistle a favourite tune (which involves acoustic information processing) while simultaneously listening to another tune on the radio.

Before concluding this section, it is important to explore the issue of whether attention is better regarded as a *unitary* central resource or as a set of "modules" (i.e. attentional sub-systems) which have different yet specific resource limitations. In other words, are attentional resources unitary or multiple? According to Kahneman (1973), attention is best understood as a central, undifferentiated reservoir of mental energy. This "pool" of energy can be "drained" off between different concurrent tasks depending on such factors as the specific priorities and the prevailing arousal level of the performer. An alternative theory, however, is that particular processing structures draw upon separate "structure-specific" capacity pools (Navon & Gopher, 1979). For example, there may be different specialised modules for the processing of visual and auditory information.

Although it is difficult to arbitrate empirically between these rival theories, evidence has accumulated from the "dual-task" paradigm (see above) which challenges the undifferentiated resources theory. As I explained, this paradigm proposes that when two tasks (e.g. A and B) are performed concurrently, and the difficulty of one of them (e.g. A) is increased, the demands on the pool of attentional resources should become greater. Therefore, if performance of task A is to be maintained at a consistent level, then performance of task B is likely to suffer. Unfortunately, research evidence suggests that when task A is made more difficult, and when the same standard of performance on this task is required, adverse effects do not necessarily occur on task B. For example, as we learned above, skilled pianists can simultaneously play written musical scores and engage in verbal shadowing with no disruption of either task (Allport, Antonis, & Reynolds, 1972). In addition, recent neuroscientific evidence also raises doubts about the plausibility of the undifferentiated resources model of attention. Thus a recent review by Hartley (1992) concluded that "the evidence strongly supports the claim of a modular organisation. There are a variety of different structures and systems ... carrying out attentional functions" (p. 10). Accordingly, it seems "unlikely that there is some general attentional resource". So, perhaps attention is better understood as a series of *separate resource pools* (e.g. Wickens, 1984) each with unique attention-performance limitations. This approach views attention not as some general purpose energy source but rather as a series of dedicated modules within the information processing system. One obvious implication of this view is that it questions the validity of attempts to measure "absolute" amounts of attention demanded by performance of some primary task in sport (Abernethy, 1993). What evidence would support a multiple-resources view of attention?

Several lines of evidence can be adduced in this regard. First, in dual-task research, mutual interference effects increase when tasks share common sensory or output modalities (McLeod, 1977). Conversely, when the primary and secondary tasks are in different sensory modalities, little or no interference effects are observed. In addition, neuropsychological evidence (from studies of regional cerebral blood flow, rCBF) indicates that different parts of the human prefrontal cortex are activated selectively during different aspects of attentional task performance (Allport, 1989). Apparently, this finding favours the view that there is "a multiplicity of attentional functions, dependent on a multiplicity of specialised subsystems. No one of these subsystems appears uniquely 'central' " (Allport, 1989). Unfortunately, the major difficulty with multiple resource theory is that it is difficult to test or falsify. Almost any pattern of interference between two tasks can be explained by postulating some pattern of attentional resources (Anderson, 1995b).

ATTENTION AS A SKILL

Having explored the nature, types and theories of attention, it may be helpful to outline an issue which arises from current research on this construct. This issue concerns the relationship between attention and practice and it is important as it has implications for the proposition that attention may be regarded as a skill—a recurrent theme of this book.

Attention and practice

Earlier, I suggested that practice may offer people a way of overcoming their mental capacity limitations. Let us now examine this idea more closely. Ever since James (1890) described the transition from novice to skilled performance in terms of "habit development", it has been agreed that the performance of any skill, whether cognitive or motor, changes as a function of practice (Schneider, Dumais, & Shiffrin, 1984). What seems to happen is that deliberate or intentional learning (i.e. "controlled" processing) of a given sequence of movements is gradually replaced by effortless (or "automatic") performance. For example, whereas a novice typist may initially display a slow and laborious approach to keyboard skills, an experienced typist can hold a conversation with someone while typing 100 words per minute. Likewise, skilled pianists often claim to practise musical pieces "in their fingers" so that their minds are free to pay attention to other matters. But these anecdotal observations are no substitute for empirical evidence. Therefore, consider what Spelke, Hirst, & Neisser (1976) discovered about the value of practice in skill learning. This study showed that following an 80-hour, four-month series of training sessions, two people were able to achieve "automatic" performance of two initially demanding, concurrent mental skills—reading texts and copying down unrelated words dictated to them by the experimenter. Interestingly, these researchers concluded "people's ability to develop skills in specialised situations is so great that it may never be possible to define general limits on cognitive capacity". In summary, there is strong support for the idea that the practice of a given task tends to reduce the amount of cognitive resources which it requires.

But why does practice change performance? Although no clear answer to this question exists, Logan (1988) proposed that practice works by changing the nature of the task to be performed. Specifically, each episode of practice creates a new memory trace which is a new "instance" of the skill. As a result, performance becomes effortless because there are more opportunities to recall instances (Haberlandt, 1994). Thus practice increases a person's knowledge base by producing more instances of the skill to be learned. Unfortunately, the exact reasons why repetitions are effective are not fully clear. However, research shows that practising with knowledge of results (KR) is one of the best ways of acquiring a skill (Annett, 1991).

The principal change which practice brings is a reduction in one's awareness of mental effort in performing the skill in question. To explain, at first, novices must devote considerable effort and attention to each stage of the skill to be learned. Therefore, their initial attempts to master it are slow, error-ridden and clumsy. But with sufficient practice, their skills become fluent, effortless and accurate. This stage of skill mastery is called "automatic processing" and refers to a "fast, fairly effortless process that is ... not under direct subject control, and is responsible for the performance of well-developed skill behaviours" (Schneider, Dumais, & Shiffrin, 1984).

Although considerable theoretical debate exists about the criteria of automaticity (see Hampson, 1989), two main features appear to characterise automatic behaviour (Pashler, 1994). First, it proceeds without voluntary control (i.e. it is "obligatory"). In addition, it does not require processing resources. A common example of automatic processes is the perceptual recognition of familiar objects: It takes place without intentional effort and seems to require little or no processing resources. The concept of automaticity, according to Treisman, Vieria, & Hayes (1992), refers to a state of skilful, fluent and effortless performance which people achieve through extended practice of a given task. Several theories have been postulated to explain this phenomenon. First, some theorists (e.g. LaBerge, 1973) interpreted automaticity as a form of perceptual learning in which features of stimuli become perceived in larger units which makes them independent of expectation. Another theory (e.g. Schneider, Dumais, & Shiffrin, 1984) proposes that automaticity is linked to attentional processes. A third approach treats automaticity as analogous to the compilation process of a computer. Specifically, in automaticity, declarative knowledge is transferred to procedures through production routines (Anderson, 1983). Finally Logan (1988) suggested that automaticity results from the accumulation of specific "instances" across repeated trials. These instances are directly retrieved under conditions which foster automatic responses.

Intriguingly, as Carr (1992) noted, early psychologists like Huey (1968) observed that in learning a skill, "repetition progressively frees the mind from attention to details, makes facile the total act, shortens the time, and reduces the extent to which consciousness must concern itself with the process" (p. 104). A good example of automaticity in sport comes from gymnastics. Thus Peter Vidmar, a silver medal winner in gymnastics in the 1984 Olympic Games, explained what he thought about when performing: "The only thing I am thinking about is ... the first trick. And, as I start the first trick, then my body takes over and hopefully everything becomes automatic and all I have to do is worry about those little adjustments" (cited in Schmidt, 1987, p. 85).

What are the main criteria of automatic behaviour? According to Haberlandt (1994), automatic processes are involuntary, easy, consume relatively little mental capacity, and can be carried out concurrently. Conversely, "controlled" processes are usually "effortful" or demanding, difficult, have a longer latency and are susceptible to disruption. In more detail, Kahneman & Treisman (1984) suggested that automatic processes (such as reading familiar words): (i) are involuntary (can be triggered without intention and once started cannot be stopped intentionally); (ii) do not draw on general resources; (iii) do not interfere with each other; (iv) are usually unconscious. Therefore, automatic processes (i.e. those which do not require attention) are regarded as unavoidable and occurring without capacity limitations.

Although this distinction between "controlled" and "automatic" cognitive processing is plausible intuitively, it has received growing criticism from attention researchers (Summers & Ford, 1995). Two problems are especially noteworthy. First, it may be somewhat simplistic to propose that attentional resources are homogeneous. Thus Navon & Gopher (1979) proposed that different processing resource modules may become available for different kinds of mental activities (e.g. depending on the sensory modality involved). In addition, researchers like Abernethy (1993) have questioned the validity of the boundary between controlled and automatic processes. For these theorists, degrees of automaticity are possible. Therefore, perhaps controlled-automatic processes reside on a continuum rather than in a rigid dichotomy.

Attention and individual differences

As we learned in Chapter 1, the general goal of cognitive psychology is to understand how the mind acquires, stores and uses knowledge (Neisser, 1967). Unfortunately, in their search for general principles underlying knowledge-seeking activities, cognitive researchers have devoted relatively little attention to studying individual differences in mental processes. This neglect of how people differ from each other in cognitive strategies has been noted by Eysenck & Keane (1990) who lamented cognitive scientists' reluctance to take individual differences seriously. Indeed, they observed that, for most cognitive researchers, the typical research strategy is "to use analysis of variance to assess statistically the effects of various experimental manipulations on cognitive performance, but to relegate individual differences to the error term" (p. 500).

Fortunately, not all cognitive psychologists have been blind to the value of studying individual differences in mental processes. For example, studies have shown that individual differences in attention are significantly related to performance on such "real-world" tasks as piloting an airplane (Gopher & Kahneman, 1971) and driving a car (Arthur & Doverspike, 1992). These applied studies usually employ some version of the traditional dichotic listening task to measure attentional abilities (Arthur et al., 1995). For example, Gopher & Kahneman (1971) tested cadets in the Israeli air force using an auditory "shadowing" task which required Subjects to identify target digits presented against a background of words. Results showed that the cadets' performance on this task was one of the best predictors of success in their training programme. The concept of "individual differences" in attentional ability suggests that the construct itself may be regarded as a skill. Indeed, this view is endorsed by such researchers as Hirst (1986). But is that description valid? What exactly is a "skill" anyway?

As I proposed in Chapter 1, a skill is a form of goal-directed behaviour (Fitts & Posner, 1967) or a form of "problem solving" (Glencross, 1992). To explain, the task facing any skilled performer is to use their knowledge (both declarative and procedural) to satisfy the demands of the situation. Similar views are expressed by other theorists. For example, Fitts & Posner (1967) identified three criteria of skilled behaviour. It must be (a) organised sequentially, (b) purposeful or goal-directed and (c) involve feedback. For them, "skilled" behaviour designates the co-ordination of some set of actions to achieve a specific goal (Hirst, 1986). So, what is gained by adopting a view that attention is a mental skill? According to Hirst (1986), there is a crucial difference between viewing attention as a "resource" and as a "skill". To explain, if we regard attention as a resource (the standard view since Kahneman, 1973), then it becomes important to explore the way in which people allocate this resource to various task demands. But in accepting this position, the psychological processes underlying people's ability to do two or more things at once takes only a secondary role. However, according to Hirst (1986), proponents of a "skills" approach to attention are interested in describing what people *do* when performing two tasks simultaneously. For example, a small child cannot put on a coat while talking. But an adult can do so rather easily. Why? Resource theorists might say that frequent practice in putting on one's coat has reduced the attentional resources required by this task to negligible amounts. Therefore, it is no longer difficult to perform this action. However, researchers who view attention as a skill may explore how practice with putting on coats leads people to co-ordinate a series of actions (e.g. moving one's arms, swinging one's torso) into a single fluent movement. Here, the emphasis lies in understanding what *precisely* happens in people's behaviour as a function of practice.

Is attention a trainable skill? To answer this question, Gopher (1992) suggests that we require evidence to show that: (i) attention can be controlled voluntarily; (ii) problems and failure can arise from inadequate attentional control; and (iii) that attentional control can be improved with practice. With regard to the first of these criteria, he concluded that "several lines of experimental data support the ability of performers to adopt a selective set, divide and switch attention at will, and produce graded priority levels for two concurrent performed tasks" (p. 303). With regard to the second criterion, namely attentional control problems and failures, there is evidence that some of these deficiencies may be attributable to inadequate attentional control (e.g. performers may invest their attentional resources inefficiently between the concurrent tasks). In summary, Gopher (1992) concluded that many performance difficulties stem from "insufficient knowledge about the efficiency of allocation or from deficient control abilities". Finally, he claimed that the ability to control attention can improve with practice. But what about this last criterion: Can people really benefit from attentional control training? One promising line of evidence on this question comes from the work of Gopher (1992) who recently explored the effect of 10 hours of practice with a specially designed computer game called "Space Fortress" on the subsequent flight performance in the Israeli flight-training school. The computer game was devised to simulate a complex and dynamic aviation environment. Briefly, it poses a difficult and continuous manual-control task while also eliciting such skills as visual monitoring, decision making and attentional resource management. Results showed that relative to a control group, "flight performance scores showed large and significant advantages for trainees who received emphasis-change game training". Not surprisingly, therefore, Gopher (1992) concluded that "the potential to control attention and develop attention strategies exists".

Overall, it seems plausible to propose that attention is a skill. Thus a recurrent theme in this book is that sport offers attention researchers a "natural laboratory" in which to explore this hypothesis. For example, a study by Castiello & Umilta (1992) on the attentional abilities of expert volleyball players suggests that these athletes have developed the ability to quickly re-orient their attention during matches. To explain, as a result of extensive practice, proficient volleyball players have mastered the capacity to shift their visual attention *covertly*—by processing what is happening in the *periphery* of their visual field without shifting their gaze to that location. Therefore, these authors conclude that "attention is a flexible process, subject to changes in practice, and that expert athletes are characterised by a higher attentional flexibility, which allows them to reduce the effects of unexpected events" (p. 307).

SUMMARY

Cognitive psychology is concerned with the scientific study of how the mind works in receiving, storing and using knowledge in everyday life. Within this field, the study of "attention", or the concentration of mental effort on sensory or cognitive events, is extremely important. Clearly, without some central executive system for allocating cognitive resources to what we perceive and do, our lives would be completely chaotic. Therefore, the attentional system may be viewed as a bridge between perception, cognition and action. Its nature and characteristics must be examined if we wish to make any progress in understanding the concentration processes of athletes. Therefore, this chapter attempted to explain what cognitive psychologists have discovered so far about the human attentional system.

I began by identifying three key components of the construct of attention: selectivity of processing (focused concentration), mental "time-sharing" of actions (co-ordination of skilled behaviour) and regulation of alertness (arousal-control). Then, I provided a brief review of the historical treatment of this multi-dimensional construct. Next, I distinguished between two main types of attention: selective and divided. Each type of attention has generated its own sub-field of research. "Selective" attention refers to our ability to process information preferentially or to direct and focus the beam of our "mental spotlight" (commonly known as "concentration") voluntarily. "Divided" attention, however, denotes our capacity to perform several different tasks simultaneously (e.g. listening to the radio while reading). Another aspect of attention—alertness—was also examined. This analysis led to a brief review of the main brain processes which are implicated in the regulation of sustained attention.

Theories of attention comprise both "filter" and "capacity" models. In general, "filter" theories of selective attention (e.g. those of Broadbent) are concerned with identifying the location and characteristics of certain structural limitations (e.g. a hypothetical bottleneck) in the information processing system. Capacity theorists, however (e.g. Kahneman), adopt a less mechanical view of attention. In particular, they suggest that it is best understood as a form of mental resources or "fuel" which can be allocated strategically to concurrent actions according to such principles as "automaticity" (i.e. the finding that with sufficient practice, skills become fluent, effortless and unconscious). One recent controversy in this field, however, concerns the precise nature of these hypothetical central resources which are alleged to be distributed across concurrent actions. Are these attentional resources undifferentiated or modular? As yet, no clear answer has emerged to this question. I concluded this chapter by marshalling some empirical support for a recurrent theme of this book: The proposition that attention may be regarded as a skill which can be enhanced through appropriate practice and instruction. This theme will be considered again in Chapter 6.

SECTION TWO

Concentration in sport

Section Two (which comprises Chapters 3, 4 and 5) attempts to answer three main questions about concentration in "sport performers" or "athletes". Firstly, why is the ability to concentrate effectively such a vital prerequisite of successful performance by athletes (Chapter 3)? Secondly, if concentration is such a crucial mental skill, why do sport performers "lose it" so easily (Chapter 4)? Finally, can concentration processes be measured accurately (Chapter 5)? Each of the chapters in this section attempts to provide answers to these questions using relevant empirical research findings.

In Chapter 3, I consider the reasons why attentional processes are vital to athletes. More precisely, based on evidence derived from anecdotal testimonials of world-class performers, descriptive research on "flow state", expert-novice differences and studies of attention-performance relationships, I argue that concentration is a key cognitive substrate of sporting excellence. Next, in Chapter 4, I explore the nature and impact of a plethora of common "distractors" which divert the attention of sport performers away from their intended thoughts or actions. As well as analysing these factors, this chapter also addresses the theoretical question of why the mind is prone to attentional lapses at all. Finally, in Chapter 5, I review the adequacy of various empirical strategies for measuring attentional skills in athletes. Among the tests evaluated are instruments derived from the psychophysiological, experimental and psychometric measurement traditions.

CHAPTER THREE

Concentration in sport performance

"The ability to selectively attend to the appropriate stimuli is critical in most athletic situations ... Selective attention is perhaps the single most important cognitive characteristic of the successful athlete"

(Cox, 1994, pp. 66–67)

"Attending to appropriate stimuli is believed to be one of the most important cognitive characteristics distinguishing expert from novice performers"

(Landers et al., 1994, pp. 313–314)

"Klinsman brought home to me how you have to concentrate all the time, so when a chance comes you're going to take it"

(Teddy Sheringham, English international soccer striker, cited in Lovejoy, 1995, p. 19)

"I was never more focused for a race. No looking about, tunnel vision all the way ... my concentration was so intense that I almost forgot to look up to see my time after touching the finishing pads"

(Michelle Smith, 1995 European 200 metres swimming champion, cited in Roche, 1995, p. 1)

"I just took it ball by ball, trying to give every delivery 100% concentration"

(Michael Atherton, England cricket batsman, after his remarkable ten and three-quarter hour innings against South Africa, cited in They all agree, 1995, p. 25)

INTRODUCTION

In the preceding chapter, I examined the construct of attention and discussed the principal theories and issues surrounding it. This analysis was necessary for two reasons. First, the conceptual distinction between selective and divided attention helps us to classify research on concentration in athletes. In addition, a review of research findings on the nature of the attentional system offers a scientific counterpoint to the tendency towards "naive phenomenology" (Summers & Ford, 1995) which characterises many studies in contemporary sport psychology. To explain, all too often, sport psychologists appear to be willing to accept uncritically athletes' subjective, retrospective accounts of their own mental processes. Although these reports constitute a valuable source of evidence on certain mental states (e.g. those characterised by distracting thoughts), they must be validated scientifically before being accepted because they are often biased or incomplete. For example, athletes engaged in racquet sports may be convinced that their eyes follow the ball continuously during play. But this subjective experience may be illusory as it is challenged by objective evidence that squash and tennis players tend to look *away* from the ball at crucial moments during its flight towards them (Summers & Ford, 1995). For similar reasons, Brewer, Van Raalte, Linder, & Van Raalte (1991) urge caution in the interpretation of athletes' post-hoc reports. To summarise, athletes' insights into their concentration processes should be carefully evaluated against what we already know about the human attentional system. It is to this task that I turn now.

The purpose of the present chapter is to review psychological research on the concentration processes of athletes. As confirmed by the quotations above from psychologists and sport performers, such processes are regarded as being crucial determinants of athletic success. I shall proceed as follows. To begin with, I shall examine what the term "concentration" means in sport psychology. Then, I shall explain why attentional skills are valued highly by athletes. Next, I shall review research findings on selective and divided attention in sport performers. This section will also feature a brief treatment of the issue of expert-novice differences in concentration skills. Finally, I shall sketch some of the theoretical and methodological benefits for sport psychology which stem from conducting research on concentration in athletes.

The main theme of this chapter is the idea that the ability to concentrate effectively is the mental key to successful performance in sport. Support for this proposition comes from several sources. For example, Cox (1994) remarked that few topics in sport psychology are as important as understanding "attention or concentration" in athletes. Likewise, Abernethy (1993) observed that it is difficult to imagine anything more important to the performance of sport skills than "paying attention to the task at hand". Similarly, Summers, Miller, & Ford (1991) suggested that attentional factors such as "sustained alertness and freedom from distraction" are vital ingredients of athletic performance. To illustrate these claims, consider some of the attentional skills required by cricket players (Gordon, 1990). To begin with, bowlers have to identify quickly whether an opposing batsman is right- or left-handed. This information is vital for choice of bowling delivery. In addition, as with other closed-skill performers, bowlers must be able to disregard thoughts of previous or future actions while focusing entirely on the present delivery. But above all, they must be able to regulate their concentration at will, or to "switch on at every delivery and switch off during periods of inactivity" (Gordon, 1990). Not surprisingly, batsmen in cricket require similar concentration skills. They may have to maintain alertness for periods ranging from between four and eight hours in order to achieve a good score (Summers & Ford, 1995). Indeed, occasionally, they have to hold their concentration for even longer durations. For example, in a remarkable rearguard innings on the second day of a test match against South Africa in December 1995, Michael Atherton, the England captain, batted for *ten and three-quarter hours* to help his team to secure a draw which had seemed impossible after the previous day's play. Significantly, according to Johnson (1995), Atherton's face during this marathon innings "was so screwed up in concentration that it looked like a road map".

In view of the importance of concentration to athletes, many performers have developed informal psychological theories about how to achieve an optimal mental "focus" for competition. For example, Ian Botham, the former England cricket captain, advises athletes to expend their limited attentional resources sparingly in cricket due to its indeterminate duration. Specifically, he claims that "how you conquer the concentration barrier is an individual thing. Some people chew gum, others talk, others keep quiet. Some talk to themselves. My personal way is to switch off the moment the ball is dead. I concentrate totally from the moment the bowler starts his run until the ball is dead—then I relax completely and have a chat and a joke with another fielder. But as soon as the bowler reaches his mark I switch back on to the game. I think anybody who can concentrate totally all the time is inhuman. I certainly can't. So I try to keep the light moments to times when they won't affect my performance in the game" (Botham, 1980, p. 5). A similar approach to concentration was displayed by the famous golfer Lee Trevino who used to laugh and joke with the crowd on the fairway but adopt a totally "focused" approach when addressing the ball. Clearly, both Botham and Trevino understood the value of being able to exert mental effort at the right times. But how do they know when to switch on their concentration skills? Unfortunately, little research has been conducted on how athletes either monitor or change their attentional processes in the moments that precede skilled performance.

In summary, attentional skills are vital in sport. But what exactly do sport psychologists mean by the term "concentration"? Furthermore, what empirical findings have emerged from research on concentration in athletes? The purpose of this chapter is to provide answers to these important questions.

NATURE AND IMPORTANCE OF "CONCENTRATION" IN SPORT

Most sport psychologists use the terms "attention" and "concentration" interchangeably (Bond & Sargent, 1995). To establish the validity of this practice, it may help to review the meaning of the term "attention". Recall from Chapter 2 that cognitive researchers usually define this term as the concentration of mental effort on internal or external events. Most sport psychologists (e.g. Landers et al., 1991) accept this definition, emphasising two crucial features of this construct in particular. To begin with, they stress the *selectivity* of attention (Summers & Ford, 1995). Thus in order to concentrate effectively, athletes must endeavour to exclude irrelevant stimulation while focusing on what is deemed to be important at that moment. Secondly, in agreement with Ian Botham, sport psychologists recognise that considerable "mental effort" is required in order to maintain alertness for prolonged periods. By exerting such mental effort, distractions which might impair performance can be avoided (Castiello & Umilta, 1988). But what does the term "mental effort" mean? According to Paas, Van Meerienboer, & Adam (1994), it refers to the amount of mental resources allocated to task demands. In other words, it involves "controlled processing" (see Chapter 2) of task-relevant stimuli. Intriguingly, the focus of our mental effort is believed to be "shiftable" (Summers & Ford, 1995). In other words, we can change both the direction (i.e. where it is pointed—at either internal or external targets) and width (i.e. how much information is detected) of our beam of concentration when necessary (see Chapter 2). Combining these features of selectivity and mental effort, we can see why sport researchers like Schmid & Peper (1993) define concentration as the ability "to focus one's attention on the task at hand and thereby not be disturbed or affected by irrelevant external and internal stimuli". As an example of this skill in action, consider how a quarterback in American football must distinguish very rapidly between relevant and irrelevant information before throwing a pass (Weinberg & Gould, 1995). Initially, the player must glance at the opposing defence in order to determine its formation. Then, if he decides that the linebackers are going to "blitz", he will probably replace the long pass he had intended to throw with a shorter pass. But being aware of this likely change, the linebackers often fake their movements in order to send irrelevant messages to the quarterback. Therefore, it becomes critical for the quarterback to be able to distinguish rapidly between valid and spurious signals for a particular "play".

Because it seems reasonable to use the terms "attention" and "concentration" synonymously, I shall now consider the construct of attention in more detail. Most sport psychologists recognise the fact that attention is a multi-dimensional construct (see Chapter 2). For example, Etzel (1979) has identified a number of attentional components of sport performance. To begin with, "capacity" refers to the amount of mental energy available for task-related information processing in a given sport situation. In other words, "attention" is simply situational processing capacity. Next, the "duration" dimension of attention refers to the ability to sustain concentration over time—a characteristic also known as "vigilance" (Perry & Laurie, 1993). Third, attentional "flexibility" refers to the ease with which a sport performer can "direct and alter the scope and focus of attention" (Etzel, 1979). For example, as we shall see in Chapter 5, marathon runners may switch from concentrating on their own bodily sensations (an attentional strategy known as "sensory monitoring") to focusing instead on features of the environment in which they are running (a "dissociative" strategy). Finally, "selectivity" designates the most obvious feature of attention (see Chapter 2), namely, analytical information processing activities. Unfortunately, the preceding conceptual distinctions involving the construct of attention are not well understood by sport psychologists. For example, some sport researchers fail to understand that there are at least two different types of attention: selective and divided (see Chapter 2). To illustrate, Gauron (1984) claims that "all of us *suffer* from divided attention" (italics mine). Indeed, he goes on to say that "one way of knowing that you are not concentrating is when you are experiencing divided attention. Your mind will be split as you attempt to do more than one thing at a time" (p. 44). Rather than complaining about this experience, however, cognitive psychologists use it as a starting point for their research on how attentional resources may be spread between concurrent activities (Pashler, 1994).

At the outset, I proposed that concentration skills are vital prerequisites of success in sport. It is now time to adduce some evidence to support this assertion. This evidence comes from four sources: (i) the views of experienced sport psychologists and athletes; (ii) descriptive studies on the phenomenology of "peak performance" experiences; (iii) attempts to construct distinctive psychological profiles of successful athletes; and (iv) research on the relationship between attentional strategies and performance in sport.

Opinions of sport psychologists and athletes

To begin with, as I indicated at the beginning of this chapter, testimonials to the importance of concentration to athletes abound among sport psychologists. For example, according to Nideffer (1993b), the ability to concentrate on a task is "almost universally recognised as the most important key to effective performance in sport". These sentiments are echoed by Winter & Martin (1991) who warn athletes that "without good concentration, no amount of skill, fitness, or motivation is going to get you to your peak". Likewise, Singer et al. (1991) proposed that the ability to concentrate on the present task, "without being distracted by irrelevant information, thoughts or physical cues, leads to better accomplishments". Perhaps most emphatically, Orlick (1990) explains that if he were asked to choose one mental skill that distinguishes successful from unsuccessful athletes, it would be "their ability to adapt and refocus in the face of distractions".

Complementing these opinions from psychologists are the views of two former tennis champions, Rod Laver and Bjorn Borg. These legendary performers attributed their success largely to their extraordinary powers of concentration (Weinberg, 1988). A similar testimony to the importance of focused mental effort was provided by Judy Hashman, the former US badminton international and ten-times All-England champion, who claimed that "concentration is the greatest single factor which brings you success" (Hashman, 1982). Conversely, but equally convincingly, attentional deficiencies are blamed widely for unsuccessful performances in competitive sport. To illustrate, John McEnroe said that "mentally, my concentration cost me that match" after his defeat by Andrei Cherkasov in the French Open in May 1991 (McEnroe blames lack of concentration, 1991). More generally, Abernethy (1993) identified three consequences of poor concentration in athletes. To begin with, performers who cannot differentiate between relevant and irrelevant task-related cues are hampered by adopting too *broad* an attentional focus: They are not selective enough in their perception. For example, a soccer defender who boots the ball aimlessly up the field, under no pressure from opponents, instead of attempting to direct it to an unmarked team-mate, shows evidence of having an attentional "beam" that is too wide for what is required optimally by the situation. In such circumstances, when ones' attentional focus is too wide, distractibility is highly likely. On the other hand, mistakes can occur if one's attentional spotlight is directed at the "wrong" (i.e. task-irrelevant) target. To explain, if a golfer were to pay too much attention to muscular sensations while preparing to putt, the resultant stroke would probably suffer. Here, the mistake lies more in the *direction* of attention (in this case, internal rather than external) than in its "narrowness". A third problem may arise if an athlete takes too long to switch attention from one target to another. For example, the fact that a soccer player may get "caught in possession" (i.e. is robbed of the ball by an opponent) suggests a failure to alternate attention swiftly enough between the skills of receiving and passing the ball. Taken together, these examples indicate that the efficiency of sport performers' concentration is determined largely by their capacity to identify task-relevant cues to action as quickly and as accurately as possible. As well as being able to detect task-relevant cues, athletes must be capable of knowing what to *do* when performance anxiety occurs. Interestingly, one of the cognitive principles underlying strategies for dealing with "nerves" (see also Chapter 4) is that performers should instruct themselves to perform some task which takes their mind off the anxiety experienced. The logic here is that as the mind can only concentrate on one mental target (or idea) at a time, one cannot simultaneously focus on an instruction to perform some specific action (e.g. a tennis player may give themselves an instruction to "go down the line with the next return") and engage in self-destructive worry ("My opponent is too good for me—I'm bound to lose this match") at the same time. In summary, our analysis has shown that deficiencies in attentional skills among athletes are often associated with decrements in skilled performance.

Descriptive studies of peak performance states

Stronger evidence on the role of concentration in sport comes from studies of "peak performance" in sport (e.g. see Garfield & Bennett, 1984; Privette, 1981). In this coveted yet elusive state of mind, also known as "the zone" (Brewer, Van Raalte, Linder, & Van Raalte, 1991), "flow state" (Jackson, 1995) or "ideal performance state" (Williams, 1986), the athlete is absorbed totally in task-relevant concerns

(Mahoney, 1989). As Kimiecik & Stein (1992) declared, a "focusing of attention on the task to be completed is an important element of flow". Likewise, Mahoney (1989) claims that peak performers have developed "exceptional concentration abilities appropriate to their sport". These observations led Gould, Eklund, & Jackson (1992a) to conclude that optimal performance states "have a characteristic that is referred to, variously, as the ability to focus, concentration, a special state of involvement, awareness and/or absorption in the task at hand".

The importance of establishing an appropriate cognitive "set" for competition was emphasised in a study of the mental preparation strategies used by members of the 1984 Canadian Olympic Squad (Orlick & Partington, 1988). For these athletes, it was not until "focusing skills were refined that their dreams became reality". In a similar vein, McCaffrey & Orlick (1989) interviewed top professional golfers about the thoughts and feelings which were reported to have accompanied their best-ever performances. One of these golfers reported that "for my best rounds, my focus was on the shot that I was hitting every time. Nothing else. Nothing else entered my mind ... No thought at all". Another example of this focused mental state emerged from an experience reported by the late world-champion racing driver, Ayrton Senna, as he took "pole position" in a race in Monaco in 1988. Specifically, he claimed that "I suddenly realised I was no longer driving the car consciously. I was kind of driving it by instinct, only I was in a different dimension ... I was going and going, more and more and more and more ... It frightened me because I was well beyond my conscious understanding" (Williams, 1992, p. 27). A third illustration of the role of concentration in peak performance comes from the Irish snooker player Fergal O'Brien who defeated world-champion Stephen Hendry in the quarter-finals of the 1994 Irish Masters' Tournament. After this victory, O'Brien reported that "my concentration never wavered—it was like I was in a trance" (Stylish O'Brien, 1994). This reference to a trance-like state endows the flow experience with a mystical air. Perhaps the mysticism comes from the "automated" character of the skills involved. Thus "flow states" tend to be impervious to conscious introspection or attempted control (Mahoney, 1989). Therefore, paradoxically, efforts to analyse "flow" states usually produce impaired performance. Put simply, athletes are better advised to "let it flow" than to try to "make it flow". Theoretically, psychologists believe that the attempt to re-invest conscious mental effort in a skill which is already automatic tends to be counter-productive because it serves to "unravel" that skill. In other words, as Potter (1947) observed so shrewdly, "conscious flow is broken flow" (see also Chapter 4 for a discussion of "paralysis by analysis"). Other psychological experiences commonly reported to accompany "flow states" include a feeling of having abundant energy, a sense that time has slowed down and an overall sensation that one has and can exert complete mastery over the situation (Browne & Mahoney, 1984).

Unfortunately, due to their rather mercurial nature, peak performance experiences have attracted relatively little scientific interest from sport psychologists. On methodological grounds alone, however, subjective insights into these states should be treated with great caution by researchers. This circumspection is necessary because people's retrospective accounts of their own mental processes are vulnerable to various attributional biases (Nisbett & Wilson, 1977). To illustrate, Brewer, Van Raalte, Linder, & Van Raalte (1991) have shown that when people receive spurious feedback concerning the outcome of their performance on certain laboratory tasks, they tend unwittingly to distort their recall to corroborate this experience. In such circumstances, they may claim to have experienced such qualities as the focused concentration which is characteristic of the peak performance state. In view of such distortions, Brewer, Van Raalte, Linder, & Van Raalte (1991) urged researchers to be cautious in their interpretation of results from self-report studies of athletes' mental experiences. To paraphrase Berry & Broadbent (1984), we cannot describe all that we can do and we cannot do all that we can describe.

Profiles of successful athletes

A third source of evidence on the importance of concentration skills in sport performance comes from research which attempts to construct psychological profiles of successful athletes. As one might expect, successful performers in such sports as gymnastics (Mahoney & Avener, 1977) and wrestling (Highlen & Bennett, 1979) have been shown to possess greater attentional skills than their less successful counterparts. In a related vein, Gould, Eklund, & Jackson (1992b) interviewed members of the US wrestling team shortly after they had competed in the 1988 Olympics in an effort to elicit the thoughts and emotions which they had experienced during their athletic contests. Content analysis of the interview data suggested that the "best performance" experiences of competitors were accompanied by "a special sort of concentration and involvement in the match that featured an effortless awareness". Clearly, this experience bears a strong resemblance to other accounts of previously discussed "flow states". Not surprisingly, one of the themes which emerged from accounts of the wrestlers' "worst performances" during the Olympics concerned their distractibility through engaging in "task-irrelevant thoughts". Among the distractions experienced in these situations were thoughts about previous losses, speculations about possible future encounters, excessive awareness of officials or coaches and a tendency towards distractibility from external sources (e.g. watching the clock while the wrestling match was in progress). Another study of the mental characteristics associated with athletic success was conducted by Mahoney, Gabriel, & Perkins (1987). Briefly, these researchers found that elite athletes (comprising national and world championship winners) differed from less successful counterparts in the capacity to "efficiently deploy their concentration before and during competition". But this finding should be interpreted cautiously because between 25% and 31% of the elite athletes reported experiencing concentration *problems* during competitive encounters. Either way, concentration featured prominently in these athletes' experiences.

Attentional strategies and performance in sport

The last source of evidence on the importance of concentration comes from studies which indicate associations between the use of certain attentional strategies and successful performance in sport. For example, Morgan & Pollock (1977) found that elite marathon runners used an "associative" mental strategy while competing. Using this technique, the runners directed their mental focus towards their own bodily sensations (e.g. leg muscles) instead of allowing their mind to wander (see also Chapter 5). In addition, some researchers (e.g. Kerr & Cox, 1991) have found that skilled competitive squash players were better able to "narrow" their attention on relevant cues in the match than were less successful players. But apart from its value as a performance-enhancement technique, concentration is also important for athletes who are confronted by stressful situations. To illustrate, Gould, Finch, & Jackson (1993) found that among the techniques reportedly used by elite US figure skaters to cope with competitive pressure, practical focusing strategies were especially prominent. Thus one skater highlighted the value of "getting my mind focused. Being really efficient with my thoughts. Not letting anything interfere. Not becoming distracted. I found a way of doing this by talking to myself, by visualisation, by taking my time, by staying away from people who were most distracting to me" (p. 459). An additional source of similar practical advice for athletes is provided by Moran (1994a).

To summarise, there are at least four strands of evidence which may be woven together to show that concentration is justifiably regarded as a crucial mental skill in sport. Unfortunately, despite such evidence, relatively little empirical research has been conducted to test exactly what types of concentration processes are required by athletes in different sports. It is not surprising, therefore, that Boutcher (1992) concluded that "research ... examining the role of attention in sport is underdeveloped". Similarly, Maxeiner (1987) observed that "attention ... has been widely neglected in sport science, even though its relevance for sport performance is self-evident". Likewise, Hardy & Nelson (1988) concluded that "despite the importance placed upon attention control by practitioners of sport psychology, empirical studies of attention control in sport are a rarity". To illustrate this neglect, Klinger, Barta, & Glas (1981) reported that a search of *Psychological Abstracts* between the mid 1960s and the late 1970s produced only one reference to a controlled study of concentration in athletes (Sheedy, 1971).

As I explained in the preface to this book, the neglect of attention by sport researchers is attributable mainly to the fact that much research in sport psychology is atheoretical in nature. In other words, it is influenced more by intuition than by conventional hypothetico-deductive methods, with theoretical interpretation being *post hoc* rather than before the data are collected (Landers, 1983). Throughout this book (especially in Chapter 1), I have suggested that cognitive psychology can provide a "suitable framework" (Boutcher, 1992) for future research on attention in sport.

RESEARCH ON CONCENTRATION IN SPORT

Before I review what researchers have discovered about attention in sport, I shall consider the best way to classify empirical studies in this field. According to Kremer & Scully (1994), five sub-fields of concentration research may be identified. To begin with, the selective attentional processes of athletes have been studied on the assumption that attention involves the skill of detecting "advance cues" that are relevant to the task in hand while "screening out" distractions (Abernethy, 1987). Next, other scholars (e.g. Rose & Christina, 1990) have investigated "divided attention" or the ability of athletes to perform two or more actions simultaneously (e.g. a soccer player running with the ball while scanning opportunities for a possible pass). A third category comprises research (e.g. by Easterbrook, 1959) which has examined the effects of physiological arousal on attention and performance. Usually, studies in this area reveal that arousal causes an involuntary *narrowing* of the attentional focus which, in turn, leads to a deterioration in performance. Yet another strand of attentional research in sport is that which explores individual differences in concentration strategies among athletes (e.g. see Morgan & Pollock, 1977). I shall review this approach in Chapter 5. Finally, a variety of psychophysiological studies on attention have been conducted (e.g. Landers et al., 1994; also discussed in Chapter 5). A simpler classification system for concentration studies has been proposed by Abernethy (1993). This system, which distinguishes between research on selective attention, divided attention and arousal-performance effects, is appropriate for our purposes because it is compatible with the typology of attention which I outlined in Chapter 2. Using this typology, I shall now review what is known about selective and divided attentional processes in athletes. I shall delay a discussion of arousal-concentration relationships until Chapter 5.

SELECTIVE ATTENTION IN ATHLETES

As I explained in Chapter 2, "selective" (or "focused") attention involves the mental process by which some input is selected for further processing while other sources of information are ignored. It is a covert process by which stimulus details are filtered so that "only the most relevant information gets processed" (Abernethy, 1987). As sport provides many dynamic situations which challenge people's selective attentional skills, some psychologists have used this topic to explore the nature of athletic expertise. For example, if the human visual system has difficulty in "tracking" targets moving faster than 70 degrees per second, how can professional baseball players have time to detect, let alone hit, balls that travel with angular velocities exceeding 500 degrees per second (Bahill & La Ritz, 1984)? More generally, how do expert athletes in any fast-ball sport (e.g. tennis) transcend structural information processing limitations (see Chapter 2) by appearing to have "all the time in the world" (Bartlett, 1947) when they perform their skills?

The answer to this puzzle is that, compared to novices, expert athletes in fast-ball sports seem to attend earlier to, and extract more information from, "advance" cues provided unwittingly by their opponents. This finding helps us to understand at least two aspects of athletic expertise (Abernethy, 1993). First, by focusing attention on relevant advance cues, expert performers can prepare to initiate responses *earlier* than novices. This makes them *seem* faster than less experienced performers. In addition, early cue detection allows experts to recognise redundancy in the stimuli to be processed and so reduces the "load" on their working memories. For example, an experienced tennis player knows that they do not have to watch all of the movements of an opposing server. In fact, the direction of the ball toss may be the most important factor to consider when anticipating a serve. For example, if the ball is tossed to the right by a right-handed server, an experienced tennis player will automatically prepare to step to the right hand side in preparation for the return of serve. This discovery that experts "pick up" advance cues earlier than do novices raises an interesting question. For how long do experts actually look at the ball in fast-ball sports? Contrary to popular wisdom (and also to coaching advice; see Seiderman & Schneider, 1985), research suggests that top players in such sports do *not* "track" the ball all the time. To illustrate, studies on the eye-movements of international table-tennis players have shown that it is *not* necessary to watch the ball continuously in order to respond successfully to opponents' shots: Scanning the predicted landing-position of the ball seems to work just as well as attempting to view it while it is in flight (Ripoll & Fleurance, 1988). Of course, anticipation is inextricably linked with experience and knowledge. Therefore, in this section, I shall explore the extent to which expertise in sport is associated with efficiency in selective attentional processes. But to begin with, let us consider some aspects of the temporal constraints of some fast-action sports.

Many sports require high-speed processing of, and response to, dynamic arrays of stimulus information. These "detection-and-response" activities take many forms. For example, in some sports (e.g. baseball) the player uses equipment (e.g. a bat) to intercept a moving object at some optimal point. But in other sports, the task is to ensure that one's *body* coincides with the arrival time of a projectile (e.g. as when one prepares to head a ball in soccer). In both cases, anticipation and timing are crucial aspects of successful performance. To illustrate, consider examples from soccer and cricket. In soccer, a goalkeeper who has decided to come off the goal-line to catch a corner-kick must be able to process such information as the flight of the ball, and its relative position to their own body, despite the presence of dynamic peripheral distractions (arising from the movements generated by up to 20 jostling figures in the penalty-area). This skill in co-ordinating information reception and response initiation is known popularly as "timing" by athletes and coaches. Cricket is another sport which demands quick reactions and highly selective attention. In particular, research has been conducted recently to explore how batsmen (McLeod & Jenkins, 1991) and wicket-keepers (Houlston & Lowes, 1993) can respond so quickly to balls that are bowled at them at such high speeds (which can reach up to 40 metres per second; see McLeod & Jenkins, 1991). To appreciate the temporal constraints involved, consider that McLeod & Jenkins (1991) have estimated that a batsman has only about 700 milliseconds (msec) to "time" an action. In the light of these examples from soccer and cricket, it is widely believed that "perceptually quick" athletes, or people who can process a greater amount of salient information in a shorter period of time than their opponents, will have a distinct competitive advantage over their rivals. Thus Deary & Mitchell (1989) found that successful batsmen in cricket were faster at picking up information from briefly presented visual displays than were less proficient colleagues. However, this result is rather unusual as most studies in this field have found that expertise is highly domain-dependent (Abernethy, 1994b). In other words, a standard finding is that expert sport performers display superior perceptual skills *only* in sport-specific situations (see some examples below). However, different methodological paradigms may be responsible for these results. Thus whereas high-speed visual processing paradigms employ a duration of milliseconds, typical sport-specific perceptual paradigms use times of 4–5 seconds. In summary, as expected, sport psychology shows that the ability to perceive rapidly what is important in a given situation and to respond to it successfully is the hallmark of athletic expertise (Ericsson & Charness, 1994). But what cognitive factors promote such processing efficiency? Also, what role does selective attention play in regulating this system?

Expertise and attention in athletes

In Chapter 1, I considered the rival claims of "hardware" and "software" theories of athletic expertise. The former approach suggested that elite sports performers are equipped with faster information processing systems than those of novices. For example, they may have *shorter reaction-times* than beginners. This impression is supported anecdotally when tennis coaches praise the reflexes (e.g. "quick" eyes, "fast" hands or impressive "foot speed") of top-class players. On the other hand, perhaps expertise lies more in the mind than in the body of sport performers: Maybe they *anticipate* better, and prepare earlier, than do novices.

As I indicated, the first of these explanations appears to be untenable. Research fails to yield consistent evidence that expert athletes have reaction times that are significantly faster than those of relative novices. To illustrate, consider a case study from the sport of cricket (McCrone, 1993). Peter McLeod (University of Oxford) has tested the reaction-times of several top-class batsmen (including such outstanding performers as Allan Lamb and Wayne Larkin) to determine how well they could cope with cricket balls bowled at them by a machine. The balls were pitched at them on a mat which covered a series of wooden rods. These rods were necessary in order to simulate the unpredictable bounce, and change of direction, of a good bowler's delivery. Results indicated that none of the batsmen under study could react to a sudden change in the flight of the ball in less than 200msec—the figure which represents the typical reaction time of an adult in the general population. McLeod discovered that if the ball deviated unpredictably from its original path in *less* than 200msec, even the best batsmen were beaten every time. According to this type of evidence, therefore, elite cricket players do *not* appear to have significantly faster simple reaction-times than control subjects.

But what about the second hypothesis—the idea that anticipation generates "all the time in the world" (Bartlett, 1947) for experts? Some support for this theory is evident from empirical research. Thus McLeod (1987) found that expert batsmen are much better than beginners at anticipating the ball-flight, and likely landing position, of rapidly bowled cricket balls. Put differently, McLeod believes that top-class batsmen have accumulated sufficient "cricket knowledge" to be able to predict where a ball will be in the final 200msec when they will be "blind" to its path. They will then be able to "time" their reactions accordingly and deliver a smoother swing than beginners in order to connect with the ball. So, as I indicated at the beginning of this chapter, research suggests that, contrary to age-old coaching advice, experts in fast-ball sports like cricket and tennis do *not* simply "look at the ball" until a response is required (see also Bahill & La Ritz, 1984). This latter feat is perceptually impossible given that the sum of the receiver's reaction time and movement time usually exceeds the flight-time of the ball. Instead, what appears to happen is that experts in these sports are uniquely skilled in "anticipation". But what does this word mean?

The construct of "anticipation" is somewhat loosely understood in sport psychology. In fact, several different definitions of it may be identified. First, in fast-ball sports (e.g. tennis, cricket), it signifies "the early prediction of the terminal location of the ball" (Isaacs & Finch, 1983). Alternatively, "anticipation" refers to "efforts to forecast the future intentions of one's adversary" (Buckolz, Prapavessis, & Fairs, 1988). But one can anticipate in non-adversarial sports also. So, perhaps the most acceptable definition of "anticipation" is that it designates the "process by which performers utilise advance information in order to co-ordinate consequential behaviour" (Houlston & Lowes, 1993). This skill involves the ability to recognise the probabilities underlying what is happening in a given sport context. In tennis, for example, expert receivers use contextual (e.g. knowledge of opponent's tendencies) and body language (e.g. stance) aspects of the server's behaviour to predict ball-flight. Thus receivers "carefully study the action of the server's racquet and are able to predict approximately where in the service area the ball will land even before the server has hit the ball" (Ericsson & Charness, 1994, pp. 736–737). In short, experts have greater *anticipatory*, rather than reaction-time, skills than novices. Speed of response appears to be in the head, rather than the hands, of expert sport performers.

From the research reviewed above, a tentative principle emerges. To explain, given the time-constraints imposed by factors such as the velocity of the ball, the relatively short distances it must travel and the inherent limitations of the information processing system in "tracking" moving targets, expert performers of fast-action sport skills must use *anticipatory* processes to guide their responses. Therefore, expertise in sport depends considerably on the ability to make rapid and efficient use of minimal perceptual cues from opponents (Abernethy, 1987). Accordingly, expert athletes tend to perform better in situations which require rapid decision making. For example, consider how an expert tennis player prepares to return a slice serve. In this situation, the player will move diagonally rather than parallel to the baseline because this movement allows reduction of the angle of the serve. Similar observations apply in squash. Thus evidence is available to suggest that for expert squash players, "the important decision is made *before* instead of *after* the attack". Cues such as the angle that the attacking player's body makes with the front wall are especially revealing for proficient players who are trying to anticipate shots in a game (see Alain & Sarrazin, 1990). On the basis of studies like this, Cox (1994) claims that "selective attention is perhaps the single most important cognitive characteristic of the successful athlete".

But it is not only athletes who must focus precisely on task-relevant cues. *Referees* in sport are also required to display the same skills as athletes in processing information selectively. To illustrate, Weinberg & Richardson (1990) remind us that "all officials need to focus on the action and be sensitive to the relevant cues that dictate exactly what aspects of the activity they should focus on". Obviously, what makes refereeing exceptionally demanding as a cognitive task is that this selectivity of attention must be displayed in the face of a host of distractions arising from such sources as hostile spectators, belligerent coaches and volatile players. Interestingly, there is evidence that expert and novice judges of sport skills may focus on different cues when evaluating the performances of competitors. For example, Bard, Fleury, Carriere, & Halle (1980) examined the visual search patterns of gymnastics judges when scrutinising a film of competitors performing a balance-beam routine. Results showed that there was a significant difference between the experienced and novice adjudicators in the location of their visual fixations. Specifically, novice judges tended to scrutinise the lower limbs of the gymnasts whereas these cues were of little concern to the experienced judges.

Expertise and the cue-occlusion paradigm

One of the hallmarks of expertise is cognitive efficiency or the ability to "take in" large amounts of information in brief periods of time (Allard & Burnett, 1985). But how is this skill achieved? One way of exploring it is by examining the cues which experts pay attention to when presented with complex yet realistic stimulus displays in sport. In the "cue-occlusion" paradigm, associated largely with the work of Abernethy (e.g. Abernethy & Russell, 1987), expert and novice athletes are shown films of athletes performing various sport skills (e.g. serving in tennis, drop-shots in badminton). Extrapolating from these films, subjects are required to predict such details as the likely landing position of the ball. In some conditions of this paradigm, the experimenter deliberately occludes certain visual cues (e.g. by obscuring details of the performer's arm and racquet). Following such "cue-occlusion", subjects are expected to make predictions (e.g. about the terminal location of the ball) from the information available. The effect of selective cue-occlusion on the accuracy of subjects' responses helps to identify anticipatory cues used by athletes. Indeed, the fact that certain response decrements occur reliably when a given cue is occluded suggests that this cue could be a potentially valuable source of predictive information for the performer. However, the ecological validity of this paradigm is questionable for several reasons (see Summers & Ford, 1995). To begin with, subjects do not *actually* move or *physically* return a shot when they "respond" to their "virtual" opponents in this paradigm. In addition, the film simulations do not replicate the psychological conditions which prevail in a typical sporting contest (e.g. with regard to crowd noise and/or performance anxiety—factors which are known to affect attentional processes; see also Chapter 4). Therefore, critics like Mestre & Pailhous (1991) suggest that Abernethy's experimental technique contaminates (or "uncouples") the perception-action link which is thought to characterise real-life sporting skills.

Despite these criticisms, Abernethy (1993) claims that evidence gathered from the cue-occlusion paradigm suggests that, within their sporting domain, experts are superior to novices in their ability to "pick up" advance cues about relevant details like ball-flight information or the relative positions of opponents. For example, expert racquet sport performers have been shown to use advance cues (e.g. from arm and racquet positions) more frequently and earlier than do relative novices (Abernethy & Russell, 1987). Additional evidence to support the proposition that expert performers use anticipatory cues to predict the flight and landing position of balls has been gathered from studies of experienced performers in soccer (Morris & Burwitz, 1989), badminton (Abernethy & Russell, 1987), squash (Abernethy, 1990), cricket

(Abernethy & Russell, 1987) and tennis (Isaacs & Finch, 1983). In each case, experts have been found to "pick up" task-relevant cues earlier and more systematically than do less proficient colleagues. The advantages of early detection of relevant cues by athletes are obvious. First, advance cue utilisation tends to cause faster decision times and superior accuracy among experts (Summers & Ford, 1995). In addition, it facilitates the identification of possible redundancy among the cues which are sampled. This identification serves to reduce the "load" on the athlete's working memory, thereby allowing greater mental capacity to plan and implement strategic actions.

Expertise and athletes' eye-movements

Another clue to the perceptual cues used by athletes in sport performance comes from their eye-movements, whose function is to bring information into central or "foveal" vision. The assumption here is that the manner in which people inspect stimuli visually in sport situations reveals how their selective attentional system operates. Furthermore, it is believed that expert sport performers should differ from novices in such ocular variables as fixation time, visual search strategy, visual search rate and in the type of cues fixated. Most of these variables can be measured by studying the patterns of eye-movements displayed by people as they view slides or film-simulations of sporting encounters. Interestingly, one finding that has emerged from such studies is that the visual strategies used by performers often depend on the situation in which they are playing. For example, consider some research on eye-movement patterns in table-tennis players. Ripoll (1989) analysed the visual search patterns of a sample of French international players as they played a particular stroke (the forehand) in two different situations—while performing practice drills and when playing competitive matches. Results showed some interesting differences between the eye-movement patterns revealed in these different situations. Specifically, during match conditions, when stimulus uncertainty was highest, players tended to fixate their opponents more frequently and to "track" the ball for longer periods than in practice situations. The average visual tracking duration was 240msec in the match but only 150msec in the practice drill. In passing, Abernethy (1988) pointed out a curious misnomer pervading eye-movement studies. Specifically, he suggested that more can be learned from how the person allocates focal attention through ocular *fixations* rather than through ocular movements: Hence, as Mackworth (1976) remarked, the "pause is mightier than the move" in eye-movement research!

On the basis of the cognitive characteristics associated with expertise in other fields (e.g. see Bedard & Chi, 1992), it might be expected that the visual search patterns of sport experts should be more constrained (being guided by heuristic strategies indicating *where* to look) and more efficient (i.e. they should "sample" the visual array more systematically) than those displayed by novices. Unfortunately, there is surprisingly little evidence that there are consistent differences in visual search variables between expert and novice sport performers (see Abernethy, 1988, for a brief review). Most of the studies in this field have been conducted by comparing the manner in which performers of different ability levels view either slides or film-simulations of sport-specific information. For example, Abernethy & Russell (1987) recorded the eye-movements of expert and novice badminton players while they viewed a film-simulation of a competitive situation that was presented as part of the cue-occlusion paradigm. From these data, expert-novice differences in visual search strategies were analysed. Results showed that although the experts were superior to the novices in extracting early anticipatory cues from the filmed display, no differences between these groups were apparent in visual search strategies. So, these authors concluded that the factors which appear to be crucial in discriminating experts from novices lie not in visual search strategies but rather in "what use the performers can subsequently make of this available environmental information". This point was highlighted neatly by Abernethy (1990) who found that although expert squash players were superior to novices in picking up advance cues (e.g. from opponents' racquets and racquet-arms) from opponents, their visual search patterns were "indistinguishable from those of novices". Therefore, he concluded that the distinguishing feature of expert squash players lay not in *where* they looked but rather in what they *saw*: Their ability to "extract and utilise the information available at key fixation locations (such as the opponent's racquet, arm and head)". However, a study by Bard & Fleury (1976) challenges this conclusion. These authors discovered that, when presented with slides of basketball match situations, ocular fixation data indicated that expert players accorded priority to the empty space between the ball-carrier and the basket whereas novices ignored this cue. So perhaps Abernethy (1990) over-stated his conclusion that the visual search patterns of sport experts are different from those of beginners. A more detailed treatment of this issue is presented by Bard, Fleury, & Goulet (1994).

Research on eye-movements in athletes is notoriously difficult to interpret. To begin with, the assumption that ones' gaze and ones' concentration are synonymous is dubious on several grounds (Abernethy, 1988). For example, anyone whose mind has wandered while reading knows that "looking" at a book is not necessarily the same as "seeing" the meaning of the words. Whereas "looking" involves some degree of visual fixation on a target, "seeing" entails the detection of relevant information from it (Abernethy, Neal, & Koning, 1994). Similarly, it is possible for people to shift their attention without changing their fixation-point. Thus research on "covert" attentional orienting suggests that the focus of attention is often different from the target which is fixated visually. Indeed, this phenomenon can be used strategically in sport. For example, Castiello & Umilta (1992) showed that expert volleyball players were superior to novices in dividing their focal visual attention between non-contiguous regions of space. In particular, they can deceive opponents by pretending to pay attention to one location (e.g. the centre of the visual field) while directing their attention covertly to another place (e.g. the periphery of the field). Clearly, there are compelling reasons for failing to accept any simplistic notions of attention which underlie research on eye-movements. Yet another problem in this field is that standard eye-movement recording equipment is rather insensitive to cues in the periphery of the visual field. Furthermore, substantial individual differences in eye-movement patterns are apparent (e.g. Petrakis, 1987). Last, but not least, eye-movement recording instruments are notoriously difficult to use: They are intrusive, difficult to calibrate (especially if portable) and may induce the person being tested to adopt a spurious mode of looking at things. In summary, a variety of conceptual and methodological obstacles afflict attempts to measure and draw conclusions from the eye-movements of athletes.

DIVIDED ATTENTION IN ATHLETES

In Chapter 2, I explained that "divided" attention refers to the cognitive resources which govern our capacity to perform several concurrent actions equally well. Clearly, sport offers many opportunities for exploring the nature and consequences of this skill. For example, how is it possible for a basketball player to dribble with a ball and monitor an opponent's movements at the same time? Unfortunately, less research has been conducted on divided attention than on selective attention in athletes. Perhaps this imbalance reflects the view of concentration which permeates the "first wave" of theories in this field (see Chapter 2)—namely, the idea by Broadbent (1958) that attention is a system for "filtering" perceptual experience rather than one which regulates action-control. However, Allard & Burnett (1985) used the dual-task paradigm (also explained in Chapter 2) to investigate which types of secondary task interfered with the automated skill of batting in softball. They argued that the less expert batters, being more reliant on consciously calculated (declarative) information, would be more susceptible to the disruptive influence of a concurrent task than would the more expert players (whose skills were assumed to be more automated). As expected, the performance of the novices deteriorated in the presence of concurrent tasks. This finding suggests that for the less skilful players, batting consumed working memory resources which were required to analyse the pitch of the ball coming towards them and so they were unable to perform a concurrent cognitive task.

Dual-task paradigm

Many sport psychologists believe that the best way to explore the divisibility of athletes' attention is by examining situations in which task performance is studied in relation to the combined demands of two or more concurrent activities. Let us now evaluate the application of this idea in sport (see Abernethy, 1993, for a more detailed review). Before doing so, however, I shall recapitulate some details of the principal methodological strategy used in this field—the "dual-task" paradigm (see also Chapter 2). In its original form, this paradigm involves the presentation of two tasks (a "primary" and a "secondary" task) over three conditions. In condition 1, the person is required to perform the primary task on its own. In condition 2, the secondary task is performed on its own. In condition 3, both tasks are performed concurrently. When this paradigm is applied to sport, the "primary task" usually consists of some closed skill (e.g. target-shooting in archery) whereas the "secondary task" typically assesses the subject's latency of making a pre-determined response (vocal or manual) to some "probe" signal (e.g. an auditory tone). Following comparison of performance between these three conditions, conclusions may be drawn about the attentional demands of the primary and secondary tasks. Among sport psychologists, most interest concerns performance in the condition 3, the concurrent task situation. In this condition, subjects are required to perform a primary task which is interrupted periodically by the presentation of a "probe" stimulus (e.g. an auditory tone). When this probe signal occurs, the person has to respond to it as rapidly as possible. It is assumed that the speed of responding to the probe is related inversely to the momentary attention devoted to the primary task. Therefore, if a primary task is cognitively demanding, then a decrement should be evident in secondary task performance. But if the performance of the secondary task in the dual-task condition does not differ significantly from that evident in the relevant control condition, then it may be assumed that the primary task is relatively effortless (or automatic). In summary, the dual-task paradigm is an attempt to measure the *spare mental capacity* of a person while they are engaged in performing some task or mental activity.

Dual-task paradigm in sport

Although the dual-task paradigm has been used extensively in cognitive psychology, it has attracted relatively little interest from sport scientists. However, the meagre literature in this latter field seems to be organised around two main questions (Abernethy, 1993). First, sport psychologists have explored the circumstances under which the division of attentional resources changes as a function of skill-learning. In addition, dual-task techniques have been used to examine the manner in which attentional processes fluctuate during the performance of a particular sport skill. I shall now provide some brief examples of each of these lines of research.

Changes in the allocation of attentional resources during skill learning have been examined by Parker (1981). In this study, netball players of different levels of expertise were required to perform two concurrent tasks. The primary task consisted of passing the ball to a designated target and returning as many catches as possible within a 30 second period. The secondary task consisted of detecting peripheral lights. Structurally, these tasks have reasonable "face validity" because they mimic some of the cognitive demands that occur in competitive netball, where players must be able to catch and pass the ball while simultaneously monitoring the relative positions of team-mates and opponents on the court. Results showed that little variation occurred between players of different skill levels in catching and passing the ball in the "primary task alone" condition. This evidence suggests that "ball catching" is an automatic skill among the netball players tested. However, as anticipated, performance on the *secondary* task helped to discriminate significantly between players of different levels of expertise. In particular, the expert players made significantly less peripheral detection errors apparent in the secondary task. Parker (1981) interpreted this finding as evidence that expert netball players have more "spare" attentional capacity to devote to the secondary task than do less proficient counterparts. An interesting feature of this study is that it shows that dual-task methods can reveal subtle differences in attentional division between performers of different skill levels. To explain, if the players had simply been compared on their ability to perform the primary task alone, no effects of expertise would have been apparent. However, in the concurrent task condition, the superiority of experts was clearly evident from the greater accuracy they displayed in *secondary* task performance. In other words, the dual-task paradigm is valuable in allowing differences in skill acquisition to be revealed in situations in which expertise effects are not readily apparent from observation of primary task performance on its own (Abernethy, 1993).

Dual-task methods were also used by Rose & Christina (1990) to examine expert-novice differences in the way in which pistol shooters allocated attention during the preparatory stages of their performance. Performers of three different levels of expertise were studied: elite, sub-elite and novice shooters. The primary task for these subjects consisted of a precision-shooting activity whereas the secondary task involved making a manual response, as rapidly as possible, to an auditory probe. As usual in this paradigm, the authors assumed that the time required to react to the secondary probe would serve as a measure of the level of attention allocated to the primary task at the time of probe presentation. Results showed that probe reaction time increased as shot time approached for performers at all three levels of expertise. This finding suggests that, not surprisingly, all shooters concentrated more intensely on the primary task as shot time approached. But expertise effects were found in secondary task performance. Specifically, the elite pistol shooters failed to respond to the secondary probe significantly more often than did the novices. Also, the experts were significantly more likely to abort shooting trials if they felt unprepared to complete a shot. Thirdly, performers in the relatively skilled groups (i.e. the elite and sub-elite subjects) tended to miss significantly more probes than novices during the aiming stage of their shot preparation. The authors interpreted this latter finding to indicate that the more proficient performers were beginning to focus more intently on task-relevant cues (rather than on secondary distractions) at this stage than were the novice performers.

Another application of dual-task methodology in sport concerns the study of how athletes' concentration may change during the performance of a given sport skill. For example, Castiello & Umilta (1988) presented athletes with two simultaneous tasks to perform: A "primary" task comprised a typical sport skill (e.g. reception of a volleyball serve, doing a 110 metre run, competing in a 110 metre hurdle run and returning a tennis serve) and a "secondary" task that consisted of making a vocal response to an auditory signal. Performance of these skills was assessed at different temporal stages of skilled performance. The authors expected that the speed of the response to the auditory signal would be inversely correlated with the resource demands of the primary task. In general, this hypothesis was corroborated because it was found that resource demands changed as a function of the moment during which they were probed. To illustrate, for athletes trying to return a tennis serve, it was concluded that *all* component stages of this skill were attentionally demanding (based on evidence that RT in the secondary task increased significantly during the dual-task condition as compared with a control condition). Interestingly, there was one stage in the execution of this skill that appeared to require most concentration. This occurred when the served ball was hitting the court. Castiello & Umilta (1988) suggested that this stage requires most attention because it is at this point that the receiver must evaluate the trajectory of the ball in order to anticipate how best to play the appropriate return shot. Interestingly, this discovery of the importance of paying attention to the destination of a serve in tennis is supported by evidence, mentioned earlier in this chapter, that expert table-tennis players do not keep their eyes trained on the ball during play but try instead to predict its likely landing position (Ripoll & Fleurance, 1988).

Different types of serve in volleyball also make different attentional demands on receivers. For example, Castiello & Umilta (1988) discovered that the reception of a "floating" serve requires more concentration than does that of a "jump" serve—even among professional volleyball players. A possible explanation for this finding, according to the authors, is that the floating serve is less *predictable* than the jump serve. In the latter shot, the trajectory of the ball can change unpredictably. But in the "jump" serve, ball speed is critical whereas ball trajectory can be estimated quite easily. In general, it seems that volleyball receivers' "mental effort" (concentration) tended to increase as the ball passed over the net, reaching its maximum when the ball was about to be received.

In the late 1980s, it seemed likely that the study by Castiello & Umilta (1988) would have heralded renewed interest in the dual-task paradigm in sport. Unfortunately, due to several flaws in this approach (e.g. see Abernethy, 1993; Fisk, Derrick, & Schneider, 1986–1987), such an upsurge of interest has not occurred in the intervening decade. Three seemingly intractable problems have been identified in this paradigm. To begin with, problems may arise in the choice of secondary task(s) to be coupled with the primary activity. Specifically, if performance on secondary tasks is shown to improve with practice (which tends to occur when subjects experience repetitions of the same stimulus-response patterns over time—what Shiffrin & Schneider (1977) call "consistent mapping"), then erroneous assessments of the primary task's attentional demands may occur. Put differently, Fisk, Derrick, & Schneider (1986–1987) advocate that the information processing "load" of the secondary task must remain constant throughout the experiment. Perhaps the best way to ensure that this happens is to arrange for the secondary task to have "inconsistent mapping" of (i.e. an unpredictable pattern between) stimuli and responses. A visual search task, for example, would satisfy this criterion. Another problem with dual-task methodology concerns the possibility that performance on the primary task might vary across the experimental conditions. Under the logic of this paradigm, performance on the primary task must remain constant relative to the single-task control conditions. As Fisk, Derrick, & Schneider (1986–1987) pointed out, without a sensitive measure of primary task performance, "little meaningful information can be inferred from secondary task performance". Accordingly, these authors recommend that there should be equivalence of single and dual primary task performance. A third difficulty with this paradigm is that appropriate baseline measures must be taken for each task if the data are to be interpretable. Therefore, Abernethy (1993) recommended that the baseline conditions should match precisely the dual conditions "with respect not only to the stimulus-response configurations used but also with respect to the spacing and relative frequency of stimuli".

In summary, research on divided attention in sport has been facilitated mainly by the use of the "dual-task" paradigm. Using this approach, some advances have been made in identifying the amount of attentional "spare capacity" available to expert performers when performing a primary sport skill. In addition, this paradigm has led to objective analysis of specific stages of skilled performance which appear to demand most attention from performers during skill execution. Clearly, this evidence may have important implications for coaching practice (e.g. coaches could try to give priority to the automation of those aspects of the skill which require most attention initially). However, as I explained, several conceptual and methodological problems hamper the accuracy with which results from dual-task research may be interpreted in sport psychology.

IMPLICATIONS OF RESEARCH ON CONCENTRATION IN SPORT

The preceding research on concentration processes in athletes has yielded at least three benefits to sport psychology. First, the concept of selective attention as a "skill" (see also Chapter 2) has been helpful to sport coaches who have sought to improve performers' ability to extract maximum information as quickly as possible from the limited set of cues available in sport situations. Secondly, sport psychologists have begun to examine the circumstances under which the "beam" of our attentional "spotlight" (see Chapter 2) is either narrowed or expanded. Finally, the search for expert-novice differences in selective attention has raised interesting issues about the extent to which sporting expertise is "hard wired" (i.e. a product of physical aspects of our nervous system) or based on cognitive "software" (i.e. the knowledge which athletes acquire through coaching, practice and competitive experience). I shall now consider each of these topics briefly.

Selective attention as a skill

In Chapter 2, I introduced the proposition that attention may be regarded as a cognitive skill. This theme is supported not only by sport psychologists such as Cox (1994) but also has practical implications for coaching. For example, instead of requiring athletes to pay equal attention to all aspects of a given sport situation, coaches may be better advised to train them to "zoom in" selectively on cues which provide the greatest amount of specific, task-relevant information. These cues may serve as prediction "keys" which could activate programmed responses (see Yandell, 1990). For example, in volleyball, "blocking" may be a powerful attacking weapon because a team is usually blocking when it is serving and, of course, can only gain points when it is serving. To benefit from this situation, blockers must attend selectively to their assigned attackers and must "screen out" the actions of the setter or those of other spikers.

Another implication of this idea is that coaches may be able to help players to identify the most salient "advance" cues in a sport situation. Appropriate practice drills may then be used to consolidate this skill. For example, if a wrist movement in a racquet sport is regarded as an important predictive cue by a coach, then it would be possible to create drills in which a model wears a brightly coloured wristband to attract attention to this stimulus. In this way, the efficient usage of "advance" cues, which is one of the hallmarks of sporting expertise (see earlier in this chapter) may be modelled through theoretically driven instructional drills.

Attentional "narrowing" under pressure

Another development which has stemmed from the selective attention literature in sport is the discovery that certain emotional factors (e.g. anxiety) may restrict the "width" of our attentional beam—a phenomenon known as involuntary "attentional narrowing" (see Easterbrook, 1959). This attentional constriction is prevalent in competitive sport because of the highly charged emotional atmosphere in which many games are played. Indeed, when large crowds are present, anxious players participating in team-sports may fail to perceive better-placed colleagues simply because the emotional "heat of the moment" appears to hamper their peripheral vision. For example, Boutcher (1992) suggests that if an aroused point guard in basketball is looking for team-mates outside the key, attention may narrow so much that the player may fail to notice "open" players in the periphery.

Overall, anxiety seems to affect our attention in at least two ways: first, it restricts the *scope* of our attention span, and second it changes the *direction* of our concentration beam. Specifically, anxious people tend to attend more to internal stimuli (especially, thoughts of failure and imaginary catastrophes) than to external stimuli when they are required to perform complex tasks under pressure. Many experiences in everyday life confirm our tendency to "take in" less information when we are aroused than when we are relaxed. The usual explanation for this phenomenon is that the cognitive act of worrying (which tends to involve the creation of unpleasant imaginary "causal scenarios") is attentionally demanding and consumes considerable working memory resources. Therefore, less "spare capacity" is available for concentration on task-relevant information, such as the critical advance cues evident in the sporting situation. A fascinating field-study on the extent to which anxiety impairs concentration was conducted by Webster (1984) who discovered that *not one* member of an Australian Rules football team could recall all of the coach's instructions just *five minutes* after his pre-match address! Apparently, in this case, pre-match anxiety among the athletes impeded their retention of the coach's directions. An important implication of this finding is that pre-competitive instructions for sport performers should be short, clear and repeated. Interestingly, this advice is similar to that expressed in the guidelines advocated by cognitive psychologists for the presentation of emergency evacuation instructions to commuters (see Reed, 1996).

What theoretical mechanisms are involved in attentional narrowing? One of the earliest and most influential models of this process was proposed by Easterbrook (1959). Briefly, he postulated that arousal narrows attention, restricting the range of incidental cues that are used. But the effects of this restriction on subsequent performance are quite complex. For example, in complex sporting tasks, where there are a large number of vital cues available, a narrowing of attention may cause the person to ignore potentially valuable information. But in a simpler task, with fewer cues available, a restriction of attention may not be as detrimental to performance. Specifically, for any task "provided that initially a certain proportion of the cues in use are irrelevant cues ... the reduction (in the number of cues in use) will reduce the proportion of irrelevant cues employed and so improve performance. When all irrelevant cues have been excluded, however, ... further reduction in the number of cues employed can only affect relevant cues, and proficiency will fall" (p. 193). To illustrate Easterbrook's theory about how anxiety affects attention, consider an example supplied by Baumeister &

Showers (1986). A non-aroused goalkeeper may think about the fans' reactions as well as catching the ball and hence allow it to slip into the net; the moderately aroused goalkeeper may follow the game closely and be alert to the threat to the goal; but a highly aroused goalkeeper may fail to compensate for a "bad" bounce of the ball and allow it to enter the net.

An interesting study of the effects of emotional factors on attention was conducted by Rose & Christina (1990) using the dual-task paradigm. Briefly, these researchers discovered that as the time to perform a skill gets closer, attentional narrowing tends to occur. Using a sample of rifle-shooters, they found that reaction time to a secondary task (pressing a button with the non-shooting upon detection of an auditory signal) increased as "shot time" approached. The authors interpreted this result as indicating that the shooter was attending more narrowly to the primary task (shooting) as the time to begin shooting came nearer. So far, we have seen that attentional selectivity is important in sport, but that it can be affected adversely by such factors as anxiety.

Cognitive processes of expert athletes

The study of concentration in athletes is part of a wider attempt to understand the nature and determinants of expertise in sport. As I explained in Chapter 1, this field has attracted an upsurge of research interest from sport psychologists in recent years (see reviews by Abernethy, 1993; Abernethy, 1994a; Allard & Starkes, 1991). In fact, expertise is currently a "hot topic" in cognitive psychology also (see Ericsson & Charness, 1994). Perhaps the most important discovery here concerns the "hardware/software" distinction (see Chapter 1). To recapitulate, it seems that it is differences in *knowledge* rather than in physical factors which underlie expert-novice differences in sport. Put differently, despite common-sense predictions, there appears to be little evidence that expert athletes differ from relative novices in such "hardware" factors as visual acuity, depth perception, range of peripheral visual field or even reaction time (Regnier, Salmela, & Russell, 1993). But there is growing evidence that experts in various sports differ significantly from novices in "software" factors such as the ability to extract advance-cue information from relevant perceptual displays, the ability to make sport-specific decisions quickly and the ability to memorise structured game situations.

Consistent with research findings in other cognitive domains (such as chess; see Chase & Simon, 1973), skilled athletic performers differ from less proficient counterparts in a variety of "software" processes (see

Allard & Starkes, 1991). For example, experts tend to perceive and recall more information than do novices when shown game-related information for brief durations (4–5 seconds). To illustrate, Garland & Barry (1991) discovered that expert coaches of American football "took in" and remembered more information from schematic diagrams of football positions than did novices. Likewise, Allard, Graham, & Paarsalu (1980) investigated the memories of inter-varsity and intra-varsity basketball players for "structured" (e.g. a point-guard about to make a pass at the top of the "key") and "unstructured" (e.g. a scramble for a ball) game situations presented on slides for 5 seconds. Results showed that the inter-varsity players recalled more of the structured "plays" than their colleagues. However, no differences were evident between the groups for "unstructured" situations. This finding illuminates the general principles that when material is meaningless or presented randomly, experts cannot remember it any better than novices.

This principle that the advantages of expertise are domain-specific is illustrated by the discovery that the recall superiority of chess experts over novices was not a function of greater memory ability but rather reflected the use of different encoding and retrieval strategies (Chase & Simon, 1973). In other words, chess experts could remember more, but only about chess, than could novices. Apparently, the chess masters attended to the *structure* of the array presented to them rather than to the separate positions of the individual pieces. Therefore, their superior domain-specific (i.e. chess) knowledge allowed them to "chunk" the stimulus array more efficiently than novices. Accordingly, the standard explanation for the superiority of experts in memory tasks is the proposal that they have access to a richer and more extensive knowledge base than do novices. This knowledge base allows them to identify connections between what they are required to learn and what they already know. Put differently, the experts used knowledge of higher-order groupings of the material ("schemata") to "chunk" the information presented to them. Therefore, they were able to "take in" more information from a single glance (provided that the stimulus information was meaningful) than were novices.

Let us now consider the question of whether or not expertise in sport is associated with superiority in attentional skills. Two aspects of this issue may be identified (see Abernethy 1993). First, researchers have explored expert-novice differences in the manner in which information is sampled or *selected* for perceptual analysis. In addition, research has been conducted on expert-novice differences in the way in which this perceptual information is subsequently *interpreted* and used in real-life settings. According to Abernethy (1993), far more research has been conducted on the former issue than on the latter one. But there is some evidence that the decision-making processes of sport experts are superior to those of novices. For example, the subjective estimates of event probabilities developed by expert performers appear to be more accurate than those provided by novices in a given sport (see Whiting, 1979). This finding suggests that expert athletes, by virtue of having a richer procedural "knowledge base", can anticipate domain-specific events more efficiently than can novices. In other words, "knowing" facilitates "doing". But does this theory provide an adequate *explanation* for athletic excellence? Unfortunately, the expert-novice paradigm is essentially a descriptive system rather than an experimental level of analysis (Gagne, Yekovich, & Yekovich, 1993). Yet it suggests that some cognitive mechanisms underlie this relationship between "knowing" and "doing". But what exactly are these mechanisms?

As I indicated in Chapter 1, the theory of "production systems" (Anderson, 1983) may offer a useful way of thinking about the link between "knowing" and "doing" in sport. In particular, "doing" could be regarded as the action evoked by a particular knowledge-state. But Allard & Starkes (1991) argued that "knowing" and "doing" are different aspects of motor skills (e.g. skill in tying one's shoelaces is not related to being able to tell someone about how to do it) and can develop and be influenced separately. To explain, they claimed that whereas the cognitive components of many complex skills appear to be situation-specific (e.g. mnemonic codes developed for number recall may not generalise to face recall), those of the motor system appear to be "general purpose" in nature. Without the knowledge component, it would be "difficult for the motor system to perform actions consistently". Clearly, the the use of constructs like "production systems" illustrates the influence of the information processing approach on research in sport. As I explained in Chapter 1, however, some theorists (e.g. Clark, 1995; Williams, Davids, Burwitz, & Williams, 1992) reject the notion that hierarchical executive processes (e.g. centrally stored "productions") underlie skilled behaviour. Instead, they argue that perception cannot be studied independently of the action it subserves. Therefore, these theorists believe that specific motor control structures are temporarily assembled to cope with the contextual demands of a given sport situation. By this view, the concept of a "mental representation" of a skill is implausible. However, the information processing perspective is still in the ascendancy among most sport psychologists. According to this perspective, expertise in sport is held to depend upon the accumulation of an extensive knowledge base. But can this knowledge base be imparted instructionally to novices in an effort to enhance their skills?

Unfortunately, few researchers have evaluated the extent to which instruction in the skills associated with athletic expertise actually leads to an improvement in sport performance relative to control conditions. But how likely is it that expertise in sport performance will be hastened through programmes designed to train novices to pay attention to anticipatory cues that have been shown to be favoured by experts? Although the idea of "training" expertise may appear plausible, it is beset by problems. For a start, it takes a considerable length of time (in fact, by common consent, at least 10 years) to become an expert in any domain. As Whiting (1978) observed, "it becomes necessary for the beginner to experience the selection and rejection of information over an extended period in order to reach the information processing potential of the expert" (p. 33). In particular, during this cognitive "apprenticeship", the novice must learn how to incorporate "the statistical properties of information sources into an internal model of the task". Therefore, for cognitive reasons, there are seem to be no obvious shortcuts to the development of expertise. Overall, therefore, the knowledge base of sport performers (e.g. a tennis player) is thought to contain three types of knowledge: "declarative" knowledge (including knowledge of the general rules of the game of tennis together with knowledge of the specific score at any point in the match—"episodic" and "semantic" information, respectively); "procedural knowledge" (or non-verbal skills to execute actions such as serving in tennis); and "strategic knowledge" (i.e. knowing when to use heuristic techniques such as approaching the net). Not surprisingly, therefore, experts in sport are regarded as athletes who can use each of these different types of knowledge to solve "problems" in their sport domain. It should be noted here, however, that most research in this field has been restricted to the *visual* perceptual domain. Little or nothing appears to be known about the advance auditory or tactile cues that are used by athletes to make predictions in their sport. Bearing this limitation in mind, certain research findings have emerged. Most of these findings come from studies using either the "cue-occlusion paradigm" or some form of eye-movement recording technology.

SUMMARY

According to many athletes, coaches and sport psychologists, the ability to concentrate effectively is a vital prerequisite of successful performance in sport. Although this proposition is widely accepted, few authors have tested it empirically. Accordingly, evidence on the importance of concentration in athletes is rather sparse and fragmented. Despite this difficulty, this chapter attempted to evaluate the role of attentional processes in sport performers. I began by weaving together several strands of evidence which highlight the importance of concentration skills in sport. These sources of evidence included anecdotal testimonials from world-class performers, empirical studies of "peak performance" experiences among athletes, comparisons between the psychological profiles of expert and novice performers and studies of the relationship between concentration techniques and sport performance. Next, I reviewed available evidence concerning the selective (or "focused") and divided attentional skills of athletes. In general, less research has been conducted on divided attention than on selective attention among athletes.

With regard to selective attention, we discovered that expert athletes tend to detect relevant anticipatory cues from opponents quicker and more accurately than do relative beginners. This principle emerges largely from research using the "cue-occlusion" paradigm in which athletes (e.g. squash players) are required to predict ball-flight information from incomplete details on film (i.e. some critical cues have been deliberately omitted). Interestingly, it also emerged that, contrary both to the introspective accounts of performers and to some coaching principles, athletes do *not* usually "watch the ball" continuously as it approaches them in fast-ball sports such as cricket or tennis. Instead, they appear to use perceptual cues (e.g. from the stance of an opponent) to anticipate the likely flight path and destination of the ball, co-ordinating their responses accordingly. In other words, they appear to be guided more by what they *know* rather than by what they see. Divided attention in athletes has been studied experimentally using the "dual-task" paradigm. Here, subjects are required to perform two tasks ("primary" and "secondary") concurrently. Performance on the secondary task (e.g. responding to an intermittent "probe" stimulus such as an auditory tone) is usually inversely related to the attentional demands of the primary task. I explained how dual-task methodology can be used to monitor changes in allocation of attention by athletes as they prepare to perform important skills. For example, there is some evidence that skilled pistol-shooters make more mistakes than relative beginners in performing a secondary task in the seconds which precede shot execution. This finding suggests that these skilled athletes have learned to deploy their attentional resources effectively on task-relevant activities. By contrast, novices behave as if all tasks in the preparatory period were equally important.

I concluded this chapter by considering three implications of the research reviewed above on the attentional processes of athletes. First, if we consider selective attention as a cognitive skill, perhaps coaches could encourage sport performers to practise it by learning to "zoom in" on relevant advance cues from opponents whenever possible. In addition, research on attention in athletes shows that emotional factors (e.g. anxiety) can restrict the "beam" of one's concentration. This finding explains why anxious athletes often make errors in perception and decision making during competitive encounters. Finally, I explored the degree to which athletic expertise is associated with superiority in attentional skills. Although little empirical research has been conducted on this question, it seems likely that expert athletes have greater insight into, and control over, their attentional resources than do relative novices. In order to resolve this issue, however, further research is required on the topic of "meta-attention" (or knowledge about one's own attentional processes) in athletes.

CHAPTER FOUR

Losing concentration in sport: External and internal distractions

"The manner in which we conceded a try early in the second half was due to a lack of concentration at a scrum. You cannot afford that against a side such as England"
(Irish rugby manager Donal Lenihan, cited in Van Esbeck, 1995, p. 18)

"When you're wrong in your attitude, everything's bloody wrong then. The cameras keep moving all the time. The table's hopeless. People keep moving up and down the steps. The other player is getting in your way. The referee keeps getting in your way. Everything's wrong. It all goes then. Of course there's nothing wrong in all these things. It's you who are wrong"
(Snooker player Terry Griffiths, cited in Burn, 1992, p. 21)

"My mind started getting ahead of me and that was a mistake ... I started thinking, wow, I was beating the No. 1 player in the world"
(Lisa Raymond, after she had lost to Steffi Graf in the Pathmark Tennis Classic, July, 1994, despite leading 6–4, 4–3; cited in Cavanaugh, 1994, p. c7)

"They urged me to pile up some points but I knew I could only win the fight by a knock-out. I waited and waited, until Moorer lost his concentration and gave me an opening"
(George Foreman, after his defeat of Michael Moorer in the World Boxing Association championship, cited in Jones, 1994, p. 1)

"It was three-all in the first set, and I had break points in every game. It should have been 4–2 at the least. I wasn't focused, my mind was all over the place ... All those thoughts are going through my mind. The problem is they are going through my mind on the court "
(Martina Navratilova after her 7–5, 6–4 defeat by Helena Sukova in the 4th round of the US Open at Flushing Meadow, cited in People's favourite departs, 1993)

"I choked under pressure"
(John McEnroe, 1992, after his shock defeat by Italian Stefano Pecosolido, in the German Open Tennis Championship, cited in Shock wins for Italians, 1992)

INTRODUCTION

As the quotations above illustrate so vividly, lapses in attention can upset the performance of even the world's best athletes. In view of this problem, one of the greatest challenges confronting competitive performers is the task of maintaining concentration in the face of distractions. To illustrate, the United States Olympic Committee (1994) developed a self-help booklet, entitled *"Staying Focused at the Olympic Games"*, which offers practical advice for athletes about how to counteract the host of "on site" distractions which may arise before and during international competitions. But what exactly are "distractions" (or "distractors")? Where do they come from and how do they affect athletic performance? The purpose of this chapter is to provide some answers to these questions by exploring the nature and consequences of "losing" concentration in sport. As little or no empirical research exists on this topic, I shall include a variety of examples of distractors in different sports to illustrate the material discussed.

My plan is as follows. I shall begin by considering what "distraction" means and raise the question of why mental "wandering" occurs at all. Next, I shall classify the main factors which precipitate attentional lapses in athletes. Finally, I shall review what is known about the effects of each of these distractors on sport performance. Included in this section is a brief coverage of a common problem which may arise when anxiety affects concentration, namely, that of "choking" under pressure.

WHAT IS "DISTRACTION"?

Throughout the past century, theorists have vacillated between the interpretation of "distraction" as a response and as a stimulus. From the former perspective, a distraction may be regarded as a mental experience in which one's attention is diverted from some intended target. Thus James (1890) observed that "distraction" is "a confused, dazed, scatter-brained state". But a distraction may also be viewed as a stimulus. To illustrate, *The New Shorter Oxford English Dictionary* (Brown, 1993) defines distractions as situations, events and circumstances which divert our minds from some intended train of thought or from some desired course of action. Perhaps the best way to resolve this disagreement is to point out that both perspectives have merit. As we shall see, many of the factors which precipitate a state of attentional diversion come from our own minds. Clearly, when a distractor arises internally (e.g. from intrusive thoughts), it can be difficult to distinguish between stimulus and response interpretations of the state which it engenders.

Lest we become too embroiled in theoretical debate on this matter, perhaps I should begin with a definition of distraction favoured by many sport psychologists. Specifically, Nelson, Duncan, & Kiecker (1993) suggested that a distraction occurs when competing stimuli "interfere with or divert attention from the original focus of attention". Applying this definition to the quotations at the start of this chapter, we can see that athletes such as Terry Griffiths, Lisa Raymond, George Foreman, Martina Navratilova and John McEnroe attributed their mental turmoil to "competing stimuli" which sprang from their own thoughts. We may call such task-irrelevant thoughts "internal" or "self-generated" distractors. They are less obvious, but no less pervasive or upsetting, than distractions which arise from external sources (e.g. crowd noise). Regardless of their origin, however, distractors tend to disrupt athletic performance. For example, according to Ian Botham, the former English cricket star: "There is nothing more certain than that the moment you let your mind wander elsewhere the game will be unkind to you. You can stand in the slips and do nothing all day—but it is odds-on that the one ball you let your mind wander from will be the one that brings a catching chance" (Botham, 1980, p. 5).

In view of the adverse consequences of attentional lapses, Orlick (1990) claimed that "distraction control" is probably the most important mental skill required for success in sport. Of course, this skill has been cultivated by many top athletes. For example, in the final of the 1992 French Open tennis championships, the former world-champion Monica Seles displayed nerves of steel when "refusing to let either Graf's never-say-die attitude or the biased crowd, who were constantly chanting 'Steffi, Steffi', get at her" (Radford, 1992). This incident raises an interesting question. Specifically, under what circumstances do athletes actually *notice* distractions? Curiously, it seems that what performers actually notice while they are competing depends significantly on how absorbed they are in the competitive situation itself. Thus Pennebaker & Lightner (1980) observed that most athletes agree that "cuts, bruises, and feelings of fatigue are more painful and intense *following* a sporting event than *during* the event", because, in the latter, "the contestants are so immersed in the game itself that they are often unaware of internal physical sensations". Anecdotal evidence to support this claim is evident in both soccer and golf. For example, Andy Townsend, captain of the Irish international soccer team, remarked that injuries seem worse when the score is unfavourable in a match: "Go one down and start chasing the game and they can seem almost crippling but they are never half as bad with a 1–0 lead and the ball at your feet" (Townsend, 1995). Likewise, research suggests that top golfers may allow their score to affect their susceptibility to distractions (McCaffrey & Orlick, 1989). To illustrate, an anonymous player claimed that "everything distracts you when playing bad. The player that is not playing well is backing off shots, telling people in the gallery to move and they're hearing every noise on the golf course. Whereas the player who is playing well, you could drop their bag at the top of their back swing and it wouldn't bother them" (McCaffrey & Orlick, 1989, p. 267).

Unfortunately, despite its practical importance, people's vulnerability to distractions has attracted relatively little interest from cognitive researchers. For example, consider the term "distraction" itself. It is not listed in the subject indices of most contemporary textbooks in cognitive psychology (e.g. Anderson, 1995b; Best, 1995; Haberlandt, 1994; Hampson & Morris, 1996; Matlin, 1994). This neglect is probably attributable to a combination of two problems. On the one hand, as we have seen, "distractors" are rather nebulous constructs because they reflect an interaction between "internal" (i.e. mental) processes and "external" (i.e. environmental) events. For example, Gould, Eklund, & Jackson (1992b) found that US wrestlers' worst performances during the 1988 Olympic Games were preceded by such reported distractions as thinking about previous losses, anticipating the next match, becoming aware of the presence of team coaches and watching the clock while the wrestling match was in progress. Clearly, this finding shows that almost *anything* can be perceived as distracting for an athlete. Therefore, "distractors" appear to be defined retrospectively (i.e. by their apparent effects) rather than by the possession of a distinctive set of objective features. A second reason for the neglect of "distractibility" in psychology arises from a historical reluctance on the part of cognitive researchers to explore such "internal" experiences as daydreams and reverie in everyday life. As Eysenck & Keane (1995) explained, for methodological convenience, most research on concentration "has been concerned only with attention to the external environment". As a consequence, researchers have been unwilling to seek explanations for our mundane tendency to allow our thoughts to wander in spite of our best efforts to concentrate fully. In order to appreciate this anomaly of mental control, consider how difficult it can be sometimes to suppress an intrusive or distressing thought. As Dostoyevsky observed, "try to pose for yourself this task: Not to think of a polar bear, and you will see that the cursed thing will come to mind every minute" (cited in Wegner, 1992). Analogous experiences of mental reversals can occur in sport when tennis players tell themselves *not* to "double fault" on a key point or when golfers try to suppress the image of a threatening water-hazard while preparing to pitch to a green. Sadly, in most cases, these attempts at mental control prove counter-productive and people end up doing the exact opposite of what they had intended.

WHY DOES THE MIND TEND TO WANDER?

Have you ever had the experience of discovering suddenly that you have been reading the same sentence in a book or newspaper over and over again—and yet its meaning has not been "registered" by your mind? Hopefully, this phenomenon is not happening to you right now! But if this experience *has* occurred to you in the past, then you know at first hand what "losing" your concentration is all about! Of course, strictly speaking, one's concentration is never really "lost"—only misdirected. But if there is one thing that is *worse* than becoming distracted, it is not being aware that your mind has "wandered" in the first place! Imagine staring at this page indefinitely—not realising that you are lost in your own thoughts. Clearly, without a capacity to monitor our own awareness (a skill which involves "meta-attention"—see also Chapter 8), we would not know when a concentration "lapse" had occurred. But why does the mind wander "all over the place", as Martina Navratilova discovered to her cost?

According to James (1890), the mind wanders involuntarily because of the presence of a profusion of interesting stimuli in the world which "capture" our attention. However, although this proposal seems plausible, it cannot account for the fact (see Pope, 1978) that our minds also tend to wander during *sleep*—when our awareness of external stimulation is minimal. Thus Wegner (1994) concludes that "wandering is not just the result of weakness of will in the face of absorbing environmental stimulation ... but rather it is compelled somehow, perhaps even required, by the architecture of the mind" (p. 3). In other words, certain "design features" of the mind, rather than the capricious nature of our will, may be responsible for attentional lapses. Therefore, in a provocative theory, Wegner (1994) proposes that the mind wanders because we try to control it: Trying *not* to think about something may paradoxically increases its prominence in our consciousness. For example, trying to force oneself to fall asleep usually produces a prolonged and fitful state of wakefulness. In sport, mental wandering has been documented by Herrigel (1953) who noted that "as though sprung from nowhere, moods, feelings, desires, worries and even thoughts incontinently rise up, in a meaningless jumble, and the more far-fetched and preposterous they are, and the less they have to do with that on which one has fixed one's consciousness, the more tenaciously they hang on" (p. 53). Supporting this view, Wegner (1994) proposed that consciousness tends to wander "when we try to hold it in place while we check to make sure it has not moved. In checking ... we inadvertently draw our minds toward precisely where they least intend to go". Furthermore, he suggests that in certain circumstances (e.g. when conscious attentional resources are depleted by emotional factors) the mind not only wanders away from where we want it to go but also heads *towards* that which we wish it to avoid. As we shall see, the former part of this proposition is supported empirically by evidence (e.g. see Eysenck, 1992) that anxious people's attentional focus is "primed" to detect any signs of the stimuli which they fear. This attentional bias is thought to occur automatically.

In an effort to explain why attentional lapses occur, Wegner begins with the idea that consciousness comprises two complementary systems: An "intentional operating" process and an "ironic monitoring" system. The former is a conscious (or "controlled"; see Chapter 2) cognitive system which searches for mental contents that will yield a desired mental state. But the latter system, which is "automatic" or unconscious, is designed to detect any *failure* to achieve desired mental states. For example, consider what happens when, using Dostoyevsky's famous example, we try to suppress a thought of a white polar bear. On the one hand, our intentional operating system engages in a consciously driven, "controlled" search for thoughts which are different from the thought we wish to avoid. Simultaneously, however, our "ironic monitoring system" embarks on an automatic search for any signs of the unwanted thought.

Normally, the intentional operating system exerts more control over the mind than does the ironic monitoring process. But under certain circumstances, especially when there is a drain on our attentional resources (e.g. when we suffer from fatigue or stress), a paradoxical state of mind may arise in which "unattended items are especially accessible". In other words, the ironic system prevails over the intentional operating system and we experience a "rebound" of the thought that we had tried to suppress. This hypothesis is supported by evidence that people who had tried to concentrate while being distracted ended up memorising, rather than ignoring, the distractors (Zukier & Hagen, 1978). These findings led Wegner (1994) to conclude that "the intention to concentrate creates conditions under which mental load enhances monitoring of irrelevancies". As I shall explain later in this chapter, this idea that fatigue or stress may enhance distractibility is well supported by the anecdotal testimonies of athletes. Under such circumstances, athletes often experience a loss of control. This phenomenon was acknowledged by Fiske & Emery (1993) who pointed out that "mental control will be threatened if a person's ability to concentrate attention is disrupted". In summary, when our mental resources are plentiful, the "intentional operating system" will override the ironic monitoring system. But when our attentional resources are depleted by anxiety or fatigue, our capacity for "controlled" information processing is reduced. Accordingly, the ironic monitoring prevails in these situations and unwanted intrusion of irrelevant thoughts may occur.

GENERAL EFFECTS OF DISTRACTORS

By definition, distractions induce people to "lose" their concentration and engage in thinking which is irrelevant to the task at hand. Discovery of this mental lapse usually provokes agitation in the performer—an emotion neatly encapsulated in the remark by the snooker player, Terry Griffiths, that "everything's bloody wrong" (see beginning of chapter). This agitation is associated with a decline in performance. For example, in the 1995 Wimbledon Championship, the American tennis player Jeff Tarango literally walked out of his third-round match against Alexander Mronz after he had been censured by the umpire for screaming "shut up!" at the spectators whom he accused of distracting him. Not surprisingly, Tarango's "audible obscenity" to the crowd had followed several unforced errors on his part.

Why do distractors usually hamper task performance? One theoretical possibility in this regard is that distractors compete with task-relevant stimuli for our limited pool of attentional resources. This explanation assumes that our attentional system is limited in its capacity (see Allport, 1989; Shiffrin & Schneider, 1977), that distractors "eat up mental capacity" (Fiske & Emery, 1993) and that an increase in the allocation of resources to one task leads inevitably to a *decrease* in the resources available for a concurrent task. To illustrate, Seibert & Ellis (1991) claimed that distracting thoughts interfere with successful task performance because "attention is diverted, perhaps leaving fewer resources to perform the criterion task". This theory is supported by two main findings (Graydon & Eysenck, 1989). First, distraction effects are more pronounced for complex than for simple tasks. In addition, distraction effects become more apparent as the similarity of distractors to task-relevant stimuli increases. But not all psychologists agree with the idea that distractors always impair task performance. Thus Allport (1924), in attempting to explain "social facilitation" findings (i.e. the fact that under certain circumstances, the performance of a task is enhanced or "facilitated" by the mere presence of other people), suggested that people may react to distraction by redoubling their efforts—by over-compensating for intrusions.

Another theory in this field which invokes the idea of competition for limited resources was provided by Cioffi (1991). She raised the question of why we tend to experience a sudden "worsening" of an ache or pain at night as the house grows still. According to her, this phenomenon can be explained by a variation of the "competition-of-cues" theory (Pennebaker, 1982). Briefly, when the external environment provides relatively little information, our tendency to elaborate on somatic information increases. Further support for this theory was provided by Pennebaker & Lightner (1980) who found that when subjects who had been jogging on a repetitive oval track were compared with subjects who had run the same distance on a cross-country route, the former athletes were more aware of their physical fatigue and effort than were the runners who traversed the more varied cross-country route—despite the fact that track-joggers ran at a slower pace. But distractions are not always debilitating for the person involved. For example, consider how some people learn to cope with pain. Theoretically, pain processing is assumed to be a "controlled" cognitive process (as it demands conscious attentional resources; Eccleston, 1995). In other words, the detection and monitoring of pain sensations consumes mental energy. However, most people try to distract their minds from painful sensations. This common use of distractors to alleviate pain is based on the idea that focusing on a distractor consumes attentional resources which would otherwise be directed at the experience of pain itself. According to McCaul & Malott (1984), tasks that require greater use of attentional resources "will be more powerful reducers of pain-related distress" than those which do not tax our mental effort. Available evidence suggests that a distraction strategy is most effective when the pain is acute and the stimulation is persistent (Eccleston, 1995).

Interestingly, self-generated distractions are sometimes used to cope with the pain of prolonged or strenuous exercise. For example, Morgan, Horstman, Cymerman, & Stikes (1983) found that people who had focused on the rhythm of their footfalls while on a treadmill exercised 32% longer than did control subjects who had not been trained in the use of this distraction strategy. However, as Cioffi (1991) noted, the efficacy of any distraction strategy is limited by both the intensity and the length of the unpleasant stimuli clamouring for attention. Obviously, we may not be able to withstand indefinitely the pain caused by noxious stimuli simply by distracting ourselves. By implication, distraction techniques may not be entirely appropriate for athletic endurance events (e.g. marathon running). In such situations, a technique called "sensory monitoring" may be useful. This term refers to instructions to pay attention to the sensory aspects of the sensation (Cioffi, 1991). For example, Suls & Fletcher (1985) discovered that deliberately paying attention to somatic sensations is preferable to distraction when the stressor is *chronic* rather than acute and when the strategy focuses on the concrete aspects of the physical sensation rather than on diffuse physical states (like fatigue). I shall return to this strategy of monitoring physical sensations in Chapter 5 when I explore the attentional processes of marathon runners.

DISTRACTIONS IN SPORT: INTERNAL AND EXTERNAL

What is the best way to classify the distractions commonly encountered in sport? Perhaps the most obvious distinction is that between "internal" and "external" threats to our attention. For example, an anxious thought provides a different source of distraction from that presented by a loud noise. Not surprisingly, many attentional researchers (e.g. Johnston & Dark, 1986) distinguish between "external" (data-driven or "bottom up") and "internal" (concept-driven or "top-down") processes also. The former involve "sensory" activity while the latter entail "cognitive" processing (See, Howe, Warm, & Dember, 1995). Although this "internal-external" distinction is by no means conclusive (because distractions usually involve the interaction cognitive and environmental factors), it is convenient for our purposes. Apart from its convenience, this "internal-external" classification of distractors has a long history in psychology. It was proposed originally by James (1890) who referred to "external" objects of attention like pictures and tunes and "internal" objects of awareness like memories and trains of thought. Other theorists (e.g. Duval & Wicklund, 1972; Hartley, 1992) have supported this distinction. For example, Wachtel (1967) notes that attention is discussed "as focusing not only upon external stimuli but upon internal processes as well". In a similar vein, Eysenck (1993) says that "we all know that we can choose between attending to the external environment or to the internal environment (i.e. our own thoughts, and information in long-term memory)". Likewise, Abernethy (1993) suggests that distractors "come not only from external sources (e.g. crowd noise, the fakes of an opponent) but also from within (e.g. subjective feelings of fatigue or excessive thinking about past successes or failures)" (p. 152).

Interestingly, this distinction between paying attention to "internal" and "external" stimuli may have some physiological basis. For example, Lacey (1967) proposed the "intake-rejection" hypothesis which suggested that there is a direct relationship between heart-rate deceleration and the *direction* of one's attentional focus. Specifically, he found that in situations in which attention is devoted to the external world (e.g. watching a flashing light—an example of "intake" of environmental information) heart-rate *deceleration* tends to occur. Conversely, in situations where external information is ignored (e.g. when performing mental arithmetic tasks—deemed to reflect the "rejection" of environmental information) cardiac *acceleration* is likely to occur. This hypothesis has received some empirical support from Ray & Cole (1985; see also Chapter 5).

EXTERNAL DISTRACTIONS

"External" distractions may be defined as stimuli from the environment which divert people's attention away from its intended direction. Typical distractors in this category in sport include (i) noise (ii) the behaviour and tactical ploys of opponents ("gamesmanship") (iii) weather and playing conditions and (iv) visual distractions. Each of these factors will be considered below.

Noise as an external distractor

Noise, which may be defined broadly as "unwanted sound" (Kjellberg, 1990), has long been considered a major source of distraction for anyone endeavouring to perform some important or mentally demanding activity. Furthermore, people exposed to noise cannot simply re-orient their sensory receptors as they might do when faced with visual distractions. In sport, most competitive encounters take place in clamorous circumstances. Common auditory distractions in this domain includes crowd noise, airplanes flying overhead, announcements on the public address system, the "clicks" and "whirs" of supporters' cameras, mobile telephones, "beepers" (see Irvine, 1994) or other electronic paging systems and loud conversations among spectators. Accordingly, athletic success may hinge crucially on the ability of players to ignore such distractors while focusing on what is most important for the task at hand. For example, if extraneous noise prevents an expert tennis player from hearing the sound of an opponent's racket strings making contact with the ball, then his or her ability to "read" the shot will be impaired because of the loss of important auditory cues. In fact, during a quarter-final match in Wimbledon in 1992, Nathalie Tauziat, of France, complained to the umpire about the distraction posed by Monica Seles' sonorous grunting (Thornley, 1992a). Martina Navratilova supported this complaint, alleging that Monica Seles never grunted in practice. She added that players find it distracting when they cannot hear the ball leaving their opponent's strings. This observation by Navratilova has received empirical support from research on expert-novice differences (see also Chapter 3). To illustrate, as I explained in Chapter 3, Abernethy (1994a) concluded that expert athletes make greater use of advance cues than do relative novices. Also, Goulet, Bard, & Fleury (1989) found that expert tennis players tend to use advance cues derived from the racquet and racquet-arm of opponents whereas relative novices focused on the tennis ball.

Ironically, when Monica Seles, the former World tennis champion, was asked about her defeat in the 1992 Wimbledon final by Steffi Graf, she complained that her attempts to control her own grunting had impaired her concentration during the rather one-sided match. This attentional lapse resembles that "unravelling" of skills which occurs when people become conscious of behaviour that was previously automatic. In passing, it may be noted that the practice of grunting has some foundation in Japanese martial arts where "any attack must take place when breathing out (yang) if possible while the adversary is breathing in (yin), because then he is most vulnerable" (Deshimaru, 1982). Grunting was also practised in contact sports as early as 100 BC. Thus in *Disputations*, Marcus Tullius Cicero (106–43 BC) suggests that boxers exhale audibly when striking their opponent in order to endow their blow with greater force. A similar practice exists in Japanese martial arts, where fighters are taught the benefits of "Kiai"—the shout which they utter as they strike or throw an opponent. As before, the alleged purpose of this shout is to concentrate the force of one's movement.

Paradoxically, our awareness of a given sound is often increased by its absence. To illustrate, we may become conscious of the existence of a clock in a room only when it has *stopped* ticking. This phenomenon indicates that contrast effects are especially captivating in auditory perception. By implication, unexpected changes in ambient noise levels may distract athletes in sporting environments. For example, sudden *reductions* in noise may prove disruptive. Accordingly, in rugby, the eerie silence which a partisan crowd maintains while a "home team" player prepares to kick a penalty may be just as deleterious to performance as a "wall of sound" greeting them as they walk out onto the pitch. This point is supported by Ieuan Evans (the Welsh and Lions player) who commented on the difficulties confronting visiting teams' penalty-kickers in matches against Ireland in Lansdowne Road. Specifically, he felt that "if you win a penalty (in Lansdowne Road) that could sink them, the crowd goes dead silent. It is the ultimate in sportsmanship but it is also very disturbing" (Lansdowne, 1993).

A good example of auditory distractions comes from the world of golf. This distraction occurred when Greg Norman, one of the world's leading players, was playing in the 1982 Martini International Tournament in Lindrick. Suddenly, on the relatively easy 17th hole, the click of a photographer's camera shutter upset his swing so much that he sent his ball into uncharted territory and ended up with a *14* on the hole! (Gilleece, 1992). Another common auditory distraction in golf comes from mobile telephones. To illustrate, in the 1995 Spanish Open championship in Madrid, Eamon Darcy, the Ryder Cup player, was disturbed during his downswing by the loud ringing of a mobile telephone. Unfortunately, this unexpected noise caused Darcy to send his ball "out of bounds". Afterwards, he commented angrily that "telephones should not be allowed on a golf course. It completely upset my stroke and I never got my rhythm back after that" (Darcy asks for whom, 1995). Interestingly, some golfers have trained themselves to become oblivious to background noises. For example, consider what happened to the British Ryder Cup golfer, David Gilford, in the 1992 Moroccan Open Championship in Rabat. Victory in this event had looked a formality for Roland Karlsson of Sweden as he approached the final hole one stroke ahead of Gilford. But the British player pitched the ball to eight feet on this hole and calmly rolled in the pressure putt for a "birdie" which levelled the match. The most remarkable aspect of this shot, however, was the fact that Gilford played it only seconds after a child had driven a motorised buggy into spectators circling the green of this final hole! Oblivious to the noise created by this incident, Gilford claimed that "I didn't hear a thing. I was concentrating so hard that I couldn't let anything upset me. It would have taken a diesel train to have disturbed me" (see Golf, 1992). Gilford went on to win the third playoff hole and earned a substantial cheque.

Why do changes in noise levels affect sport performance? According to Broadbent (1971), changes in ambient levels of noise increase a person's arousal level. As I explained in Chapter 3, this increased arousal is thought to narrow attention (Easterbrook, 1959). Under conditions of low arousal, a broad array of information is absorbed, including task-relevant and task-irrelevant cues. But with increased arousal, less information is taken in, with the result that performance often improves since distractors are excluded. Therefore, Easterbrook (1959) claimed that "for any task ... provided that initially a certain proportion of the cues in use are irrelevant cues ... the reduction (in the number of cues in use) will reduce the proportion of irrelevant cues employed and so improve performance. When all irrelevant cues have been excluded, however, ... further reduction in the number of cues employed can only affect relevant cues, and proficiency will fall" (p. 193).

Gamesmanship and distraction

FATHER: "You know, John, if you want to be a good putter, you need total concentration".

SON: "Please explain, Dad"

FATHER: "Well, son, a barking dog, a blaring car horn or even the snap of a twig can upset your concentration on the green. Get the picture?"

SON: "Sure, Dad. So—should I cough during my opponent's back-swing or just as he hits the ball?"!

As the joke above shows, there are many situations in sport where competitors use strategic behavioural ploys in an effort to disrupt the concentration of their opponents. This tactical practice is known as "gamesmanship" (Potter, 1947) and has been defined as "the art of winning games without actually cheating". For example, the former Wimbledon tennis champion Jimmy Connors was notorious in his latter years for eliciting sympathy from the crowd in an effort to boost his confidence while upsetting the momentum of younger adversaries. Not surprisingly, Michael Stich, another Wimbledon champion, found this practice to be disconcerting. Thus he remarked, after a famous four-hour match with 39-year-old Jimmy Connors in the first round of the 1992 French Open championships, "I don't like playing him ... You're not just playing against Connors, you're playing against other things—the way he talks to the crowd, the way he talks to the linesman. You have to concentrate. If you let those things affect you, you lose the game" (Roberts, 1992b, p. 15).

Technically, gamesmanship is designed either to distract one's opponents or "to raise his (sic) pitch of arousal beyond the optimum level, into the sphere of blinkered anger or anxiety" (Syer, 1986). It is assumed here that such emotions disrupt sport performance—an assumption which echoes Virgil's remark that "anger carries the mind away". A good example of this tactic occurred when Stephen Collins, the Irish boxer, defeated Britain's Chris Eubank in the World Boxing Organisation's super-middleweight championship title fight in Millstreet, Cork, in March 1995. Put simply, Collins "psyched out" Eubank by pretending to him that he had been hypnotised prior to the fight. So upset was Eubank at the prospect of facing an opponent who, he believed, was impervious to pain that he threatened to withdraw from the match. "It is unfair", he said, "to fight someone who is behaving in a mechanical way. I prepared naturally for the fight. I think hypnosis is legalised cheating" (cited in Hayes, 1995). In fact, although Collins had hired a hypnotist to advise him, no hypnosis had been conducted prior to the contest. But Collins *acted* as if he had been hypnotised before the fight. As he explained afterwards, "I stared manically at him and told him I was going to win. I kept repeating that I was going to win and he got such a fright ... and when he went public about his worries, I knew he was losing his bottle" (Cooney, 1995).

Gamesmanship is common in boxing. Thus Mohammed Ali distracted Ernie Terrell when they fought in Houston in 1967 by calling out "what's my name?" every time he landed a punch on him. This tactic caused Terrell to lose his concentration. Similarly, "psych outs" occur regularly in top-class tennis. For example, in Wimbledon 1994, Christian Bergstrom claimed that Boris Becker raised his arm, signalling a ball was outside the line on set point—a gesture which allegedly caused a distraction. Bergstrom missed the return to lose the set and eventually the match, 7–6, 6–4, 6–3 (Becker's gesture, 1994). Another unusual distraction occurred in a professional snooker match in England when Alex Higgins broke the momentum of his opponent by making the rather unusual complaint that the referee, John Williams, had been standing in his line of vision during play (Gilleece, 1994).

One of the most subtle and intriguing ways in which gamesmanship may be practised is through a pseudo-compliment or covert "psych out". For example, in an apparently spontaneous remark, one golfer may say to another: "It's amazing how well you can hit that ball with that strange grip you have!" (see Fox & Evans, 1979). This comment usually causes the performer to engage in a form of "paralysis-by-analysis". They look again at their grip and become excessively conscious of it, thereby disrupting the rhythm of a previously effortless and fluent stroke! More generally, the idea of distracting one's opponent through *praise* may be traced back to Potter (1947), the progenitor of the theory of gamesmanship. As we shall see, praise affects performance by creating self-consciousness, which, in turn, affects one's attentional focus and upsets the rhythm of the skill one is performing. This cycle of "praise-dissection-discussion-doubt" (Potter, 1947) is the essence of gamesmanship. Similarly, in tennis, by praising an opponent's success with a given stroke, one is encouraging him or her to become aware of this shot. Accordingly, the shot loses its fluent or effortless character. Yet another example of verbal gamesmanship occurs when players try to distract their opponents by talking to them during matches. For example, according to Newcastle defender Darren Peacock, the Manchester United and England striker Andy Cole is an expert at "trying to wind me up. One of his tricks is to stand in the middle of the pitch with his hands on his hips, looking as if he's not interested in what's going on, then he's off and you've lost him. He does it to try and get defenders to become complacent" (Cole's comments, 1993).

Intimidation by opponents is another strategy designed to make a performer "re-focus" on some task-irrelevant feature of the situation. Examples of this practice may be found in both "open" (or reactive) and "closed" (or individual) sports. In soccer, intimidation is also widely encountered in contact sports like soccer. For example, as a player with Leeds United in the 1960s, Jack Charlton, a World Cup winner for England in 1966, pioneered the practice of standing on the opposing team's goal-line for corner kicks in order to prevent the goalkeeper from "tracking" the flight of the incoming ball. This form of intimidation of the goalkeeper is now widespread in soccer. Intimidatory tactics are also prevalent in cricket—especially among bowlers. For example, Richard Hadlee, of New Zealand, claimed that "I never bowled a ball in my life that was intended to hurt a batsman. Shake him up a bit, terrify him a little, sure. But at Test level, the batsman is there to be tested" (Line, 1978). Similarly, the bowler Harold Larwood, said that he "never bowled to injure a man ... frighten them, intimidate them, yes" (Frith, 1977).

Verbal intimidation of opponents is evident in sports like cricket and basketball. In fact, the term "sledging" has been coined to represent a tactic pioneered by the Australian fast-bowler Merv Hughes in which there is "direct, personalised belligerence ... of trying to bad-mouth opponents into a loss of concentration" (McIlvanney, 1993). As Ian Botham commented: "Intimidation is part of a fast-bowler's make-up. When you lose the power to intimidate, it's like losing three yards of pace. Merv uses it well and it works for him" (ibid.). Meanwhile in basketball, the term "talking trash" has been coined to describe the tendency for players to try to upset the concentration of opponents by insulting them throughout the match. Thus a basketball coach, George Raveling, warned his players that "guys are trying to make you lose your focus, to play head games with you" (cited in Maxwell, 1994). Sports like cycling are also famous for the frequency with which competitors engage in tactical intimidation. For example "blocking", or deliberately obstructing the progress of cyclists chasing the leader, is a legitimate ploy in this sport. But sometimes, this tactic is supplemented by more robust obstruction. For example, in the final stage of the 1992 FBD Milk Race in Ireland, a number of Irish riders hampered the progress of the Italian race-leader, Giuseppe Guernini. Subsequently, six of them were penalised for dangerous cycling (Brennan, 1992a).

In individual sports (e.g. tennis), attentional disruption in opponents may be caused deliberately by engaging in such ploys as time-wasting or stalling play (e.g. tying one's shoelaces in tennis, replacing the ball several times before taking kick outs in soccer), insulting one's opponents (e.g. by abusive language) or by using verbal gamesmanship (such as pseudo-compliments). In each case, the purpose is "to unsettle the opponent's confidence in his judgement, to get him guessing, to grub at the roots of his game" (Patmore, 1986). Intimidation is also commonplace in such sports as diving. For example, Nideffer (1985) reported an incident in which an opponent attempted to "psych him out" when he was diving competitively. During the competition, this opponent casually remarked to Nideffer that he should watch out for the end of the diving board which was very slippery. This remark caused Nideffer to worry about the possibility of slipping and hence led to a poor performance in the event. But why does gamesmanship tend to impair concentration in sport? In order to answer this question, I shall refer to theories by Reason & Mycielska (1982) and Vallacher (1993).

To begin with, skills become disrupted when we are induced to pay attention to the "wrong" features of the task in question. Thus Eysenck & Keane (1990) suggested that "automated activities can sometimes be disrupted if too much attention is paid to the details of task performance. For example, it can become very difficult to walk down a deep spiral staircase if attention is paid to the leg movements involved" (pp. 128–129). Likewise, Reason & Mycielska (1982) concluded that paying "too much attention to some component of a highly-skilled performance is a sure way of making it falter, as every top-class musician or athlete will know ... In such cases of over-attention, the outcome can be a complete rendering of the delicate fabric of the skill..." (p. 139). Interestingly, Potter (1947) cleverly anticipated this cognitive principle when he observed that "conscious flow is broken flow". In other words, he understood intuitively that excessive self-consciousness impairs a person's performance by re-directing their attentional focus. Here, task-consciousness has been replaced by excessive self-consciousness. This attentional unravelling effect is the converse of the normal flow of skill learning (see Fitts & Posner, 1967) because it forces the performer to think consciously about a skill which had been previously automatic.

Another version of this theory of "paralysis-by-analysis" was provided by Vallacher (1993). He proposed that a major function of consciousness is to hold a series of complex, time-consuming behavioural actions in an organised queue pending their execution. Accordingly, consciousness can *subvert*, rather than facilitate, performance under certain circumstances. Specifically, actions that "can be discharged directly—simple movements, for example—are probably better left alone. The same can be said of an over-learned skill. Ironically, sometimes the best way to control an action is not to control it at all". Again, this idea supports the theory of ironic mental control (Wegner, 1994) which I outlined in Chapter 3. More generally, "gamesmanship" can be interpreted as inducing a faulty "mental calibration" (Vallacher, 1993). To explain, the attempt to control one's actions at either too low or too high a representational level can be disruptive. This "faulty mental calibration" is a term which describes what happens when "people are sometimes led to monitor and control what they are doing with respect to a level in the queued action hierarchy that is inappropriate for the co-ordinated discharge of action" (p. 459). Put differently, every action takes place in a context which provides cues for the identification of the skilled components required. Situations involving competition, audience evaluation, or other pressures to do well, "may keep the person mindful of high-level identities of a self-evaluative nature (e.g. 'demonstrating my skill', 'trying to win', 'impressing others') at the expense of the action's more molecular representations" (p. 459). In summary, it seems that "performance can be disrupted when attention is drawn to the over-learned details of an action ... The more over-learned the action is, the greater the performance impaired by a conscious concern with how to perform the act ... A proficient piano player, for instance, can become completely derailed in the middle of a familiar piece if he or she looks at the music and tries to think about how to play a section. In effect, consciousness is trying to micro manage a problem that is best left to lower-level echelons to work out among themselves" (Vallacher, 1993, p. 460). Similarly, Norman (1982) observed that "there is no better way to ruin performance than to think simultaneously about the details of its execution". This idea that over-analysis can lead to performance breakdown has been known since the beginning of this century (e.g. Bliss, 1892–1893). Indeed, for a long time, it has been known that the secret of effective performance is knowing when to let go of the action—when to allow the sequence of movements "to be run off without further conscious intervention" (Vallacher, 1993). The same point was made by Schmidt (1988) who claimed that asking a pianist to describe what their hands are doing while they are reading music will focus attention on the finger movements to the detriment of the total performance.

Various terms have been coined to describe the phenomenon in which a preoccupation with the "mechanics" of an automated procedural activity can hamper its performance. To illustrate, Deikman (1966) coined the term "deautomatization" to designate the "undoing of automatization, presumably by reinvesting actions and percepts with attention" and Klatzky (1984) noted the fact that "awareness of performance decreases with practice, and that becoming more aware impairs execution of a skilled act". A theoretical analysis of this phenomenon was provided by Reason & Mycielska (1982) who suggested that a deterioration in cognitive performance can result from an incompatibility between our "intention system" and our "control system". Specifically, they claimed that "over attention, or attention paid at the wrong moment can also produce slips. In this case, the Intention System goes closed-loop at a time when it would have been better to have stayed in the open-loop mode. Or to put it bluntly, there are occasions when the Intention System should have minded its own business" (ibid., p. 139). Interestingly, it is not just sports stars who have discovered that paying attention to an intuitive act may "derail" concentration and performance. Thus the renowned Irish short-story writer William Trevor once confessed that "I'm very curious, noticing details, but as soon as you start to analyse what you do, you begin to lose it" (Adair, 1994).

Distractions from playing / weather conditions

It has long been known that the novelty and complexity of stimuli make them especially captivating (Berlyne, 1960). These factors are evident in certain weather or playing conditions encountered in sport. For example, the Russian tennis player Alexander Volkov blamed his defeat by Thomas Muster in the 1994 Australian Open on the excessive heat in the stadium. Having lost his match thorough a string of unforced errors (e.g. 14 double faults), Volkov complained afterwards that "as soon as I came on to the court, I realised it was too hot for me. During the match, I was just thinking how hot it was" (Volkov finds Muster, 1994). Many aspects of competitive sport situations are distracting to athletes simply because they are *unfamiliar* to the performers involved. For example, Orlick (1990) explains how Greg Joy, a world-class high jumper, was dismayed to learn, before a competition, that the runway differed in orientation from the one he had practised on in training. This upset his concentration so much that his subsequent performance suffered. More generally, factors which cause most disruption of concentration include unfavourable weather (e.g. wind, snow or rain) and unfamiliar surfaces or surroundings. In either case, "negative transfer" of learning (i.e. when a skill learned in one situation is detrimental to performance in another context) may occur. For example, many leading tennis players experience problems in transferring from relatively fast surfaces (e.g. hard courts) to slow courts (e.g. clay). Thus three-times Wimbledon champion Boris Becker claimed that "to adapt from clay to a surface where I can serve and volley quite easily takes me about half an hour. To go to clay takes me four or five weeks!" (Becker had to struggle, 1992).

Familiarity with local environmental conditions may help to explain the "home advantage" phenomenon in sport (i.e. the tendency for teams to win more games played at their home venue than when played away; see Courneya & Carron, 1992). Thus "home" players may be able to "settle down" quicker than visiting players and, as a consequence, be less susceptible to distractions during the match.

Visual distractions

Perhaps the most obvious way of dealing with distractions is for people to orient their sensory receptors (e.g. eyes) towards desired information and away from unwanted stimulation. Unfortunately, sport is replete with situations in which the object of our visual scrutiny serves to distract us from the task in hand. For example, in the 1994 Kremlin Cup tennis tournament in Russia, American player Chuck Adams (who was runner-up) complained that he had been distracted in the final by the sight of Russian president Boris Yeltsin taking his seat during the first set. "His hair is so white", Adams remarked, "I thought it was reflecting off the lights and it broke my concentration. It was good to see him but it was a distraction" (Sampras back, 1994). Likewise, Jim Courier, who won the French Open tennis championship title in 1992, reported an unusual distraction which occurred during the final against Petr Korda—namely, the sight of the face of American television celebrity Johnny Carson. As Courier remarked, "it was a little disturbing at first actually, because every time Petr would serve to me in the deuce court, I would see Johnny right behind him, so I saw a lot of Johnny today" (Roberts, 1992a). Clearly, visual distractions can be distracting for performers. This idea is supported by research in experimental psychology. For example, Eriksen & Eriksen (1974) found that the visual "noise" created by neighbouring letters hampered reaction time in a visual search task. Interestingly, this phenomenon may have biological substrates. Thus Kosslyn & Koenig (1992) claimed that there is a "stimulus-based attention shifting" system in the brain which draws one's eyes towards a novel stimulus. An example of this phenomenon comes from tennis star Ivan Lendl's explanation for losing to Sergei Bruguera in the third round of the Monte Carlo Open in 1993. He claimed that a television crew had distracted him: "with lights straight on to the court, blinding even in the daylight" (Roberts, 1993b).

Other examples of visual distraction in sport occur when athletes (e.g. soccer players, golfers) look at either "instant replay" television screens or electronic scoreboards during competitive encounters. To illustrate, the English soccer club Tottenham Hotspur has been criticised for allowing instant replays of controversial moments in football matches to be shown while the game is in progress—thereby causing a distraction both to the players and to the referee (Harris, 1995). Similarly, sport performers often consult electronic scoreboards to obtain information about the progress of rival competitors. Not surprisingly, this practice is potentially disruptive. For example, Frank Clark, the Nottingham Forest manager, complained in 1994 that the electronic scoreboard at his club's stadium (the City Ground) provided an unnecessary distraction for his players. In his opinion, the practice of "flashing up" scores from other matches "can be a major distraction for the players—and it can be a dangerous practice if, as sometimes happens, an incorrect score is flashed up. Our skipper is in complete agreement with my stand on this. He went berserk about it at half-time. *The last thing you need is to be worrying about other people's results*" (Thornton, 1994, p. 55, italics mine). Clark's observation is insightful and is supported by the following incident concerning Sylvie Bernier, the 1984 Olympic champion diving champion. In order to perform to her full potential, Bernier had to overcome a susceptibility to distraction caused by a habit which she had developed of paying attention to the scoreboard instead of focusing on her own dive: "I knew that every time I looked at the scoreboard, my heart went crazy. I couldn't control it. I knew that I dove (sic) better if I concentrated on my diving instead of concentrating on everyone else" (cited in Orlick, 1990). Likewise, McCaffrey & Orlick (1989) reported that many professional golfers are distracted by the sight of the leader board when they play in tournaments.

Novel stimuli present compelling distractions for many sports performers. For example, in the 1993 Wimbledon championship, during a marathon battle between Goran Ivanisevic and Chris Bailey, an unusual incident occurred which appeared to change the course of the match. In the fourth set, with Bailey 2–0 up and leading by two sets to one, a pigeon suddenly glided into the stadium and flapped around the court for a moment. This movement distracted Bailey who gently lobbed a ball in its direction. However, Ivanisevic took full advantage of this momentary lapse of attention and proceeded to take both that set and the final one (Roberts, 1993a). In some sports, players may lose their concentration by looking at their opponent rather than the ball. That is why some athletes (e.g. in a tennis doubles match) jump around in order to upset their opponents. Also, as one is preparing to return an approach shot in tennis, one may be distracted by the sight, in one's peripheral vision, of one's opponent approaching the net. Related to this difficulty is the problem of being distracted by officials in the vicinity of the sport arena. For example, in a Federation Cup tennis match between Britain and Finland in Frankfurt in 1992, Sarah Gomer, the British number two, became distracted by a service judge who had forgotten to take up the correct position. As Thornley (1992b) reported, "her concentration gone, Gomer sprayed her shots wildly wide, lost the game to love and trailed 2–3"—before losing the match 6–4, 6–0.

An interesting consequence of the fact that sports performers may become distracted by certain visual stimuli is the notion that clever opponents may exploit this tendency. Thus it can be beneficial to competitors to engage in deceptive manoeuvres which distract visual attention. Consider a recent example of this ploy in the IBF/WBA championship title fight between the 46 year-old George Foreman and his 28 year-old opponent, Michael Moorer. Foreman won the fight by knocking Moorer out in the 10th round. In this round, Foreman pretended to jab Moorer with his left hand but instead, hit him unexpectedly with a straight right. This "knockout blow" came as a result of a lapse in Moorer's concentration (see quotation at beginning of this chapter).

On the basis of the preceding research, what exactly should performers pay attention to in their competitive environment? Many sport psychologists (e.g. Nideffer, 1985; Yandell, 1990) recommend that athletes in "open" sports should focus on "keys" or specific patterns of opponents' movements. For example, if a tennis player tosses the ball to the side when serving, then a slice serve should be expected. This advice is theoretically justifiable because there is growing evidence that athletic expertise is associated with the early detection of task-relevant cues (see also Chapter 3).

INTERNAL DISTRACTIONS:
HOW MENTAL FACTORS AFFECT CONCENTRATION

Sport performers are familiar with many of the distractions described in the previous pages simply because these threats to our concentration are both visible and audible. But as I explained earlier, "internal" sources of distraction can disrupt attention as powerfully as can external stimuli. For example, as Jackson (1995) has shown through interviews with elite athletes, worries and irrelevant thoughts can cause people to withdraw their concentration "beam" from what they are doing to what they hope will not happen. Similarly, as I explained in Chapter 1, Klinger, Barta, & Glas (1981) discovered that certain events which occur during games (e.g. either setbacks or unusual runs of success) may induce attentional lapses simply because they encourage the players to think excessively about themselves or about the likely results of their skills. Taken together, these studies by Jackson (1995) and Klinger, Barta, & Glas (1981) show that thinking too much about oneself ("self-consciousness") and/or about what might happen in the future ("result-consciousness") inhibits skilled performance. These studies are supported by Carver & Scheier (1990). By contrast, a concern with task performance is usually associated with an appropriate mental "focus" for competition. As Loehr (1986) observed, "we have the right focus when what we are doing is the same as what we are thinking".

In this section, I shall explore how "internal" sources of distraction (e.g. thoughts about future results) affect athletic performance. This topic is important because as Dalloway (1993) suggested, "mastery over thoughts, fears and worries (i.e. the internal noise) frequently poses a greater challenge than overcoming external distractions". Likewise, Seibert & Ellis (1991) concluded that any factors that "take the focus away from thoughts appropriate to, and necessary for, criterion task performance could interfere with performance". An interesting demonstration of this principle was provided by Fenz (1975) who explored expert-novice differences in parachute jumping. Briefly, this study showed the less skilled jumpers were so preoccupied with thoughts about the possible physical danger posed by the impending jump that they were prevented from "focusing" effectively. Some success has been obtained in the measurement of thoughts which tend to disrupt a performer's attention during competitive performance. For example, Schwenkmezger & Laux (1986) have developed the 10 item "Cognitive Interference Questionnaire" which may be administered to athletes immediately after performance in an effort to establish what they had been thinking about during the contest. This scale includes such items as "I thought about my failure to follow the coach's instructions" (item 6) or "I was concerned about previous mistakes" (item 8). Unfortunately, the utility of such measures is questionable as many of the thoughts experienced by anxious people are automatic, and hence inaccessible to retrospective analysis.

In passing, it is possible that paying too much attention to internal cues can increase athletes' susceptibility to injury. For example, Anshel (1995) suggests that when athletes focus their attention too narrowly instead of scanning the entire stimulus field, they may be vulnerable to physical injury from fellow competitors in contact sports. To illustrate, Bond & Sargent (1995) explained how an Australian Rules Footballer was knocked unconscious by a tackle which he had not anticipated due to his intense concentration on a potential match-winning goal.

Distraction and regrets: Thinking about the past

One of the biggest challenges facing competitive sports performers is to "let go" of incidents and opportunities which have passed. Of course, this skill in disregarding what one can no longer control is difficult to master. Naturally, athletes tend to ruminate over past events. For example, goals that strikers know they *should* have scored could play on their mind for an entire football match. This problem was highlighted by Landers, Boutcher, & Wang (1986) who found that archers who were preoccupied with past mistakes tended to produce poorer performances than those whose minds were focused on the present. Interestingly, one of the factors that make individual sports so challenging mentally is the fact that they provide ample opportunity for rueful reflection about past mistakes or misfortunes. By contrast, the rapid and unpredictable action occurring in most team sports forces players to pay attention to what is happening at that moment. Otherwise their team-mates or coach will berate them.

Distraction though "Fortune telling": Thinking about the future

Thinking about the future can also upset one's concentration. For example, a baseball player may go for a home run rather than try to make clean contact with the ball. Similarly, soccer strikers who miss important goal chances are often accused of "reading tomorrow's headlines" and golfers who have a tendency to anticipate their victory speeches while still playing the final hole rarely win tournaments. An insight into this proclivity to think too far ahead comes from the 1994 Australian Open tennis championship when Pete Sampras was serving for the tournament victory. Leading 7–6, 6–4 and serving at 5–2, he double-faulted and lost two more games, before holding out by 6–4 in the third set. Interviewed afterwards, Sampras explained that his lapse in concentration was caused by speculating about the future: "I was thinking about winning the Australian Open and what a great achievement, looking ahead and just kind of taking it for granted instead of taking it point by point" (Roberts, 1994). In each case, the same principle applies: Thinking about the future usually causes a deterioration in present performance.

In general, thoughts about possible future events—especially the likely result of a match in which the player is engaged—are very common in competitive sport (e.g. a golfer may wonder while preparing to tee off what will happen if they fail to hit the fairway). The frequency of such thinking may reflect an understandable desire to plan our lives. But it also indicates the importance which we attach to results: We are constantly tempted to extrapolate from what we are doing to what will eventually happen (the result). In addition, players may try to guess *how others might react* to the eventual result of the match (e.g. "How can I face my coach if I lose to this player?"). In each of these cases concentration has been lost by engaging in a form of "fortune telling". The player is more worried about a possible future outcome than about controlling a current activity or task (e.g. by focusing only on the shot being played). In many sports (e.g. soccer, hockey), teams may concede a goal soon after they have scored one—simply because they are thinking too far ahead.

Interestingly, one way of encouraging thinking (especially about the importance of a given shot) is to create a situation in which the performer has plenty of time to consider the consequences of what they are about to do. For example, in basketball, coaches have traditionally used a psychological ploy of calling a "time out" before an opposing player attempts a "free throw". Clearly, the purpose of this strategy is to give this player more time to "think" (or more accurately, worry) about the impending shot. It is anticipated that this delay will cause a performance error through loss of concentration. However, a recent empirical test of the utility of this strategy found no evidence to support it. In short, calling a time-out was not found to be effective in reducing the percentage accuracy of free-throws by opposing players (Kozar, Whitfield, Lord, & Mechikoff, 1993).

Distraction through inadequate motivation

Motivational factors also play a role in optimal concentration. For example, it may be difficult for athletes to concentrate properly if they are not sufficiently motivated by the challenge which they face. An illustration of this problem comes from the world of golf. Thus Jack Nicklaus admitted that "whenever I am 'up' for golf—when either the tournament or the course, or best of all both, excite and challenge me—I have little trouble concentrating ... But whenever the occasion doesn't stimulate or challenge me, or I'm just simply jaded with golf, then is the time I have to bear down on myself with a vengeance. What I suppose I'm really saying is that, in my case, lack of concentration ... can result from becoming stale (too much golf in any one short period without sufficient time to rejuvenate) as much as from pressure" (Nicklaus,

1974, p. 95). In a similar vein, Weinberg (1988) explained how inadequate motivation in tennis players may cause their attention to wander. He claimed that players who are not sufficiently challenged by a particular opponent (e.g. because of perceived differences in ability) may suffer lapses in concentration as a consequence. Thus "it takes a lot of motivation to concentrate when you do not feel challenged". This point is echoed by Rod Laver who says that "throughout my career, I've always had trouble in the early rounds of tournaments mainly because it was hard for me to psychologically get up until I got to the quarters or the semis" (cited in Weinberg, 1988).

Laver's observation may help to explain the difficulties faced by tournament favourites when drawn against lower-ranked opponents in "knock out" competitions in either individual or team sports. Willie Thorne, the snooker player, attributed his inconsistent performances against lower-ranked rivals to a lack of motivation: "The problem I think is my motivation. It's common knowledge that I'm half-looking for an excuse sometimes when I'm playing these players I should beat ... I mean (Steve) Davis if he plays a bad player, and he can beat him six-nil, he'll beat him six-nil. He slaughters them, whoever they are. You've got to play the same all the time, which is something I've not been able to do" (cited in Burn, 1992, pp. 58–59). A final example of the link between motivation and concentration comes from a comment by the 5000m world-champion athlete Sonia O'Sullivan, who had to struggle in order to qualify for the semi-finals of this event in the 1992 Olympic Games in Barcelona. She said "I like time to warm to things and I could not really concentrate since I reckoned I could qualify handily enough" (Brennan, 1992b).

Fatigue and distraction

Given that attention involves "mental effort" (see Matlin, 1994), it is not surprising that concentration can be lost simply through fatigue. This is confirmed by many sports performers. For example, all-Ireland Gaelic football winner, John O'Keeffe noted that "when you get tired, your concentration goes. Loose marking and inaccurate passing then follow" (O'Keeffe, 1993). Like fatigue, sleep deprivation can also upset concentration. In general, it appears that the performance of any task that is long or tedious is likely to deteriorate after loss of sleep.

Theoretically, fatigue upsets concentration by reducing the amount of processing resources available for deployment in a demanding situation. Interestingly, however, fatigue has little impact on skills which are rendered automatic by sustained practice. Thus reductions in mental energy (e.g. from fatigue) should hamper controlled processes more than automatic processes. Interestingly, the tennis star, Rod

Laver, discovered this principle for himself as he used to practise *harder*, rather than take a break, when he was tired: "What I used to do was to force myself to concentrate more as soon as I'd feel myself getting tired, because that's usually when your concentration starts to fail you. If I'd find myself getting really tired in practice, I'd force myself to work much harder for an extra ten or fifteen minutes, and I always felt as though I got more out of those extra minutes than I did out of the entire practice" (cited in Weinberg, 1988, p. 57).

Another danger to concentration comes from waiting for a long time to play. Thus Judy Hashman, a former US ladies' badminton champion, acknowledges "the effort of acquiring the necessary degree of concentration something like five or six times in one day, with meals in between". Also, in the 1992 French Open tennis championship, the holder of the women's title, Monica Seles, had to wait for four hours for rain to clear before playing a quarter-final match against Jennifer Capriati. After her victory, Seles complained that "When I got on the court, I kind of became dizzy. I was really disoriented from waiting for a long time" (Roberts, 1992c).

Distraction through anxiety: "Choking" under pressure

Emotional factors (e.g. anxiety) play a vital role in creating "internal" sources of distraction. In general, emotional factors affect cognition by encouraging task-*irrelevant* processing. Not surprisingly, abundant evidence exists concerning the deleterious effects of anxiety on performance in competitive sport. Indeed, the terms "choking", "icing" (in basketball, see Kozar, Whitfield, Lord, & Mechikoff, 1993) and "performance anxiety" are used interchangeably by sport psychologists to denote situations in which athletic performance is impaired by fears associated with the possibility of impending failure or defeat (Leith, 1988). Technically, "choking" involves "the failure of normally expert skill under pressure" (Masters, 1992) or "the occurrence of sub-optimal performance under pressure conditions" (Baumeister & Showers, 1986). Interestingly, these definitions highlight the fact that a key feature of "choking" is that the athlete in question is highly motivated to succeed and yet performs badly. Paradoxically, therefore, "choking" seems to occur when people try *too hard* to perform well.

As competitive sport imposes the pressure to be a winner, "choking" is widespread among athletes at all levels. For example, in the 1993 French Open tennis championships, Gabriela Sabatini lost a quarter-final match to Mary-Jo Fernandez despite the fact that, at one stage, she needed just one more point for victory. In fact, she "double-faulted" twice in a row at that point (Thornley, 1993). What happened? The most plausible explanation for this unexpected collapse is that when Sabatini served for the match at 6–1, 5–1, anxiety ca\ her to think too far ahead (i.e. about the result of the match) rather tɪɪan to focus only on actions which she could control and execute at that moment (e.g. the choice of serve to play). As Loehr (1986) noted, when what we are doing is different from what we are thinking, our concentration will lapse and our performance will suffer. Sabatini acknowledged such an attentional lapse later when she admitted later that "I had the match in my hands and I was playing great tennis. I think probably ... I lost my concentration" (see Moran, 1994c). Another example of "choking" in tennis comes from the 1993 Wimbledon Ladies Singles final between Jana Novotna (the Czech Republic) and Steffi Graf (Germany). Serving at 4–1 in the third set, with a point for 5–1, Novotna began to lose control. She produced a double-fault and some wild shots to lose that game. Later, she served *three* consecutive double faults in her anxiety to increase her 4–3 lead over Graf. Curiously, Novotna, who lost to Graf in that match, subsequently denied that she had "choked". However, she conceded that if Graf had crumbled in a similar manner, she would probably have concluded that Graf had "choked" (see Thornley, 1993). Interestingly, Novotna behaved in a similar fashion in the third round of the 1995 French Open championship in Paris when she contrived to lose a match (against the American player Chanda Rubin) in which she had 9 match points when leading 5–0, 40–0 in the third set. Most of the errors she committed at that stage of the match were unforced. The eventual score was 6–7, 6–4, 8–6 to Rubin. Another example of "choking" comes from snooker where the ability to handle anxiety is critical. Consider what snooker star Jimmy White said after nervous tension had caused him to miss an easy shot to win the 1994 World Championship final (which he lost to Stephen Hendry): "I couldn't believe it. I didn't even cue it properly. I hurried the shot ... It was just 'quickly, quickly' give me the cup. I got excited" (Hodgson, 1994).

According to Anshel (1995), "choking" is caused by a combination of internal and external factors. The former include such variables as over-arousal and a lack of confidence whereas the latter include factors like the perceived demands and expectations of coaches, spectators and team-mates. However, for many theorists (e.g. Weinberg & Gould, 1995), "choking" is best regarded as an *attentional* problem which typically arises from thinking too much about what one is doing. To explain, anxiety seems to affect the *direction* and *width* of the beam of our attentional "spotlight". Specifically, when we are anxious, we look inwards and focus on self-doubts rather than on actions. Thus Bonanno & Singer (1993) observed that "anxiety is associated with a preoccupation with internally generated fears, worries or expectations". In addition, anxiety causes us to narrow our attentional "beam", encouraging us to dwell on task-irrelevant features of the situation. Therefore, as Rotella & Lerner (1993) suggest, "athletes who are intimidated by being nervous are in trouble because they are assured of wasting their attention on their nervousness rather than focusing their mind on the more appropriate task" (pp. 535–536). In accordance with these views, Eysenck (1992) explained how anxiety may lead to task-irrelevant thinking. Briefly, worry consumes cognitive resources associated with the "central executive" in working memory—the attentional component of the system. Accordingly, the effects of worry on performance depend on the extent to which the task in question places demands on the central executive: The more cognitively demanding the task, the more vulnerable it is to disruption by worry. By implication, therefore, tasks which have become automated should be less vulnerable to disruption by conscious activities like worrying. Another perspective on this issue is provided by Easterbrook (1959) who proposed that anxiety restricts "cue utilisation" (see discussion earlier in this chapter).

As one might expect, performers other than athletes also suffer from "choking". For example, consider the experience of "stage fright" among actors and musicians. The term "stage fright" refers to any form of severe anxiety about performance in public (Steptoe & Fidler, 1987). It is characterised by a variety of symptoms ranging from memory disturbances and apprehensive thoughts (e.g. "I am sure to make a dreadful mistake which will ruin everything") to physical signs of nausea, such as hyperventilation, increased muscle tension, dizziness and trembling (Steptoe et al., 1995). The problem of stage fright is, as these authors observe, that it diverts the attention of the performer away from the task in hand, increasing the likelihood of errors.

Technically, "stage fright" occurs when performers become excessively aware of themselves or of what might go wrong. This heightened degree of self-focused attention is often found in pathological mental states (e.g. see Ingram, 1990). It may be elicited experimentally by certain environmental conditions such as cameras, mirrors, tape recordings of one's voice, photographs and the presence of spectators. Interestingly, these "triggers" of anxiety were cited as distractions by the Olympic wrestlers interviewed by Gould, Eklund, & Jackson (1992a). Of course, stage fright is also found among athletes—especially those who "freeze" in competition. For example, Victor Costello, the Irish shot-putter who set an Irish national record of 20.04m in this event was overawed by his first experience of the Olympic Games in Barcelona in 1992. In attempting to explain his poor performance of only 17.01m, he claimed that "my legs just turned to jelly when I stood in the circle and nothing happened" (Brer 1992c).

At least two attentional explanations have been offered in attempting to explain "choking" (Baumeister & Showers, 1986). First, "distraction" theorists (e.g. Baumeister) suggest that choking occurs because the performer may stop paying selective attention to task-relevant cues (e.g. ball flight in tennis) and instead engage in task-*irrelevant* (e.g. "what if?") thinking (e.g. worrying about results). According to Baumeister & Showers (1986), *worry* is one of the primary causes of this task-irrelevant thinking. Some theorists (e.g. Wine, 1971) believe that self-focused attention impairs performance by reducing attention to task-relevant features. For example, people experience test-anxiety when they are preoccupied with "self-evaluative" thoughts ("I'm going to fail") to the relative neglect of task-relevant details. But how does worry or self-doubt affect our attention? As I explained earlier, anxiety tends to restrict our concentration. According to Syer (1986), when we are anxious, our attention becomes constricted and we tend to notice only those things which increase our fear. In a similar vein, Orlick (1990) claims that worry raises anxiety, drains energy and "diminishes your performance focus".

Alternatively, self-awareness theories (e.g. Fenigstein, Scheier, & Buss, 1975) propose that when performers become aware of themselves, the resultant self-consciousness disrupts task execution. To explain, perceived pressure may cause the performer to focus disproportionately on the *process* of performance—leading to a state in which automaticity is reversed (see explanation above): Under pressure, "the individual begins thinking about how he or she is executing the skill, and endeavours to operate it with his or her explicit knowledge of its mechanics" (Masters, 1992, p. 345). Other theorists (e.g. Kimble & Perlmutter, 1970) believe that self-awareness causes an exaggerated concern with the mechanics underlying the execution skilled behaviour, thereby "robbing it of its normal fluidity and rhythm" (Vallacher, 1993).

The concept of self-focus has great relevance for elite sports performers because they are constantly surrounded by the conditions which engender this mental state. To illustrate, they face the presence of spectators, television cameras and tape recorders. Paradoxically, the presence of such *external* stimuli may exaggerate performers' sensitivity to their *internal* mental states. In such circumstances, self-doubt and worry may occur. In turn, these feelings may upset the performer's concentration. Indeed, available evidence indicates that self-focused attention is associated with a variety of psychological problems, such as poor self-esteem, depressed mood, increased anxiety and impaired concentration (see Ingram, 1990).

From the self-awareness perspective, concentration may be upset for several reasons (Baumeister & Showers, 1986). First, perhaps "performance-contingent rewards" cause performers to think too much about the consequences involved. Thus an athlete may "choke" because they have already imagined what it would be like to be celebrating the victory or lamenting the defeat. Second, a performer may be distracted by worry—by a self-focused fear of failure. A third theory is that, by definition, attention to the self is a distraction because one cannot be aware of oneself and of one's environment at the same time. In summary, each of these theories tries to explain "choking" in terms of the performer's attentional mechanisms.

It is generally agreed that highly anxious people are more susceptible to distraction than are less anxious counterparts. Furthermore, Eysenck (1988) suggested that there are significant attentional differences between people who are classified as "high" and "low" in trait anxiety. Specifically, the former are thought to display greater attentional selectivity, to have less attentional capacity available and to suffer from greater distractibility than people who are relatively low in trait anxiety. He also proposed that distraction will affect highly anxious people most strongly when the task-irrelevant stimuli are threat-related. In summary, Eysenck (1992) suggests two possible explanations for the detrimental effects of anxiety on concentration and performance. First, "hypervigilance" (the hallmark of anxiety) leads to rapid environmental scanning which causes the allocation of attentional resources away from the current task and towards extraneous sources of distraction. In other words, the distractibility of anxious people may reflect environmental scanning for threatening stimuli. Second, anxiety consumes working memory resources. Therefore, anxious people have less available attentional capacity than low-anxious people. So they are more distractible simply because they have less processing capacity available to counteract the disruptive effects of distractors. I shall return to this issue in Chapter 8.

SUMMARY

Distractions (or "distractors") may be defined as factors which divert our attention from its intended "focus" or target. As I explained, these factors are ubiquitous in competitive sport. Surprisingly, however, few attempts have been made to understand either their origin or their typical effects on athletic performance. Therefore, the objective of this chapter was to evaluate the causes and consequences of lapses of attention among athletes.

I began by considering the general question of why people's thoughts tend to wander—especially in situations in which they are tired, stressful or otherwise cognitively over-loaded. Briefly, according to Wegner (1994), the intention to concentrate on something activates two mental processing systems simultaneously. The "intentional operating system" seems to drive a controlled search for cognitive contents which satisfy the desired mental state (i.e. "wanted" thoughts) whereas the "ironic monitoring system" is an automatic mechanism designed to detect incompatible mental states (i.e. "unwanted" thoughts). Normally, our conscious intentions exert greater influence over our mental states than does our ironic monitoring system. But when stress or fatigue consume some of our limited attentional resources, the ironic system may prevail. Under these circumstances, paradoxical lapses of attention may occur. For example, people may find that the more they try to suppress an unwanted thought, the more tenaciously it clings to consciousness.

Distractions may be distinguished on the basis of whether they originate in the outside world ("external" variables) or in the performer's own mind ("internal" factors). Frequently, these factors combine to divert one's attentional focus from task-relevant thoughts or actions. Common "external" distractors include environmental factors like changes in noise and heat. Similarly, tactical ploys (e.g. gamesmanship) by opponents and the presence of visual distractions may cause athletes to lose their "focus". But athletes also contrive to distract *themselves* when they engage in regrets (e.g. thinking about missed opportunities) or when they speculate about events in the future ("fortune-telling"). Of course, concentration can also be impaired through emotional influences. Specifically, it seems that emotional factors (e.g. anxiety) can affect the direction and breadth of athletes' concentration. Specifically, anxiety causes sport performers to narrow their concentration beam and to direct it inwards. Accordingly, pressure situations may cause athletes to become either too self-conscious or excessively result-conscious. Both of these attentional foci are equally unhelpful as they take the performer's mind away from the task at hand. Therefore, "choking" under pressure is widely regarded by sport psychologists as an attentional problem. Other internal distractors which tend to disrupt athletic performance include inadequate motivation and fatigue. Unfortunately, despite their theoretical and practical importance to athletes, internal distractors have received little research attention from psychologists.

CHAPTER FIVE

Measuring attentional processes in athletes: From brain states to individual differences

INTRODUCTION

In Chapter 2 of this book I indicated that the construct of attention is multi-dimensional in character. Specifically, it refers to cognitive ("mental effort"), behavioural (action control) and physiological (alertness) aspects of concentration behaviour. Not surprisingly, these separate attentional components have been assessed by psychologists using a variety of different measurement paradigms. For example, psychophysiological correlates of attention have been measured using such indices as heart rate (HR) and the electroencephalogram (EEG). Similarly, measurement of attentional "narrowing" as a result of anxiety has been achieved largely through experimental psychological techniques such as the "dual-task" paradigm (see Chapter 3).

Unfortunately, although they are valuable in their own ways, neither the physiological nor the experimental paradigm is designed to address an important question for sport psychologists: How do athletes differ from each other in concentration skills and strategies? In order to answer this question, several self-report measures of attentional processes (e.g. the "Test of Attentional and Interpersonal Style", TAIS; Nideffer, 1976a) have been developed by sport psychologists in recent years. These tests are being used increasingly in the selection and evaluation of athletes. For example, the TAIS has been employed in the Australian Institute for Sport for almost a decade (see Bond & Sargent,

1995). But how valid and reliable are these psychometric tests of concentration? More generally, what findings have emerged from the various attempts to measure attentional processes in athletes? Specifically, what is known about the relationship between concentration strategies and sport performance? The purpose of this chapter is to provide some answers to these questions.

I shall begin by outlining key assumptions and examples of the psychophysiological, experimental and psychometric (self-report) measurement paradigms used for the assessment of concentration skills in athletes. Then I shall evaluate the reliability and validity of one of the most popular attentional scale used in sport psychology, namely, the Test of Attentional and Interpersonal Style (TAIS; Nideffer, 1976a). Next, using the attentional processes of marathon runners as a case-study, I shall explore the relationship between self-reported concentration strategies and athletic success. This section will feature an analysis of "associative" and "dissociative" concentration strategies. Finally, I shall evaluate the psychometric adequacy of the attentional sub-scales which are contained in two general self-report inventories used in sport psychology (i.e. the Psychological Skills Inventory for Sports, PSIS R-5; Mahoney, Gabriel, & Perkins, 1987 and the Bangor Sport Psychological Skills Inventory, BSPSI; Nelson & Hardy, 1990).

PSYCHOPHYSIOLOGICAL MEASUREMENT TECHNIQUES

Although psychophysiological aspects of athletic performance have been studied extensively (see review by Hatfield & Landers, 1987), the most popular biological indices of attention used by sport psychology researchers have been electroencephalogram (EEG) measures, heart rate (HR) parameters and event-related cortical potentials (ERP). These techniques are helpful to sport scientists because they provide a continuous record of physiological activity while the athlete is performing.

In general, physiological measures of attention have been administered most frequently to performers of "closed" skills (i.e. those in which the key movements are self-paced, repetitive and performed in a relatively unchanging environment; e.g. archery, pistol-shooting or bowling; see Brady, 1995). For example, in target shooting, the preparatory period which occurs 3–7 seconds before skill execution is regarded as critical for optimal performance. During this period, "the shooter makes the final adjustments to his or her preshot set" (Konttinen, Lyytinen, & Konttinen, 1995). As one might expect, there is evidence that a distinctive pattern of physiological activity occurs in this preparatory period as the shooter intensifies his or her concentration. Below, I shall consider some of the physiological characteristics associated with these changes in the concentration patterns of archers and shooters.

Electroencephalogram (EEG) measures

The electroencephalogram (EEG) provides a record of the spontaneous electrical potentials that are generated continuously by nerve cells in the brain. This electrical activity is typically measured by electrodes placed at different sites on the surface of the scalp. Overall, EEG patterns comprise different bandwidths or wave-forms ("brain waves") that are believed to reflect different states of physiological arousal. For example, "alpha" wave activity (lying between 8 and 13Hz) is associated with relaxed wakefulness. Usually, suppression of EEG alpha-wave activity is thought to indicate increased physiological activation (Abernethy, 1993).

Many studies have been conducted on the pre-shot EEG patterns of pistol and rifle shooters and archers. One consistent finding which emerges from this literature is that accuracy of shooting performance (i.e. shots which landed closer to the centre of the target) tends to be associated with alpha frequencies in the left cerebral hemisphere. For example, Hatfield & Landers (1987) reported that top-class, right-handed marksmen displayed increased EEG alpha-wave activity as they expended more mental effort up to the moment at which they pulled their triggers. This increased EEG activity was most evident in the left-temporal region of the brain of the shooter in the 3–5 seconds immediately preceding shot execution. Similarly, Salazar et al. (1990) reported that the best performances of Olympic and top US archers occurred in association with increased alpha activity in the left hemisphere during the 3 seconds prior to arrow-release. Hemispheric asymmetries in the preparatory period have also been reported in the case of rifle shooters (Hatfield, Landers, & Ray, 1984). Here, a surge of left hemisphere EEG alpha activity was detected prior to trigger pull. In summary, these studies show that as shooters or archers prepare to fire, there is a marked shift from left to right hemispheric activation.

According to Summers & Ford (1995), this change in physiological activation reflects a shift in executive control from the verbally-based left hemisphere to the more visual-spatial right hemisphere prior to skill execution. This finding suggests that elite shooters have gained such control over their attentional processes that they can voluntarily reduce cognitive activity in their left hemisphere. Such selective suppression of cortical activity may lead to a lowering of task-irrelevant cognitive distractions (or mental "chatter") which could otherwise disrupt shooting performance (Boutcher, 1992). Unfortunately, the EEG is regarded as a somewhat blunt technique because it is not formally connected with external stimulus events. Accordingly, the use of this physiological index has been compared by Eysenck & Keane (1995) to the task of trying to monitor conversations between people in another room by putting one's ear to the wall!

Despite this criticism, the EEG has been valuable in mapping patterns of electrical activity that precede optimal shooting performance. From this research, an interesting question arises. Would the performance of archers or shooters improve if they were trained to alter their brain states through biofeedback? Landers et al. (1991) attempted to answer this question using a sample of archers. Briefly, these authors provided "incorrect" (i.e. right-hemisphere), "correct" (i.e. left-hemisphere) or no alpha feedback to different groups of archers. Results showed that, relative to control conditions, the performance of the left-hemisphere feedback group improved most significantly (see also Chapter 6). Interestingly, when asked to describe what they had been thinking about in the final seconds of their pre-shot preparation, many archers in this study replied that their minds had been "blank" or that they had been totally focused on the target. Although these comments appear to reflect the elusive fusion of thinking and action which characterises optimal "flow" states in performers (see Chapter 3), they must be interpreted cautiously in view of the biases which are known to afflict athletes' retrospective accounts of their own mental processes (Brewer, Van Raalte, Linder, & Van Raalte, 1991). Still, this study suggests that biofeedback training may enhance the performance of certain repetitive skills in sport. Additional details of research in this field are provided in a review by Petruzzello, Landers, & Salazar (1991).

Heart rate measures

Interest in the psychological significance of heart-rate (HR) dates back at least as far as ancient Greece. The physician Galen is alleged to have used direct observation of a patient's pulse to determine that she was suffering from love-sickness (Coles, 1972). However, it is only in the recent past that researchers have begun to use changes in heart-rate, which is controlled by the autonomic nervous system, as an index of attentional states in sport performers.

In Chapter 2, when reviewing the structure of the attention system, we learned that the orienting response (or involuntary "startle" reaction) occurs as a function of stimuli that are novel or intense. Usually, this response is accompanied by certain physiological changes. One of these changes concerns the slowing down (or "deceleration") of heart-rate. This observation influenced Lacey (1967) to suggest that when people pay attention to environmental tasks, their heart rate decreases whereas when they attend to internal stimuli, their heart rate usually accelerates. Among the tasks for which cardiac acceleration occurred were mental arithmetic and anagram solving. This finding indicated to Coles (1983) that HR acceleration was related to information processing and decision making activity. Conversely, there is evidence that cardiac deceleration occurs during the foreperiod of reaction time tasks, when subjects are presumably preparing to respond to environmental events (Coles, 1972).

The idea that the directionality of the "beam" of our concentration has a physiological basis (see Lacey, 1967) is supported by several studies. First, Coles (1972) gave subjects a visual search task involving different degrees of discriminability of the target stimuli. As low discriminability tasks require greater "sensory intake", Lacey's (1967) hypothesis predicts that HR should be *lower* under conditions of low- versus high-discriminability tasks. In general, this hypothesis was corroborated since heart rate was found to decrease during the foreperiod for each level of discriminability. Also, as predicted, HR decreases were greater for low- than for high- discriminability tasks. Second, as with EEG studies, research has been conducted on cardiac changes in athletes as they prepare to perform sport skills. For example, Wang & Landers (1986) and Helin, Sihvonen, & Hanninen (1987) reported that heart rate decreased in the period preceding the arrow release in archery and the trigger pull in gun shooting, respectively. This cardiac deceleration was also found by Konttinen & Lyytinen (1992) and may be interpreted as support for the Lacey hypothesis that HR deceleration occurs during attentional anticipation of an external event. Lacey (1967) would explain HR deceleration during the preparation period in shooting as being caused by the fact that the shooters at that time are directing their attention *outwards*—focusing not only on the visual target but also on the best way to stabilise and align the gun (Konttinen & Lyytinen, 1992).

Among highly-skilled golfers, significant decelerations in heart rate (of the order of 4–11 beats per minute) have been reported within 3 to 7 seconds of the execution of a putting stroke (Boutcher & Zinsser, 1990; Molander & Backman, 1989). Similar results have been found among players of miniature golf (Molander & Backman, 1989). Likewise, Wang & Landers (1986) discovered a significant deceleration in HR in archers immediately prior to their release of the arrow. This finding is consistent with the theory that during this preparatory stage, archers tend to focus predominantly on the *external* environment in order to align their sights with the target (Landers et al., 1994). Likewise, Landers, Christina,

Hatfield, Daniels, & Doyle (1980) reported evidence that heart-rate decelerated in elite rifle shooters just before they pulled the trigger. Interestingly, Lacey's (1967) "intake-rejection hypothesis", which states that "external" attentional states are accompanied by heart rate (HR) deceleration and that "internal" attentional states are correlated with HR acceleration patterns, was invoked by Fenz (1975) to explain expert-novice differences in parachute jumping. Further research on heart-rate and sport performance was conducted by Pelton (1983) who found that elite shooters tended to squeeze the trigger consistently *between* heartbeats. Apparently, the tiny tremor caused by a heartbeat is sufficient to send a shot wide of the intended target. A major advantage of psychophysiological techniques like biofeedback, therefore, is that they may provide both pistol- and rifle-shooters with a method of timing their shots so that they occur *between*, rather than at the same time as, their heartbeats.

Although archery and other forms of target-shooting are precision sports, it may be argued that they are *responsive* rather than *self-paced* tasks. Thus Boutcher & Zinsser (1990) explained that archers and shooters are trained to focus their attention on external cues which "prime" them to respond. For example, archers respond to a "clicker" which lies on the bow handle and indicates when the archer is at "full-draw". Likewise, shooters pull their triggers when their sights are aligned with the target. Another difference between archery or target shooting and skills like golf putting is that the former require more physical exertion than the latter (Crews & Landers, 1993). Indeed, top-class archers must possess considerable arm and lower-body strength to draw back bow-strings which carry a force of approximately 20 kilograms. Also, archers must have strong leg and stomach muscles in order to maintain a steady bodily position while shooting. In golf putting, on the other hand, performers is not obviously waiting for any external cue to prime their behaviour. Boutcher & Zinsser (1990) were interested in testing Lacey's (1967) hypothesis using the self-paced skill of golf-putting. They monitored cardiac, respiratory and behavioural patterns of elite and novice golfers both before and during performance of a number of 4-feet and 12-feet putts. Both groups of golfers showed significantly decelerated heart-rates while performing both lengths of putt. But for the 12-feet putts, elite golfers recorded significantly slower heart-beats for the inter-beat intervals before, during and after striking the ball. Two other findings of this study were noteworthy. First, the top golfers showed less variation in their "pre-shot routines" (i.e. in the sequence of preparatory actions which they executed prior to their performance; see also Chapter 6), and took longer ball-address time, than did the beginners. In addition, interview data indicated that the elite performers tended to focus their attention on single, task-relevant cues (e.g. "back of the ball") whereas the beginners were more concerned with the mechanics of the action or with the adverse consequences of hitting the ball too hard. Indeed, there was some evidence that the expert golfers focused more on kinaesthetic cues (e.g. "feeling" the putt) than on technical ones (e.g. stroke mechanics). In summary, Boutcher & Zinsser (1990) concluded that the differences in heart rate deceleration patterns between these groups highlighted the greater attentional control of the elite golfers in comparison with the beginners.

So far, we have seen that certain physiological changes occur reliably as expert performers try to focus their attentional resources in the seconds preceding their performance. But is there any evidence that such mental effort is beneficial to skilled performance? A study by Landers et al. (1994) addressed this issue. These researchers set out to assess the psychophysiological (i.e. EEG and HR) changes occurring among a sample of right-handed novice archers who participated in a 12-week archery training programme (including practice and instructional modules). Results comparing pre-test at week 2 to post-test at week 14 showed two important changes. First, a pre-shot pattern of HR *deceleration* was evident among the novices at the end of the training period. This suggests an improvement in concentration skills among these performers. In addition, after the training programme, during the 3-second duration preceding shot execution, more *left hemisphere* than right-hemisphere EEG activity was apparent. This corroborates the prediction (Lacey, 1967) that both heart rate deceleration and left hemisphere EEG activity should become more evident as performers learn to focus their attention more effectively on specific cues in the external environment. These changes in psychophysiological activity over a 12-week training programme led the authors to conclude that "as archers became more proficient their attentional skills improved" (Landers et al., 1994).

In summary, slowing of the heartbeat (or "cardiac deceleration") is frequently evident in athletes immediately prior to the performance of "closed" sport skills (e.g. the golf putt). Moreover, the extent of this decrease seems to be related to the level of proficiency of the performers involved. Specifically, expert athletes appear to display greater deceleration than do relative novices (Summers & Ford, 1995). This finding suggests that expert athletes know how to regulate their physiological processes in order to prepare optimally for skilled performance.

Event-related cortical potentials

Although EEG measures have been valuable in monitoring the attentional processes of athletes, they suffer from being relatively independent of external stimulus events. But this limitation can be circumvented by the use of "event-related cortical potentials" (ERPs; see Rugg & Coles, 1995). These potentials are based on electrical activity in the brain that is "time-locked" to some eliciting event or stimulus. Unlike the EEG, which indicates continuous electrical activity in the brain, ERPs reflect transient changes in the brain's electrical activity that are "evoked" by certain information-processing events. Also, unlike EEG measures, event-related potentials reflect neural activity which is "time-locked" to these specific stimuli.

In general, an ERP is best defined as a pattern of brain wave activity obtained by averaging EEG waves recorded over as many as 100 trials (Haberlandt, 1994). Typically, ERPs display characteristic peaks of electrical activity that begins a few milliseconds after the onset of a stimulus and continue for almost a second afterwards. These electrical peaks and troughs are labelled as either positive ("P") or negative ("N") and designated by their latency in milliseconds from stimulus onset (e.g. 300msec). For example, consider the ERP known as "P300". For attentional researchers, this ERP, which reflects a latency recorded over the parietal scalp 300 milliseconds after stimulus onset, is a potentially valuable index of attention because it is apparently sensitive to the resource demands of the "primary" task in the dual-task paradigm (Abernethy, 1993). A study which has explored the P300 index in athletes was conducted by Zani & Rossi (1991). These researchers reported differences in this index between clay-pigeon shooters specialising in different events (i.e. either trap or skeet shooting). A comprehensive review of the nature and implications of the P300 index was provided recently by Polich & Kok (1995).

MEASURING ATTENTION EXPERIMENTALLY: THE DUAL-TASK PARADIGM

So far, I have explained how sport psychologists have tried to assess attentional processes through psychophysiological measures. But there is another approach to attentional measurement—one derived from the "dual-task" paradigm in experimental psychology (described in Chapters 2 and 3).

For example, consider a study by Landers, Qi, & Courtet (1985) on rifle-shooting. Briefly, these authors tested the hypothesis (Easterbrook, 1959) that, under conditions of increased arousal, performance on a primary task would improve or be maintained whereas performance of a secondary task would deteriorate. Here, it is assumed that when people show deficits in performance of the secondary task, some attentional "narrowing" has occurred. Therefore, performance on this secondary task has been interpreted as an index of an athlete's "peripheral" awareness. Using this logic, Landers, Qi, & Courtet (1985) compared rifle-shooters' performance on a primary target shooting task with that on a secondary auditory task, while they competed under low-stress and high-stress conditions. Results showed that when the difficulty of the primary task was increased (by increasing time demands), subjects in the high-stress condition took longer to react to the auditory stimuli (secondary task) than when they performed in the low-stress condition. This result suggests that with increased arousal, the shooters had less spare attentional capacity available to monitor the peripheral auditory task.

Another example of dual-task performance in sport comes from Weltman & Egstrom (1966) who discovered that novice scuba divers who were undergoing training in underwater submergence in the sea took longer to react to a peripherally presented light than when they performed in a diving tank. In passing, it should be noted that the "dual task" paradigm has been used most frequently to measure the "breadth" of attention (i.e. whether the "beam" of one's concentration is broad or narrow; Wachtel, 1967) rather than its direction (i.e. whether one focuses on internal or external events).

MEASURING ATTENTION THROUGH SELF-REPORT PROCEDURES

The psychophysiological and experimental paradigms use objective techniques for the measurement of attentional processes in athletes. Unfortunately, neither of them assesses directly the insights and experiences of the performers themselves. By contrast, the self-report approach is based on the idea that people can provide valuable evidence on their own attentional habits and preferences in different sport situations.

Unfortunately, paper-and-pencil tests of attention have encountered both theoretical and methodological problems. Theoretically these scales assume that our knowledge about our own attentional processes is directly accessible to conscious introspection. However, as I mentioned in Chapter 3, opinions are divided among cognitive psychologists about the validity of this assumption. In particular, Nisbett & Wilson (1977) raised doubts about the extent to which introspection provides *any* form of privileged access to our mental processes. They presented evidence to suggest that when people attempt to report on their own cognitive processes, they do not do so on the basis of "true" introspection but rather on the basis of implicit, *a priori* causal theories. In other words, people often draw conclusions about mental experiences to which they may not have direct awareness. Evidence to support this argument comes from studies which show that people's introspections about the factors which influence their behaviour are often no more accurate than the speculations which are provided by other people (i.e. external observers) about it. Therefore, in many situations, what people tell us is *more* than they can validly know about their own behaviour (Nisbett & Wilson, 1977). By implication, verbal reports on mental processes are of questionable significance. This scepticism about self-reports is shared by Boutcher (1992) who acknowledged that "there are problems with the assumption that attention can be accurately described through self-analysis and language". Although this critique of introspection challenges the validity of self-report measures, it falls short of discrediting people's accounts of their own *attentional* processes. For example, Nisbett & Wilson (1977) were convinced that "an individual may know that he (*sic*) was or was not attending to a particular stimulus". Turning to methodological issues, several reviewers have claimed that self-report measures of attentional processes lack construct (especially predictive) validity. For example, Boutcher (1992) concluded that "no evidence exists to suggest that attentional questionnaires are good predictors of sport performance".

Despite these reservations about the merit of information derived from self-report measures, the brevity and convenience of attentional scales makes them appealing to applied sport psychologists. Perhaps the most popular of these concentration scales is the "Test of Attentional and Interpersonal Style" (TAIS; Nideffer, 1976a).

NIDEFFER'S THEORY OF ATTENTIONAL STYLES

At first glance, the theory of attention developed by Nideffer (1976a; 1976b) appears to be one of the most comprehensive cognitive models in contemporary sport psychology. In particular, it seems to account for many attentional phenomena (e.g. individual differences in concentration skills) in an elegant, parsimonious and plausible manner. On closer inspection, however, there is evidence that attentional style theory is not only over-simplified but is also marred by conceptual and methodological weaknesses. But before considering these issues, I shall summarise the main propositions underlying this theory and describe the test itself.

Assumptions of Nideffer's theory

At least four key propositions underlie attentional style theory (see Bond & Sargent, 1995, for a comprehensive review). To begin with, Nideffer (1976b) postulated that people have a "preferred attentional style" or propensity to adopt a characteristic focus of concentration in different sport settings. This individual preference, which may be regarded as a relatively stable personality trait, is assumed to be measurable using the Test of Attentional and Interpersonal Style (TAIS; Nideffer, 1976a). Influenced by Wachtel's (1967) typology, Nideffer proposed that attention varies simultaneously along two independent bi-polar dimensions: Width and direction. The term "width" refers to the amount of information attended to in the stimulus field. It ranges along a continuum from "broad" (where one is aware of many stimulus features at the same time) to "narrow" (where one filters out irrelevant information). The term "direction" denotes the *target* of one's attentional focus. As I indicated in Chapter 3, this target may be either "internal" (involving stimuli like one's thoughts, feelings and bodily sensations) or "external" (including such sources of information as features of the environment or aspects of the behaviour of one's opponent). Attentional "width" refers to the number of elements that the person can focus on to at a given moment whereas attentional "direction" indicates whether concentration is focused on the environment or on the self.

According to Nideffer (1986), these two dimensions of attention may be combined factorially to yield different four different "attentional styles". To illustrate, a "broad external" focus might be required when a soccer player quickly scans the field to assess the position of team-mates before passing the ball. This focus involves the ability to integrate many different environmental stimuli at once. Conversely, a "narrow external" focus is required when an archer focuses on the "bull's eye" on the target before shooting. Likewise, a "broad internal" attentional focus (which entails the ability to integrate many different thoughts and feelings simultaneously) is necessary when a player formulates a "game plan" for a forthcoming match while a "narrow internal" focus is used when a performer mentally rehearses ("visualises") a specific skill (e.g. a balance beam routine in gymnastics) before a competition.

Second, different sport skills are held to require different types of attentional foci. For example, a point-guard in basketball may need to display a "broad external" attentional style whereas a golf putter may require a "narrow external" focus. But even *within* a given sport, different attentional styles may be demanded by different skills. For example, before a race in rowing, a narrow-*internal* focus is necessary for a performer to monitor muscular tension in their arms and shoulders. However, during the race, a narrow-*external* focus is required as the rower concentrates on the coxswain's instructions (Horsley, 1989). Athletes often have to learn to switch their attention rapidly from one target to another during competition. For example, when a basketball player scans the court for an "open" (unmarked) team-mate, a broad attentional focus is used. But seconds later, when the player identifies an unmarked colleague, a narrow focus is used to ensure that the resultant pass is delivered accurately. More generally, Nideffer speculated that there should be significant attentional differences between athletes in "open" and "closed" skill sports. Specifically, he claimed that "a narrow focus of attention is necessary in closed skill and/or self-paced sports like shooting, diving, and skating" (Nideffer, 1993a). Data to test this prediction were gathered from the archives of the Australian Institute for Sport (see Bond & Sargent, 1995) where the TAIS has been used for more than a decade. Results showed that athletes involved in closed-skill sports tended to have a narrower focus of attention than that displayed by counterparts involved in open- and team-sports (Nideffer, 1990).

Third, efficient sport performance is held to depend on the degree to which a performer's preferred attentional style is compatible with the attentional demands of the sport. As Albrecht & Feltz (1987) remarked, "to the extent that one's personal attentional style matches or is congruent with the specific situational demands of a given task, the more proficient one is likely to be in performing that task". If an incongruence exists between style and task demand, lapses in performance may occur. For example, a tennis player who is about to serve (and hence requires a narrow attentional focus) risks distraction by scanning the crowd for familiar faces (an activity which inadvertently broadens the attentional focus; see also Chapter 4 for discussion of distractions provided by spectators). Similarly, in order to maintain balance, gymnasts require a narrow focus of attention that is directed mainly at "internal" cues (e.g. kinaesthetic sensations). But if their attention is captured by some "broad external" factors, then they might become distracted and fall.

Fourth, attention is affected by increased arousal in certain predictable ways (see also Chapter 3). For example, pressure may cause an the anxious performer to adhere rigidly to their attentional style. Also, arousal leads to an involuntary narrowing of attentional focus. Furthermore, Nideffer (1980) suggested that arousal increases distractibility: "The person becomes distracted by his (sic) own bodily feelings (beating heart, muscle tension, and so on) and his (sic) thoughts (why did the runners leave base, what's the matter with me, I might choke, and so on). As attention is directed internally, the ability to concentrate on their game deteriorates" (p. 103). Therefore, according to Nideffer, increased arousal leads to reduced attentional flexibility, a narrowing of attentional focus and a predominantly "internal" attentional orientation.

Having outlined the main assumptions underlying Nideffer's theory, let us now evaluate his Test of Attentional and Interpersonal Style (TAIS).

The Test of Attentional and Interpersonal Style (TAIS)

The TAIS is a 144-item, self-report, paper-and-pencil inventory designed to measure "attentional and interpersonal characteristics believed to be relevant to the prediction of performance" (Nideffer, 1987) in a variety of everyday situations (e.g. item 14 contains the statement "When I read, it is easy to block out everything but the book"). The test was developed on a sample of college students and was not designed uniquely for sport situations. An abbreviated version of the test (containing 12 items) has been developed (see Nideffer, 1976b) although no data on its psychometric adequacy are available. However, its authors claim that it is "pretty good at identifying ... tendencies" in attentional focus (Nideffer, 1985). The TAIS was designed to serve both as a research tool and as a "feedback device" (Nideffer, 1987). In this latter role, the TAIS has been used for over a decade in the Australian Institute for Sport (Bond & Sargent, 1995).

The TAIS contains 17 sub-scales. Nine of them purport to assess the manner in which a person is likely to behave in a variety of interpersonal situations (e.g. item 60, "People fool me because I don't bother to analyse the things that they say; I take them at face value"). Another six sub-scales are held to assess attentional processes (specifically, various combinations of attentional "width" and "direction") and the remaining two scales are alleged to measure behavioural and cognitive control. The constructs alleged to be measured by the six attentional sub-scales are: (i) "broad external focus", BET, or the capacity "to effectively integrate many external stimuli at one time" (Nideffer, 1976b); or "good environmental awareness and assessment skills" (Nideffer, 1987)—measured by such items as "I am good at rapidly scanning crowds and picking out a particular person or face" (item 44); (ii) "external overload", OET, external distractibility, or the performer's propensity to make "performance errors due to attending to irrelevant external distractions" (Nideffer, 1987), as measured by items like "At stores, I am faced with so many choices I can't make up my mind" (item 35); (iii) "broad internal focus", BIT, or the ability to think of several things at once when it is appropriate to do so, as measured by such items as "I theorise and philosophise" (item 20); (iv) "internal overload", OIT, internal distractibility, or a susceptibility to "performance errors due to distractions from irrelevant internal sources" (ibid.), as assessed by items like "When people talk to me I find myself distracted by my own thoughts and ideas" (item 1); (v) "narrow attentional focus", NAR, or the ability to narrow attention effectively when required, as assessed by statements like "When I read it is easy to block out everything but the book" (item 14) and (vi) "reduced attentional focus", RED, or "a breakdown in shifting from an internal focus of attention to an external focus, or vice versa", as assessed by "I make mistakes because my thoughts get stuck on one idea or feeling" (item 62). Incidentally, Nideffer (1993a) claims that the RED scale measures the tendency to fail to shift attention from an internal to an external focus.

Relatively high scores on the broad-external (BET), broad-internal (BIT) and narrow-internal (NAR) scales are thought to reflect an effective deployment of attention while relatively high scores on the overload-external (OET), overload-internal (OIT) and reduced-attention (RED) sub-scales are held to suggest an ineffective attentional style. Three of the six attentional sub-scales claim to measure effective use of attention. These are BET, BIT and NAR. The other three sub-scales assess the performer's tendency to adopt an inappropriate attentional focus. In particular, these latter scales claim to measure the extent to which people have a reduced attentional focus (RED) and are susceptible to being overloaded by external (OET) and internal (OIT) stimuli.

Some empirical support for this theory is evident. For example, Nideffer (1976a) reported that unsuccessful swimmers were overloaded by external (high OET) and internal (high OIT) stimuli relative to successful counterparts. Similarly, Landers, Furst, & Daniels (1981) found that poor rifle shooters were overloaded by external stimuli (high OET) and displayed restricted attention (high RED) relative to proficient colleagues. Furthermore, Wilson, Ainsworth, & Bird (1985) reported evidence supporting the convergent validity of the TAIS. To explain, they discovered that volleyball players who had been rated by their coaches as "good concentrators" under competitive stress scored significantly lower on the BET ("broad external" focus) and BIT ("broad internal" focus) sub-scales than did "poor concentrators", thereby suggesting that such players can narrow or "focus" their attention when pressure occurs. Surprisingly, however, there was no significant relationship in this study between the players' self-ratings of their concentration abilities and those provided by their coaches. This finding reinforces the doubts I expressed earlier in this chapter about the validity of any self-report scale of attention. Specifically, it suggests that people are not very reliable or accurate judges of their own mental abilities. Indeed, other studies (e.g. Reisberg & McLean, 1985) show that people may not be accurate judges of their own attentional processes. Accordingly, we should be cautious about research (e.g. Etzel, 1979) in which it is assumed "that subjects could articulate the extent to which attention influences their shooting".

Another source of evidence in support of Nideffer's test comes from studies which have tested his proposition that a specific attentional style is necessary for optimal performance in a given sport. In this vein, significant relationships have been reported between TAIS scores and performance in swimming (Nideffer, 1976b), golf (Kirschenbaum & Bale, 1984) and shooting (Landers, Furst, & Daniels, 1981). Unfortunately, Summers, Miller, & Ford (1991) discovered that the TAIS failed to discriminate between athletes (i.e. basketball players, fencers and cricket players) of different levels of expertise. I shall return to this point later in the chapter.

How successful is the TAIS in measuring attentional processes in athletes? At the outset, we must be clear that this test assesses *perceived*, rather than actual, attentional skills. Unfortunately, few researchers have tried to validate these attentional beliefs against objective evidence. However, in an effort to establish the convergent validity of the TAIS, Turner & Gilliland (1977) correlated the six attentional sub-scales of the TAIS with two indices of concentration derived from an IQ test, namely, the Block Design and Digit Span tests of the Wechsler Adult Intelligence Scale (WAIS; Wechsler, 1955). Significant positive correlations were expected between these tests and the BET, BIT and NAR scales of the TAIS. Furthermore, significant negative correlations were expected between the two IQ sub-tests and the OET, OIT and RED components of the TAIS. Unfortunately, of the 24 correlations calculated to test these predictions, only one was significant statistically (i.e. BIT with performance on Block Design). These disappointing results highlight the need for validation of the TAIS against behavioural and/or other psychometric indices of attention. In response to these problems, Nideffer (1993a) defended the TAIS on the rather odd grounds that validation studies of this test have been conducted on "the performance of *relatively normal individuals* and have not systematically manipulated the level of arousal in their subjects" (p. 548, italics mine). Apparently, he believes that measures of attentional style are not sufficient, by themselves, to predict performance: An arousal manipulation is also required in order "to increase the trait behaviour of that dominant style". By this reasoning, it seems clear that Nideffer (1993a) regards arousal as a variable which mediates attention-performance relationships.

Conceptual and methodological issues surrounding the TAIS

Overall, the TAIS needs to address a variety of conceptual and methodological problems before it can be recommended as a valid and reliable test of the attentional skills of athletes. These problems can be summarised as follows.

To begin with, the rationale underlying this test appears to contradict one of the tenets of Nideffer's theory. Specifically, although Nideffer claims that sports vary considerably in the attentional demands which they make on performers, the TAIS is a *generic* concentration test which was not designed solely for athletes. Therefore, as Van Schoyck & Grasha (1981) observed, TAIS items "lack reference to any sport and it would be difficult to quickly translate them into a sport frame of reference". To counteract this difficulty, sport-specific versions of the TAIS have been developed for tennis (Van Schoyck & Grasha, 1981) and baseball/softball (Albrecht & Feltz, 1987). The advantage of such tests is that items "are given a context pertinent to the specific sport being studied" (Summers, Miller, & Ford, 1991). Preliminary results suggest that these tests display slightly greater predictive validity than that of "general" TAIS (Summers & Ford, 1990). Second, the factorial validity of the test is questionable. Specifically, factor analyses conducted by several researchers (e.g. Landers, 1982) have failed to replicate the six independent attentional factors alleged to underlie the attentional sub-scales of the test. This failure to replicate a desired factor structure raises doubts as to psychometric "purity" of the TAIS. Indeed, according to Abernethy (1993), the breadth dimension of the TAIS is probably multidimensional rather than homogeneous. Third, the TAIS fails to differentiate between athletes of different skill levels in sports in which selective attention is known to be important (Summers & Ford, 1990; Vallerand, 1983). Likewise, when expert-novice differences in TAIS performance have been discovered, they have often been on sub-scales which are different from those which had been expected to yield differences (Landers, Furst, & Daniels, 1981). These results reinforce the need to "tune" the TAIS more explicitly to sport-specific situations (Kirschenbaum & Bale, 1984). Perhaps not surprisingly, the tennis-specific version of the TAIS devised by Van Schoyck & Grasha (1981) is reported to have greater internal consistency and higher test-retest reliability than the general TAIS. Next, as Hardy (1989) reminded us, Nideffer's (1976a) theory does not distinguish between task-relevant and task-*irrelevant* information in sport contexts. This crucial neglect is alarming in view of the conventional definition of attention as the capacity to focus on task-*relevant* information while ignoring distractions (see Chapter 2). Fifth, Summers, Miller, & Ford (1991) suggested that Nideffer has neglected the dimension of "attentional flexibility" in his theory. This term refers to the "ability to move attention from one spatial position to another" (Castiello & Umilta, 1992) or the ability to "vary the span of visual attention from a focal to a diffuse mode and vice versa" (ibid.). In other words, the TAIS ignores athletes' capacity to *switch* their concentration rapidly from one target to another. This omission is surprising because in many sports, performers have to change rapidly from one attentional focus to another. For example, when competing in a marathon, runners may alternate between the use of distractions to cope with pain and the use of "sensory monitoring" (i.e. focusing deliberately on bodily sensations; see also later in this chapter) to develop a suitable rhythm (Morgan & Pollock, 1977). Other important aspects of attention which have not been addressed by Nideffer are "selectivity" and "duration" of concentration (Vallerand, 1983).

A further problem for the TAIS concerns the issue of attentional narrowing (see Chapter 3). Briefly, Cote, Salmela, & Papathanasopoulu (1992) disputed Nideffer's theory that attentional narrowing occurs as a function of increased arousal. In particular, these authors required subjects to respond to a 5-choice reaction verbal reaction time task while engaging in physical exercise (i.e. pedalling a stationary bicycle). Results showed that increased heart rates from the physical exercise were not associated with a narrowing of attention. Yet another difficulty with the TAIS is the fact that it is unclear who respondents should compare themselves with when they are answering the test items. Nideffer (1987) acknowledged this difficulty.

Perhaps more damaging than the preceding criticisms, however, is the issue of the validity of a key assumption of self-report assessment techniques. As I have indicated earlier, self-report measures of concentration assume that people can evaluate their own attentional processes. But is this assumption valid? Research on "meta-attention" (i.e. people's knowledge of, and control over, their own attentional pro- cesses; see also Chapter 8) indicates that people are often poor judges of their own concentration skills—especially with regard to the impact of distractions upon their performance of a given task (Reisberg & McLean, 1985). Even if athletes could comment accurately on their atten- tional processes, would they do so truthfully? Cratty (1983) suggested that social desirability "response sets" are likely in such assessment because athletes may not wish to acknowledge or divulge their atten- tional limitations. Furthermore, a problem arises because the TAIS does not assess the *motor* responses of the subject. Therefore, Cratty (1983) concluded that the TAIS was only "marginally useful, and the data it produces are not much better than the information a coach might obtain from simply questioning athletes or observing their performance" (p. 100).

What conclusions are warranted with regard to the validity of the TAIS? Overall, despite its popularity in applied sport psychology, this measure has received only meagre support from empirical studies in which it has been evaluated. Cox (1994) concluded that the test is primarily a measure of *personality* and, as such, is a poor predictor of athletic performance. Landers (1982) on the other hand, was more optimistic in his appraisal of the TAIS. Specifically, he concluded that it is a useful measure of the *breadth* of people's attentional focus. But he identified the main flaws of this scale as a failure to assess adequately either attentional direction or attentional flexibility. Interestingly, although the TAIS may be challenged on psychometric criteria (but see Nideffer, 1990, for a rebuttal of these criticisms), the theory of attentional style is a useful *instructional* aid in applied sport psychology. Because Nideffer's theory "makes intuitive sense to coaches and athletes" (Bond & Sargent, 1995), it encourages them to explore the different types of concentration demanded by their particular sports. Overall, therefore, empirical evidence indicates that although Nideffer's theory of attentional style has substantial "face" validity, its construct validity is questionable.

Having explored the physiological, experimental and psychometric approaches to the measurement of attention, I shall now consider some research on the relationship between concentration strategies and athletic performance.

ATTENTIONAL PROCESSES IN MARATHON RUNNERS

For sport psychologists, the minds of endurance event athletes (e.g. marathon competitors) are especially intriguing because these athletes choose to compete over distances (usually ranging from 10km, or 6.2 miles, to 42.2km, or 26.2 miles) that exceed those which are necessary to maintain adequate physical fitness. In addition, by competing strenuously for long periods of time, marathon runners expose themselves to sources of stress (e.g. inordinate levels of fatigue and pain) that are not usually encountered in most other forms of running.

To illustrate these demands of marathon running, consider the mental resolve and physical stamina required to participate in the Western States 100 mile Endurance Run which is undertaken in the Sierra Nevada mountains. This race has been described as the world's ultimate test of stamina (Acedevo, Dzewaltowski, Gill, & Noble, 1992) because it includes a total ascent of 19,000 feet, a total descent of 21,000 feet and considerable changes in air temperature en route (e.g. 30

degrees to 110 degrees Fahrenheit). How do athletes who compete in such endurance events maintain their concentration despite the fatigue, pain and monotony which they are likely to encounter? By exploring this question, we can illuminate the relationship between selected attentional strategies and athletic success.

Association and dissociation in marathon runners

In a seminal study, Morgan & Pollock (1977) explored the attentional techniques reportedly used by elite and non-elite "distance" runners. The sample consisted of two groups of runners: An "elite" world-class group (comprising 11 middle- and long-distance runners and 8 marathon runners) and an outstanding collegiate group (made up of 8 middle-distance runners from universities). The athletes in the elite group were very serious competitors, each of whom trained seven days a week and was capable of running a marathon in less than 2 hours and 15 minutes. All subjects were evaluated on a variety of measures. These included psychometric tests (e.g. mood state scales), ratings of perceived exertion, physiological tests conducted during treadmill running, and post-exercise interviews. The physiological data were collected as the subjects ran on a motor-driven treadmill at speeds of 10–12 mph. Perceived exertion ratings were obtained during the last 15 seconds of each 2 minute laboratory exercise block. The athletes were also interviewed about the cognitive strategies that they tended to use while competing. Specifically, the runners were asked to "describe what you think about during a long-distance run or marathon: What sort of thought processes take place as a run progresses?" (Morgan & Pollock, 1977).

Results showed that there were no significant differences between the elite group and the middle distance runners on any of the physiological variables tested. Equally, no differences emerged between these groups on perceived exertion ratings. However, at each exercise period, the physiological "costs" for the collegiate athletes were higher than for the elite group. More dramatically, however, there were significant differences between these groups in the cognitive strategies which they claimed to have employed during races. In particular, the elite athletes claimed to have engaged in "associative" monologues while running. These strategies involved paying explicit attention to bodily signals (e.g. heart beat, respiratory processes and muscular sensations in calves, thighs and legs), concentrating on race strategy, reminding themselves to replenish fluids regularly and deliberately trying to maintain a relaxed physical state. This attentional strategy was called "association". Its trademark, according to Pargman (1993), is a "tendency to adopt an internal focus of attention (i.e. maintaining awareness of performance factors)". Using this strategy, the elite runners focused continuously on such signals as "respiration, temperature, heaviness in the calves and thighs, abdominal sensations" (Morgan, 1978). As one might expect, skilful execution of this strategy is difficult for athletes as it requires them to maintain a narrow, internal focus for protracted periods of time (Schomer, 1987). However, experienced runners seem to be adept at using it—perhaps because they are more sensitive to their bodily states than are novices. To illustrate, Schedlowski & Tewes (1992) discovered that expert parachute jumpers were more competent in assessing their level of physiological arousal (as measured by heart and respiration rates) during a jump than were relative beginners.

A field study of the efficacy of associative techniques was conducted by Schomer (1986). He equipped marathon runners with micro-cassette recorders in order to obtain a continuous record of their thoughts while they competed. The results revealed a strong relationship between associative attentional strategies and perceived exertion. Specifically, the more difficult the race became, the greater was the perceived exertion and the stronger was the likelihood of using associative thinking. In passing, there is some anecdotal evidence (Merrill, 1981) that athletes who use associative strategies manage to avoid the notorious "wall" experience which afflicts many marathon runners. This term refers to a painful experience which is allegedly encountered by marathon runners at some point around the 20th mile of the distance. For example, in the Boston marathon, this pain barrier is associated with a location known as "Heartbreak Hill".

Returning to the study by Morgan & Pollock (1977), it emerged that the non-elite athletes reported a preference for using distraction-based (or "dissociative") strategies while running. In this way, these athletes were able to reduce "anxiety, effort sense and general discomfort" (Morgan, 1978). In general, dissociative concentration techniques involve the attempt to *disengage* the mind from any physical discomfort experienced during the race. By using an external focus of attention, the runner "purposely cuts himself off from the sensory feedback he (sic) normally receives from the body" (Morgan, 1978). Common dissociative procedures included attempting to recall the names of former teachers, composing fictitious letters to friends, doing mental arithmetic, counting lamp-posts on the competition route, building imaginary houses, creating lists of jobs to perform and listening to imaginary music during races. Using these techniques, athletes are able to "negotiate temporary pain zones and distract (themselves) from the monotony of the running process" (Schomer, 1986).

Dissociative techniques have a long tradition in oriental cultures. For example, consider the *"lung-gom"* (literally, "swiftness of foot") method of running which was allegedly practised by Tibetan (Mahetang) monks who were required to travel rapidly over long distances in mountainous regions (Sachs, 1984). This technique involves attempting to breathe in synchrony with the repetition of a sacred mantra. By practising this skill, the monks apparently learn to ignore sensations of pain or fatigue. According to Watson (1973), one skilled exponent of this method was able to travel 300 miles in 30 hours. This is a remarkable feat as it entailed averaging speeds of 10 miles per hour over rough terrain in very cold conditions. Expressed differently, this performance would be equivalent to completing eleven and a half consecutive marathons at approximately 2 hours 37 minutes per marathon (Morgan & Pollock, 1977)! A vivid description of this mysterious technique in action was provided by David-Neel (1967): "I could clearly see his perfectly calm impassive face and wide-open eyes with their gaze fixed on some invisible far-distant object situated somewhere high up in space. The man did not run. He seemed to lift himself from the ground, proceeding by leaps. It looked as if he had been endowed with the elasticity of a ball and rebounded each time his feet touched the ground" (pp. 225–226). Not surprisingly, a link has been discovered between dissociative mental states and a susceptibility to hypnosis (Masters, 1992). Indeed, Morgan (1978) referred to dissociation as a form of self-hypnosis. Interestingly, analogies between running and hypnosis have also been noticed by Webster & Smith (1984) who suggested that, due to the rhythmic nature of the sport, "runners, joggers, and gymnasts go spontaneously into altered states of consciousness".

In summary, Morgan & Pollock (1977) concluded that the use of different attentional strategies was "the major distinguishing psychological dimension of the elite marathoner". Interestingly, in view of our discussion of external and internal distractions in Chapter 4, the major difference between associative and dissociative strategies seems to concern the *direction* in which the athlete focuses their attention. Specifically, associative attentional styles involve focusing on "internal" stimuli such as thoughts, feelings and bodily sensations whereas a dissociative attentional style encourages the performer to concentrate on objects and events which lie *outside* the body.

Association and dissociation: Which strategy is better?
Following the study by Morgan & Pollock (1977) on attentional processes in marathon runners, considerable research has accumulated on the relative efficacy of associative and dissociative techniques. Which of these strategies is preferable as a concentration technique for athletes?

Unfortunately, contrary to the findings of Morgan & Pollock (1977), associative strategies are not always apparent among expert performers in endurance sports. To illustrate, whereas Summers, Sargent, Levey, & Murray (1982) reported that most of the athletes they surveyed had used dissociative strategies during training runs, Schomer (1986) discovered that *association* was a more popular attentional strategy among marathon runners. This study was interesting because it used "thought-sampling" techniques (see also Chapter 8) to assess runners' thoughts *while* they exercised rather than relying on post-hoc measures (which had been used by Morgan & Pollock, 1977). Similarly, Acedevo, Dzewaltowski, Gill, & Noble (1992) found that, contrary to what Morgan & Pollock (1977) had reported, a majority of "ultra-marathoners" (who run average distances of at least 100 miles) claimed to adopt an external attentional focus (dissociative) while competing.

To complicate matters, there is evidence which challenges the intra-individual consistency of athletes' choice of either associative or dissociative strategies. Thus Morgan, O'Connor, Ellickson, & Bradley (1988) found that 72% of a group of elite distance runners reported using an associative strategy during competition while 28% claimed to have used both associative and dissociative techniques. In other words, some runners think differently in training, as distinct from competitive, situations. Interestingly, none of these athletes reported sole usage of a dissociative attentional strategy. However during training runs a different picture emerged. Thus only 21% of the group reported using an associative strategy during training whereas 43% reported a preference for a dissociative strategy in these circumstances. Similar findings were reported by Masters & Lambert (1989). Briefly, these researchers discovered that 94% of the runners in their sample chose to use associative strategies. Unfortunately, these investigators did not use statistical procedures (e.g. proportions tests) to establish the significance of percentage differences which they reported.

Additional comparative data were reported by Summers, Sargent, Levey, & Murray (1982), who found that although 69% of their sample of novice marathon runners adopted a dissociative strategy during training runs, only 6% of them reported using it during competitive events. Almost a third of the sample preferred to use associative strategies during competitive races. However, over 60% of the runners surveyed reported no clear preference for one or other attentional style. One problem with this study, however, is that it relied on memory data of unknown duration (a difficulty which also affected the research by Morgan & Pollock, 1977). These studies by Masters & Lambert (1989) and Summers, Sargent, Levey, & Murray (1982) support the view that marathon runners of all levels tend to use associative strategies while competing but rely more on dissociative strategies when training. More recently, Ogles, Hoeffel, Lynn, Marsden, & Masters (1993–1994) explored the extent to which a preference for a given attentional style in runners may fluctuate between training and racing sessions. Briefly, in line with previous research by Masters & Lambert (1989), these authors found that marathon runners reported using a dissociative (externally-focused) attentional strategy more frequently during training runs than during actual races.

The alleged utility of associative techniques among marathon runners has also been challenged. For example, Okwumabua, Meyers, Schlesser, & Cooke (1983) compared the performance of runners who had been trained in either associative or dissociative strategies. Although most of the runners preferred to adopt associative methods, the fastest performance times were recorded by people who had used relatively more *dissociative* techniques. Similarly, Gill & Strom (1985) discovered that athletes performing an endurance test on a leg-extension (quadriceps) machine performed more repetitions when their attention was *externally*, rather than internally, focused. Additional support for the merit of an external attentional style comes from Padgett & Hill (1989) who required subjects to ride a stationary bicycle for 30 minutes at a fixed speed. Whereas one group (the "associative" performers) was instructed to attend to internal sensations while they rode, another group was subjected to external distractions by being required to focus on answering a concurrent survey. Results indicated that the latter group (i.e. the "distracted" cyclists) performed significantly better than did the associative group. They also perceived the cycling task to be significantly shorter than did the associative group. These results suggest that the adoption of an "external" focus appears to be the best cognitive strategy for increasing endurance performance. Taken together, these studies challenge the original finding (by Morgan & Pollock, 1977) that an associative attentional style is linked with superior performance in marathon running.

Explanations for inconsistency in research on association-dissociation

Why has there been such inconsistency in research findings on the attentional styles of endurance athletes? Several possible explanations have been proposed. These theories usually invoke some key intervening variables which were not considered by previous authors.

To begin with, Brewer, Van Raalte, & Linder (1992) claimed that the level of expertise of the athlete is a critical mediating variable. Thus they suggested that associative attentional strategies may be more effective in the case of *experienced* athletes performing familiar endurance tasks whereas dissociative techniques may be more effective when inexperienced athletes are required to perform relatively novel endurance tasks. Emotional factors may also be involved in determining the relative efficacy of the two attentional "styles". To explain, Brewer, Van Raalte, & Linder (1992) proposed that people who initially dislike endurance events may be over-sensitive to any "distress cues" which might arise during the run. For such people, an associative attentional focus would probably be unhelpful because it would encourage them to interpret certain bodily sensations (e. g. a pounding heart) as harbingers of catastrophe. With additional experience, however, the athlete should be able to interpret such arousal sensations more optimistically. Accordingly, at this point, an associative attentional focus may be suitable for the athlete because it usually has greater relevance for task performance than does a dissociative technique.

Another potentially important intervening variable in this field concerns the climatic environment of the event. Thus Sachs (1984) proposed that athletes may shift their attentional styles in accordance with environmental conditions. For example, he found that the excessive heat and humidity of Florida led runners there to place a premium on maintaining their awareness of their bodily functions, thereby facilitating an associative attentional strategy. But dissociation was used during the middle section of these races. As Sachs (1984) concluded, "it is clear that we cannot provide a simple characterisation of the cognitive strategies of runners".

Interestingly, this theme of attentional flexibility was taken up by Silva & Applebaum (1989). Specifically, these authors studied the attentional strategies employed by top-50 finishers in the US Marathon Trials. Contrary to what Morgan & Pollock (1977) had found, other studies (e.g. Silva & Applebaum, 1989) suggest that top-50 finishers tended to *shift* their attentional focus between associative and dissociative techniques. Specifically, the evidence suggested that the successful runners switched between associative and dissociative strategies during the early section of the marathon (i.e. the first 5–8 miles). However, during the 18–24 mile section of the marathon, the top runners showed a preference for dissociation to counteract the pain (i.e. "the wall" experience) which usually arises at this stage of the race Overall, Silva & Applebaum (1989) concluded that "top 50 placers modify their cognitive style in an adaptive manner as a function of changes in race demands whereas individuals finishing 51st or lower tend to adopt a dissociative strategy early and maintain this strategy throughout the race". Another test of Morgan & Pollock's (1977) theory was conducted recently by Couture et al.(1994). These authors examined the effects of different mental training (including attentional) strategies on the performance by Canadian Army soldiers of a three-hour, weight-loaded endurance march. Results indicated that, as had been reported by Summers, Sargent, Levey, & Murray (1982) in the case of marathon runners, the soldiers alternated between associative and dissociative styles of attention during the march.

In summary, there is some evidence that elite marathon runners prefer to use associative (internally focused, body monitoring) rather than dissociative (externally focused, cognitive disengagement) attentional styles during competition. But there is little evidence that association leads to significant benefits in race performance. However, a significant advantage of an associative focus is that it is usually safer for the athlete as it may warn them of injury signs. It may also serve as an index of the "mental work" which has been exerted during a run. In general, therefore, if we regard attentional strategies as ways of coping with endurance-event stress, perhaps an external focus (dissociation) facilitates a temporary relief from sensory discomfort whereas an internal focus (association), provided it is directed at the "right" stimuli (see Clingman & Hilliard, 1990), may provide bodily feedback which facilitates tactical or technical adjustments by the performer.

Current issues in research on association-dissociation

At least three issues need to be resolved before further progress can be made in understanding the attentional processes of marathon runners. First, different researchers have used different techniques for the measurement of attentional strategies. For example, whereas Morgan & Pollock (1977) and Summers, Sargent, Levey, & Murray (1982) have relied on retrospective accounts by athletes of strategy adoption, other investigators (e.g. Schomer, 1986) have used portable tape-recorders to collect verbal protocols from athletes during marathons. As these approaches differ considerably, it would be helpful if a standardised measurement tool were devised for this domain. In this regard, Brewer, Van Raalte, & Linder (1992) have developed a self-report scale called the Attentional Focusing Questionnaire (AFQ) for the measurement of concentration processes in runners. As yet, however, its validity and reliability are unknown. The second issue concerns the tendency to regard an "external focus" of attention (described in Pennebaker & Lightner, 1980) as being synonymous with a dissociative strategy (Morgan, 1978). As Padgett & Hill (1989) pointed out, these concepts refer to different phenomena. To explain, the adoption of an external focus requires one to look for cues that stem from specific environmental stimuli (e.g. a lamp-post on a marathon course) whereas the use of dissociative techniques involves letting the mind wander *randomly*—

not in some directed fashion. The third issue confronting researchers in this field is the challenge of exploring different types of attentional focus *within* a particular concentration technique. This issue was raised empirically by Clingman & Hilliard (1990). These researchers explored the efficacy of different types of *internal* attentional focus on race-walking performance. A sample of experienced race walkers was randomly assigned to walk four half-mile segments on a track under different instructional conditions. Two types of instructions were used. Those which advocated adopting an "external focus" emphasised paying attention to things which were unrelated to the walk, such as the environmental features surrounding the track. Conversely, "internal" instructions required participants to focus on either their stride or their "cadence" (i.e. speed of leg movement). Results showed that when the walkers were asked to focus on cadence, they walked faster than when they focused on stride-length. This effect was similar for both high- and low-ability performers. Accordingly, these researchers concluded that "the advantage gained from an internal attentional focus is dependent upon what the athlete is attending to"—even though both of the foci of concentration involved may be regarded as "associative" in nature.

Interestingly, this finding may help us to understand better the findings of Morgan & Pollock (1977). To explain, perhaps an "internal" attentional strategy is effective only when the athlete knows which particular bodily signals to monitor. In other words, associative techniques may work best for athletes who can "listen" accurately to their bodily processes. Conversely, an athlete may benefit more from an external attentional strategy when unaware of the precise bodily signals to which attention should be paid. To conclude, a promising line for future research in this field concerns the possibility that different *types* of *internal* attentional focus may have different effects on performance.

ATTENTIONAL SUB-SCALES IN PSYCHOLOGICAL SKILLS INVENTORIES

Before concluding this chapter, it should be noted that attentional skills can also be measured psychometrically through selected sub-scales from general sport psychological screening inventories. Two such inventories are the "Psychological Skills Inventory for Sports" (PSIS R-5; Mahoney, Gabriel, & Perkins, 1987) and a recent instrument called the "Bangor Sport Psychological Skills Inventory" (BSPSI; Nelson & Hardy, 1990). I shall discuss these tests because both of them contain scales which purport to measure "concentration" in sport performers.

The Psychological Skills Inventory for Sports

The "Psychological Skills Inventory for Sports" (PSIS R-5) is a 45-item, self-report test which claims to measure six psychological skills that are thought to be associated with exceptional athletic performance. These mental skills are anxiety control, concentration, confidence, mental preparation, motivation and "team emphasis". In each case, a higher score is held to reflect greater competence in the execution of the mental skill in question. The concentration sub-scale contains six items (e. g. item 2, "I often have trouble concentrating during my performance").

Originally, the PSIS R-5 comprised 51 items administered using a dichotomous response format ("true-false"). However, two changes have resulted from the thorough psychometric appraisal to which it was subjected by Mahoney, Gabriel, & Perkins (1987), using a large sample (n=713) of male and female athletes from 23 different sports. First, the test was abbreviated to 45 items. In addition, its response format was changed from a "true-false" mode to a 5-point Likert scale. Because of the relatively recent origin of the PSIS R-5, data concerning its psychometric adequacy are somewhat scanty. On the basis of the limited evidence available, however, the following conclusions are warranted.

To begin with, although the factor structure of this test was thought originally to be stable across athletes of different ages and levels of ability (Mahoney, Gabriel, & Perkins, 1987), recent research (see Chartrand, Jowdy, & Danish, 1992) suggests that the predicted 6-factor solution did not materialise for a sample of collegiate athletes. This lack of structural clarity led the authors to appeal for a theoretical revision of the PSIS R-5. Thus they proposed that "it may be necessary to return to a theoretical level and reassess the constructs represented in the instrument".

With regard to reliability, data are available to evaluate both the internal consistency and test-retest reliability of the test. First, estimates of the internal consistency of the six scales, as reported by Chartrand, Jowdy, & Danish (1992), were largely unsatisfactory. Specifically, the following Cronbach's alpha coefficients were reported for the scales: Anxiety control (0.59); concentration (0.52); confidence (0.85); mental preparation (-0.34); motivation (0.62) and team emphasis (0.53). Clearly, only one value here (i.e. for the "confidence" sub-scale) exceeded the minimum criterion of 0.70 commonly advocated in this field. Another disappointing finding here was the *negative* internal consistency coefficient discovered for the "mental preparation" scale. In an effort to explain this surprising result, Chartrand, Jowdy, & Danish (1992) conducted an item-analysis of this scale and found that item 33 ("When I mentally practise my performance, I 'see' myself performing just like I was watching a videotape") correlated *negatively* with its companion items. This may indicate that this item is scored incorrectly at present. In contrast to these results, White (1993) reported more favourable internal-consistency values for the PSIS R-5 sub-scales in a recent study of collegiate skiers. In particular, she found that Cronbach's alpha values for these scales were uniformly higher than those obtained by Chartrand, Jowdy, & Danish (1992) as they ranged from 0.69 (for the mental preparation scale) to 0.84 (for the confidence scale). Although these data lend support to the claim that the PSIS R-5 is reasonably reliable, they also confirm doubts about the adequacy of the mental preparation scale (which again displayed the lowest internal consistency of all six sub-scales). Turning to test-retest reliability, relevant data were reported by Lesser & Murphy (1988) who had administered the test to a large (n=301) sample of US athletes training for the Olympic Games. These researchers found that test-retest coefficients of 0.60 were obtained for three sub-scales: Mental preparation, confidence and motivation. However, disappointingly low values were evident for the other three scales (anxiety control, concentration and team emphasis). Finally, another psychometric problem identified by Chartrand, Jowdy, & Danish (1992) concerned the "purity" of the PSIS R-5 sub-scales. Put simply, some items from different scales appeared to overlap significantly. This observation led the authors to conclude that the anxiety-control, concentration and confidence scales were "confounded".

How valid is the PSIS R-5? As this test is a self-assessment instrument, convergent validation data (preferably from objective behavioural sources) are necessary. Unfortunately, criterion-related validation data on this test are equivocal. On the one hand, Lesser & Murphy (1988) claimed that the test was successful in differentiating between US Olympic athletes of different ability levels—a finding which supports the construct validity of the PSIS R-5. However, on the other hand, Mahoney (1989) reported that non-elite athletes scored *higher* than their elite counterparts on all but one sub-scale (i.e. "motivation") of the PSIS R-5. The discrepancy between these results has not been resolved yet. To compound this problem, no published data on either the convergent or predictive validity of this test could be located. Accordingly, attentional researchers must be very cautious in interpreting results derived from this test.

The Bangor Sport Psychological Skills Inventory

The Bangor Sport Psychological Skills Inventory (BSPSI) was developed "for use by applied sport psychologists for the purpose of psychological skills profiling" (Nelson & Hardy, 1992). It consists of 56 items which purport to assess seven different psychological skills. These skills are attentional control, mental preparation, imaginal skills, self-efficacy, cognitive anxiety control, relaxation, and motivational skills. There are eight items in each scale. Respondents are required to rate each item using a 7-point Likert scale. The concentration skills sub-scale contains eight items (e.g. item 12, "My thoughts are often elsewhere when I am competing"). Curiously, all of them must be reverse-scored because as they are presented, they reflect problems of distractibility.

Due to the recent origin of this test, evidence on construct validity is rather scarce. However, some data on this issue have been reported by Nelson & Hardy (1992). Briefly, these authors claim that each of the 7 scales has adequate internal consistency, ranging from 0.78 (for the mental preparation scale) to 0.90 (for the relaxation scale). In particular, the concentration scale appears to be highly consistent, with a Cronbach's alpha coefficient of 0.85. The concurrent validity of this test was assessed through its relationship with the TAIS (Nideffer, 1976a). Although the correlations between these scales were significant statistically, relatively little variance was accounted for as the obtained correlations ranged from only 0.33 to 0.49. Unfortunately, no published evidence is available on the predictive validity of this test. Therefore, as with the PSIS R-5, great caution must be taken when interpreting the results yielded by Bangor Sport Psychological Skills Inventory.

SUMMARY

The construct of attention is regarded as multi-dimensional because it refers to cognitive (e.g. "mental effort"), behavioural (e.g. concurrent task performance) and physiological (alertness) processes. Not surprisingly, depending on the nature of the dimension under scrutiny, different paradigms have evolved for the measurement of concentration processes in athletes. These measurement approaches consisted of psychophysiological techniques, task performance measures and psychometric scales. This chapter attempted to review these three approaches, devoting special consideration to the assessment of individual differences in attentional skills among athletes. In addition, as a case study of measurement in action, I explored the attentional strategies used by marathon runners.

The first attentional indices examined were the psychophysiological measures. These consisted of electroencephalographic (EEG) and heart rate (HR) indices as well as event-related potential (ERPs; or "cortical evoked potentials"). As I explained, these indices have been used most frequently to monitor attentional changes in athletes who perform precise and self-paced skills like archery, rifle marksmanship and golf putting. From such studies, a distinctive pattern of physiological changes seems to occur in athletes in the moments leading up to performance of closed skills. Specifically, during the pre-shot period of intense concentration, experienced athletes tend to show an increase in left hemisphere alpha activity and some signs of cardiac deceleration. The next attentional measures considered were those derived from the dual-task paradigm. Although not widely used in sport psychology, this paradigm facilitates assessment of the attentional demands of different sporting tasks. Furthermore, it allows researchers to investigate the effects of increased arousal on the performance of selected sport skills. Using this paradigm, evidence has emerged to suggest that physiological arousal may serve to "narrow" attention in athletes. For example, rifle-shooters who had been performing under stressful conditions showed poorer performance on a secondary task than did low-stress counterparts. The final measurement approach that I evaluated was the psychometric paradigm. This approach has given rise to Nideffer's "Test of Attentional and Interpersonal Style" (TAIS) which is one of the most widely used tests in sport psychology.

The TAIS is a self-report, paper-and-pencil inventory which purports to assess a variety of different types of attentional foci (e.g. "narrow internal" and "broad external" orientations). Although some aspects of the theory which underlies this test are intuitively appealing (e.g. the idea that different sport skills demand different types of attentional focus), the construct validity of the TAIS is questionable. In support of this conclusion, I summarised several conceptual and methodological issues which hamper accurate interpretation of TAIS scores. For example, a major conceptual problem with this test is that it fails to distinguish between attending to task-relevant and to task-*irrelevant* information. Likewise, a methodological issue is raised by the assumption that athletes can comment accurately on their own attentional processes. Overall, the substantial face validity of Nideffer's theory of attentional style must be balanced against its questionable construct validity. Next, I explored the attentional strategies used by marathon runners. In particular, I reviewed available evidence concerning the strengths and limitations of "associative" and "dissociative" concentration techniques. The former strategy involves paying deliberate attention to bodily signals (e.g. muscular sensations) whereas the latter consists of disengagement techniques (e.g. writing imaginary letters to friends). Originally, it was believed that expert marathon runners tended to adopt associative strategies during races whereas less proficient colleagues preferred to use dissociative procedures. However, recent research casts doubt on the validity of this conclusion. Indeed, it seems that some athletes alternate between the two types of concentration strategy, depending on technical and tactical considerations. Therefore, attentional flexibility, or the capacity to alternate between different attentional styles, is now attracting increasing interest from researchers in this field. Finally, I reviewed the adequacy of two attentional sub-scales of generic psychological skills inventories used by sport psychologists. These tests were the "Psychological Skills Inventory for Sports" (PSIS-R5) and the Bangor Sport Psychological Skills Inventory (BSPSI). On the basis of published evidence, the psychometric adequacy of the PSIS R-5 is perhaps better established than that of the BSPSI. Unfortunately, neither of the attentional sub-scales derived from these tests can be recommended unequivocally to concentration researchers in sport.

SECTION THREE

Concentration techniques

If concentration is a skill, then it can be improved by appropriate instruction and practice. Therefore, the purpose of Section 3 of this book (Chapters 6 and 7) is to evaluate the background to, and efficacy of, various psychological exercises and techniques which purport to improve the attentional skills of sport performers.

In Chapter 6, I shall begin by identifying the key assumptions underlying any programme of mental skills training. Then I shall examine the theoretical rationale underlying the use of various training exercises (e.g. the "concentration grid" and adversity training) which are alleged to enhance attentional skills. Next, I shall review the adequacy of four psychological "concentration techniques" for sport performers. The techniques include goal-setting, pre-performance routines, arousal-control strategies (e.g. progressive muscular relaxation) and the use of "cue-words" (a form of instructional self-talk). Overall, I conclude that these techniques, while plausible superficially, have not yet been validated sufficiently by controlled empirical evidence.

In Chapter 7, I evaluate the nature and efficacy of another popular concentration technique used by athletes. This strategy is called "mental practice" (MP, or "visualisation") and it involves the systematic use of mental imagery in order to rehearse symbolically physical movements prior to their actual execution. I shall begin by explaining the nature and characteristics of mental practice. Then I summarise the history of research on this topic. Next, I shall review the claims and evidence surrounding MP as a performance-enhancement strategy. This discussion leads to an evaluation of the main theories of visualisation effects. Finally, I shall consider the adequacy of mental practice as a concentration technique. Overall, I conclude that although attentional mechanisms probably mediate MP effects, the evidence currently available is inadequate to justify the claim that the systematic practice of visualisation will improve concentration skills.

CHAPTER SIX

Improving concentration in sport I: Assumptions, exercises and techniques

"The great thing, then, in all education, is to make our nervous system our ally instead of our enemy ... For this we must make automatic and habitual, as early as possible, as many useful actions as we can"

(James, 1890, p. 122)

"Behaviour influences consciousness. Right behaviour means right consciousness"

(Deshimaru, 1982, p. 89)

"I must get perfectly set up—it's almost a compulsion—before I can pull the trigger. My mind simply will not let me start the swing until I'm right', no matter how long it takes"

(Nicklaus, 1974, p. 78)

"The only thing I have learned is the ability to control my mind"

(Darrell Pace, 1976 and 1984 Olympic Champion, cited in Vealey & Walter, 1994, p. 436)

INTRODUCTION

Within the past decade, there has been a growth of interest among performers, coaches and sport psychologists in the design and implementation of programmes of "mental skills training" (MST) or "psychological skills training" (PST) for athletes (Seiler, 1992; Vealey, 1994; Weinberg & Gould, 1995). In general, the purpose of these programmes is to provide formal instruction in various psychological techniques (e.g. goal-setting) that are believed to enhance both mental processes (e.g. concentration) and athletic performance. Many of these techniques are described in popular "self-help" books designed for sport performers (see bibliography by Sachs, 1991) and coaches (Martens, 1987). The increasing popularity of these programmes suggests that psychological skills training is now an integral part of sport psychology (Hardy & Jones, 1994).

Given the importance of concentration in sport (see Chapter 3), it is not surprising that many MST programmes (e.g. see Hardy & Fazey, 1990; Winter & Martin, 1991) include strategies and exercises which purport to increase attentional skills in athletes. The purpose of these techniques is to help the performer to achieve a "focused" state in which the mind "is cleared of irrelevant thoughts, the body is cleared of irrelevant tensions, and the focus is centred only on what is important at that moment for executing the skill to perfection" (Orlick, 1990, p. 18). At first glance, the emergence of programmes which purport to increase "concentration skills" is a welcome development. Unfortunately, on closer examination, it is apparent that few of these concentration programmes have been subjected to either conceptual or empirical evaluation. This oversight is worrying because it confirms the suspicion that much of the popular literature in sport psychology is based on shaky theoretical foundations. Indeed, according to Singer et al. (1991) attentional skills programmes have been based more on "intuition and practical experience" than on empirical psychological principles. If these programmes lack a firm theoretical foundation, how can they be validated scientifically?

The purpose of this chapter is to review the adequacy of the various psychological strategies alleged to improve athletes' concentration skills. To pursue this objective, I shall address three key questions. First, what is the theoretical rationale underlying concentration skills training programmes in sport psychology? Next, what is the justification for the main psychological techniques advocated in these programmes? Finally, how effective is "concentration training" for athletes? Before answering these questions, however, let us outline briefly the assumptions underlying "mental skills training" for sport performers.

ASSUMPTIONS OF MENTAL SKILLS TRAINING PROGRAMMES

As explained earlier, the purpose of mental skills training (MST) programmes for athletes is to help them to perform consistently to their full potential—especially in competition. Two main assumptions underlie such efforts.

First, certain mental states are thought to be associated reliably with successful performance in sport. Evidence to support this assumption comes from anecdotal and descriptive sources. Anecdotal data include the results of "peak performance" research (already discussed in Chapter 3) while descriptive studies have been conducted on the distinctive psychological profiles of elite athletes. To illustrate the latter line of inquiry, Mahoney & Avener (1977) and Mahoney, Gabriel, & Perkins (1987) reported that top-class sport performers, when compared with less successful counterparts, displayed stronger motivation, greater self-confidence, greater anxiety-control skills, stronger concentration and were more likely to engage in mental rehearsal. Unfortunately, as such studies are correlational in nature, it is impossible to tell whether these mental skills were causes or effects of athletes' sporting success. But additional support for the idea that certain mental states are correlated with success in sport comes from interviews with athletes. For example, Orlick & Partington (1988), in a survey of Canadian Olympic athletes and coaches, discovered that although "readiness" can be considered using physical, technical and mental criteria, only "mental readiness" was significantly associated with Olympic performance. In combination, these sources of evidence corroborate the assumption that certain mental characteristics are important for success in sport. These characteristics may be regarded as necessary but not sufficient conditions for sporting excellence. But even if we accept this proposition, how do we know that these qualities may be regarded as "skills" which are "trainable"? This question brings us to the second issue.

A key principle of sport psychology is the idea that the mental qualities associated with athletic success are "trainable" (Weinberg & Gould, 1995). For example, Jones (1995) claimed that "psychological skills are like physical skills" and that "performers can learn to be more confident, they can learn to concentrate better, and they can learn to be more composed in pressure situations". Burke (1992) suggested that "concentration is a skill and therefore it can be improved with proper training". Also, Moran (1995) discovered that some of the world's most experienced tennis coaches believe that mental skills can be trained in tennis players. Furthermore, Loehr (1986) proposed that "concentration is a learned skill". But it is not just sport psychologists who have adopted a "skills" approach to attention. Athletes and cognitive researchers endorse similar sentiments. For example, the legendary golfer Jack Nicklaus claimed that "concentration can be developed and strengthened with training and self-discipline" (Nicklaus, 1974). Furthermore, cognitive psychologists like Bartlett (1958) suggested that all cognitive activities may be enhanced through special training: he believed that thinking itself is a form of skilled activity. Specifically, it is "an extension of evidence, in line with the evidence and in such a manner as to fill up gaps in the evidence". In the light of such views, many psychologists (e.g. Gopher, 1992) believe that concentration skills may be enhanced through appropriate instruction. For example, Eysenck (1990) concluded that the "efficient control of attention in complex situations is a skill that can be trained and improved". In summary, considerable support is available from athletes, sport psychologists and cognitive theorists for the assumptions underlying MST programmes for athletes.

CONCENTRATION EXERCISES AND TECHNIQUES

If we accept the idea that concentration is a skill, then how can it be improved? Unfortunately, as I mentioned earlier, few theoretical guidelines exist on this matter. As Boutcher (1992) observed, MST programmes in this field "have not been developed within a theoretical framework and have largely proceeded by trial and error". Despite this atheoretical approach, a variety of "concentration techniques" have been promulgated in various "self-help" books in sport psychology (e.g. see Albinson & Bull, 1988; Dalloway, 1993; Hardy & Fazey, 1990; Harris & Harris, 1984; Nideffer, 1992; Orlick, 1990; Weinberg, 1988; Winter & Martin, 1991). They are also described in more scholarly sources (e.g. Bond & Sargent, 1995; Schmid & Peper, 1993; Weinberg & Gould, 1995). In general, these concentration techniques advocated by sport psychologists fall into two categories: Exercises recommended for use during athletes' training sessions (which I shall call "concentration exercises"; see Table 6.1) and those which are recommended for use during competition itself ("concentration techniques"; see Table 6.2 on page 174). Let us now consider briefly the theoretical rationale underlying each of these categories.

Concentration exercises

To begin with, consider the "training exercise" category. This consists of various activities (see Table 6.1), such as the "concentration grid" (Harris & Harris, 1984), which appear to be borrowed mainly from experimental psychology.

Although the tasks listed in Table 6.1 are invariably challenging and entertaining, their status as tools for enhancing concentration is un-substantiated. For example, consider the "concentration grid" which is recommended both by Dalloway (1993) and by Schmid & Peper (1993) as an aid to attention. In this exercise, athletes are required to scan as many digits on a sheet as possible within a given time limit. Unfortunately, empirical evidence is rarely adduced to support claims made by proponents of this grid. For example, no references are cited to corroborate either the claim that the grid has been used "extensively in Eastern Europe as a pre competition screening device" (Weinberg & Gould, 1995) or that top athletes can obtain scores "in the upper 20s and into the 30s" (ibid) on it. Unfortunately, in advocating this grid as an attentional training technique, Boutcher & Rotella (1987) fail to provide any evidence to justify their claim that "athletes who can concentrate and scan effectively will typically score more points than those who are unable to concentrate efficiently". The absence of such evidence casts doubt on the theoretical foundation of popular exercises such as the concentration grid. Put simply, we have no valid reasons to believe that by engaging in such visual search activities as "watching a clock face" (Albinson & Bull, 1988) or looking continuously at a sport-related object (Burke, 1992), athletes' concentration abilities will improve. Sadly, despite their dubious theoretical status, many of the exercises listed in Table 6.1 are promoted uncritically by sport psychologists.

TABLE 6.1 **General training exercises alleged to enhance attentional skills in athletes**			
	Exercise	*Alleged benefit*	*Source*
1.	"Concentration grid"	scanning	Harris & Harris (1984)
2.	Pendulum	"mental concentration"	Weinberg (1988)
3.	Watching clock face	focusing	Abinson & Bull (1988)
4.	Visual search tasks	scanning	Hardy & Fazey (1990)
5.	Focus on sport object	concentration awareness	Burke (1992)
6.	Simulation training	concentration	Orlick (1990)

Although scepticism is justified with regard to many of the "concentration exercises" listed in Table 6.1, there is one procedure which merits closer inspection. This technique is known under a variety of terms such as "adversity training" (Loehr, 1986), "simulation training" (Orlick, 1990), "simulated meet training" (Dalloway, 1993) and "dress rehearsal" (Schmid & Peper, 1993). The assumption here is that athletes may become inured to, or "inoculated" against, the adverse effects of "external" distractions (e.g. noise) during competition by practising systematically in their presence during training.

Anecdotal testimonials to the value of adversity training are plentiful in sport. For example, Darrell Pace, twice Olympic archery champion, reported that as a novice he used to practise shooting arrows under noisy and distracting conditions in order to simulate competitive situations: "I shot by railroad tracks, had cars driving by etc., to practise dealing with distractions. I had to learn to block everything out" (cited in Vealey & Walter, 1994). Similarly, Jimmy White, one of the world's leading snooker players, suggested that simulation training can help to reduce performance anxiety. Specifically, he claimed that "the more you can remove in your mind the feeling that practice and 'the real thing' are different, the better your chances of cutting down some of the tension induced by feeling that you have to play differently when it's for real" (White, 1988, p. 151). Additional testimonials to this exercise emerged during the 1992 Olympic Games in Barcelona. The South Korean rifle shooting team revealed that they had practised systematically under adverse conditions before the finals. Specifically, the gold-medal winner Lee Eun-Chul attributed his success in the small-bore rifle event of this competition to the fact that "we practise the finals every day" and "we train a lot to get used to the situation" (Korean shooter reveals secrets, 1992). Likewise, the victorious Olympic Chinese table-tennis doubles team praised simulation training after their narrow defeat of the former world-champions, Germany, in a five-set final. Lu Lin attributed their success to the fact that "as part of our programme, we have learnt to put up with this kind of pressure psychologically" (Korean shooter, 1992). Another example of pre-Olympic simulation training occurred in the case of the Australian women's hockey squad before the 1992 Games. Among the experiences simulated for these athletes were climatic and playing conditions, the competition schedule, tournament rules, media exposure and transport conditions (Bond & Sargent, 1995). Furthermore, in American football, coaches often "simulate opposing team fans and stadium loud noises during practice to acquaint their players with the potential distracting situations in the subsequent competitive game" (Singer et al., 1991).

Unfortunately, despite the preceding array of persuasive examples, no controlled empirical tests of "adversity training" have been undertaken by sport psychologists. However, some support for adversity training may be found in cognitive psychology. For example, research on the "state-dependency" of learning shows that information is recalled best "when there is a close match between the conditions in which it was originally learnt and the conditions in which the person tries to remember it" (Brewin, 1988). The implication of this principle is that by simulating competitive situations in practice, athletes can learn to transfer their training experiences optimally. Also, adversity training can be justified on the grounds that it counteracts the tendency for novel or unexpected factors to distract sports performers in competition (see Chapter 4). Simulating these factors in training will reduce their subsequent attention-capturing qualities subsequently. For this reason, Anshel (1995) recommends that practising under "game-like" conditions reduces the likelihood that athletes will "choke" under pressure (see analysis in Chapter 4). Taken together, there are several theoretical grounds to justify the claim (Orlick, 1990) that simulation training "helps you to prepare mentally for competition conditions and likely distractions". Before concluding this section, however, it should be noted that applied sport psychologists have largely ignored the ethical issues surrounding adversity training. For example, Bond & Sargent (1995) appear to be oblivious to the potential stress to athletes which may have been generated by the hoax bomb-scare which they reportedly used as part of a simulation exercise for the Australian women's hockey squad before the 1992 Olympics.

Concentration techniques

Let us now examine a variety of "concentration techniques" that are recommended for use by athletes in competitive situations. From an inspection of relevant mental skills programmes, five psychological techniques alleged to improve attentional skills were identified. These techniques, which are presented in Table 6.2, include goal-setting, pre-performance routines, arousal-control, cue-words and mental practice.

Over the next two chapters, I shall evaluate the merits of these five concentration techniques. Methods one to four above (i.e. goal-setting, pre-performance routines, arousal-control and cue-words) will be considered in this chapter. Mental practice (or "visualisation") will be examined separately (in Chapter 7) because of the large volume of research which it has generated.

TABLE 6.2
Psychological techniques alleged to improve athletes' attentional skills and performance

Technique	Alleged benefit to performer
1. Goal setting ("performance goals")	Focuses mind on task-relevant thoughts
2. Pre-performance routines	Helps athlete to concentrate only on what one can control
3. Arousal control (e.g. "centering")	Relaxes body/expands awareness
4. Instructional self-talk Cue-words ("triggers")	Helps to re-focus quickly on task-relevant cues
5. Mental practice ("visualisation")	Rehearse what one wants to achieve

GOAL-SETTING AS A CONCENTRATION STRATEGY

Ever since the work of Tolman (1932), a central proposition in cognitive psychology has been the belief that human actions are better understood as the outcome of internally represented goals than as the direct result of external factors (Jeannerod, 1994). Within this tradition, "goals" are understood as mental representations of outcomes which people strive to attain (Dweck, 1992). Therefore, "goal-setting" in sport refers to the process by which people establish desirable objectives for their performance and achievements.

Goals help sport performers in a variety of ways. For example, they motivate athletes "by focusing attention and promoting increased intensity and persistence" (Burton, 1992). To illustrate, rather than shooting mindlessly at the basket during a training session, a basketball player might concentrate on achieving a goal of scoring twelve consecutive free throws. More convincingly, a recent meta-analytic review of research on the efficacy of goal-setting concluded that, overall, it improved athletic performance by over one-third of a standard deviation relative to baseline conditions (Kyllo & Landers, 1995).

Most studies on goal-setting have been based on the theories of Locke & Latham (1985). These authors predicted that relative to either "no goal" or vague "do your best" conditions, performance should be enhanced when athletes use goals that are specific, short-term and difficult yet realistic. Unfortunately, research designed to test the predictions by Locke & Latham (1985) in sport have produced equivocal findings (Weinberg, 1992). For example, several studies have failed to establish the allegedly beneficial effects of specific and realistic goals on people's performance of motor tasks. Thus Weinberg, Bruya, Garland, & Jackson (1990) found that performance of hand strength and "sit-up" tasks was neither related to goal difficulty nor to goal specificity. This anomaly highlighted certain conceptual and methodological issues in research on goal-setting in sport (Weinberg, 1992). To illustrate, some authors question the conceptual suitability of goal-setting principles that are developed from organisational, rather than sporting, theories of behaviour. For example, Kremer & Scully (1994) observed that the extrinsic rewards arising from the world of work "stand in contrast to the intrinsic motivators which have been identified as being so crucial to maintaining an interest in amateur sport". Allied to such conceptual problems are a host of methodological difficulties. For example, a recurrent problem in research in this field is the tendency of subjects in control and/or "do your best" conditions to engage in *spontaneous* goal-setting activities (Weinberg, 1992). Clearly, this practice contaminates the design of experiments on this topic. Even more disappointing is the fact that, until recently (e.g. Weinberg, Stitcher, & Richardson, 1994), almost all research on goal-setting was laboratory-based. Rarely have researchers sought to explore how different *types* of goals affect athletes in competitive settings.

"Performance" goals and concentration

According to Weinberg & Gould (1995), there are two types of goals in sport. "Outcome" (or "result") goals typically specify the desired competitive result of an event (e.g. to win a race) in which people compete against others. "Performance" goals, however, refer to self-referenced behavioural standards (e.g. achieving 80% accuracy in sinking golf putts from two metres).

Most authors of MST programmes suggest that "result" goals fail to enhance performance. For example, by focusing only on the results of their actions, athletes may distract themselves by thinking too far ahead (see also Chapter 4). In other words, future consequences replace present actions in the mind of the athlete. Also, result goals encourage the performer to concentrate on factors outside their control (e.g. the quality of their opponents). However, "performance" goals are believed to be particularly effective in improving attention (see Locke & Latham, 1985) because they are clear, specific and controllable. Accordingly, athletes are encouraged to use any extra time (e.g. from breaks in play) to re-focus their minds on these action-goals. For example, Winter & Martin (1991) claimed that "top players use these natural segments to help them to concentrate. They do this by setting fresh goals and plans for each segment. The main aim of these fresh goals and plans is to keep the focus of concentration on what is happening at that moment" (p. 28). But is there any empirical evidence to support this hypothesis? Although data on this issue are meagre, a study by Jackson & Roberts (1992) explored the type of goals that collegiate athletes had in mind during either their "best" or "worst" sporting performances. Results showed that whereas 66% of the athletes reported experiencing "performance" (or "process") goals during their best performances, nearly 88% of athletes claimed that they had been "outcome focused" during their worst performances. Accordingly, Jackson & Roberts (1992) concluded that the adoption of a "result" focus was associated with poor concentration and performance.

In summary, it seems plausible that the establishment of specific performance goals should improve athletes' concentration because such objectives encourage present-focused, strategic and task-relevant thinking. Unfortunately, little research has been conducted by sport psychologists on the relationship between goal-setting and attentional processes.

PRE-PERFORMANCE ROUTINES AS CONCENTRATION STRATEGIES

The ability to perform to one's full potential consistently, despite variable competitive circumstances, is the hallmark of athletic expertise. Therefore, in an effort to display "a consistent motor pattern" (Allard & Burnett, 1985), most athletes have developed stereotyped preparatory routines which they follow before they perform. For example, top tennis players like to bounce the ball a standard number of times before serving. Likewise, expert rugby place-kickers tend to take the same number of steps in the lead-up to important kicks in matches. Golfers may display consistent action-sequences (e.g. "waggling" their club in a characteristic fashion or taking a set number of practice swings) before executing a shot (see Clay, 1988; Perry & Morris, 1995). Interestingly, Crews & Boutcher (1986a) found that successful professional golfers repeatedly took the same length of time, and the same number of practice swings, before playing each shot during tournament play. In a similar vein, archers use pre-shot routines to ensure that they never get distracted by looking at fellow competitors. To illustrate, consider how Darrell Pace, the former Olympic archery champion, prepares to shoot: "I look in two places. I look either straight down at the ground in front of me or I'll see the centre of the target ... From the time I cross the line, a switch goes on. They blow the whistle, I shoot, and then the switch turns off like a machine. It's like tunnel vision—nothing can interfere with it" (cited in Vealey & Walter, 1994, pp. 435–436). In summary, the preceding examples show that many athletes believe that adherence to pre-performance routines will facilitate optimal mental preparation for competition—especially when the performance of "closed" skills (i.e. those which are performed at one's own pace in a relatively static environment) is required.

The popularity of performance routines stems largely from the belief that they enable athletes "to concentrate more efficiently" (Boutcher, 1992). Many theorists accept this proposition. For example, routines are alleged to help performers "to minimise distractions and focus concentration" (Weinberg, 1988) in the seconds leading up to the execution of a given skill. Moreover, Gould & Udry (1994) suggested that pre-performance routines work by "helping athletes to divert their attention from task-irrelevant thoughts to task-relevant thoughts". Likewise, Moore & Stevenson (1994) proposed that a pre-shot routine helps "to increase the likelihood that the golfer will not be distracted, internally or externally, during swing execution". But what empirical evidence exists to justify such claims? Before I answer this question, I shall outline briefly the nature and functions of performance routines in sport.

Routines: Nature and functions

The term "pre-performance routine" refers to a systematic sequence of task-relevant thoughts and actions which an athlete engages in systematically prior to his or her performance of a specific sport skill (Gayton, Cielinski, Francis-Keniston, & Hearns, 1989). It is a "systematic, routinised patterns of physical actions and preplanned sequence of thoughts and arousal-related cues" (Gould & Udry, 1994). Usually, routines comprise both cognitive and behavioural elements (Cohn, 1990). The former include such strategies as mental imagery (see Chapter 7) and the use of instructional "self-talk" (e.g. reminding oneself to achieve a "smooth tempo" in one's swing—see later in the present chapter) whereas the latter components involve such activities as physically rehearsing the movement to be performed (e.g. taking a practice swing), glancing at the target, "grounding" oneself and aligning one's feet or shoulders appropriately.

In general, the cognitive and behavioural content of a pre-shot routines varies considerably from sport to sport, depending on the nature of the skill to be executed and the level of expertise of the performer (Cohn, 1990). To illustrate the former factor, a basketball player who is preparing for a free throw may align his or her feet squarely with the hoop whereas a golfer who is about to putt will adopt a completely different stance. Likewise, weight-lifters may use self-talk to increase arousal ("psych up") during a pre-lift routine whereas archers may endeavour to calm themselves (or relax) prior to shooting. With regard to level of expertise, the content of a routine should be appropriate to the stage of skill-mastery achieved by the performer. To explain, Fitts & Posner (1967) suggested that people pass through three stages when learning a skill—a "cognitive" phase (which involves attempting to understand the nature and demands of the task), an "associative" stage (habits are tried out and new patterns begin to emerge) and an "autonomous" phase (where component processes become "less directly subject to cognitive control, and less subject to interferences from other ongoing activities or environmental distractions"). Thus whereas a novice bowler may require specific cue words which tell them to "extend the arm" or "follow through" on delivery, an experienced bowler may rely only on a kinaesthetic image of the appropriate feeling which allows the correct delivery to be "run off" automatically.

Traditionally, pre-shot routines have been deemed to be most beneficial for "closed" or "self-paced" sport skills (which are performed in a relatively unchanging environment; e.g. the golf putt). However, some researchers (e.g. Boutcher & Rotella, 1987) propose that routines may also be used to enhance the performance of closed-skill activities in "open" sport environments (where the performer must respond to dynamic stimuli, e.g. batting in cricket). Examples of self-paced sports include archery, golf, shooting, diving, gymnastics and weightlifting. "Closed" skills include such activities as putting in golf, serving in tennis, free-throwing in basketball or penalty-taking in rugby or soccer.

Routines are alleged to provide at least five benefits for sport performers (Boutcher, 1990). First, they are believed to improve concentration by encouraging athletes to focus their thoughts on task-relevant cues (e.g. having an appropriate "swing thought" in golf) rather than on extraneous distractions such as noise. Thus Crews & Boutcher (1986b) suggested that they serve to divert attention away from negative or irrelevant thoughts and to establish "the appropriate physical and mental state for the ensuing task". Next, they may help athletes to overcome their natural tendency to dwell on the negative consequences of a recent, unsuccessful performance (e.g. a missed putt on the previous hole in golf; see Boutcher & Rotella, 1987). Third, Cohn (1990) claimed that the pre-performance routine allows the athlete to select the appropriate motor schema which is required to "run off" the skill to be performed. Fourth, routines are believed to prevent "warm up" decrements. To explain, it is widely known that temporary decrements in performance can occur after a period of rest. But Anshel & Wrisberg (1993) found that such decrements were reduced significantly among golfers by taking practice swings. Therefore, pre-shot routines may function as important "warm up" activities for athletes. Finally, the possession of a routine may prevent athletes from devoting excessive attention to the mechanics of their automatic skills or movements—a habit which can "unravel" automaticity (see discussion of "paralysis by analysis" in Chapter 4).

On the basis of these alleged benefits, pre-performance routines are valued highly by athletes. In a recent study of psychological factors which appear to influence the occurrence of "flow" states, Jackson (1995) (see also Chapter 3) found that elite athletes in a variety of sports relied heavily on such routines when preparing for competition. In a similar study, Gould, Eklund, & Jackson (1992a) discovered the perceived importance of routines to wrestlers who competed at the 1988 Olympic Games in Seoul. In particular, before a tournament, elite wrestlers liked to isolate themselves from colleagues, to employ a standard "warm up" routine and to visualise themselves wrestling their opponents. This study highlighted the fact that athletes usually combine routines with other mental preparation strategies (e.g. visualisation; see Chapter 7).

Efficacy of pre-performance routines

Do pre-performance routines improve performance? Anecdotal evidence supports this possibility. For example, the Welsh rugby international place-kicker Neil Jenkins claims that routines help him to ignore distractions. For example, he revealed recently that "I just try and make sure that everything I do on the training ground is repeated on the big day: the angle of the ball, the steps, the strike—and when you do that, it's not that hard to block the crowd out of your mind" (cited in Shalvey, 1995, p. 25). Some empirical research also exists on this question. For example, Crews & Boutcher (1986b) compared the performances of two groups of golfers: Those who had been given an eight-week training programme which focused on swing practice only and those who had participated in a "practice-plus-routine" programme for the same duration. Results showed that the more proficient golfers benefited more from routines than did less capable colleagues. So perhaps skill-level mediates the effects of pre-shot routines on golf performance. This hypothesis receives support from other sources. For example, there is evidence that the pre-performance routines of highly-skilled players are executed more consistently than are those of less proficient counterparts (Boutcher & Crews, 1987). Furthermore, Boutcher & Zinsser (1990) found that experienced golfers display consistently longer pre-putt routines than do beginners. Similar results have been reported for basketball players (Wrisberg & Pein, 1992). In this study, expert performers (i.e. higher "percentage" shooters) took consistently longer to prepare for free-throw shots than did less skilful colleagues. Taken together, these studies suggest that expert athletes differ from novices not only in "outcome" variables (e.g. accuracy) but also in *preparatory* processes. Another source of evidence on the efficacy of pre-performance routines comes from a qualitative study of Olympic athletes conducted by Gould, Eklund, & Jackson (1992a). Briefly, using structured interviews, these researchers found that US wrestling medal winners at the 1988 Olympic Games "were characterised by very systematic pre-performance routines that were relatively consistently adhered to throughout the Olympic tournament. Nonmedalists reported deviating from their pre-performance routines prior to matches that were considered less challenging or less important" (pp. 377–378).

What theoretical mechanisms have been postulated to explain the effects of pre-performance routines on performance? At least five relevant theories are apparent. To begin with, it is possible that pre-shot routines may facilitate consistency of performance simply because they reduce the variability of the performer's movements prior to skill execution (Lobmeyer & Wasserman, 1986). Biomechanically, skill execution requires a great deal of consistency of movements in a performer. For example, in golf, a tiny variation in the angle of the club face may mean the difference between a perfect pitch to the green or a "blade" to the nearest bunker. Similarly, the trajectory of a bullet or arrow is affected by even the tiniest tremor in the hand of the shooter or archer. Therefore, the finding (by Hatfield & Landers, 1987) that elite rifle-shooters tend to squeeze the trigger between heart-beats suggests that their pre-performance routines have a sound theoretical basis (see also Chapter 5). Clearly, any technique which standardises preparatory movements in the seconds leading up to a shot is desirable for an archer or a pistol-shooter. Another possible explanation for the apparent success of routines is that they may simply increase the *confidence* of performers, thereby enhancing their sense of perceived control over the competitive situation. This theory is supported somewhat by the fact that the basketball players tested by Lobmeyer & Wasserman (1986) tended to *over-estimate* the value of using routines relative to the actual benefits obtained. A third possible explanation for the effects of routines is couched in terms of "schema theory" (Schmidt, 1975; see also Chapter 1). Briefly, this theory holds that motor movements are represented as "schemas" in memory. These schemas are thought to contain unique parameters which define how a "motor program" will be executed for a given skill. So, it is possible that pre-shot routines allow the performer to establish the initial conditions which "trigger" the appropriate motor program automatically from procedural memory (Cohn, 1990). This explanation resembles the theory of "production systems" (Anderson, 1983) in which "conditions" trigger "actions" (see Chapter 2). A fourth explanation for routines concerns the "set hypothesis" (Cohn, 1990). In particular, this hypothesis suggests that a pre-shot routine serves to protect the performer's mental "set" against decrements in performance that are known to occur in sports where the action is punctuated by frequent breaks (e.g. as happens in golf or tennis). In other words, routines may exert their effects by "reducing the effect of warm-up decrement" and by developing an "appropriate internal set that matches the requirements of the task". Incidentally, the warm-up decrement refers to a temporary decline in skilled performance that tends to follow a brief rest period. The fifth explanation for the effects of routines was offered by Boutcher & Crews (1987). These researchers suggested that stereotyped preparation prevents sport performers from engaging in the negative self-talk which is allegedly elicited by stressful situations. Instead, by conducting a well-learned set of "cue" thoughts and actions, athletes learn to focus on what they need to *do* rather than on what they hope to avoid.

The next step in exploring routines is to assess their potential value as concentration techniques for athletes. According to Boutcher (1990), at least three theoretical principles may be adduced to support this possibility. First, routines may help to reduce distractibility and increase the likelihood of processing task-relevant cues. To explain, assuming that each step of a routine is task-relevant, performers who focus deliberately on key pre-performance activities will be less likely to be distracted than those who do not know which cues to process. As Boutcher observed, the ability to "offset task-irrelevant processing could be improved with the use of an effective pre-performance routine that consistently directs attention to task-relevant cues". Second, adherence to behavioural routines might increase athletes' concentration by preventing two well-known sources of distraction for performers (especially in pressure situations; see Chapter 4): Worrying about themselves (excessive self-consciousness) and speculating about what might happen in the future (i.e. "result consciousness"). Third, engaging in pre-performance routines may prevent lapses in attention caused by the "warm-up decrement" (described earlier in this chapter). In summary, there are some theoretical grounds for believing that adherence to routines may help athletes to improve their ability to "focus" effectively. But can we be sure that such a practice is not simply a form of superstitious behaviour?

Routines or superstitions?

How can we distinguish between pre-performance routines and superstitious rituals? In order to answer this question, some conceptual clarification is required. "Superstitious" behaviour occurs when people interpret random associations between events (e.g. wearing a particular colour of socks and winning a match) in causal, rather than correlational, terms. More formally, a superstition is a belief that one's fate is in the hands of unknown external powers and is governed by factors outside one's control (Jahoda, 1969). Such beliefs are widespread among athletes. To illustrate, Ernie Els, the South African golfer, has superstitions about the balls that he uses in tournaments. In particular, he never plays with a ball that is marked with the number "2" because "I have a bad, bad memory of the 2 ball. The first South African Open I played, back in 1983, was at the Durban Country Club. I was 18. I hit three identical shots off the first tee, all out of bounds, and made a nine on the hole. From that day onwards, I've never played a 2 ball" (Doust, 1995, p. 7). Incidentally, Els also has a ritual about discarding a golf ball as soon as he achieves a "birdie" with it because "Sam Torrance once told me that there is only one birdie in each golf ball" (ibid.).

This phenomenon of random associations between events raises an interesting question for pre-performance routines. Is it possible that they mask *superstitions* in the minds of sport performers? Lahey (1992) considers this possibility in relation to the pre-throw rituals of a discus thrower. To explain, he argued that initially the behaviour that occurs before a discus is thrown is relatively random. But when the thrower delivers a particularly good throw (which constitutes a major reinforcer for a discus thrower), any of the random behaviour that occurred just before the throw will be reinforced through superstitious reinforcement. This backward-chaining is called "superstitious" because the reinforcement of the good throw had nothing to do with some random behaviour like touching one's shoulder before beginning the action. However, unless the discus-thrower is careful, a whole series of behaviours could become "glued" together as apparently essential requirements of a successful throw.

The problem of disentangling routines from superstitious rituals is difficult because almost all sport skills involve a *chain* of responses. In addition, the reinforcement for executing a successful performance affects not only the last component of the response chain, but also *earlier* responses. As Coon (1994) remarked, if a golfer taps the club on the ground three times and then hits a prodigious drive, the success of the shot rewards not only the correct swing but also the three taps. Overall, two issues are relevant to distinguishing pre-shot routines from superstitions. First, how long is the pre-shot response chain? The longer it is, the greater is the probability that it will have some superstitious elements. Second, does each component of the behavioural routine have a clear technical function in the execution of the skill? If some of the components of a routine have no rational basis (e.g. whether a footballer puts on the left boot before the right boot in the dressing room), then superstitious behaviour may be involved. In summary, in this section, I have explained the nature, characteristics and conceptual foundations of the pre-performance routines used by athletes in an effort to enhance their performance. Unfortunately, until consistent evidence is available from controlled empirical studies in this field, claims made on behalf of routines as concentration techniques should be treated with great caution.

AROUSAL-CONTROL AS A CONCENTRATION TECHNIQUE

In Chapter 2, I mentioned that "alertness" is a biological component of the construct of attention. Subjectively, this state is associated with feelings of energy. But can this energy be regulated voluntarily? If so, what effect does such self-regulation have on one's ability to concentrate effectively? In this section of the chapter, I shall examine the possibility that arousal-control techniques may serve as concentration strategies for athletes.

The term "arousal" refers to a "general physiological and psychological activation of the organism that varies on a continuum from deep sleep to intense excitement" (Gould & Krane, 1992). Sometimes, this construct is associated with athletic success (Weinberg & Gould, 1995). For example, without adequate alertness, athletes may complain of feeling "flat" or sluggish before competitive encounters; conversely, if they are too "psyched up", the resultant tension may impair their performance. Depending on how it is interpreted by the athlete, arousal may either facilitate or inhibit sport performance. Therefore, the ability to *regulate* arousal levels is widely regarded as an important mental skill in athletes (Gould & Udry, 1994). To illustrate, Mahoney & Avener (1977) found that successful gymnasts (i.e. those who qualified for the 1976 US Olympic squad) tended to interpret pre-competitive anxiety as a form of anticipatory excitement—a view which facilitated subsequent performance. Conversely, less successful counterparts (i.e. athletes who failed to qualify for the team) tended to treat their arousal levels with trepidation, interpreting them as unwelcome signs of impending panic and disaster. This study highlighted the importance of arousal-control for athletes. More generally, performers who are engaged in strength and power sports such as wrestling and weight-lifting may favour "psych up" strategies while preparing for competition (Jacobson, 1932). On the other hand, precision sport performers like archers and snooker-players may prefer to engage in "psych down" or relaxation techniques. For example, the American athlete Darrell Pace, an Olympic gold-medalist in archery on two occasions, revealed that he uses a controlled breathing technique (in which the pattern of inhalations and exhalations is synchronised with the cue word "relax") to help him to concentrate before competitions (Vealey & Walter, 1994). Likewise, the brilliant basketball player Michael Jordan claimed that before matches, "you try not to get all psyched up. You try to relax. You try to make it fun" (cited in Stauth, 1992). Clearly, world-class athletes Pace and Jordan believe that their attentional skills can be improved through arousal-control. The assumption here is that by gaining increased control over their physiological processes, sport performers can learn "to recognise earlier when they are not focused or aroused appropriately" (Ravizza, 1989). Is this claim substantiated by empirical research? In order to answer this question, I shall examine the construct of arousal and evaluate the extent to which arousal-control strategies may enhance concentration.

The construct of arousal

Traditionally, arousal has been regarded as a form of bodily energy which prepares the organism for action. For example, Landers & Boutcher (1993) referred to the "energising function" of arousal. More precisely, it is regarded as a psychological state, varying in intensity and mediated by the sympathetic nervous system, in which changes in bodily processes prepare an individual to respond to a perceived demand for action (Whelan, Epkins, & Meyers, 1990). However, this definition of arousal fails to acknowledge its multi-dimensional character. Thus Anshel et al. (1991) emphasised the fact that arousal is not only experienced but *interpreted* by the person involved. Moreover, they claim that it may "include positive or negative emotions". To illustrate, a high degree of arousal in an athlete (e.g. rapid heart rate in a sprinter on the "blocks") may sometimes give rise to a feeling of being "psyched up". On other occasions, however, it may be interpreted as a sign of "nervousness" (e.g. when a golfer experiences a sudden flutter of the heart as she steps up to take a putt on the 18th green). Conversely, a low level of arousal may be experienced either as a relaxed state or alternatively, it may be labelled as a "flat" feeling by an athlete. In short, the same degree of arousal is amenable to different interpretations or cognitive labels. Therefore, the construct of arousal is *multidimensional* because, at the very least, it contains a physiological "energy" component and a psychological "interpretation" component.

A considerable amount of research has been conducted on the role of arousal in sport performance (see reviews by Crews, 1993; Gould & Krane, 1992; Jones, 1991; Zaichkowsky & Takenaka, 1993). From this research literature, several issues are apparent. First, the homogeneity of the construct of arousal has been called into question by the discovery that there is relatively little agreement between physiological and self-report measures of this construct (Gould & Udry, 1994). Second, few general principles have emerged to describe the relationship between arousal and skilled performance. This uncertainty is attributable to a variety of methodological and conceptual problems in the field. For example, many arousal-performance studies have used only one measure of arousal despite the fact that the construct is widely accepted as being multi-dimensional in nature (Hardy & Nelson, 1988). Furthermore, the arousal-performance relationship is mediated by a host of intervening variables (e.g. the nature of the skill to be performed) which have not been controlled adequately to date. As a result of these problems, it is almost impossible to predict accurately how a specific level of arousal will affect the performance of a given sport skill. This leads us to consider the relationship between arousal and performance.

Arousal, performance and attention

Historically, the two most prominent arousal-performance theories in sport psychology have been "drive theory" (Hull, 1943) and the "inverted-U" hypothesis (based on Yerkes & Dodson, 1908). Although a detailed review of these theories is beyond the scope of this chapter, a brief explanation may be helpful here (but for additional details, see Anshel, 1995; Gould & Krane, 1992).

According to drive theory, a direct positive and linear relationship exists between motivation, arousal level and performance. Specifically, motivational drives are held to elevate arousal levels which, in turn, lead to improved performance. Unfortunately, when tested in sport settings, this theory has received only meagre empirical support (Anshel, 1995). For example, although "psyching up" strategies (e.g. a rousing "pep talk" before a game) may increase arousal, there is little or no evidence that they improve skilled performance. Meanwhile, according to the "inverted-U hypothesis", increased arousal is believed to improve performance up to a certain point (sometimes referred to as the "zone of optimal functioning"; Hanin, 1980). But beyond this hypothetical stage, further increases in arousal are predicted to impair performance. This theory is derived from the Yerkes-Dodson law (Yerkes & Dodson, 1908) which proposed that there is an optimal level of arousal for performance on any task. Specifically, performance tends to be poor at low or high levels of arousal but is best at intermediate levels of arousal. Translated into the domain of sport, athletic performance which occurs under conditions of either high or low arousal should be inferior to that displayed at intermediate ("optimal") levels. The problem with this theory is that it is difficult to test empirically due to a scarcity of independent measures of key constructs. For example, how can we assess objectively whether an arousal level is "too low" or "too high" for a given performer? Clearly, the point of "diminishing returns" for the effects of arousal on performance is not measurable in advance. Therefore, as Neiss (1988) suggested, "the inverted-U hypothesis is effectively immune to falsification". Furthermore, he claims that it "has not received clear support from a single study" in the research literature. A more detailed critique of this theory is provided by Jones (1991) and Neiss (1988). Despite its questionable validity, the "inverted-U" theory has been promulgated as an established fact by many applied sport psychologists. For example, Winter & Martin (1991) present a diagram of the Yerkes-Dodson law as a prelude to their advice to tennis players on "controlling 'psych' levels". Similarly, Gauron (1984) uses this graph to support his contention that "intermediate or moderate levels of arousal are most conducive to peak performance". In summary, it seems that the popularity of the "inverted-U" theory in sport psychology owes more to its intuitive plausibility than to its scientific validity.

At first glance, the failure to find clear principles governing the relationship between arousal and sport performance is disappointing because it suggests that there is no single arousal state which facilitates optimal performance for all athletes. But, given the multi-dimensionality of arousal, perhaps it is somewhat naive to expect to find some "zone of optimal energy" (Martens, 1987) or "ideal performance state" (Loehr, 1989) for all athletes. After all, as sport skills vary widely in their demands for power and precision, is it reasonable to expect that arousal-performance relationships should be universal? Also, given the number of intervening variables in the relationship between arousal and performance (e.g. athletes' previous experiences with arousal changes, their perceived ability to control arousal, and the presence of others; Whelan, Mahoney, & Meyers, 1991), how can we expect simple laws to emerge? As Whelan, Mahoney, & Meyers (1991) concluded, "while arousal ... appears necessary, the athlete's perception ... and ability to manage it may be the variables most highly related to performance gains". For these reasons, a closer inspection of relevant research literature reveals a rich source of data which has, until recently, been approached rather simplistically.

To explain, if arousal is interpreted simply as a uni-dimensional construct, it is hardly surprising that few robust generalisations have emerged concerning its relationship with sport performance. But if it is regarded as a *multi-dimensional* construct with cognitive, affective, physiological and behavioural correlates, then a different picture may emerge. In this picture, the role of cognitive factors in arousal states is emphasised. These factors are acknowledged in the "catastrophe" model of arousal-performance relationships (Fazey & Hardy, 1988). According to catastrophe theory, physiological arousal is associated with sport performance in a manner described by the "inverted-U" function—but only when the athletes are not worried (i.e. when they have a low level of cognitive anxiety). With greater worry, however, increases in arousal tend to improve performance up to a certain point beyond which further increases in arousal may produce a swift and discontinuous ("catastrophic") decline in performance rather than a slow and gradual deterioration (as predicted by traditional linear models). Thus Fazey & Hardy (1988) suggested that the effects of arousal on performance may be either facilitatory or catastrophic depending on the cognitive processes of the sport performer. For example, when an athlete is engaged in routine training, his or her cognitive anxiety is usually relatively low. Accordingly, modest increases in arousal should enhance his or her performance (in line with predictions from the Yerkes-Dodson principle). But under competitive pressure, when cognitive anxiety tends to rise, the "inverted-U" curvilinear relationship may not describe accurately what actually happens. Under these circumstances, increased arousal may impair performance suddenly and dramatically (i.e. "catastrophically"). Some support has been received for this prediction that arousal hampers sport performance when cognitive anxiety is high but not when it is relatively low (Hardy & Parfitt, 1991).

Let us consider now the relationship between arousal and attention. These constructs have been linked in several theories of human information processing (e.g. see Eysenck, 1992). To illustrate, in the "capacity model" of attention (Kahneman, 1973; see also Chapter 2), a person's level of arousal is thought to be directly related to the amount of attentional resources available to them. As Reddy (1991) explained, available capacity may be regarded as a pipe of flexible diameter: "If you are tired and/or under aroused you will have less processing capacity than when you are at a peak of wide-awake alertness". An obvious implication of this theory is that arousal-control can expand or restrict the availability of attentional resources.

Two general categories of arousal-control techniques can be identified in sport psychology (Gould & Udry, 1994; Harris & Williams, 1993). On the one hand, "arousal reduction" strategies (e.g. "psyching down" or relaxation techniques) purport to help sport performers to *lower* their arousal levels and thereby increase their concentration. Conversely, arousal enhancement techniques ("psyching up") are alleged to *increase* athletes' activation levels. However, it is not clear how this latter strategy would affect concentration. I shall now examine briefly each of these strategies for regulating arousal.

Arousal reduction strategies as concentration techniques

Arousal reduction strategies are advocated in sport because relaxation is assumed to counteract the narrowing of athletes' attentional spans under competitive pressure (see Easterbrook, 1959; also Chapter 2). Chief among these strategies are controlled breathing, progressive muscular relaxation, various meditation techniques and biofeedback training (Kremer & Scully, 1994; Zaichkowsky & Takenaka, 1993). These techniques, which are outlined below, are believed to induce a relaxed state which is characterised by decreases in oxygen consumption, lowered heart and respiration rate together with increases in skin resistance and alpha wave EEG activity (Gould & Udry, 1994).

But do relaxed states actually facilitate optimal athletic performance? Unfortunately, research reviews are equivocal on this question. Gould & Udry (1994) concluded that "performance enhancement resulting from relaxation based training is possible": Hardy & Jones (1994) claimed that "there is relatively little literature that shows a direct effect of relaxation upon sports performance". One reason for this confusion is that methodological problems afflict research in this field. For example, many studies on relaxation fail to include manipulation checks to ensure that subjects are actually following assigned treatment instructions (Gould & Udry, 1994). Despite these difficulties, the following arousal reduction techniques are regularly used in applied sport psychology programmes in an effort to enhance concentration skills.

Controlled breathing. Controlled (i.e. "deep") breathing, which is conducted using the diaphragm rather than the chest, is used by athletes both to induce feelings of relaxation and to increase the amount of oxygen available for circulation to active muscles. Zen meditators believe that diaphragmatic breathing enables them to inhale larger amounts of air than is possible using chest breathing (Zaichkowsky & Takenaka, 1993). Unfortunately, many athletes have never learned the skill of diaphragmatic breath control. Accordingly, when faced with competitive pressure, they tend to hold their breath for too long or else breathe too rapidly and shallowly. Both of these types of breathing are thought to impair sport performance.

On account of these hazards, Nideffer (1985) recommended that athletes should learn breath control skills for two reasons. First, anxiety may cause athletes to breathe faster than is desirable in competition. Therefore, by checking on how they breathe, performers can counteract the tendency to "speed up" under pressure. Second, the conscious effort of paying attention to one's breathing may relieve anxiety as one "cannot simultaneously, consciously attend to both breathing and worry"

(Nideffer, 1985). Breath control forms part of a relaxation technique called "centreing". This technique, which involves adjusting the location of one's centre of gravity, has been defined by Nideffer (1985) as "learning to direct your thoughts toward the centre of gravity in your own body". Subjectively, the experience of being "centred" resembles a feeling of being firmly anchored or "grounded" solidly. Conversely, the tense or "uptight" position is inappropriate for the execution of most sport skills. For Nideffer, the relevance of centering for attention is that it provides "a brief time out that gives you momentary control over concentration and tension" (ibid.). Theoretically, breath control may help to increase concentration by helping athletes to achieve a relaxed state which should "free" the mind to focus on task-relevant information. Technically, relaxation reduces the amount of working memory resources which are consumed by worrying about the consequences of one's performance (see Eysenck, 1988). By implication, breath control may have some theoretical merit as a concentration strategy for athletes.

Progressive muscular relaxation.   Progressive muscular relaxation (PMR; Jacobson, 1938) is a technique which teaches people to focus their awareness systematically on discrete muscle groups in order to reduce bodily tension in these areas (Neiss, 1990). It is often practised by athletes during stretching exercises. In practice, PMR involves a series of exercises in which athletes learn to identify the difference between tense and relaxed bodily sensations by alternately contracting and loosening designated muscle groups. The exercise usually begins with muscular contractions in the dominant hand and progresses to other muscle groups in the body. For each part of the body, practitioners are required to feel and then "hold" the feelings of tension produced as they deliberately contract them. Then they are asked to relax the muscles and to notice the resulting sensations. Through this systematic procedure, which usually lasts for 20–30 minutes, a state of muscular relaxation is usually achieved. Practical scripts for athletes using PMR are available in such popular sources on mental skills training as Albinson & Bull (1988) and Orlick (1990).

Advocates of progressive relaxation claim that it improves concentration by training practitioners to focus their minds selectively on that which they can control. Accordingly, this technique has some justification for being included as a putative concentration technique. However, no empirical studies could be located in which this proposition was tested. There is evidence, however, that gymnasts may benefit from relaxation training. Thus Ravizza (1989) developed a progressive relaxation technique called "awareness stretching" for these athletes.

Briefly, this procedure requires the performer to focus on contracted muscle groups and then to exhale as the tension was released. Gradually, the gymnasts were trained to control their muscle tension during stretching using breath control. In this way, athletes can "develop concentration as they stretch before practice by feeling the stretch and breathing into it". This idea of coupling stretching with attentional processes is also emphasised by Hackfort & Schwenkmezger (1993) who noted that "it seems necessary ... to refer to the focus of concentration of the athlete" during muscular relaxation.

Recent reviews of PMR (e.g. by Onestak, 1991) confirm its utility as an anxiety-reduction strategy. However, despite its popularity among athletes, its efficacy on sport performance is largely unknown. Thus Zaichkowsky & Takenaka (1993) claim that research on progressive relaxation in sport is "quite sparse". Therefore, in the absence of relevant empirical data, the status of progressive muscular relaxation as a concentration technique for athletes is questionable.

Meditation.   It is widely accepted that the regular practice of meditation may lead to a variety of psychological benefits. In particular, these benefits include decreased blood pressure, metabolic rate and heart rate as well as increased blood-flow to the skeletal muscles (Hall & Hardy, 1991). Furthermore, interest in the use of meditation as a concentration technique in sport dates back as far as the work by Herrigel (1953) on Zen techniques in archery. Using this practice, people attempt to change their consciousness by using a series of physical and mental exercises. According to Harris & Williams (1993), the regular practice of meditation "facilitates concentration by disciplining the mind". In this vein, Schmid & Peper (1993) recommend the meditative practice of "one pointing". This technique requires athletes to focus on "one point" in a sport situation (e.g. on the seams of the ball in tennis) in order to reduce distractibility. These authors claim that practice with this technique helps "athletes eliminate their concentration-breaking thoughts". Unfortunately, no empirical evidence is cited in support of these opinions.

In general, the term "meditation" incorporates a variety of different approaches (e.g. Zen meditation, transcendental meditation) which share a common concern with the use of breath control, bodily posture, mental imagery and "focused" thinking in an effort to increase relaxation, reduce self-awareness and improve powers of concentration. With regard to the last-mentioned claim, Deikman (1963) proposed that by training people to see something "as it exists in itself", practitioners of meditation claim that they can rid their minds of unwanted thoughts and feelings and hence improve their concentration. In this regard, a

Zen metaphor likens the exclusion of unwanted thoughts to observing birds fly across the "sky" of one's mind: One simply watches as they disappear (Samuels & Samuels, 1975).

In general, effective systems of meditation share four key elements, according to Benson, Beary, & Carol (1974). First, the meditation should take place in a quiet, distraction-free environment. Second, a mental strategy (e.g. repetition of a 'mantra' like "one") should be used to focus one's attention while one is relaxing. Third, a passive attitude should be adopted. Finally, the meditator should sit in a comfortable manner. Although procedures which satisfy these criteria can reduce arousal levels, there is little evidence that they can actually improve athletic performance (Zaichkowsky & Takenaka, 1993). In fact, some studies have found counter-productive effects for meditation interventions. For example, Hall & Hardy (1991) compared the relative efficacy of a programme of Transcendental Meditation (TM) and a programme of "visuo-motor behavioural rehearsal" (Suinn, 1972; a form of mental practice—see also Chapter 7) on pistol-shooting performance. Results showed no significant benefit for the meditation intervention. Indeed, there were signs of a deterioration in some aspects of the shooting performance of this group. Conversely, the shooters who had been exposed to a mental practice treatment programme displayed improvement in certain aspects of their performance (e.g. greater accuracy and control in firing). Overall, little empirical evidence has been gathered to support the claim that meditation is an effective concentration strategy for athletes.

Biofeedback training. The term "biofeedback training" refers to a special form of operant learning in which people use electronic equipment (e.g. special computers) to acquire information about their own physiological states or processes (Hackfort & Schwenkmezger, 1993). This physiological information (e.g. cardiovascular, electrographic and/or electrodermal activity), which is not ordinarily available because it is involuntary, is then used (or "fed back") to help people to regulate specific parameters of arousal (Petruzzello, Landers, & Salazar, 1991). In sport psychology, biofeedback training has been used most extensively in the treatment of performance anxiety. Although commercial biofeedback instruments and programmes for athletes have been developed, the ultimate goal of biofeedback training is to encourage behavioural "self-regulation" whereby the practitioner can regulate desired bodily changes without the assistance of any instrumentation.

Several studies have used electromyographic (EMG) feedback in an effort to improve athletic performance by decreasing the muscular tension of the performers involved (Druckman & Swets, 1988). The assumption here is that reduction of bodily tension is associated with performance enhancement. Unfortunately, as sport skills vary considerably in their muscular requirements, little evidence has emerged to support this proposition. In Chapter 5, I explained that left hemisphere EEG activity is associated with proficiency in precision sports like archery, target shooting and golf. We also learned that under certain circumstances, left-hemisphere biofeedback training can improve archery performance (Landers et al., 1991). However, two issues obstruct further progress in this field (Petruzzello, Landers, & Salazar, 1991). First, biofeedback is usually employed as a component of a larger "package" of mental skills interventions. Therefore, it may be difficult to disentangle the relative contribution of biofeedback from that of other arousal-control strategies applied (e.g. progressive muscular relaxation). In addition, there is little agreement among sport researchers as to appropriate criteria for biofeedback training. To explain, in order to enhance athletic performance using biofeedback, sport performers must be trained to identify optimal arousal levels for such indices as EEG or heart-rate. But as Petruzzello, Landers, & Salazar (1991) remarked, "there is often no prior knowledge regarding optimal levels of activity in these measures". Taken together, these problems explain why there has been a dearth of well-controlled studies of biofeedback effects on sport performance (for reviews of available literature, see Petruzzello, Landers, & Salazar, 1991; Zaichkowsky & Fuchs, 1988).

In summary, two conclusions appear to be warranted by the research literature explored above. First, psychological techniques such as controlled breathing, progressive muscular relaxation, meditation and biofeedback can facilitate a reduction in the arousal levels of athletes. However, little or no empirical evidence is available, as yet, to support the claim that such techniques can help athletes to improve their concentration or sport performance.

Arousal enhancement strategies as concentration techniques

Most athletes recognise the need to engage in some psychological activities that serve both to increase the energising capacity of their bodies and to "sharpen" their attentional focus before they participate in competition. For example, a long-jumper may make vigorous running movements "on the spot", as fast as possible, as a preparatory strategy. Likewise, a marathon runner may use some arousing imagery (e.g.

visualising energy being pumped from a physical landmark on the route, such as a service station, into one's body) in order to re-vitalise his or her flagging spirits when fatigue beckons. Similarly, an entire team may try to activate their energy levels symbolically. To illustrate, the famous "haka" dance of the New Zealand All-Black Rugby team serves this purpose successfully (Kremer & Scully, 1994). Coaches also have a role in helping athletes to "energise" themselves. For example, the delivery of emotionally-charged "pep talks" before competitive encounters is a venerable "psych up" strategy which is assumed to lead to increased autonomic arousal (e.g. Weinberg, 1989). Typical instructions provided during these pep talks encourage the performer to "get yourself emotionally prepared ... psych yourself up by getting mad, aroused, pumped-up or charged up" (Gould, Weinberg, & Jackson, 1980). Theoretically, such "psych up" strategies are regarded as being especially useful for activating the energy required for strength or power skills (e.g. weightlifting) and also for physical contact sports (e.g. American football). Energising techniques may be used *during*, as well as before, competitions. For example, a cyclist may require a "psych up" technique to counteract "dead leg" sensations brought on by fatigue. Similarly, a tense rower may feel that they have no reservoirs of power before a race. Here, cue-words like "go" or "explode", when combined with appropriate images of strength, may help to increase arousal levels (Harris & Williams, 1993).

Among the most popular arousal-enhancing techniques advocated by sport psychologists (see Albinson & Bull, 1988) are pre-game workouts to music, rapid breathing, "self-talk" (e.g. the use of cue words like "power" or "explode") and various stretching exercises (which may increase blood circulation). But does "psyching up" actually enhance athletic performance? Unfortunately, research on the efficacy with which energising techniques improve performance is "minimal" (Zaichkowsky & Takenaka, 1993). However, there is some laboratory evidence which suggests that such strategies work. For example, Caudill, Weinberg, & Jackson (1983) found that a one minute "psych up" condition produced better performances among sprinters and hurdlers than did a one minute duration of instruction from coaches or a one minute talk by the experimenter. Similarly, Shelton & Mahoney (1978) found that "psych up" techniques helped a group of weight lifters to increase their hand-dynamometer scores relative to a control group which had not received any "energising" intervention. Also, "psych up" instructions have been found to improve performance in tasks involving leg strength (Gould, Weinberg, & Jackson, 1980) and muscular endurance.

Despite the preceding evidence, several difficulties curtail conclusions drawn from studies in this area. First, the precise theoretical mechanisms by which "psych up" effects occur are unknown. For example, contrary to Weinberg's (1989) assumption that these strategies boost autonomic arousal, no evidence of a heart-rate increase was found by Whelan, Epkins, & Meyers (1990) in people who used "psych up" techniques. In addition, no field studies have been conducted on the use of arousal enhancement techniques among athletes. Finally, no empirical studies have been conducted on the effects of "energising" techniques on the concentration skills of athletes. However, attentional factors were invoked by Wilkes & Summers (1984) in exploring the effects of different cognitive preparation strategies (e.g. attentional focusing instructions which urged subjects to "block out all outside thoughts and think only of just how you are going to extend your leg") on strength performance. Results showed that these techniques enhanced strength performance. Post-experimental interview data suggested that these strategies had succeeded in narrowing subjects' attention to the key elements of the task involved. Therefore, mental preparation techniques may help to re-direct the attentional focus of sport performers. As with the arousal reduction techniques, however, available evidence is not adequate to support the claim that these techniques could help athletes to concentrate more effectively.

INSTRUCTIONAL SELF-TALK AS A CONCENTRATION TECHNIQUE

Athletes often talk to themselves while they train or compete, especially during individual sports (e.g. marathon running). Sometimes, this "dialogue" is audible, as when a golfer shouts out loud following a costly mistake. Usually, however, athletes talk to themselves covertly—a practice known as "self-talk". For example, a gymnast performing a floor routine may say the word "forward" to remind herself to push ahead at a certain stage of the movement (Weinberg & Gould, 1995). Likewise, swimmers may imagine such technical trigger phrases in their minds as "head pop" or "kick hard" while competing (Green, 1994). Reliance on self-generated instructional commentary is also practised extensively by golfers. For example, the legendary Sam Snead used the word "oily" to remind himself to concentrate on his fluid swing (Vealey & Walter, 1993). Not surprisingly, the relationship between this type of auditory imagery and sport performance has attracted interest from many applied sport psychologists. For example, Bunker, Williams, & Zinsser (1993) proposed that self-talk can be used for "attentional control". In particular, they claimed that "by using a specific set of verbal cues, athletes can keep their minds appropriately focused". Likewise, Nideffer (1993a) claimed that self-talk leads to a "redirection of attention to task-relevant cues". Also, Williams & Roepke (1993) proposed that self-talk "can influence factors such as concentration, confidence, and persistence". But what evidence is available to support these claims? In this section of the chapter, I shall attempt to answer this question and evaluate the adequacy of instructional self-talk as a concentration strategy in sport (see Weinberg, 1988).

In general, self-talk can take the form of praise (e.g. "Well done! That's good"), criticism (e.g. "You fool! Another stupid mistake") or neutrally-toned, task-related instruction (e.g. a sprinter might say "stay low" while preparing on the blocks). An example of "positive" self-talk comes from Meyers, Schleser, Cooke, & Cuvillier (1979) who coached gymnasts to use such phrases as "That's easy :.. I know I can do a good front walkover". The effect of this intervention is unclear, however. In a later study, Rushall (1989) suggested that three types of self-talk statements are especially helpful to athletes. First, "task-relevant" statements may be helpful in "triggering" correct technique. For example, performers may use "cue words" (e.g. "low to high") to remind themselves to perform a key movement during skill execution (e.g. in order to hit a solid backhand drive in tennis, the racket must be swung from a "low" to a "high" position). Next, "mood words" may evoke images of certain movements which are necessary for skilled performance (e.g. a figure skater may use the word "glide" to remind herself to retain her balance between jumps; Weinberg & Gould, 1995). Third, "positive self-statements" may be used to encourage a performer (e.g. "Come on! Let's go!").

On what theoretical basis do "self-statements" affect sport performance? Cognitive behavioural theorists (e.g. Meichenbaum, 1977) assume that a person's "self-statements" may be viewed as indices of their beliefs and that such beliefs play a mediational role in behavioural performance. Theoretically, therefore, it is possible that instructional self-statements (e.g. "keep your eyes on the ball") could enhance performance whereas negative self-statements (e.g. "I hope I won't choke") should impair it (McLean, 1986). In this regard, it has been found that "defeatist" self-talk is detrimental to performance (Rotella, Gansneder, Ojala, & Billing, 1980). It has also been reported that "thought-stopping" techniques (i.e. those in which athletes use a trigger word, such as "STOP", to eliminate unwanted thoughts) can be used to change self-statements (Meyers & Schleser, 1980). However, it is disappointing to discover that few empirical studies have been conducted on the relationship between self-talk and sport performance (Hardy & Jones, 1994).

Self-talk and performance

Theoretically, athletic performance has been viewed as an exercise in cognitive self-regulation (Kirschenbaum & Wittrock, 1984). According to this perspective, "self-talk" and other forms of cognitive behaviour modification (e.g. Meichenbaum, 1977) should enhance sport performance. Endorsing this proposition, several researchers (e.g. Gould, Hodge, Peterson, & Giannini, 1989) have used such cognitive intervention techniques as "thought stopping" (Dalloway, 1993) with athletes. But little systematic research has been conducted to evaluate these techniques.

In order to explore the effects of self-talk on task performance, two main research paradigms have been used (Van Raalte, Brewer, Rivera, & Petitpas, 1994). On the one hand, some researchers (e.g. Rotella, Gansneder, Ojala, & Billing, 1980) have used athletes' self-reports to examine how self-talk affects sport performance. Meanwhile, other researchers (e.g. Schill, Monroe, Evans, & Ramanaiah, 1978) have used controlled experiments to investigate similar questions. Unfortunately, little consensus exists about the findings which emerge from these paradigms. For example, Highlen & Bennett (1983) discovered that whereas the use of self-talk distinguished between divers who qualified for a major event and those who did not, it failed to discriminate between qualifying and non-qualifying wrestlers. Qualifiers tended to use instructional self-talk whereas non-qualifiers simply praised themselves. This finding is somewhat counter-intuitive as positive self-talk is usually associated with successful athletes. Meanwhile, in controlled experimental studies, "negative" self-talk is associated with poor performances (e.g. Schill, Monroe, Evans, & Ramanaiah, 1978) and "positive" self-talk is related to successful performances (e.g. Johnston-O'Connor & Kirschenbaum, 1986). What factors account for this apparent conflict between studies from these alternative paradigms? Van Raalte, Brewer, Rivera, & Petitpas (1994) suggest that task familiarity is an important intervening variable. Specifically, they proposed that negative self-talk may be more detrimental to the performance of *unfamiliar* tasks (e.g. mirror tracing) than to the performance of well-learned tasks (e.g. "closed" sport skills).

Interestingly, there is evidence that self-talk may improve performance. For example, Rushall, Hall, & Rushall (1988) investigated the effects of different types of self-talk on the performance of elite cross-country skiers. The first type of self-talk advocated was the use of instructional task-relevant statements designed to enhance mechanical efficiency (e.g. "feel really long and powerful" or "up hill, quick and grip"). The second self-talk category included mood induction phrases aimed at increasing capacity (e.g. "go, blast, punch" or "drive, drive"). The final self-talk strategy was to use positive self-affirmation statements (e.g. "feel great") which are alleged to improve physiological efficiency. Results showed that all of these self-talk statements produced a significant improvement in skiing performance relative to a control group. Unfortunately, caution should be expressed about the validity of these results as no manipulation checks were included to establish whether or not the participants had followed experimental instructions.

Instructional self-talk and performance

Many cognitive psychologists believe that self-talk has an instructional significance. For example, Luria (1961) proposed that as skill learning becomes more automatic, self-talk is used less overtly and more covertly. Initially, children's motor actions receive verbal encouragement from other people (e.g. parents). Next, they talk to themselves aloud while practising the skill alone. In later childhood, according to Luria (1961), self-regulation is achieved and "self-talk" becomes covert. Turning to adult learning, we can quickly appreciate the value of self-talk as an instructional tool. For example, consider how most people learn the skill of driving. In your first lessons, did you notice how your instructor used *key words* to emphasise the sequence of actions to be followed? For example, you may have been encouraged to say "mirror...brake...clutch...gear...mirror...accelerator" before driving away from the kerb. In this case, by synchronising certain phrases with desired actions, the driving instructor is verbally "programming" your procedural skills.

Recently, Van Raalte, Brewer, Rivera, & Petitpas (1994) conducted a descriptive analysis of the audible "self-talk" and observable gestures exhibited by a sample of junior tennis players during competition. Using an unobtrusive rating scale, these authors recorded a variety of vocalisations and gestures which were evident during matches. The score of the match at the time was also recorded. Several findings emerged. First, more "negative" (i.e. self-critical) than "positive" (i.e. encouraging) self-talk was apparent among the players. Not surprisingly, these negative cognitions (e.g. "Why can't I serve?" or "You're so slow!") were mainly displayed after mistakes. Second, no significant association was found between audible, positive self-talk and performance. It is possible, however, that point-winners used covert self-talk in the match. Third, and consistent with findings from the experimental paradigm, negative self-talk was associated with poor performance on court. Overall, surprisingly little instructional self-talk (e.g. "move your feet") was apparent among these players. This finding suggests that many of these players lacked self-monitoring skills.

EFFICACY OF ATTENTIONAL SKILLS
TRAINING PROGRAMMES

How effective are programmes of concentration skills training for athletes? Before I attempt to answer this question, an allegory may be instructive. A famous Irish politician, who was known for his obscure analyses of economic problems, was once alleged to have remarked about a proposed Bill, "That's all very well in practice, but will it work in theory?!" Although it is apocryphal, this tale offers an interesting way of looking at the issue of attentional skills research in contemporary sport psychology. Briefly, although there is a great deal of literature on the claims surrounding the training of concentration skills, there is a dearth of underlying theory and research to support much of the practical advice offered. Thus Hardy & Nelson (1988) claimed that "despite the importance placed upon attention control by practitioners of sport psychology, empirical studies of attention control in sport are a rarity". Similarly, Singer et al. (1991) complained that "the paucity of research on the nature and effectiveness of attentional training is surprising considering the apparent recognition of effective self-generated attentional processes". Overall, it seems that "attentional research in sport is still at a very early stage of development" (Hardy, 1989). However, Lee (1990) examined the degree to which an concentration training programme (consisting of a 12 minute tape of instructions on relaxation, visualisation and attentional re-focusing) helped people to counteract auditory and visual distractions (coming from noise and lights) when performing a ball-throwing task. Subjects in a control condition were given general task instructions for the same duration. Results showed that the people who had listened to the "focusing" tape achieved greater consistency and accuracy of ball-throwing than their control-group counterparts.

In a similar vein, a handful of other studies which have been conducted on attentional skills were reviewed recently by Nideffer (1993a). He concluded that the results of these investigations were "generally supportive". But this conclusion is questionable in view of the fact that few of these studies included any attempt to measure the *pre*-treatment attentional skills of the athletes involved. As a result of this design flaw, how can we be sure that the athletes' attentional skills improved at all? Clearly, the experimental designs of future studies in this field will have to deal with this flaw. In summary, despite a wealth of anecdotal and descriptive evidence in this field, it has not yet been established conclusively that psychological techniques can improve the concentration of athletes. However, this possibility can be tested more rigorously if increased collaboration occurs between sport psychologists and cognitive researchers (see also Chapter 8).

SUMMARY

Within the past decade, there has been a remarkable upsurge of interest in the development and implementation of programmes of "mental skills training" (MST) for athletes. The impetus for this trend comes from two main sources. On the one hand, some research psychologists are interested in testing the proposition that mental processes such as attention and imagery may be regarded as cognitive skills which can be enhanced through appropriate training. On the other hand, most athletes and coaches are interested in exploiting the alleged advantages of MST in the domain of performance enhancement. Taken together, this convergence of interests has led to a profusion of psychological exercises and techniques which purport to enhance mental skills and competitive performance. But how effective are these techniques in improving concentration in athletes? Unfortunately, few researchers have addressed this question. Therefore, in this chapter, I set out to review the nature and foundations of attentional skills training programmes for athletes. In addition, I attempted to evaluate the adequacy of four psychological techniques which are alleged to increase the concentration skills of sport performers. These techniques included goal-setting, pre-performance routines, arousal-control and the use of "cue-words" (or instructional self-talk).

Initially, I identified two main assumptions underlying any efforts to improve athletes' mental processes. On the one hand, it is believed that certain psychological characteristics are significantly associated with athletic success. On the other hand, these characteristics are regarded as "skills" which can be improved through special training experiences. I concluded that both of these assumptions were tenable. Then, I reviewed the principal psychological exercises and techniques which are alleged to enhance athletes' concentration processes. The exercises consisted of such activities as the "concentration grid", visual search tasks and "adversity training" (i.e. the simulation of competitive conditions in training environments). Unfortunately, with the possible exception of adversity training, little theoretical or empirical evidence could be located to support the efficacy of these exercises. Therefore, considerable scepticism is warranted about the extent to which psychological games and exercises can enhance the concentration skills of athletes. Next, I reviewed the evidence available to support four "concentration techniques" commonly advocated in programmes of mental skills training. Although the plausibility of these techniques is supported by a persuasive blend of anecdotal and descriptive evidence, empirical data from controlled evaluation studies are lacking. Therefore, additional research is required to test the adequacy of these procedures as concentration strategies for athletes.

Overall, this chapter shows that concentration training programmes for athletes are at an early stage of development and validation. Before further progress can be made, at least three issues must be addressed. First, at a theoretical level, sport psychologists need to understand more about the nature and behavioural correlates of the construct of attention before they can hope either to assess it accurately or to or improve it. At present, attentional skills training programmes are difficult to validate mainly because they are not derived clearly from established theoretical principles. As a consequence, many popular concentration techniques recommended by sport psychologists (e.g. the "concentration grid") are based more on intuition than on solid conceptual or empirical principles. Second, the research designs used to evaluate attentional skills training programmes must be careful to include suitable "baseline" (or pre-test) measures. Finally, if certain psychological techniques are found to enhance concentration in athletes, research is required to establish the best ways in which to "prime" athletes to use these methods when they compete in actual competitive settings.

CHAPTER SEVEN

Improving concentration in sport
II: Mental practice

"We marked the pitch; four jackets for four goalposts, that was all.
The corners and the squares were there like latitude and longitude
Under the bumpy thistly ground to be agreed about or disagreed about when the time came,
And then we picked the teams and crossed the line our called names drew between us.
Youngsters shouting their heads off in a field as the light died
And they kept on playing because by then, they were playing in their heads..."

(Heaney, 1991)

"I visualise what the guy I'm guarding is going to do, what his tendencies are, and how am I gonna play against that"
(Basketball star, Michael Jordan, cited in Stauth, 1992, p. 79).

"I did dives in my head all the time. At night, before going to sleep, I always did my dives ... Sometimes I would take the weekend off and do imagery five times a day"
(Sylvie Bernier, former Olympic diving champion, cited in Orlick, 1990, p. 68)

"The only limits on what a player can score are imposed by
his own imagination. I believe it takes a vivid imagination
to *shoot low scores ... I know that Johnny Miller felt the same
way. He would talk about the mental images that would flash
before him, drawing him onwards towards a really low score*"

(David Feherty, professional golfer,
cited in Gilleece, 1991, p. 14)

INTRODUCTION

In Chapter 6, I reviewed four psychological techniques (i.e. goal-setting,
performance routines, arousal-control methods and cue-words) that are
alleged to enhance the concentration of athletes. In the present chapter,
I shall consider the concentration-enhancing properties of another
technique commonly used by sport performers—namely, "mental practice"
(MP) or "visualisation". This technique, which is used extensively by
athletes as a form of mental preparation for competition (Hall, Rodgers,
& Barr, 1990), involves "seeing" and "feeling" oneself performing skilled
movements in one's imagination prior to their actual execution.

Due to its reliance on simulated movements and experiences, mental
practice is dependent on the cognitive process of "mental imagery". This
construct refers to our capacity to represent in the mind experiences of
things which are not physically present (Matlin, 1994). Interestingly,
mental imagery has been described as "a central pillar of applied
sport psychology" (Perry & Morris, 1995) because it is used widely by
athletes for purposes ranging from confidence building to anxiety
control. Although many of the claims made on behalf of visualisation
lack scientific support, the use of imagery to enhance skill learning and
performance is well established. To explain, there is now abundant
evidence that, under certain circumstances, the systematic practice of
imagery (i.e. "mental practice") can improve the performance of
cognitive and motor skills (see review by Driskell, Copper, & Moran,
1994). Interestingly, this mental practice effect was highlighted recently
in a special issue of the *British Journal of Psychology* which was devoted
to the topic of motor skills imagery (see Annett, 1995). Apart from its
utility in skill learning, visualisation has also been promoted as a
method for improving other *mental* processes. For example, regular
imagery practice is thought to produce a "cognitive focusing effect"
(McLean & Richardson, 1994) which may lead to enhanced attentional
skills. In view of this claim, the purpose of the present chapter is to
review the efficacy of mental practice as a strategy for improving
concentration in athletes. In other words, I shall examine the claim by

Bond & Sargent (1995) that "imagery is an effective tool in facilitating concentration".

The chapter is organised as follows. I shall begin by examining what the term "mental practice" (MP) means in sport psychology and outline briefly the history of research on this topic. Next, I shall review the claims surrounding, and evidence supporting, the use of visualisation in sport. In this regard, the conclusions which receive strongest empirical support will be summarised. Then, I shall evaluate the main theoretical explanations for MP effects on skilled performance. Here the role of attentional mechanisms will receive special scrutiny. Finally, I shall evaluate the adequacy of visualisation as a concentration technique for athletes. In passing, it is notable that although the possibility of a link between mental imagery and attention has been raised by previous researchers (e.g. Finke, 1989), no empirical research could be located on this topic.

WHAT IS "MENTAL PRACTICE"?

It is difficult to find examples of artists and scientists who have reached similar conclusions about human experience (although Sir Walter Raleigh remarked in 1879 that poets "anticipate science"). But most contemporary sport psychologists would agree with the Nobel Prize-winning Irish poet Seamus Heaney (quoted at the beginning of this chapter) that sport is played as much in the *imagination* as with the body. Thus in *Markings*, Heaney observes the magic of children "playing in their heads" as darkness falls. But what is the significance of such imaginative play for adult sport performers? Specifically, is it helpful for athletes to "practise" mentally as well as physically? The objective of this chapter is to answer this question.

In general, I shall use the term "mental practice" (MP, or "visualisation") to refer to the deliberate and systematic use of mental imagery in order to rehearse physical actions. More precisely, it denotes the cognitive rehearsal of an action without overt performance of the physical movements involved (Driskell, Copper, & Moran, 1994). It has also been defined by Richardson (1967a) as "the symbolic rehearsal of a physical activity in the absence of any gross muscular movements". A related definition proposes that mental practice is "the mental simulation of a voluntary movement on the basis of visuo-spatial and kinaesthetic memorised patterns" (Decety & Michel, 1989). Technically, this imagery phenomenon is also known as "visuo-motor behavioural rehearsal" (VMBR; Suinn, 1994) and by a variety of other terms such as "symbolic rehearsal"; "imaginary practice"; "implicit practice"; "mental rehearsal"; "covert rehearsal"; "mental training" and "cognitive practice" (see Murphy & Jowdy, 1992 for a full list of synonyms). It has also been called the "mental simulation of motor behaviour" (Decety & Ingvar, 1990) and "motor imagery" (Decety & Michel, 1989). A selection of practical "scripts" and guidelines for mental practice is provided by Dalloway (1992), Korn (1994), Miller (1994) and Vealey & Walter (1993).

Strictly speaking, a distinction may be drawn between "mental practice" and "imagery rehearsal" (Murphy, 1994). The former term is generic and refers to the use of any form of cognitive activity (e.g. instructional self-talk; see Chapter 6) to facilitate the covert rehearsal of a task or skill. For example, Meyers, Schleser, Cooke, & Cuvillier (1979) used a mental rehearsal intervention programme with gymnasts which included not only visualisation of specific skills but also a series of encouraging self-statements. However, the term "imagery rehearsal" refers more narrowly to the use of mental imagery as the primary technique for achieving mental practice. Therefore, as imagery is a multi-sensory experience, "mental practice" involves the people "seeing", "hearing" and "feeling" themselves performing a given skill in their imagination. For present purposes, however, as these two terms "mental practice" and "imagery rehearsal" are used as synonyms in the research literature (McLean & Richardson, 1994), I shall also use them interchangeably.

HISTORY OF RESEARCH ON MENTAL PRACTICE

Although it may appear to be a modern discovery, the phenomenon of mental practice (MP) has been explored for over a century (see Isaac & Marks, 1992). For example, Wiggins (1984) referred to a series of studies of mental practice in gymnastics which were conducted by Anderson between 1897–1898 (Anderson, 1899). Furthermore, towards the end of the last century, James (1890) observed that, through imaginative anticipation, people can learn to skate in the summer and to swim in winter. During that era, various expressions of the "ideo-motor principle" (which stated that thoughts have muscular concomitants) were also evident. For example, in 1899 Beaunis (cited in Washburn, 1916) suggested that "it is well known that the idea of a movement suffices to produce the movement or make it tend to be produced". Similarly, Carpenter (1894) proposed that low-level neural impulses are produced during imagined movement and that these impulse are identical in nature (but lower in amplitude) to those emitted in actual movement. Jacobson (1932) obtained some empirical support for this idea when he found that when subjects were asked to imagine contracting their right arms, low-level muscular activity was detectable. Unfortunately, as a result of the Behaviourist manifesto (Watson, 1913) which attacked "mentalistic" constructs such as imagery, the embryonic research topic of mental practice perished. Indeed, it was not until the 1960s that the first comprehensive reviews of this field emerged (Richardson, 1967a; Richardson, 1967b). Fortunately, this decade, which witnessed the first textbook of cognitive psychology (Neisser, 1967) also heralded the advent of objective techniques for the measurement of mental imagery abilities (e.g. see Moran, 1993; Shepard & Metzler, 1971). Since then, research interest in mental practice has grown enormously. Accordingly, over the last 30 years, hundreds of studies have been published on the relationship between mental imagery and skilled performance.

The typical research paradigm used in research on mental practice compares the pre- and post - treatment performance of various groups of subjects (Feltz & Landers, 1983). Four groups are typically used. In particular, these involve people who have only physically practised the skill in question (the "physical practice" group, PP); those who have mentally practised it (the "mental practice" group, MP); those who have alternately physically and mentally practised it (PP/MP); and, finally, people who have been engaged in some placebo control condition. Usually, subjects are randomly assigned to one of these conditions after completion of some pre-treatment test (baseline) on a given motor task or sport skill. Typical instructions for the mental practice conditions require subjects to sit quietly, without moving, and to "see", "hear" and "feel" themselves performing a target skill. After the treatments, participants' performance on this skill is tested again. If the performance of the MP group exceeds that of the control group, a "positive" effect of mental practice is imputed. Unfortunately, the vast majority of studies on MP have used relatively simple target tasks (such as dart throwing or mirror tracing) rather than complex sport skills such as tennis serving or rugby place-kicking. Another limitation of published research in this area is the relative paucity of field studies (Isaac, 1992). I shall return to this issue later.

So far, I have argued that MP effects on skilled performance can be demonstrated reliably. But are these effects really due to *practice*? Is it not possible that they reflect motivational processes? It may be that people are encouraged to perform well once they have visualised themselves achieving a successful outcome. As Kavanagh (1987) suggested, the act of envisaging a successful performance may serve as an incentive or reinforcer, thereby increasing the probability of the imagined event. Thus an athlete who daydreams of success may be receiving self-generated encouragement during long training periods where "objective incentives and reinforcements are likely to be rare or improbable" (Paivio, 1985). This motivational explanation of MP comes from the view (see Paivio, 1985) that mental imagery serves both *affective* (e.g. motivational) as well as cognitive functions. Thus it could be argued that the mechanisms by which visualisation works are *affective* rather than cognitive in nature. So perhaps MP improves performance by either enhancing the performer's expectation of success or by lowering their fear of failure (McLean & Richardson, 1994). Some support for this position comes from a recent study by Martin & Hall (1995) which found that imagery use helped novice golfers to persist longer than a control group on a golf putting task. However, a purely motivational interpretation of MP has been challenged by several scholars. For example, Nigro (1983) found that attempts to manipulate the motivation of the performer had no effects on the efficacy of imaginary rehearsal on dart-throwing. More convincingly, Finke (1979) reported that people who imagined themselves pointing at visual targets while wearing laterally displacing prisms showed the same after-effects as when they had actually pointed with the prisms. This directional bias in executing the adapted movements cannot be explained by motivational factors.

In passing, one interesting and perhaps ironic trend in recent research on mental rehearsal (given the fact that imagery was anathema to Watson, 1913) has been the attempt by behaviourists to conceptualise it as a form of "covert conditioning". For example, Cautela (1993) referred to athletes' use of this procedure as "imagaletics". The significance of behaviourists' interest in imagery processes is that in future, we may consider mental images as something which people do (i.e. engaging in covert "simulation" of overt actions) rather than as something which people *possess* (e.g. we often speak of "*having* a vivid imagination").

DOES MENTAL PRACTICE WORK?
CLAIMS AND EVIDENCE

At the outset, we should realise that although physical practice is by far the oldest performance-enhancement strategy used by athletes, it has begun to be supplemented in recent years by the covert or cognitive rehearsal that is achieved using mental imagery (Hird, Landers, Thomas, & Horan, 1991). This development explains why world-class athletes such as the sprinter Linford Christie (Britain), the long-jumper Mike Powell (USA) and the American tennis players Andre Agassi and Jim Courier are enthusiastic advocates of mental imagery as a means of preparing for competition (Perry & Morris, 1995). More generally, mental practice has been especially useful when opportunities to engage in physical practice are curtailed by time constraints, fatigue or injury. For example, according to Suinn (1994), Jean Claude Killy, the three-times Olympic champion alpine skier, had one of his best ever performances in a race for which he had prepared only by *mental* rehearsal (due to an injury). Increasingly, therefore, sport coaches are using mental imagery programmes as a routine part of their training regimes for athletes (McLean & Richardson, 1994). Incidentally, it is important to point out that contemporary psychology offers surprisingly few theories which can explain adequately why *physical* practice serves to improve skilled performance—even though this finding has been virtually unquestioned for at least a century (Ericsson, Krampe, & Tesch-Romer, 1993).

The cornerstone of MP research is the proposition that the controlled use of mental imagery may affect subsequent actions. This idea of a bridge between the phenomenal world of intentions and the physical world of actions is simultaneously paradoxical yet familiar. On the one hand, the paradox concerns the possibility that a cognitive process (i.e. mental imagery), which does not involve motor effectors directly, can have a significant impact on motor performance. As Denis (1985) reminded us, imagery is a cognitive activity that is essentially subjective whereas motor behaviour is largely publicly observable. But most contemporary motor learning researchers (with the exception of "natural physical" theorists such as Davids, Handford, & Williams, 1994) believe that actions are controlled by centrally-stored cognitive representations such as mental images. In other words, motor control is primarily a cognitive process. Thus Heuer (1989) suggests that rules may be identified by which visuo-spatial and kinaesthetic representations of movements are transformed into motor commands. Accordingly, the paradox is not intractable—there is nothing essentially mysterious about mental practice. On the other hand, the familiarity of mental rehearsal is evident from the fact that we often use imagery to anticipate our actions and to plan motor movements in daily life. For example, we may employ mental imagery to help us to decide whether or not a sofa will fit through a door in our house before we attempt to move it from one room to another. Or we may rehearse imaginatively what we wish to do or say in a forthcoming meeting with someone we perceive to be important (see Kosslyn, Seger, Pani, & Hillger, 1990, for details of how people use imagery in daily life). In both of these cases, we are visualising intended actions in order to solve a practical problem. This is why the basketball star Michael Jordan uses mental imagery when preparing for anticipated match situations (see quotation at the beginning of this chapter). But what other problem situations in the world of sport elicit imagery use by athletes? I shall return to this question later.

Although mental practice has spawned much theoretical debate (e.g. Jeannerod, 1994), its appeal to sport psychologists lies mainly in its practical utility as a performance-enhancement strategy for athletes. Indeed, on occasions, mental practice of sport skills has been deemed *superior* to traditional physical practice because it offers "complete control over environmental conditions as well as performance outcomes" (Hinshaw, 1991–1992). More generally, at least three strands of evidence suggest that mental practice is very useful to athletes. This evidence is derived from anecdotal, correlational and experimental sources.

First, interviews and anecdotal reports suggest that sport stars such as Jack Nicklaus (golf), Dwight Stones (high-jump), Jim Courier (tennis), Michael Jordan (basketball), Jean-Claude Killy (skier) and Nancy Kerrigan (figure-skating) prepare for forthcoming competition by "seeing" and "feeling" themselves performing key actions successfully in their "mind's eye" beforehand (Janssen & Sheikh, 1994). To illustrate, consider some typical insights into imagery use among world-class athletes. For example, Dwight Stones, the 1984 Olympic champion high-jumper, remarked that "my success in the jump was directly related to the image of my body clearing the bar" (cited in Ungerleider & Golding, 1991). Also, consider the case of Greg Louganis (the former Olympic diving champion). When he dived in the qualifying round of the 1988 Olympics, he hit his head on the board as he was descending. But he did not watch the video playback of this incident simply because he was afraid that it would induce him to form a vivid "negative" mental image which could upset his subsequent performance. As he said, "I didn't want that image in my head going into the competition. I don't want the visual image of seeing me hit my head" (Bartlett, 1994). Other professional athletes have been haunted by "negative" visualisation. For example, David Leadbetter, the famous golf coach, commenting on the decline in performance of Ian Baker-Finch, revealed that this player "tells me that when he stands up there he has a mental image of disaster. Half-way down the swing a picture comes into his mind that he'll either hit it out of bounds or even miss it altogether" (cited in Edmondson, 1995, p. 8). This tendency to form "detrimental" images may be accentuated by the proclivity of coaches to tell their athletes "what *not* to do" rather than "what" precisely is required (Rodgers, Hall, & Buckolz, 1991). Interestingly, this experience parallels an important principle in research on "mental control" (Wegner & Pennebaker, 1993), namely, the idea that the content of unwanted thoughts and/or images is difficult to suppress. Evidence to support this conclusion comes from research by Wegner, Schneider, Carter, & White (1987). Apparently, when Russian novelist Dostoyevsky was young, he used to torment his brother by requesting him not to think of a white bear. Wegner, Schneider, Carter, & White (1987), in a laboratory study of this phenomenon, found that suppression of this thought proved to be extremely difficult. Worse than that, there was a "rebound" effect with reports than an initial suppression of the unwanted thought gave rise to a later recall of it. In summary, there is growing evidence that people cannot easily eliminate unwanted thoughts from their minds. Further evidence to support Louganis' reluctance to engage in "negative" visualisation emerges from studies which show that the type of image "outcome" (i.e. success or failure) may affect skilled performance. Specifically, Woolfolk, Parrish, & Murphy (1985) found that an experimental group which had received a "negative imagery" treatment performed worse than either a "positive imagery" group or a control group. Commenting on this finding, Murphy (1994) claims that it indicates that positive imagery rehearsal may "prevent attentional capacity from being devoted to negative images—thereby maintaining consistent performance". A similar finding was reported by Budney & Woolfolk (1990). Interestingly, there is some evidence that the detrimental effect of negative mental imagery is stronger than the benefits of positive imagery (Janssen & Sheikh, 1994). Another testimonial to the utility of visualisation was provided by the US Masters' champion golfer Nick Faldo—but for helicopter flying rather than golf! In particular, he described how he used mental practice to improve his flying skills: "I found that when flying the machine with the instructor, I just could not bring the helicopter down. I could not land it. I went off to a golf tournament but every day until the next lesson, *I took time off in the privacy of my room to spend 10 minutes simulating in my mind how to land the helicopter.* By the time the next lesson came around, I discovered that not only was I an expert in landing it in theory, I could suddenly land it in reality too. I conquered the mental block" (Laidlaw, 1993, p. 16). A final illustration of mental rehearsal in action comes from the Chinese gymnast Cai Huanzong: "Every time before I mounted a horse, I would go over in my mind the whole set of exercises to be performed so as to enhance my consciousness of action. I would banish everything from my mind and concentrate on my performance...In this way, I was able to stand the strains of competition with an unruffled mind" (cited in Dalloway, 1993, p. 4).

A second source of evidence on the importance of visualisation comes from survey research on how athletes perceive and use mental imagery in their training and competitive activities. For example, several studies have documented the frequency with which imagery is used by athletes. To begin with, Hemery (1988) found that 80% of a sample of the world's top athletes considered visualisation to be a vital performance- enhancement technique. Next, Ungerleider & Golding (1991) reported that 85% of their large (n=633) sample of prospective US Olympic athletes reported using imagery techniques routinely as part of their training. Even more dramatically, Orlick & Partington (1988) discovered that 99% of a sample of elite athletes claimed to use imagery techniques regularly. Next, Moran (1995) found that visualisation was rated by expert tennis coaches as being the second most valuable mental technique (behind self-talk) for improving performance "on court". Other surveys of sport experts have confirmed the perceived utility of imagery. For example, in a survey of athletes who trained at the US Olympic Training Centre in Colorado Springs, Murphy, Jowdy, & Durtschi (1989) discovered that 90% of athletes reported using imagery as part of their training for competition. Furthermore, 97% of these athletes rated visualisation as an extremely effective performance-enhancement technique. Focusing on one sport only, Barr & Hall (1992) devised a questionnaire to measure the extent to which competitive rowers used mental imagery. One finding which emerged from this study was that expert rowers tended to rely more on kinaesthetic imagery than did relative novices. For example, the former reported imaging the "feel" of the blade in the water or certain bodily movements more frequently than their less proficient counterparts. In a similar vein, other researchers have reported evidence that imagery use among athletes is directly related to their level of expertise. Thus Hall, Rodgers, & Barr (1990) found that the higher the level at which athletes competed, the more likely they were to use some form of mental imagery as a preparatory strategy. An interesting interpretation of this finding has been proposed by McLean & Richardson (1994). These researchers suggest that among expert athletes, where little technical improvement is possible, visualisation may serve a *transfer* function. Specifically, for the elite athlete, with highly established skills, "the positive effect of mental practice may have to do with maximising the transfer of skills from practice to performance". I shall discuss this issue later when considering possible explanations of mental practice effects. Taken together, these surveys of athletes' views and practices indicate that mental imagery is both widely used and highly valued as a performance enhancement technique in sport.

In view of the perceived utility of imagery, therefore, athletes employ visualisation for many different purposes. For example, Orlick (1990) explains that performers use imagery to "prepare themselves to get what they want out of training, to perfect skills within training sessions, to make technical corrections, to imagine themselves succeeding in competition, and to strengthen their belief in their capacity to achieve their ultimate goal". Some examples of these applications follow. To begin with, MP can be used for instructional purposes: To acquire, sharpen, rehearse or to transfer motor skills (Budney, Murphy, & Woolfolk, 1994). For example, mental practice can help learners to rehearse movements for the performance of such "closed skills" as the golf drive or the squash serve. In the case of the former, a leading touring professional golfer claimed that "I feel the execution of the shot, see the target area, visualise the entire sequence" (McCaffrey & Orlick, 1989). In the case of the latter, Annett (1985) explained how a squash coach used the vivid image of a "Red Indian on the warpath waving a tomahawk" to teach novice players a suitable stance for receiving a service. Second, imagery can help athletes to cope effectively with stressful situations in sport (Rishe, Krenz, McQueen, & Krenz, 1994). For example, Gould, Finch, & Jackson (1993) discovered that champion figure-skaters used mental rehearsal as an anxiety-management technique. Thus one skater reported that "I did a lot of visualisation ... It's a coping strategy ... It just gives you a calmer, ... more serene way". In this case, MP can play a "desensitisation" (Wolpe, 1958) function. To explain, athletes can be "counter-conditioned" to produce relaxation responses in situations which would otherwise evoke anxiety. Third, visualisation can be used to counteract the "warm-up decrement" (i.e. the deterioration in motor performance which usually follows a period of rest and which usually disappears with practice of the criterion skill; Adams, 1987) which can have potentially fatal consequences in such sports as gymnastics. Fourth, imagery can be used to enhance self-efficacy. Thus Feltz & Reissinger (1990) found that visualisation can enhance self-confidence in athletes. Next, MP can be used to regulate arousal levels (Budney, Murphy, & Woolfolk, 1994). Another alleged application of MP is for concentration-enhancement (Korn, 1994; Vealey & Walter, 1993). For example, Meyers & Schleser (1980) used imagery as part of an intervention programme for a basketball player who suffered from concentration problems. The efficacy of this programme was apparent in improvements in such indices as points per game and field goal percentage. Other applications of mental rehearsal (e.g. for the rehabilitation of injured athletes) are discussed by Hale (1994). Incidentally, it seems that athletes use imagery more frequently before competition than in training (Hall, Rodgers, & Barr, 1990).

Perhaps the strongest evidence confirming the value of mental practice for athletes comes from controlled empirical studies of the role of imagery in improving the performance of motor skills. In general, "closed" skills (see Chapter 5) have attracted more interest from MP researchers than have "open" skills (i.e. skills in which the performer has to react to opponents and changing environmental demands). However, many researchers have extracted "closed" components (e.g. the tennis serve and the basketball "free throw") from "open" sports. From such research, mental rehearsal has been shown to improve the performance of such sport skills as golf putting, dart throwing, tennis serving (see McLean & Richardson, 1994), pistol-shooting (Hall & Hardy, 1991) and in various aspects of gymnastics, karate, basketball, soccer, ice-hockey and golf (Rishe, Krenz, McQueen, & Krenz, 1994). More recently, however, mental practice has been explored as a technique for improving "reactive" skills which depend on counteracting an opponent's movements. For example, execution of the tackle in rugby (McKenzie & Howe, 1991) and the counter-attacking forehand in table-tennis (Lejeune, Decker, & Sanchez, 1994) have been found to benefit from mental rehearsal.

In summary, evidence to support the value of mental practice to sport performers comes from anecdotal reports, survey research and controlled empirical studies. However, although visualisation has appealed most dramatically to athletes, it has also attracted the attention of musicians (Ross, 1985) and military trainers (e.g. see Druckman & Swets, 1988; Regan & Franklin, 1994) interested in performance enhancement. Indeed, in 1992, the US Army Research Institute co-sponsored a conference on "Imagery and Motor Processes" in Britain (see Annett, 1992). Other client populations for which mental rehearsal effects have been found include the elderly, the mentally handicapped and people with neurological conditions (see Surburg, 1989). In addition, mental practice effects have been reported for congenitally blind children (Miller & Ittyerah, 1991).

EFFICACY OF MENTAL PRACTICE: CONCLUSIONS AND CAUTIONS

Evidence to support the efficacy of mental practice as a psychological technique for performance-enhancement comes from both anecdotal and scientific sources. I have already mentioned some of the anecdotal testimonials to the power of visualisation. Of course, such evidence is potentially biased due to its retrospective and selective nature (see Brewer, Van Raalte, Linder, & Van Raalte, 1991). However, a stronger source of evidence in support of mental practice effects comes from the scientific research literature. In particular, both narrative and meta-analytic reviews of laboratory and field studies of MP have been conducted by researchers such as Driskell, Copper, & Moran (1994),

Feltz & Landers (1983), Grouios (1992), Hinshaw (1991–1992), Howe (1991), Murphy & Jowdy (1992), Murphy (1994), Onestak (1991) and Perry & Morris (1995). In general, these reviewers agree that, under designated circumstances, mental practice can improve significantly the learning and performance of motor (including sport) skills. Oddly enough, however, relatively few field studies have been conducted on MP in athletes. For example, out of 146 visualisation studies reviewed by Feltz & Landers (1983), 128 used novice subjects. Clearly, additional research is required to explore MP effects in expert athletes. Also, there is a dearth of longitudinal research in this area. These oversights are disappointing in view of the possibility that the benefits of imagery training may take some time to emerge (Budney, Murphy, & Woolfolk, 1994). However, from preceding reviews of MP effects, the following conclusions appear to be warranted.

First, MP seems to have a moderate yet significant effect on skilled performance. More precisely, mental imagery improves performance somewhat less effectively than does actual physical practice but better than not practising at all. To illustrate, the meta-analytic review by Driskell, Copper, & Moran (1994) indicated that physical practice (PP) treatment conditions produced greater "effect sizes" than was evident in mental practice (MP) conditions. Indeed, the latter statistics were greater than those found with placebo controls. Statistically, the relative effect sizes of physical practice and mental practice were estimated by these authors as 0.382 and 0.261 (both Fisher's Z), respectively. But as Driskell, Copper, & Moran (1994) noted, it is not really surprising that MP seems to be less effective than PP. After all, MP does not offer the performer the same type of feedback (e.g. kinaesthetic sensations or knowledge of results of task performance) that they would derive from physically performing it. However, McLean & Richardson (1994) suggest that kinaesthetic imagery could provide feedback to performers. They cite evidence (see Henderson, 1975) which supports anecdotal reports that expert athletes "know" quickly whether a performance will be successful or not from the "feel" of the shot. For example, top golfers will often express disgust at a poor drive immediately after they make contact with the ball—long before it reaches the ground. This phenomenon suggests that expert athletes probably rely more on kinaesthetic feedback (e.g. from bodily position and tactile imagery) than on visual feedback (e.g. from knowledge of where a shot landed) when judging the quality of their own performance. For example, Brian Orser, the men's world champion figure-skater in 1987, claimed that "my imagery is more just feel. I don't think it's visual at all. I get this internal feeling. When I'm actually doing this skill on the ice, I get the same feeling inside" (cited in Orlick, 1990, p. 68). Not surprisingly, Henderson (1975) found that expert dart players could predict accurately the landing point of their throws—even when the flight of the dart and its point of impact were occluded completely (see Chapter 3 for discussion of related issues). To explain this result, McLean & Richardson (1994) argue that a combination of kinaesthetic imagery and implicit "visual" knowledge are capable of providing the "feedback" which mental practice yields to performers.

Second, it is believed that mental rehearsal, when combined and alternated with physical practice, tends to produce superior skill learning to that resulting from either mental or physical practice conducted alone (Corbin, 1972). However, this conclusion was challenged by Hird, Landers, Thomas, & Horan (1991) who investigated the effects of different ratios of physical to mental practice. Results showed that the combined imagery and physical practice were not superior to that produced by physical practice alone. With regard to sport skills, Mackay (1981) suggested that MP cannot substitute adequately for physical practice unless the performer has previously practised the skill physically. Perhaps physical practice helps athletes to acquire detailed muscular patterns whereas mental practice operates on the higher cognitive representation of the skill.

Third, although mental practice is effective for different kinds of actions, it appears (see evidence in Feltz & Landers, 1983) to improve the performance of "cognitive" tasks (i.e. those in which perceptual and sequencing skills are required—such as in pegboard, maze learning and mirror drawing tasks) more significantly than for "motor" or "physical" skills (e.g. balancing on a "stabilometer" or platform on which subjects are required to stand). Thus Ryan & Simons (1981) found that visualisation improved performance on a maze learning task but not on one involving balancing on a stabilometer. But what is a "cognitive" task? According to Hinshaw (1991–1992), it is one in which the performer is concerned primarily with sequential processing or co-ordinating actions in time (e.g. making "action plans") rather than with the execution of motor responses. For example, in maze learning, the subject has to master a sequence of choices. But we assume that they have already learned the motor components of this task (i.e. grasping or reaching). However, Hall, Schmidt, Durand, & Buckolz (1994) argued that the cognitive requirements of a task may vary as a function of the level of expertise of the performer. For example, whereas a novice performer may struggle with the motor requirements of a task, "the expert is concentrating on the strategy and tactics" of the performance. We should also note that most motor learning researchers (e.g. Schmidt, 1975) regard "cognitive" and "motor" tasks as being located at opposite ends of a continuum rather than as being mutually exclusive categories.

Next, there is evidence of an interaction between level of expertise and task type (Driskell, Copper, & Moran, 1994). To explain, expert athletes tend to benefit more from MP than do novices, regardless of task type (i.e. "cognitive" or "physical"). For example, Isaac (1992) found that experienced trampoliners benefited more from visualisation than did relative beginners. But the benefit of MP for novices seems to be confined more to "cognitive" than to "physical" activities (Driskell, Copper, & Moran, 1994).

Another finding is that the positive effects of MP on task performance tend to decline sharply over time. For example, according to Driskell, Copper, & Moran (1994), the beneficial effects of visualisation are reduced to half of their original value after approximately two weeks of time has elapsed. Obviously, this finding suggests that in order to gain optimal benefits from mental practice, "refresher" training should be implemented after this critical two-week period.

Finally, there are indications that imagery ability mediates the relationship between MP and motor skill performance (McLean & Richardson, 1994). Specifically, Weinberg (1982) claimed that athletes who display special skills in generating and controlling vivid images tend to benefit more from visualisation programmes than do those who lack such abilities. It seems plausible that the more "realistic" and multi-sensory one's mental image of a skill is, the more beneficial one's visualisation should be for subsequent physical performance. Although there has been some empirical support for this contention (e.g. Mahoney & Avener, 1977), additional research is required to establish precisely what happens when vivid and "weak" imagers (measured by standard psychometric scales of imagery vividness and control; see Moran, 1993) participate in identical programmes of MP. At present, only anecdotal evidence is available on this issue. To illustrate, Clark (1960) offered a much-quoted insight about a basketball player who suffered from inability to control a "negative" mental image. In this case, the player reported "mentally attempting to bounce the ball, preparatory to shooting, only to imagine that it would not bounce and stuck to the floor. This disturbed him to a point where he could not successfully visualise the shooting technique" (p. 567). This insight resembles the paradoxical finding from experimental psychology that the more people attempt to suppress an image which has been deliberately evoked in their minds (e.g. a "white bear"), the more intrusive it actually becomes (see Wegner, Schneider, Carter, & White, 1987). Sometimes, this inability to control one's mental imagery may be attributable to physical skill deficiencies. For example, Jowdy & Harris (1990) discovered that when subjects with "low" juggling skills were asked to visualise themselves juggling, they often reported difficulties in controlling the resultant images. Thus one participant reported that "I couldn't really focus on my arms moving and the balls at the same time".

Of course, we must be careful to avoid drawing cavalier conclusions from the preceding research findings. After all, a host of intervening variables in MP research have been identified. These factors include such key variables as the nature of the task or skill to be performed, the content of the imagery instructions provided, the duration of the imagery intervention employed, the extent of the performer's previous experience with the task, the performer's imagery abilities (see Moran, 1993, for a review of relevant measures), the level of expertise of the performer, the type of imagery perspective adopted (i.e. "internal" or "external") and the imagery outcome (i.e. success or failure) visualised (see Hinshaw, 1991–1992). Ideally, these variables should be either measured or controlled in MP research designs as they have been shown to affect treatment outcomes (Hinshaw, 1991–1992). For example, measures of movement imagery (such as the Movement Imagery Questionnaire, MIQ; Hall, Pongrac, & Buckolz, 1985) should be included in MP studies of sport skills (e.g. rowing, figure-skating) for which kinaesthetic factors are known to be important. Unfortunately, such methodological rigour is rarely apparent in MP studies (Murphy, 1994). In addition, another serious problem, which I shall call the "validation issue", confronts researchers in this field. How can we be sure that participants in MP research are actually using mental imagery? Recall that in Chapter 3, I indicated that athletes' retrospective reports about their own mental processes are not always reliable (Brewer, Van Raalte, Linder, & Van Raalte, 1991). Indeed, there is evidence that participants in imagery studies do not always follow imagery scripts (Jowdy & Harris, 1990). Therefore, despite the compelling quotations at the beginning of this chapter, we cannot accept data yielded by self-reports from athletes as conclusive evidence of imagery use.

Surprisingly, the "validation issue" has not been addressed explicitly by researchers of mental practice. This neglect is probably attributable to the fact that in order to validate athletes' reports of their alleged imagery experiences, sport psychologists require an experimental procedure for "tracking" imagery-related behaviour. But such a procedure presumes a comprehensive theoretical understanding of the cognitive and behavioural functions of imagery. Unfortunately, due to the atheoretical nature of most MP studies (Jowdy & Harris, 1990), the issue of validating athletes' imagery reports remains unresolved. However, in a recent paper, Moran (1994b) suggested that "functional equivalence" theories of imagery (e.g. Kosslyn & Koenig, 1992) may offer a possible solution to this problem. Briefly, these theories assume that imagery is a covert simulation of perceptual experiences and that as a consequence, imagery and perception share certain processing resources. This assumption is endorsed by Groden, Cautela, Le Vaseur, Groden, & Bausman (1991) who claimed that when someone is visualising, they are "responding to the absence of an external stimulus as if the stimulus were present". If imagery and perception are "functionally equivalent", then interference effects (e.g. increased errors and latency of responses) should occur when people are required to perform concurrent tasks involving imagery and perception in the same modality. Therefore, in principle, athletes' imagery reports could be validated experimentally by using a sport-specific modification of this interference paradigm (which is a variation of the "dual task" paradigm; see Chapter 5).

Pending resolution of the "validation issue", there appears to be abundant evidence that mental practice (MP) enhances skilled performance under certain circumstances. But when we examine this evidence more closely, we discover that it is derived more frequently from controlled studies of laboratory tasks (e.g. pursuit rotor performance) than from analyses of sport performance in real-life settings. In fact, as Isaac (1992) has noted, few MP studies "were conducted in actual field contexts using subjects who learned actual sport skills under the same conditions and time periods in which sports activities are typically taught". Accordingly, the efficacy of mental practice on sport skills performed in field situations is not fully established. This neglect of field research on visualisation suggests that we should treat the preceding findings cautiously.

THEORIES OF MENTAL PRACTICE EFFECTS

Why does "playing in one's head" often lead to improvements in one's skilled performance? Although number of theories have been proposed during the past fifty years (see reviews by Budney, Murphy, & Woolfolk, 1994; Murphy, 1994), the precise mechanisms which underlie MP effects are still unclear. This disappointing situation is attributable mainly to the fact that most MP studies are "one-shot", atheoretical variations of a standard experimental paradigm (described earlier in this chapter) rather than explicit hypothesis-testing investigations. Not surprisingly, this problem has been identified by several researchers as a major impediment to progress in this field. For example, Adams (1990) complained that "theory is not well articulated among investigators of mental practice". Also, Jowdy & Harris (1990) remarked that visualisation research "has primarily been atheoretical" and Murphy &

Jowdy (1992) stated that "the development of theoretical models to explain the mechanisms underlying the imagery effect has progressed slowly". Finally, Hird, Landers, Thomas, & Horan (1991) concluded that "future research needs to evaluate the underlying mechanisms of how mental practice affects performance". Despite the relative dearth of theoretical research in this field, at least two approaches have been adopted to explain MP effects (Murphy & Jowdy, 1992). These approaches postulate either a "bottom up" (e.g. "psycho neuromuscular") or a "top down" (cognitive, "symbolic") models of mental rehearsal. These rival approaches may be characterised as follows.

Neuromuscular (or "peripherally-based"; see Murphy & Jowdy, 1992) accounts of mental practice (e.g. Jacobson, 1932) suggest that visualisation causes faint "innervations" to occur in the muscles that are actually used in the physical performance of the skill being rehearsed. Accordingly, Vealey & Walter (1993) advocate that the term "muscle memory" should be used to refer to this theory when introducing mental rehearsal techniques to athletes. The "subliminal" muscular activity allegedly evoked by imagery is held to be similar to, but of a lower magnitude than, that produced by actual physical execution of the movements involved in the skill. For example, Shaw (1940) reported that, during imagined weight lifting, electromyographic (EMG) activity of forearm muscles increased linearly with the magnitude of the weight elevated. Furthermore, the tiny efferent discharge generated during imagery is held to provide kinaesthetic feedback to the learner, thereby strengthening the controlling motor program. In short, neuromuscular theories claim that imaginary rehearsal of a skill "primes" appropriate motor pathways. Clearly, the most convincing evidence in support of this theory would be the discovery that there is a consistent positive relationship between the muscular activity elicited by imagery of a given skill and subsequent performance. But as we shall see, such evidence is missing. In fact, Decety, Jeannerod, Durozard, & Baverel (1993) used nuclear magnetic resonance (NMR) spectroscopy to study the muscles involved during imagined effort. Unfortunately, no change in muscular metabolic indices was detected. This absence of overt muscular activity during mental simulation of exercise is difficult to explain using a neuromuscular theory of mental practice.

By contrast, cognitive (or "centrally-based"; Murphy & Jowdy, 1992) theories of visualisation suggest that imagery enhances the ability of the performer to code symbolically key elements of the skill being rehearsed (e.g. Sackett, 1934). Evidence to support this theory comes from research which showed that bilateral transfer of learning occurred even when the training task (involving the contra-lateral limb) was performed using mental imagery (Kohl & Roenker, 1980). Let us now provide a brief sketch of the current status of these two theories (see Murphy, 1994; Suinn, 1993, for more detailed reviews).

Physiological theories of mental practice

The earliest theories of mental rehearsal (e.g. Carpenter, 1894; Washburn, 1916) proposed that slight localised (peripheral) neuro-muscular efferent patterns or muscle movements were evident when a person imagined the performance of physical activity. An early proponent of this "neuromuscular feedback" theory was Jacobson (1932) who postulated that mental practice elicits faint electromyographic (EMG) activity in the motor output system which is similar in nature, but weaker in magnitude, to that activation evoked by actual physical performance of the task in question. This muscular activity is thought to provide feedback to the performer. As Corbin (1972) suggested, the innervation in the muscles involved in the skill being imagined "may well be capable of providing kinaesthetic feedback necessary to make adjustments in future trials, thus improving skilled motor performance".

A corollary of this theory is the claim (e.g. by Mahoney & Avener, 1977) that such kinaesthetic feedback is increased when subjects adopt an "internal" rather than an "external" imagery perspective. To illustrate perspective differences in imagery, consider two contrasting types of viewpoint or perspective which a person may adopt when visualising a golf putt. "External" imagery here would involve "watching" oneself performing this skill from the perspective of an outside observer (e.g. as if one were looking at someone performing on this skill on television—a "third person" view). Conversely, an "internal" perspective would entail a simulation of what one would actually experience in all of one's senses if one were physically performing the putt. For example, this might entail "seeing" the ball in front of oneself and "feeling" the muscular movements involved in the execution of the putting stroke. In other words, an "internal" imagery perspective entails a simulation of the kinaesthetic sensations which would be experienced by the performer. By implication, the "internal" imagery should enhance the performance of "postural" skills (e.g. gymnastics) which depend on kinaesthetic processes. However, in a recent test of this hypothesis, White & Hardy (1995) discovered that external visual imagery was more effective for subjects than was internal imagery in learning a gymnastics routine. This counter-intuitive finding serves as a timely caution to researchers to avoid drawing premature conclusions from this field.

Unfortunately, empirical support for neuromuscular theories of MP is sparse and inconsistent (Feltz & Landers, 1983). In short, there is no convincing evidence that the presence of faint muscular activity during mental practice of a skill is either similar to that recorded during overt performance of that skill or is related to the accuracy of skilled performance. For example, although EMG activity has been detected in the mental rehearsal of alpine skiers (Suinn, 1972), it is not clear whether this muscular activity is related to the specific muscles used in actual performance of this sport or is simply an epiphenomenal artifact of generalised arousal. For example, Shaw (1938) found that increased EMG activity during motor imagery was distributed across a variety of muscle groups in the body, including some which were not related to the imagined action. This finding indicates that the muscular innervations elicited by imagery may reflect generalised arousal processes. Similarly, the claim that this neuromuscular programming is facilitated by a kinaesthetically-driven, "internal" imagery perspective has been contested by subsequent researchers (e.g. Glisky & Williams, 1993; Mumford & Hall, 1985). For example, Epstein (1980) reported no significant differences between the dart-throwing performances of people who had adopted either an internal or an external imagery perspective for this task. However, the inconsistency of research findings on this issue may be explained, in part, by the presence of a crucial confounding variable, namely, the level of expertise of the performer. To explain, it has been suggested (Smith, 1987) that whereas novices may rely more on external than internal imagery when learning a skill, the converse obtains for more expert performers. As Howe (1991) explained, novice sport performers may rely on a visual (or "third person") representation of a motor action whereas experts may use "first person" kinaesthetic images. In other words, the development of sporting expertise may parallel the progressive "internalisation" of mental representations of the skills involved. Interestingly, this theory may help to explain why so many expert athletes place such great importance on developing appropriate "feel" in their sport. This point has been recognised by Murphy (1994) who explains "the importance of kinaesthetic awareness to sports performance". This kinaesthetic awareness is often called "muscle memory" by athletes and coaches. Third, neuromuscular theories suggest that the effects of MP should be greater for "physical" tasks (which are expected to produce more muscular "innervations") than for cognitive ones. Unfortunately, this prediction is not supported empirically: The effects of MP are *stronger* for cognitive than for physical tasks (Driskell, Copper, & Moran, 1994). Finally, contrary to predictions from neuromuscular theory, Jowdy & Harris (1990) found no significant differences in the magnitude of muscular activity between highly-skilled and less proficient jugglers. In summary, neuromuscular theories of mental practice have received relatively little empirical support.

Despite their shortcomings, however, neuromuscular theories of MP have been disseminated widely through commercial versions of mental rehearsal programmes. For example, "visual learning" tapes (Yandell, 1990) and the SyberVision programmes (evaluated recently by Austin & Miller, 1992) are based on the neuromuscular proposition that repeated viewing of videotaped mental practice exercises will lead to a strengthening of relevant neural pathways in the brain.

Overall, the empirical evidence gathered to date is inadequate to justify firm support for neuromuscular theories of MP. Two problems are especially prevalent in this regard. First, causal inferences cannot be derived validly from the correlational data (e.g. electromyographic and performance scores) which abound in this field. As Murphy & Jowdy (1992) concluded, "evidence to support a relationship between muscular activity during mental practice and subsequent performance in the sport-related literature has yet to be obtained". Second, some important predictions of neuromuscular theories of MP have not been confirmed. For example, Jowdy & Harris (1990) did not find expected differences between the (imaginary) muscular activity elicited in expert and novice athletes. In summary, it appears that "there exists relatively little support for psychoneuromuscular explanations of imagery's effect on motor performance" (Budney, Murphy, & Woolfolk, 1994).

Cognitive theories of mental practice

Cognitive (or "symbolic") accounts of visualisation postulate that mental practice facilitates the coding and rehearsal of key elements of the task. As Johnson (1982) suggested, "imagining movements which are already encoded in memory has the effect of consolidating the memory for that movement". Therefore, Vealey & Walter (1993) recommend that the term "mental blueprint" should be used when psychologists introduce cognitive accounts of mental rehearsal to athletes in practical settings.

One of the pioneers of this cognitive approach was Sackett (1934) who discovered that people's performance on a finger-maze task improved following mental rehearsal of the movement patterns involved. This finding was explained by postulating that mental imagery facilitates the symbolic coding of the "ideational representation of the movements involved". For example, a person encountering a finger-maze may rehearse an image of "left, then right, then left again" before beginning the task. Here, it is the cognitive system which is primarily involved in learning the appropriate movement sequence (McLean & Richardson, 1994). A similar theory was offered by Annett (1985) who referred to the possibility that visualisation helps performers to represent "critical and invariant elements of the plan" of a given task. The possibility that MP facilitates planning is also suggested by motor learning theorists such as Schmidt (1988) who speculated that during mental rehearsal, "the learner can think about what kinds of things might be tried, the consequences of each action can be predicted ... and the learner can perhaps rule out inappropriate courses of action".

In cognitive theories of MP, little importance is attached to what happens in the peripheral musculature of the performer. Furthermore, cognitive accounts of visualisation argue that repeated mental rehearsal of symbolic "keys" engenders automaticity of performance. As Murphy & Jowdy (1992) put it, MP "appears to assist the learner in developing a conceptual plan for understanding and organising the task". In summary, therefore, visualisation is deemed to be especially suitable for the learning and performance of tasks which contain many "cognitive" elements (i.e. make demands on sequential processing) such as mirror drawing.

Almost all tasks contain motor and "cognitive" components. But what makes a task cognitively demanding? Usually, what makes a task cognitively difficult is the fact that it requires the performer to learn the precise *sequence* in which a set of motor movements should be displayed. Thus activities like finger-mazes, card-sorting tasks, mirror-drawing and finger-dexterity tests are demanding mentally because they require precise sequencing skills (McLean & Richardson, 1994). In addition to posing demands on sequential abilities, many sport skills require strategic planning. Here, imagery can prove invaluable. To illustrate, former Wimbledon champion Chris Evert used visualisation to plan her match strategy. Thus she claimed that "before I play a match I try to carefully rehearse in my mind what is likely to happen and how I will react in certain situations. I visualise myself playing typical points based on my opponent's style of play" (cited in Weinberg, 1988, p. 99). Clearly, if MP is useful for performing such tasks, then it should also be suitable for the learning and recall of complex movement-sequences in dance, figure skating, synchronised swimming or gymnastics. Some evidence is available to support this hypothesis (e.g. Isaac, 1992; Palmer, 1992). As a corollary of their main assumptions, symbolic theories of MP predict that the greater the number of "cognitive" elements in the task, the more it should be amenable to visualisation. Unfortunately, little empirical evidence has been gathered to test this prediction.

Overall, several sources of evidence support cognitive explanations of mental rehearsal. First, consider recent cognitive research on the nature of mental imagery. Here there is growing evidence that mental images (at least those in the visual modality) rely on the same neural substrates as the images that are generated during normal perception (Jeannerod, 1994). For example, Farah, Peronnet, Gonon, & Giard (1988) discovered that the visual processing areas of the cerebral cortex are activated during visual mental imagery. This type of evidence suggests that mental imagery is "functionally equivalent" to perception. As Finke (1989) explained, the principle of "perceptual equivalence" states that similar mechanisms in the visual system are activated when objects or events are imagined as when the same phenomena are actually perceived. In other words, there are striking similarities between the way in which we generate and manipulate mental images and percepts (Matlin, 1994). For example, the amount of time it takes to "rotate" a mental image in our minds depends on the degree of rotation which would be required if we were to manipulate physically the real objects in question (Shepard & Metzler, 1971). In addition, it has been shown that imagery competes with like-modality perceptual processing (see Craver-Lemley & Reeves, 1992), possibly due to a sharing of common resources (e.g. the "central executive" component of working memory; Phillips & Christie, 1977). The best evidence for this theory comes from research by Brooks (1968) on the relative degree of interference between different pairs of tasks. For example, he found that a task which required visual imagery could be performed more easily while speaking than while pointing, whereas a verbal task could be performed more easily while pointing than while speaking.

Clearly, "analogical" theories of visual mental imagery (e.g. Kosslyn & Koenig, 1992) have interesting implications for understanding how motor imagery affects motor skills. Specifically, motor imagery should be related to the motor system in the same way as visual imagery is related to the visual perceptual system. There are several studies which support this proposition. For example, Decety & Michel (1989) compared the actual and mental walking times of blindfolded or normally sighted people. Results showed that mental and actual walking times were almost identical and that both increased linearly with target distance. Also, Roland, Skinhoj, Lassen, & Larsen (1980) reported that similar patterns of cortical activation occur for imagined and actual movements. Furthermore, Finke (1979) demonstrated that errors of movement produced in mental imagery were functionally equivalent to physical errors of movement in producing changes in visual-motor co-ordination. Taken together, these studies suggest that "imagery rehearsal should be expected to have some effect on learning and performance in much the same way as actual practice" (Van Gyn, Wenger, & Gaul, 1990). Theories which postulate an "analogical" representational code for mental imagery, therefore, support a cognitive interpretation of mental practice effects. As Kohl, Roenker, & Turner (1985) claim, "subjects highly competent in imagery react in a manner which is functionally equivalent to actual perceptual practice". Second, according to Feltz & Landers (1983), visualisation seems to be most effective in the earliest stages of skill learning—at the time when cognitive activity appears to be most strongly required. (Recall the cognitive, associative and autonomous sequence of stages postulated by Fitts & Posner, 1967). It is at this initial stage that, according to Adams (1990), "Subjects are learning what follows what and what goes to where, not movement subtleties". Third, researchers (e.g. Sackett, 1934) have found that tasks which are especially cognitively demanding (e.g. maze learning) appear to profit more from mental rehearsal than do tasks which require predominantly "motor" abilities (e.g. strength or balance tasks). Finally, there is evidence that imagery practice and physical practice may be functionally equivalent. To explain, Johnson (1982) argued that mental practice effects would be demonstrated if imagining a biasing condition in a perceptual task had the same effect as its actual presence. In this study, a linear positioning task was used in which novel movements were interpolated between initial presentation and recall of a criterion movement length (the "target"). These interpolated movements were either shorter or longer than the criterion movement and were either imagined or performed physically. Results revealed that similar error patterns were yielded by imagery of movements and the physical production of movements. For example, when either physically practising or imagining an interpolated movement shorter than the "target", subjects produced movements *shorter* than the criterion movement during recall. In other words, results showed that biasing errors occurred as frequently when the irrelevant movements had only been *imagined* as when they had actually been performed. Thus Johnson (1982) found that the imaging of a movement could bias later motor performance in the same manner as actual movement can bias subsequent motor reproduction. On the basis of this evidence, imaginary and physical practice were deemed to be functionally equivalent. Interestingly, a recent study by Hall, Bernoties, & Schmidt (1995) replicated this finding that imaginary practice can produce interference effects which resemble those found for physical practice effects.

Despite obtaining considerable empirical support, symbolic theories of mental practice have encountered criticism. For example, they cannot easily explain why MP sometimes enhances "motor" or "strength" tasks (Budney, Murphy, & Woolfolk, 1994) which, by definition, contain few "cognitive" components. Furthermore, symbolic theories find it difficult to explain how MP enhances the performance of experienced athletes who, presumably, possess well-established motor schemata for the movement patterns involved. In addition, most theories in this tradition are surprisingly vague about the precise cognitive mechanisms which are alleged to underlie imagery effects. Despite these criticism, Murphy & Jowdy (1992) concluded that "a strong body of research evidence exists to support centrally based mechanisms in the effectiveness of mental practice". But what precisely are these "centrally based mechanisms"? Perhaps they reflect the operation of the executive process of working memory which governs attention. This suggestion encourages us to consider the relationship between mental rehearsal and attention more fully.

MENTAL PRACTICE AND ATTENTION

Several researchers (Feltz & Landers, 1983; McLean & Richardson, 1994) contend that mental rehearsal strengthens the attentional processes of performers. In particular, it may help athletes to attain "a maximal state of readiness" (Budney, Murphy, & Woolfolk, 1994) for competition. For example, Perry & Morris (1995) suggest that a cricket batter who tends to be distracted by a bowler's run-up could use imagery to increase concentration. Specifically, by focusing regularly on an image of the cricket ball, the batter could develop a skill in maintaining a "narrow-external" focus of attention.

Attentional processes have been invoked to explain certain MP results. For example, consider the standard research finding (mentioned above) that expert athletes tend to benefit more from visualisation than do relative novices. This finding is difficult to explain if the primary function of MP is simply to strengthen the "cognitive template" or schema of a given skill. And if such skills have "ceilings", how can MP continue to enhance their performance? After all, by definition, expert athletes already possess highly efficient templates of their skills. But McLean & Richardson (1994) propose that for expert athletes, mental practice may serve an *attentional* function. Thus they suggest that MP facilitates "the cognitive focus of the athlete by improving concentration and reducing skill-disruptive levels of arousal". In other words, systematic use of imagery may help elite athletes to concentrate sufficiently well to enable their skills to transfer optimally from practice to competitive settings. Interestingly, empirical evidence exists to support this hypothesis. Thus Van Gyn, Wenger, & Gaul (1990) discovered that mental imagery rehearsal of sprint training facilitated the transfer of skills to a performance setting. Another attentional interpretation of visualisation is offered by Hale (1994) in presenting an account of symbolic theories. He suggests that "it is possible that repetitive mental practice of a skill could help the learner by focusing attention on several 'key' cues that constitute important components of successful performance". For example, a tennis player who is about to serve may need to visualise such cues as a high ball toss, a "backscratch" racquet position and a wrist-snap.

According to Feltz & Landers (1983), mental practice of a task or skill appears to play a critical role in facilitating the "attentional set" of the performer. In particular, they suggested that extended mental rehearsal of the relevant aspects of a specific skill can develop "a capacity for narrowed or focused attention". This ability "can facilitate performance by occupying the majority of the individual's attentional capacity so task-irrelevant thoughts and images are prevented from disrupting" task execution. This hypothesis has also been advanced by Hecker & Kaczor (1988). In summary, the "attention-arousal set" theory of MP proposes that imagery somehow establishes an optimal "attentional set" for task performance (Janssen & Sheikh, 1994).

This theory is a variation of the "activity set" hypothesis postulated by motor learning researchers (e.g. Nacson & Schmidt, 1971). Briefly, this hypothesis states that motor skill practice serves to adjust the performer's arousal level and attentional focus. However, following periods of rest, the performer's arousal and attentional systems may change and a deterioration in performance may occur. This decline in performance that tends to occur after periods of rest is widely known in the motor learning literature as the "warm up" decrement (WUD; explained in Chapter 6). Interestingly, there is some evidence that mental imagery may be used to counteract this deterioration in performance. For example, Ainscoe & Hardy (1987) reported that the WUD of gymnasts was eliminated in the performance of a double-leg circling on the pommel horse after subjects had warmed up by imaging themselves performing the task correctly. Also, Anshel & Wrisberg (1988) found that task-relevant imagery, but not irrelevant imagery, helped to minimise the debilitating effects of the WUD. However, contrary to these findings, Anshel & Wrisberg (1993) discovered that imaging the successful execution of the tennis serve failed to alleviate the WUD. This inconsistency of results between these studies may be attributable to methodological factors. Specifically, Anshel & Wrisberg (1993) failed to control for possible differences between subjects in imagery ability. In view of this apparent conflict, additional research is required to elaborate and test "attentional arousal" theory of mental practice.

Although there have been no attempts to test predictions derived from this "arousal-attentional set" hypothesis (Schmidt, 1988), some indirect evidence on attentional aspects of MP is available. For example, attentional focus has been reported to be a moderator of the effects of MP on task performance (Wilkes & Summers, 1984). In addition, Lee (1990) found that mental imagery which was task-relevant resulted in greater performance improvement than did task-irrelevant imagery. She concluded that imagery served "to prepare one specifically for a particular task and does not operate simply through a general effect on mood or confidence". Similarly, Eloi & Denis (1987) discovered that the learning of a motor skill can be hampered if subjects are led to form an "irrelevant" image of the task. This suggests that when the content of an image does not reflect the relevant aspects of the skill or task to be performed, its utility in MP is impaired. By the attentional-arousal theory, imagery "focuses attention on task-relevant thoughts and away from task-irrelevant cues which could disrupt performance" (Suinn, 1993). Perhaps this is what Schmidt (1988) referred to when he postulated that imagery allows the performer to "think about what kinds of things might be tried" in a mental simulation of the task.

One way of approaching the relationship between mental practice (MP) and attention is to focus on one of the key cognitive functions of imagery—namely, the fact that it facilitates covert or simulated *practice* of skills. If visualisation facilitates covert practice, and if practice leads to automaticity, then visualisation could affect performance by inducing automaticity. But what does the word "practice" mean? For psychologists (e.g. Ericsson, Krampe, & Tesch-Romer, 1993), this term denotes engaging in activities that have been specifically designed to improve the current level of performance of a given skill. Research shows that with extensive practice, almost any skill will become sufficiently "automatic" to allow it to be performed concurrently with other activities. In other words, with practice, skills become faster, more fluent and less dependent on conscious attentional control (see Chapter 2). So, practice is the means by which the mind can disengage itself from one task so that its resources are available for concurrent activities. Going back to the "spotlight" metaphor of attention (see Chapter 2), we can see that the *width* of the "beam" of our concentration is not fixed: It can be *expanded* with practice.

Although practice is a pre-requisite of automaticity, it is wrong to expect that all types of practice are equally beneficial to performance. Thus Ericsson, Krampe, & Tesch-Romer (1993) identified certain factors that improved the efficiency of practice. First, the motivation of the performer to exert effort in pursuit of improvement is a critical variable. Second, the way in which the skill is understood or "represented" in the performer's mind is important. Third, the performer should receive immediate feedback concerning the adequacy of the performance. The longer the delay between performance and feedback, the less effective is the practice. Finally, optimal practice requires that people should repeat key movements until they become automatic.

But how exactly does practice produce automaticity? Although no clear consensus exists about the answer to this question (Eysenck &

Keane, 1995), one of the most influential theories in this field has been developed by Logan (1988). He suggests that automaticity is governed by memory processes. In particular, he claims that extensive practice of any activity leads to an accumulation of procedural knowledge in the memory of the performer. This increase in the "knowledge-base" of the schema governing the skill facilitates its rapid execution later. In other words, what changes with practice is the amount of knowledge represented in memory: "only the knowledge base changes with practice" (Logan, 1988). Increased knowledge means faster retrieval: "performance is automatic when it is based on single-step direct-access retrieval of past solutions from memory" (ibid.). This theory helps to explain why automatic processes are fast and effortless: they reflect instant retrieval of motor programs from memory. Interestingly, motor skill learning researchers (e.g. Nacson & Schmidt, 1971) have proposed that practice serves to adjust the "attentional focus" of the performer. Within sport, "automatic" cognitive processes are apparent in skills (e.g. taking a golf swing) which are executed rapidly and effortlessly. By contrast "controlled" mental activities (Shiffrin & Schneider, 1977), such as planning where to aim a golf drive, are deliberate, effortful and flexible actions.

So far, I have analysed why physical practice leads to automaticity and improved performance. But is it possible that *mental* practice could achieve similar results? As we have seen, research evidence on mental rehearsal suggests that, under certain circumstances, it can enhance motor skills. Perhaps the reason it does so is that it strengthens the memory representation of the skill in question. Ever since the work of Bartlett (1932), it has been accepted that kinaesthetic experiences are stored in memory as "schemas" (see also Chapter 1). For example, in discussing the execution of a tennis stroke, he claimed that "when I make the stroke, I do not, as a matter of fact, produce something absolutely new, and I never repeat something old. The stroke is literally manufactured out of the living visual and postural 'schemata' of the moment and their interrelations" (ibid., pp. 201–202).

Borrowing ideas from Logan (1988), it seems possible that mental practice strengthens cognitive representations by helping athletes to code symbolically the sequence of movements comprising the skill. So, mental practice may serve to increase the knowledge-base in which the skill is embedded—thereby making it more fluent and effortless over time. Interestingly, Simon (1992) suggests that what appears to be "intuitive" performance by experts in any domain is really just rapid pattern recognition (i.e. memory retrieval). Conversely, according to Logan (1988), the hallmark of novices' performance is "a lack of *knowledge* rather than ... a lack of resources" (italics mine). Interestingly, the theory that practice leads to an increase in the performer's knowledge base may help to explain why expert athletes tend to benefit more from mental rehearsal than do novices (Logan, 1988). Briefly, it is possible that novices lack the ability to integrate and represent mentally the increased knowledge which systematic visualisation produces. Overall, therefore, it seems clear that mental practice researchers in sport psychology can benefit considerably from further collaboration with cognitive psychologists interested in the question of why practice leads to automaticity and improved performance of skills.

MENTAL PRACTICE AS A CONCENTRATION TECHNIQUE

Books on applied sport psychology are replete with practical guidelines alleged to ensure effective use of mental imagery by athletes. For example, recommendations on visualisation are provided by Dalloway (1992), Orlick (1990), Syer & Connolly (1987), Taylor (1993), Vealey & Walter (1993), Weinberg (1988) and Winter & Martin (1991). Unfortunately, these guidelines are somewhat premature because relatively few studies have tested the adequacy of MP interventions with athletes in field settings.

In these guidelines, however, some authors have commented on the alleged value of imagery in promoting concentration-enhancement. For example, Weinberg (1988) proposed that imagery can improve concentration in tennis: "By visualising the match and your strokes prior to playing a match you prevent your mind from wandering and thinking about irrelevant things". More specifically, he urges players to "see and feel the perfect serve" on court. Likewise, Orlick (1990) proposed that visualisation can help athletes to achieve a state in which "the mind is cleared of irrelevant thoughts, the body is cleared of irrelevant tensions, and the focus is centred only on what is important at that moment for executing the skill to perfection" (p. 18). Also, Winter & Martin (1991) stated that "as your visualisation skills develop, you will probably find that you also improve concentration". Unfortunately, no evidence or possible theoretical mechanisms are adduced to support these suggestions.

More generally, although these guidelines are often promulgated as conclusions derived from empirical research, they should be interpreted cautiously because they are often based on flimsy or equivocal evidence. For example, there is no empirical justification, at present, for the advice that imagery scripts should be written in the present tense (Syer & Connolly, 1987). Similarly, the injunction to "use internal imagery if possible" (Weinberg, 1988) is based on the rather controversial assumption that an "internal" or kinaesthetic imagery perspective invariably produces superior motor performance to that yielded by an "external" perspective (see discussion of this issue earlier in this chapter). Finally, most guidelines on imagery ignore the fact that a host of intervening variables (e.g. individual differences in imagery abilities; see Perry & Morris, 1995) affect the relationship between visualisation and skilled performance. However, there are encouraging signs of a more balanced approach to imagery research with the MP principles identified by Cox (1994). These principles are refreshing because they are based on empirical research findings rather than on intuitive assumptions.

In this chapter, we have seen that there is sufficient empirical evidence available to support the claim that mental practice (MP) can enhance the learning and performance of sport skills under certain circumstances. Until the precise theoretical mechanisms underlying MP effects have been established, however, it seems premature to conclude that visualisation is a valid concentration strategy for athletes. However, some indirect evidence has been gathered to support the link between MP and attention. Specifically, in a case-study, Meyers & Schleser (1980) used a combination of imagery and relaxation training to assist an inter-collegiate basketball player with a concentration problem. Following seven treatment sessions, the player showed improvements in overall performance. In a subsequent study (Meyers, Schleser, & Okwumabua, 1982), a more sophisticated research design was used to evaluate the same kind of imagery intervention programme for two basketball players also suffering from concentration difficulties. Using a modified multiple baseline design with a reversal on one of the athletes, these researchers discovered that, as before, the visualisation intervention facilitated improved performance. Unfortunately, no attempt was made to measure changes in concentration skills as a result of this intervention. Accordingly, only limited conclusions may be drawn from this study. So, although these studies are suggestive, controlled experimental research is required to probe more deeply the possible links between mental practice and attention.

SUMMARY

Mental imagery, or the capacity to simulate in the mind experiences of things which are not physically present, has long been recognised by psychologists as a powerful cognitive technique for the improvement of skilled performance. Put simply, what people can imagine may influence what they can do. Therefore, it is not surprising that within sport, athletes and coaches are turning increasingly to imagery-based procedures in an effort to facilitate optimal mental preparation for competitive performance. Accordingly, "mental practice" is now employed regularly as an adjunct to the physical training regime of many of the world's leading athletes. But what exactly is "mental practice"? How does it affect athletic performance? Could it help to improve concentration skills? The purpose of this chapter was to evaluate the efficacy of mental practice as a psychological strategy for enhancing athletes' concentration and performance.

The term "mental practice" (MP), also known as "visualisation", refers to the systematic use of mental imagery in order to rehearse symbolically physical movements prior to their actual execution. Alternatively, it may be defined as the cognitive rehearsal of actions without overt performance of the movements involved. Survey and anecdotal reports reveal that this type of rehearsal is used extensively by athletes for a variety of practical purposes, ranging from skill learning to anxiety control. But how effective is this technique? A large volume of experimental studies has been conducted on this issue. Most of these studies have been conducted on task performance in laboratory settings. The typical research design employed in these studies involves the comparison of the pre- and post-treatment performance of groups of subjects who have been assigned to one of four conditions: "Physical practice" only, "mental practice" only, physical and mental practice, and a placebo control. Based on several meta-analytic reviews of this research, at least four conclusions have emerged. To begin with, mental practice (MP) appears to have a moderate yet significant effect on task performance. In particular, it tends to improve skilled performance somewhat less effectively than does physical practice but is more beneficial than not practising at all. Second, there is evidence that a combination of mental and physical practice facilitates faster and better skill learning than does either mental or physical practice conducted alone. Third, MP seems to be more suitable for the learning of "cognitive" skills (e.g. mastering a sequence of movements in mirror tracing) than for "motor" tasks (e.g. tests of muscular strength). Finally, the imagery ability and level of expertise of the performer appear to mediate the relationship between mental rehearsal and performance. For example, athletes who are adept in generating and controlling vivid mental images seem to benefit more from visualisation programmes than do colleagues with less imagery skills. Unfortunately, two difficulties hamper efforts to translate these findings directly into sport psychology. Firstly, few researchers have tested the efficacy of MP techniques on athletes' performance of sport skills in field settings. In other words, sport scientists have not attempted to replicate traditional laboratory findings on mental rehearsal. As a consequence, we should treat with caution many of the guidelines for optimal MP usage advocated within popular sport psychology. In addition, a major flaw in research on mental rehearsal has been the neglect of the "validation" issue. To explain, few sport psychologists have attempted to evaluate the degree to which athletes are actually using mental imagery when they purport to be engaging in mental practice. Clearly, the absence of such research casts doubt on the validity of imagery-based explanations for mental practice effects. With regard to such explanations, I evaluated the rival claims of physiological ("neuromuscular") and cognitive ("symbolic") theories of mental rehearsal. Overall, I concluded that the latter accounts are not only compatible with current cognitive models of mental imagery but also offer a rich array of hypotheses to be tested by future MP researchers.

In the final section of the chapter, I considered the theoretical validity of mental practice as a concentration technique. I concluded that although attentional mechanisms may be involved in MP (e.g. by inducing automaticity of performance), available evidence is inadequate to justify the claim that the systematic practice of visualisation will enhance concentration skills. However, attentional processes may offer the best hope for the explanation of mental practice phenomena.

SECTION FOUR
Integration

In the final section I shall try to combine some recurrent themes in this book (e.g. the dearth of theoretically-driven research in sport psychology) with potential new directions for studies on the concentration skills of sport performers. To begin with, I shall argue that increased collaboration between sport and cognitive psychologists in this field can provide significant benefits to both disciplines. For example, the study of concentration in athletes raises interesting theoretical questions about a neglected issue in cognitive theory— namely, the relationship between mental effort and physical action (especially among expert athletes). In addition, the study of distractibility in sport performers encourages cognitive researchers to devote greater consideration to the role of "internal" factors in skilled performance. Next, I outline a number of specific new directions for further research in this field. In particular, I devote special consideration to five topics. These comprise "meta-attention" (or people's knowledge of, and control over, their attentional processes); the relationship between emotion and attention; involuntary narrowing of attention; issues in the measurement of concentration; and the attempt to identify practical principles of attention in athletes.

CHAPTER EIGHT

Concentration in sport performers: Implications and new directions

INTRODUCTION

Throughout this book, I have explored a variety of theoretical and practical themes raised by the study of the attentional processes of athletes. The purpose of this final chapter is to link these recurrent themes with some specific suggestions for further research in this field. This task will be addressed in two stages. To begin with, I shall summarise the main theoretical and methodological benefits which arise from the study of concentration in sport performers. Then I shall explore some potentially fruitful new directions for further studies in this field.

At the outset, however, a major impediment to this task must be examined. In particular, as I explained earlier in this book (see Chapter 3), research on concentration in athletes has been conducted largely in a theoretical vacuum. This unfortunate trend has been lamented by several critics. For example, Masters & Lambert (1989) regretted "the absence of a well developed theory" to explain the attentional strategies used by marathon runners (see also Chapter 5). Similarly, Boutcher (1992) bemoaned the absence of a "suitable framework to study the influence of attention on sport skills". More generally, Morris & Summers (1995) pointed out that it is rare indeed in sport psychology to find cases where a conceptual issue "has been systematically addressed through a long-term research program". Due to this dearth of theoretically-driven research in sport psychology, empirical findings on attentional processes in athletes have emerged in a segregated, "piecemeal" fashion rather than in a cumulative or coherent manner. As a result, applied sport psychologists have found few attentional principles on which to base their intervention programmes for concentration skills training (a problem discussed in Chapter 6). The remainder of this chapter will try to bridge this chasm between attentional theory and research in sport.

If we accept that attentional researchers in sport psychology require a theoretical paradigm, they can either develop one for themselves or they can borrow, and subsequently modify, conceptual assumptions from a more established field of inquiry. Although the former possibility is more desirable in the long-term, the latter proposition is easier to address at present. In particular, as attention is a cognitive process, cognitive psychology should serve as the "donor" of a suitable paradigm. This idea was suggested by Abernethy (1993) who proposed that the information processing principles of cognitive psychology (see also Chapter 1) could provide a helpful theoretical foundation for attentional research in sport psychology. So far, so good. But at this point, we encounter another difficulty. Specifically, cognitive psychologists, who possess the requisite theoretical and methodological tools for studying attention, have been reluctant traditionally to regard sport as a suitable domain in which to explore how the mind works. To illustrate, performance in sport does not merit a single reference in reviews of the literature on applied cognitive psychology (e.g. Barber, 1988; Hoffman & Deffenbacher, 1992). Similarly, the term "sport" is omitted from the "skills" headings of established texts written by Eysenck & Keane (1995) and Matlin (1994). Fortunately, in their recent textbook of cognitive psychology, Hampson & Morris (1996) rectify this oversight by including coverage of the topic of "choking" under pressure in sport performance.

To summarise, whereas sport psychology lacks a coherent theoretical paradigm, cognitive psychologists typically lack the *inclination* to study sporting phenomena. This latter difficulty can be resolved only when cognitive researchers are persuaded that studies of attention in athletes have important theoretical and practical implications for the study of how the mind works. I shall now address this issue.

BENEFITS OF RESEARCH ON CONCENTRATION IN SPORT PERFORMERS

The study of concentration processes in sport performers raises significant theoretical and practical issues for cognitive psychology. These issues may be explained as follows.

Mental effort and physical action

To begin with, research on concentration in athletes compels investigators to explore the relationship between "mental effort" (see Chapter 2) and physical action—a topic which has been neglected somewhat by mainstream cognitive psychologists, even though William James recognised a century ago that "my thinking is first and last and always for the sake of my doing" (James, 1890). This relative neglect of the physical or behavioural consequences of cognition is not accidental. It is largely a product of the advent of computational models of cognitive processes. Although these models are extremely useful, they have been criticised for their emphasis on "disembodied" thought processes (Norman, 1980), thereby reflecting an undue concern with the rational aspects of mental life (which is a legacy of Cartesian dualism; see Casey & Moran, 1989). This emphasis, together with a concern for structural ("what it is") rather than functional ("what it does") features of the information processing system, has caused many psychologists to neglect the topic of how cognition regulates action. This oversight is unfortunate because in order to gain a satisfactory understanding of what cognitive processes are *for*, research is required on the question of how people use their knowledge in order to guide their actions in everyday life (see Smyth, Collins, Morris, & Levy, 1994). This problem was detected by Allport (1992) who claimed that because attentional researchers had been preoccupied with the nature and locus of information processing limitations, they had neglected to explore "what attentional processes might otherwise be for". In order to rectify this oversight, the study of concentration in athletes may provide a natural testing ground for research on functional aspects of attention.

For example, consider the development of "automaticity" (a state of skilled processing or performance which is characterised by the apparent absence of conscious attentional effort; see also Chapter 2). Surprisingly, little research has been conducted by cognitive psychologists on how long it takes to achieve this state for a given skill. One reason for this neglect is that the typical laboratory experiment in cognitive psychology is simply too short to yield any valuable insights into long-term skill acquisition. Indeed, the role of "deliberate practice" (or time spent intentionally in trying to improve one's performance; Ericsson, Krampe, & Tesch-Romer, 1993) in skill learning has been under-estimated in cognitive theory. By contrast, in the domain of sport, where practice is crucial to performance, coaches have developed a wide array of instructional methods to help athletes to acquire complex motor skills. It could prove beneficial for cognitive theorists to collaborate with sport coaches in designing longitudinal research on the logic and efficacy of such instructional techniques. Sport psychologists can also benefit from such research. For example, longitudinal studies are quite rare in this discipline because of a traditional preference for cross-sectional research designs (Morris & Summers, 1995). By exploring how sport skills are improved through practice and instruction, sport psychologists can study the theoretical mechanisms which underlie the acquisition of procedural skills. This type of research is valuable because, as Thomas & Thomas (1994) concluded, "the way procedural knowledge develops is still a mystery".

Role of "internal" determinants of attention

Another theoretical benefit yielded by research on concentration in athletes is that it allows us to investigate the role played by "internal" (or mental) factors in producing lapses in concentration. Specifically, empirical analysis of the self-defeating thoughts which afflict athletes in competition (e.g. regrets about missed opportunities) may help to revive the interest of psychologists in the dynamic properties of certain mental states (e.g. daydreaming). An intriguing study of this domain was conducted recently by Wegner (1994) who investigated the question of why our minds tend to wander at the very time when we desire intense concentration. As I explained in Chapter 3, Wegner believes that attentional lapses are caused by an automatic monitoring system which normally works efficiently but which, under conditions of heavy cognitive load (e.g. in anxiety-provoking situations), sometimes distracts consciousness and impairs task performance. This type of research is highly relevant to understanding the reasons why athletes sometimes lose their concentration during competitive encounters (see also Chapter 4).

Unfortunately, apart from studies by Wegner (1994), few cognitive scientists have explored the internal dynamics of mental life. This neglect is attributable mainly to cognitive researchers' paradigmatic allegiance to a form of methodological Behaviourism. To explain, in the traditional experimental methods of cognitive psychology (described by Lachman, Lachman, & Butterfield, 1979), information was believed to flow into the mind from the outside world. This assumption encouraged cognitive theorists (e.g. Broadbent, 1958) to develop objective techniques (e.g. dichotic listening tasks; see Chapter 2) for the measurement of "external" sources of people's attention. Although these techniques were invaluable in linking perception and attention, they blinded researchers partially to the role played by mental factors in regulating attention. Fortunately, the importance of these "internal" factors in concentration task performance was highlighted by the vigilance research studies of the 1950s (see Chapter 2). These studies showed that when external stimulation is inadequate to maintain people's alertness, their minds tend to turn inwards. In Chapter 4, I provided an example of this phenomenon when exploring the reasons why people tend to become more sensitive to their aches and pains at night (when less external stimulation is evident) than during the day. Surprisingly, research on "self-focused" attention has attracted little interest from cognitive psychologists. This neglect is disappointing because clinical researchers (e.g. Ingram, 1990) have discovered some interesting principles which describe how our attentional system is affected by emotional distress. For example, people who are prone to panic attacks seem to spend disproportionately more time in monitoring their current bodily sensations (e.g. a rapid heart beat) than do non-anxious control subjects. By analogy, the study of cognitive processes in sport may extend this line of inquiry by helping to identify the nature and characteristics of "internal" distractors among athletes. I explored this topic briefly in Chapter 4 when I illustrated how lapses in the concentration of athletes may be caused by their own thoughts and emotions. For example, sport performance can be disrupted quite easily by indulging in regrets about the past or by engaging in idle speculation about the future. In both cases, thoughts and images which arise from long-term memory distract athletes from what they are doing at that moment. Clearly, these everyday examples of attentional diversion highlight the need for psychologists to develop methods for the study of internal determinants of concentration. Although this task may seem formidable, some encouragement should be taken from the ingenuity with which cognitive researchers have designed objective techniques for the measurement of other covert mental processes such as imagery (e.g. see Shepard & Metzler, 1971).

Expertise in sport performers

A third benefit of research on concentration in athletes is that it raises interesting questions about the nature and determinants of expertise in sport. As I explained in Chapter 1, the study of expertise in cognitive skills is a "hot topic" in contemporary cognitive science (Ericsson & Lehmann, 1996). Clearly, sport, with its ready-made, objective criteria for defining expertise (e.g. qualification times, world-ranking lists), offers cognitive researchers a unique opportunity to explore questions concerning the psychological characteristics of exceptional performers. For example, does the well-known "cognitive advantage" of expert athletes over novices in perceptual and memory skills (i.e. the fact that the former differ from the latter mainly in *cognitive* rather than in physical factors; see Chapter 1 for more details) extend also to concentration processes? Intuitively, this hypothesis seems plausible in view of the fact that experts in most domains are usually found to be more efficient than novices in performing, and in monitoring their progress on, task-relevant activities (Berardi-Coletta, Buyer, Dominowski, & Rellinger, 1995). But it has not yet been established that novices could improve their skills or performance by using the attentional heuristics used by expert athletes. Therefore, an interesting topic for further research would be a controlled experimental investigation of the degree to which novice athletes' attentional skills are amenable to instructional improvement. This type of research design would complement the somewhat descriptive approach which characterises current research on expert-novice differences (Gagne, Yekovich, & Yekovich, 1993).

Individual differences in attention
Another benefit yielded by the study of concentration in athletes is that it provides an impetus for the measurement of individual differences in mental effort—a topic which has been overlooked by cognitive psychologists in the past (Eysenck & Keane, 1995). However, just as Arthur et al. (1995) have evaluated the validity of various attentional measures (e.g. visual search tasks) in predicting simulated flight performance of trainees, so also could sport psychologists examine the relationship between a battery of concentration measures (see Chapter 5) and subsequent performance by athletes. As an example of such a test battery in action, Daniels, Wilkinson, Hatfield, & Lewis (1981) used a combination of physiological and self-report measures to assess the relationship between concentration and performance in rifle-shooters. These authors expected that such measures would be more directly related for experts than for novices. In order to test this prediction, they compared these athletes' status on physiological indices of attention (e.g. heart-rate and respiration-rate) with that on relevant self-report measures. Shooters whose subjective ratings were congruent with their physiological parameters were labelled "synchronous" and those whose self-reports were inconsistent with their autonomic data were referred to as "desynchronous". Results revealed that "synchronous" shooters displayed more accuracy than did their "desynchronous" counterparts. This finding is consistent with the theory (Morgan & Pollock, 1977; see Chapter 5) that expert athletes are likely to be more "in tune" with their physiological processes (i.e. to exhibit an "associative" attentional style) than are less proficient counterparts.

Another interesting project concerning the measurement of attentional processes would be to "map" neuroscientific correlates of athletic performance on tasks which are known to demand different types of concentration (e.g. sustained attention; rapid switching of concentration). In this regard, regional cerebral blood-flow mapping techniques (e.g. see Decety & Ingvar, 1990) could be used to establish which brain processes are activated by sport-specific tasks.

Methodological innovations

Apart from helping cognitive psychologists to pursue theoretically interesting studies, research on concentration in athletes may also encourage important methodological innovations. For example, consider the "thought sampling" research paradigm used by Klinger, Barta, & Glas (1981). These investigators tried to establish what basketball players tend to think about during a game—especially after encountering emotional situations such as periods of either "slumps" or "hot streaks" (defined as unbroken sequences of unusually successful play). Using "thought sampling" techniques, where players talked aloud into portable tape recorders immediately after substitution or while they waited to be called into action, Klinger, Barta, & Glas (1981) found that many "irrelevant" thoughts were evident among the players during the game. Furthermore, they noticed an interesting pattern in the data. Specifically, there was a difference between the thoughts of players during "gap time" (i.e. a "slump" period during which the opposing team scored two or more field goals) and "hot time" (the converse period—when the team being observed scored two or more consecutive field goals). Results indicated that thoughts which were experienced during "gap time" had switched from concentrating on the *process* of playing to either reflections on how well or how badly the team was playing or to the coach's exhortations to do better. They concluded that "something in the game—perhaps a slight reverse or strong challenge—distracts attention from the flow of concentrated play and focuses it instead on a self conscious interaction with oneself; this may then impede play further" (p. 113).

The relevance of this study for cognitive psychology is that it highlights the fact that information flows through the mind in two directions—not only from the "outside" world inwards, but also from the "inside" world outwards (Baddeley, 1990). Unfortunately, as Eysenck & Keane (1995) commented, "most of the work on attention has been concerned only with attention to the external environment". Therefore, cognitive researchers know relatively little about how people use the knowledge which travels in the opposite direction—from inside the mind outwards. Clearly, the study of the thinking processes of athletes in competitive situations may redress this neglect in cognitive research. Another interesting perspective on the use of thought-sampling techniques to study concentration processes in athletes is provided by Schomer (1986) who studied the "focusing" strategies of marathon runners.

Practical principles

Allied to these theoretical and methodological benefits, some practical principles governing concentration in athletes may be identified. In this section, therefore, I shall sketch briefly four attentional principles which emerge from empirical research on this topic. These principles, which reflect themes from the preceding chapters, may serve as a starting point for the development of practical programmes of concentration training in applied sport psychology.

Firstly, if we assume that our attentional resources are limited primarily by structural constraints on our information processing system (e.g. because we have a brief and fragile working memory; see Chapter 2), then, for practical purposes, we have sufficient mental "space" for only one thought at a time. Although some of these constraints can be overcome through practice (see Ericsson, Krampe, & Tesch-Romer, 1993), athletes and coaches must learn to focus their pre-match thoughts as efficiently as possible. In effect, this means that sport performers should be encouraged to use a combination of brief, positively phrased, self-instructional statements (i.e. "cue words"; see Chapter 6) and mental imagery (see Chapter 7) in order to train their minds to concentrate only on actions which lie within their control.

Secondly, if the harnessing of attention or "mental effort" is understood as being analogous to focusing a spotlight on something (see Chapter 2), then athletes "lose" their concentration if they are thinking about something which is neither under their own control nor helpful to the task which they wish to perform. Therefore, sport performers should strive to achieve a close correspondence between their thoughts and actions. Specifically, they need to reminded themselves to identify the specific challenge posed by imminent sporting contests. All too often, coaches upset the concentration of their athletes by inadvertently encouraging them to look too far ahead of the competition in which they are about to compete.

Thirdly, anxiety tends to disrupt our concentration in a number of ways. To begin with, it depletes working memory resources by inducing "worry"—a conscious cognitive activity involving task-irrelevant thinking. In addition, anxiety restricts the "beam" of our mental spotlight as a function of elevated physiological arousal. Furthermore, it influences the *direction* of our attentional focus. Specifically, anxiety tends to make us self-conscious. In this state, we tend to dwell on real or imagined personal weaknesses (self-focused attention) and also potential threats in the environment ("hypervigilance"). As Anshel (1995) points out, anxiety is associated with "self-preoccupation in sport when the athlete interprets an actual or potential event as threatening and is distracted from the task at hand by those non-productive thoughts" (p. 43). Another outcome of anxiety is that our attention may be re-focused on the *results* of what we are doing. This state induces a state of "evaluation apprehension" which is also likely to impair task performance. In summary, athletes must be trained to know when to switch the beam of their mental energy outwards—towards a specific, task-relevant and external target.

Finally, athletes should be encouraged to understand that self-monitoring is a necessary prelude to cognitive control. In order to become adept at this skill of self-appraisal, athletes need to acquire a combination of conceptual and methodological knowledge. At a conceptual level, they need to question and validate their meta cognitive assumptions and beliefs. Meanwhile, at a methodological level, they need to become familiar with objective techniques for the evaluation of their own performance in sport.

What techniques can be used to implement the four principles of concentration training outlined above? In Chapters 6 and 7, I reviewed the adequacy of various psychological strategies (i.e. goal-setting, pre-performance routines, arousal-control, cue-words and mental practice) which are alleged to enhance attentional skills. Unfortunately, despite their plausibility, these techniques lack support from relevant empirical evidence at present. This "validation problem" is a serious difficulty for concentration training programmes in applied sport psychology. Put simply, how can we prove that athletes' concentration skills have actually improved as a consequence of some intervention strategy? As I explained in Chapter 6, this question is difficult to answer mainly because we lack a detailed understanding of how mental effort is linked to athletic behaviour. As Reisberg & McLean (1985) remarked in a different context, psychologists "have no firm sense of what may or may not be accomplished by attending". By implication, conceptual clarification· should precede empirical validation in research on concentration in sport.

In summary, cognitive and sport psychology can benefit significantly from collaboration in the study of attention in athletes. But what directions should be taken in future research in this domain?

NEW DIRECTIONS IN THE FIELD

In the remainder of this chapter, I shall outline some fruitful new avenues for the study of concentration in athletes. Four topics will receive special attention. To begin with, I shall explain the potential benefits of studying meta-attentional processes in athletes. Then, I shall examine some new directions in the study of the relationship between emotion and attention. Next, I shall present a new perspective on the theme of involuntary attentional narrowing under conditions of perceived pressure (discussed initially in Chapter 3). Finally, suggestions will be provided to improve the validity of measures of attentional skills.

Meta-cognition and meta-attention in athletes

In Chapter 4, I explained that most athletes have developed, as a result of competitive experience, informal models of the nature and limitations of their concentration systems. For example, cricketer Ian Botham's claim that "the moment you let your mind wander elsewhere, the game will be unkind to you" (Botham, 1980) reveals a theory about how the mind works. But how accurate are such athletes' intuitive theories of mental processes? This question is very important to sport psychologists because if athletes believe fatalistically that there is nothing they can do to improve their mental skills (e.g. concentration), they will be reluctant to participate in programmes of psychological skills training. In order to explore this topic, we need to consider psychological research on "meta-cognition" (also referred to without the hyphen as "metacognition").

The construct of "meta-cognition" (literally meaning "above" cognition) refers to people's awareness of, and degree of control over, their own mental processes (Matlin, 1994). It denotes "cognition about cognitive phenomena" (Flavell, 1979) or our capacity to "know what we know". As I indicated at the beginning of this book (see Chapter 1), metacognitive processes are important in sport because as Chen & Singer (1992) observed, athletic expertise depends on "the consistent successful use of self-regulated cognitive strategies". In their view, successful athletes are performers "who constantly monitor themselves, from level of physical conditioning to mental preparation" (ibid.). From this perspective, the purpose of mental skills training (MST) is to foster self-regulatory skills in athletes (see also Chapter 6). These skills are especially important in sports (e.g. golf, marathon running) in which performers cannot receive coaching instructions while they compete. In these individual pursuits, it is vitally important for performers to be able to remind themselves to perform certain skills at key times.

In general, people's metacognitive abilities are remarkably sophisticated. To illustrate, given the vast range of information which we have accumulated in our memory system, it is quite an extraordinary feat to be able to tell someone quickly whether or not we know the answer to a simple question. For example, we can decide very fast that the word "edifice" is a meaningful word in English whereas "ledifice" is not meaningful (Cohen, Kiss, & Le Voi, 1993). This skill is impressive when we consider that our mental lexicon may contain the meanings of up to 100,000 words. Paradoxically, the speed with which we make a decision about novel word meanings suggests that we reach a conclusion *before* a search of the lexicon has begun. But our metamemory decisions are not always "all-or-none" affairs. Sometimes, we may feel that we can retrieve fragments of a desired answer but not be able to recall all the details. In this situation, we may experience a "gradient of knowing" (Cohen, Kiss, & Le Voi, 1993). A good example of this familiar experience is the "tip-of-the-tongue" phenomenon (Flavell & Wellman, 1977), or the feeling that we know something but cannot recall it exactly. To illustrate, we may be aware of the first letter of an acquaintance's name yet be unable to retrieve it fully. To summarise, metacognitive knowledge involves an awareness of what we do and do not know in a given domain. But it also involves beliefs about what we can and cannot *do* in that domain. This latter type of meta-cognitive activity may be especially relevant to performance in competitive sport (Kirschenbaum & Wittrock, 1984). For example, it seems plausible that athletes' beliefs about their own skills will affect their willingness to try a particular move or action in a competitive situation. As yet, however, this proposition has not been tested empirically. In a related vein, the issue of whether or not athletes of different ability levels have different metacognitive beliefs has not been explored either. This latter issue raises the question of the degree to which prowess in the sporting arena is associated with metacognitive sophistication. In an effort to answer this question, research could be conducted fruitfully on the similarities and differences between the informal theories of "concentration" that are held by elite athletes in different sports. It would also be interesting to examine the relationship between these metacognitive theories and subsequent competitive performance of the athletes involved.

It is well known that metacognitive skills become more sophisticated with age and experience. For example, as children receive coaching in tennis, they discover that they can not only perform various technical skills (e.g. volleying) but that they can also remain motivated for indeterminate durations by encouraging themselves through constructive "self-talk" (see also Chapter 6). However, Flavell (1979) proposed that, in contrast with adults, young children have extremely limited meta-cognitive awareness and control. In short, they are "universal novices" because they rarely monitor strategic aspects of their memory or comprehension processes. For example, Flavell & Wellman (1977) reported that five-year-old children did not spontaneously rehearse strings of digits to enhance their retention during a working memory task—even though they had the ability to do so.

Conversely, most adults appear to be more proficient meta- cognitively. For example, if they wish to remember a telephone number for a brief period, they will spontaneously rehearse the digits aloud.

Just as different cognitive processes exist, so also may different types of *meta*-cognitive phenomena be identified. For example, consider the distinction between "meta-memory", "meta-comprehension" and "meta-attentional" processes. "Meta-memory" processes involve knowing what one knows and how one's memory system operates. Thus the belief that one must exert some degree of mental *effort* in order to remember material reflects a practical understanding of a theory of memory (in this case, the "levels of processing" approach; Eysenck & Keane, 1995). Although most adults have discovered this theory from personal experience (e.g. by experimenting with different memory techniques), young children do not know it (Flavell & Wellman, 1977). Another aspect of metacognition is "meta-comprehension". This process is involved in determining whether or not we understand something which we have read or which we have been told (Matlin, 1994). The idea here is that a reluctance to "interrogate" our understanding of a passage of text or conversation will result in a failure to remember it. A third form of metacognition is "meta-attention". This term refers to people's knowledge and awareness of the operation and controllability of their attentional system (Miller & Bigi, 1979). Viewed from a metacognitive perspective, it may be argued that a vital goal of concentration training in athletes is to help them to become more adept at identifying and controlling potential distractors. Until athletes learn this skill of distraction control (see Chapter 6), they will evade responsibility for their performance by making excuses.

Of all the "executive" cognitive processes identified to date, the construct of meta-attention is perhaps the most relevant to the problem of understanding concentration processes in athletes. To understand this construct in practical terms, recall from Chapter 4 the common experience in which people suddenly discover that their attention has wandered when they become aware that they have been reading the same sentence in a book over and over again. As we saw, the puzzling aspect of this situation is not that we sometimes lose our concentration without any obvious external distractor in the vicinity. After all, we have seen how internal variables can affect our attentional focus (see Chapter 4 also). Instead, what intrigues psychologists about this common lapse is the fact that something (whether a conscious sensation or an unconscious monitoring system) prompts us to realise that we have not been paying sufficient attention to our book. The existence of this hypothetical "reminder system" suggests that we are constantly, if perhaps unwittingly, monitoring our own awareness. Unfortunately, relatively little is known by cognitive researchers about this automatic monitoring system which helps us to "re-focus" on what we were doing before we allowed our minds to wander. What is likely, however, is that meta-attentional accuracy (i.e. the precision with which we understand and can control our own attentional processes) is linked with efficient cognitive processing.

As with any meta-cognitive process, meta-attention comprises both a "knowledge" element (e.g. a set of beliefs) and a "control" system (e.g. a set of practical self-regulatory strategies). With regard to the former component, typical elements include the idea that our mind has a limited attentional capacity (e.g. "Don't confuse me—I only have one pair of hands!") or that effective concentration requires deliberate mental effort (e.g. "I'd better listen hard to this message if I want to remember it"). The latter component, which involves attentional *control* is less well understood, however. Indeed, there is evidence that under certain circumstances (e.g. when people have strong views about the factors which are likely to affect their performance on some forthcoming task), people are surprisingly poor judges of their own distractibility. For example, Reisberg & McLean (1985) found that people who had performed a visually presented arithmetic task while simultaneously listening to distracting auditory messages "did not know when they were being disrupted by distractors". In other words, they tended to make attributional errors in situations where their performance deteriorated in the presence of distractors.

The fact that people are not always reliable judges of their own distractibility has significant implications for sport performers in competitive situations. For example, it seems reasonable to assume that the efficacy of concentration techniques (see Chapter 6) depends on how well athletes can monitor their own concentration levels initially. As Reisberg & McLean (1985) pointed out so insightfully, "to benefit from knowing that distraction hurts performance, one must be able to tell *when* one is being distracted" (p. 292, italics mine). But how valid and reliable are athletes' insights into their own distractibility? Unfortunately, no published research could be located on this question. However, it seems plausible that unless athletes learn to monitor their concentration processes accurately, they run the risk of allowing disractors to remain undetected for long periods of time. Such an outcome is undesirable because the quicker performers can discover that they are being distracted, the more effectively they can strive to regain mental control.

In passing, a paradoxical issue is raised by this need for regular meta-attentional monitoring. To explain, athletes must be careful to avoid allowing the *manner* in which they check their own concentration levels to upset the "focus" for which they are striving. It would be ironic if the attempt to assess the efficacy of one's own concentration served instead to disrupt it! But as I explained in Chapter 4, this unwelcome effect can occur when people think too much about the *mechanics* of automatic skill production. Interestingly, a similar paradox was encountered when I considered the issue of why our mind tends to wander in situations when we believe that we need to concentrate most intensely. In this regard, Wegner (1994) suggested that our concentration appears to drift away from its intended target mainly in situations where our cognitive resources are depleted through anxiety or fatigue. Under such circumstances, the direction of our attention is influenced by an automatic appraisal procedure (the so-called "ironic monitoring system") which is primed to detect signs of anxiety-provoking stimuli. Support for this theory may be found in the "hypervigilance" model of anxiety (Eysenck, 1992) which suggests that anxious people's attention is drawn *towards*, rather than away from, feared environmental information. I shall return to this issue later in this chapter. Before concluding this section, however, I shall examine briefly the relationship between metacognitive processes and expertise in athletes. Recall from Chapter 1 that expert athletes tend to display a "cognitive advantage" (e.g. in perceptual and memory processes) over less skilled counterparts in many sport-specific situations. Does this superiority extend to metacognitive processes also?

Although few empirical studies have been conducted on this question, available evidence suggests that expertise in any cognitive field is associated with proficiency in the allocation of attentional resources. Skill in regulating these resources has been called "cognitive monitoring" (Chi, Glaser, & Rees, 1982). Specifically, this term refers to the ability to "accurately assess the state of information within one's own cognitive system" (Wellman, 1985). For example, Chi, Bassok, Lewis, Reimann, & Glaser (1989) discovered that proficient solvers of physics problems tended to monitor their own thinking processes more carefully than did relative novices. Thus they used more self-evaluative statements than did the less capable students. Overall, research in this field indicates that the ability to monitor one's own progress is a hallmark of expert performance. This idea is supported by Glaser & Chi (1988) who found that experts were more skilled at judging the difficulty of a problem and were more adept in allocating their time strategically to it than were novices. Likewise, Etelapelto (1993) discovered that expert computer programmers were superior to novices in monitoring their progress. There is also research evidence that expert adult readers display more skill in monitoring their comprehension as they read than do relative beginners (Baker, 1989). In summary, the research literature on expertise shows that, in general, skilled performance in cognitive domains is associated with regular self-monitoring. Therefore, it seems likely that top-class athletes will reveal a meta-cognitive superiority over relative beginners in monitoring strategic aspects of their sporting performance. Unfortunately, this hypothesis has attracted little empirical research attention to date.

There is some indirect evidence, however, to support the proposition that expert athletes will show greater strategic awareness and meta-cognitive control than less proficient performers. For example, McPherson & Thomas (1989) found that tennis experts, when compared to novices, displayed superior skills in monitoring developments during games and in planning tactical responses to these changes. Also, McPherson (1993) reported that expert baseball players were superior to relative novices in using self-regulatory strategies to update, check and modify their predictions concerning the characteristics of various pitchers. Finally, according to Abernethy (1994a), expert cyclists are more capable of monitoring personal work output from internal sources of information (i.e. physiological cues) than are relative beginners in this sport. In combination, these studies suggest that expert athletes have more awareness of, and better control over, their domain-specific knowledge and skills than do relative novices.

In summary, it seems clear that the study of meta-attentional processes in athletes is an urgent priority for researchers in cognitive sport psychology. Indeed, it could be argued that athletes who wish to use psychological skills training must first acquire some understanding of the principles by which the mind works. This understanding is essentially a form of meta-cognition. Therefore, most sport psychologists *already* accept the proposition that in order to benefit maximally from mental skills training programmes, athletes must cultivate some sophistication in meta-cognitive awareness and self-regulation. Without such metacognitive training, athletes may not know *when* to use the mental techniques that they have learned. In the language of cognitive psychology, their declarative knowledge will be inert because it has not been "compiled" in procedural terms.

But even if they acquire such procedural skills, athletes are likely to face another difficulty in translating their conceptual knowledge into effective action in competitive situations. This difficulty comes from the fact that *emotional* factors may affect attentional deployment—especially in competitive situations where the threat of failure is present. Therefore, I shall now consider how emotional factors (especially anxiety) affect concentration in athletes.

Emotion and attention in athletes

It has long been believed that "negative" mood states impair skilled performance. But is this informal theory borne out by empirical research in sport? Recent years have witnessed increasing interest among psychologists in the role played by emotional factors in everyday information processing activities. In particular, the impact of anxiety on thinking and perception has received considerable empirical scrutiny recently (Mathews, 1993; McNally, 1995). This research is potentially relevant to sport psychologists because athletic competition imposes emotional pressures which have not been considered in traditional, laboratory-based models of planning and decision-making processes. In such models, cognitive processes are typically "decoupled" artificially from emotional influences (Eysenck & Keane, 1995). However, in an attempt to rectify this oversight, some psychologists have begun to study clinical populations in an effort to explore how certain emotions (e.g. anxiety) affect thinking in various everyday settings.

In competitive sport, anxiety has been perhaps the most frequently studied influence on skilled performance. As we learned in Chapter 4, the term "anxiety" refers to a state of increased physiological arousal which is tinged by a characteristic pattern of affective and cognitive concerns. The affective changes include feelings of apprehension and panic whereas the cognitive factors involve persistent worrying about the future together with an inability to sustain a focus on task-relevant activities (Eysenck, 1992). In view of these correlates of anxiety, researchers have endeavoured to identify the theoretical mechanisms by which this emotion exerts disruptive effects on attention. Two distinct avenues of inquiry may be identified here. On the one hand, psychologists have examined the effects of anxiety on people's "controlled" or strategic attentional operations which are believed to be supervised by the "central executive" component of the working memory system. Meanwhile, other researchers have studied the automatic pattern of pre-attentive processing activities revealed by anxious perceivers when they encounter emotionally threatening information. From these parallel lines of investigation, the following conclusions have emerged about the way in which anxiety interferes with attention.

To begin with, as I explained in Chapter 4, some evidence has accumulated to suggest that worrying reduces the cognitive resources available for task-relevant information processing activities. In particular, it appears to involve a heightened degree of self-preoccupation together with a concern about the consequences of evaluation. Perhaps more insidiously, worrying entails rumination about issues which lie outside one's control. Because this activity of worrying is a conscious, effortful process, it draws upon the processing resources of working memory. Therefore, anxiety causes worry which, in turn, depletes working memory resources and drains the mind of attentional resources (Eysenck, 1992). Furthermore, research shows that worrying is consistently associated with decrements in the performance of cognitive tasks—especially under evaluative conditions (Smith, Smoll, & Schutz, 1990). Taken together, these findings suggest that anxiety interferes with attention mainly through its depletion of working memory resources. These resources are important to sport performers who rely considerably on working memory as a transient store for the perceptual information (i.e. the "condition") which triggers associated procedural knowledge (i.e. the appropriate "action"; see Chapter 1). Obviously, if working memory resources are depleted by anxiety, then less storage space is available for pattern-recognition activities. Therefore, task performance will tend to deteriorate under anxiety-provoking circumstances. In addition, the ability of athletes to engage in tactical planning will be impaired in these situations because working memory resources are required for any form of strategic processing.

So far, I have argued that worrying usually hampers performance. This proposition seems incontestable if "worrying" entails a preoccupation with unwanted, intrusive and task-irrelevant thoughts. But theoretically, perhaps worrying results from some mis-guided anticipatory processes (Eysenck, 1992). A controversial implication of this theory is the hypothesis (which has yet to be tested empirically) that under certain circumstances, worrying may enhance sport performance marginally. For example, an athlete who worries about his or her performance is effectively allocating extra mental resources to it. These resources, if properly channelled, can facilitate performance. Of course, a crucial issue here concerns the issue of effective "channelling". This issue depends largely on what exactly the athlete is thinking about when performing. As I have shown (see Chapter 4), if athletes are focused on factors lying outside their control, or if they become excessively self-conscious, then attentional lapses are likely to occur. However, if they focus their "worries" on task-relevant activities which lie under their control, they are engaging in planning behaviour.

Another point which challenges the allegedly detrimental effects of worry on performance emerges when we examine the level of attention required by the task being performed. According to Eysenck (1992), worrying has little impact on the performance of automatic tasks. In Chapter 1, we encountered a vivid example of this principle when reviewing the incident in which the tennis star Pete Sampras wept while playing brilliantly against Jim Courier in the 1995 Australian Open championship. Here, the automatic skills of serving and volleying were somehow "decoupled" from Sampras' mental anguish about the health of his coach. A practical consequence of this hypothesis is the idea that if certain cognitive skills (e.g. pattern-recognition processes) can become as automated as technical skills, perhaps the deleterious effects of anxiety on attention can be reduced. Clearly, the challenge facing sport coaches is to develop practical drills which train athletes to react automatically to task-relevant cues under simulated pressure situations. Before accepting this challenge, however, it is essential that the controversial implications of Eysenck's (1992) theory of worry should be tested experimentally in sport settings.

The preceding discussion of worry leads us to consider people's vulnerability to attentional interference from anxiety. Fortunately, some progress has been made in the measurement of individual differences this vulnerability to worry. To explain, the "Sport Anxiety Scale" (SAS; Smith, Smoll, & Schutz, 1990) contains a sub-scale which purports to measure affective influences on attention. This "concentration disruption" sub-scale of the SAS contains five items (e.g. item 6, "My mind wanders during sport competition"; and item 14, "I have lapses of concentration during competition because of nervousness") which assess the disruptive effects of anxiety on concentration. Preliminary indications suggest that the SAS displays impressive psychometric characteristics. For example, the "concentration disruption" sub-scale appears to be highly consistent internally, with a reported alpha coefficient of 0.80 (ibid.). But as yet, criterion-related validity data for the SAS are unavailable. However, in view of the fact that this test has clear theoretical foundations and is designed specifically for sport situations, the SAS merits closer investigation. Therefore, an interesting idea for further research in this field would be to establish the convergent and predictive validity of this test by evaluating its relationship with more established concentration tests (see Chapter 5) and by exploring its accuracy in predicting athletic performance in competitive sporting situations.

Another effect of anxiety concerns its capacity to exert an unconscious bias on the nature of the stimulus features which are encoded by the person's attentional system (Mathews, 1993). This finding is not really surprising in view of the theory that anxiety facilitates the detection of threatening environmental stimulation (Eysenck, 1992). In general, anxiety states tend to precipitate the selective encoding of emotionally threatening information. Specifically, they serve to direct people's attentional focus *towards*, rather than away from, emotionally significant concerns (Mineka & Sutton, 1992). This conclusion emerges mainly from laboratory studies in which people are required to perform a designated primary task while simultaneously ignoring a variety of emotionally laden words (serving as distractors). In general, these studies show that when distracted by emotionally tinged words, anxious people usually make significantly more errors on the central task than do non-anxious counterparts. To illustrate, consider how anxious people usually perform on a modified version of the classic Stroop task (Stroop, 1935). Briefly, this task requires people to name the colour of the ink in which a word is printed while attempting to ignore its meaning. On this task, it has been discovered that when anxious subjects are required to name the colour of the ink in which different types of "emotional" words are written, they tend to react slowest when the words to be ignored match their current concerns. In other words, the latency to name the colour of the ink in which the words are written provides a measure of the degree to which subjects have been able to inhibit unwanted semantic processing. Thus anxious people tend to show disproportionately longer colour naming latencies for words which express threatening content (e.g. "failure") than they do for relatively neutral words (e.g. "holiday"). This finding of latency differences between the task of colour-naming threatening words and that of colour-naming non-threatening words suggests that anxious people are "primed" to process emotionally threatening information (Mathews, 1993). In summary, results derived from laboratory research indicate that anxious people's attention tends to be diverted automatically *towards* threat-related cues in the environment when there is a mixture of threatening and non-threatening cues available. This finding is important because it may explain why anxiety leads to a "vicious circle" in which this emotion is perpetuated by perceptual factors. Therefore, in the domain of sport, if athletes expect to see threatening stimuli everywhere, then such a state of vigilance will exacerbate their experience of pre-competitive anxiety.

How could we explore experimentally the type of cognitive processing which athletes might display when they encounter emotionally threatening information? One possibility in this regard arises from the "emotional priming" paradigm (Dalgleish, Cameron, Power, & Bond, 1995). This paradigm involves the presentation of a "prime" stimulus (e.g. a statement such as "your best friend dies") immediately followed by a "probe" adjective (e.g. "shaking"). Participants are required to decide as rapidly as possible the degree to which this latter adjective describes their emotional reaction. "Facilitation" is said to occur when the presentation of the prime speeds up people's response to the probe relative to a control (non-primed) trial. Conversely, "inhibition" occurs when the presentation of the prime slows down the response to the probe in comparison with a control condition. Using this paradigm, it would be interesting to explore the effect of emotional priming on the responses of athletes. Possible "primes" here might include such statements as "you perform badly in front of a large crowd" or "you lose a match which you are expected to win". Unfortunately, as yet, no research has been conducted on this issue. Another interesting research avenue in this field concerns the examination of attentional biases displayed by sport performers in field settings. By monitoring the eye movements of athletes while they perform actual or simulated competitive skills, it may be possible to investigate visual attentional processes elicited by challenging situations. This type of research could help sport psychologists to develop psychological principles (e.g. concerning how and where to direct one's gaze in specific competitive situations) that could be used to counteract external distractions in competition.

Strictly speaking, the threatening stimuli to which anxious people are acutely sensitive may be found not only in the external world but also in the *internal* environment. For athletes, physical symptoms associated with pain or fatigue are especially salient "internal" variables (see Cioffi, 1993). These factors may occupy more of the athlete's attention as they approach a major competition. What might be happening in these circumstances is that anxious athletes are displaying attentional biases relating to their current emotional preoccupations (e.g. physical fitness). Unfortunately, little empirical research has been conducted on this topic of self-focused attention as a correlate of pre-competitive anxiety. Therefore, it would be helpful to develop a programme of field studies designed to complement laboratory research on the effects of anxiety on attention.

Anxiety and involuntary attentional narrowing

So far, I have suggested that anxiety seems to narrow the breadth of people's attentional focus, thereby making their concentration more selective. Obviously, this conclusion is consistent with the hypothesis (Easterbrook, 1959) that the arousal generated by emotional states tends to increase attentional selectivity (see Chapter 3). But is attentional narrowing an *inevitable* consequence of anxiety?

According to Eysenck (1992), anxiety does not necessarily produce a narrowing of attention. For example, consider the preceding discussion of the propensity of anxious perceivers to engage in "threat monitoring". Briefly, this perceptual bias allows anxious people to sample environmental information in such a way as to maximise the possibility of detecting threatening information. Here, the objective is to extract as much information as possible from as wide an area in the environment as possible. By this logic, under certain circumstances, anxiety may in fact *expand*, rather than constrict, the breadth of the visual attentional "spotlight". On this issue, Eysenck's (1992) "hypervigilance" theory conflicts with that of Easterbroook (1959). In an effort to resolve this apparent conflict, Eysenck (1992) suggested that anxiety may have different effects on the breadth of attentional deployment—depending on the *stage* at which the anxiety is experienced. Thus initially an anxious person may wish to extract as much information as possible from the environment in order to detect the presence of any possible threat. In this situation, a broad sampling of environmental information would be helpful to them. But when a feared stimulus is detected, the person's attentional focus may narrow considerably as they try to determine the degree of threat posed by this event or situation. Unfortunately, as Eysenck (1992) noted, there is a dearth of empirical evidence to validate this idea that attentional narrowing is stage-dependent. Perhaps a way to test this prediction is to measure the pattern of eye-fixations displayed by anxious athletes when placed in different competitive environments. Of course, this paradigm would not be sensitive to shifts in *covert* attention (i.e. the target at which one's "mind's eye" is directed) that are caused by "internal" factors (see Chapter 4). Although the hypervigilance model of anxiety may appear counter-intuitive, it makes sense from an evolutionary perspective simply because the function of anxiety is to facilitate rapid detection of actual threats or impending danger from the environment (Eysenck, 1992). Therefore, anxious people tend to become "primed" to the possible presence of the very stimuli which they fear.

So far, I have argued that anxiety affects people's information processing activities in several ways. Specifically, it reduces their memory resources, sometimes restricts their attentional focus and usually increases their tendency to encode emotionally threatening information in a selective fashion (Mathews, 1993). Perhaps the most pressing issue in this field for sport psychologists is the question of exploring the type of "internal" factors which make some people more susceptible to distractions than others. I shall now consider the issue of how distractibility may be affected by two such factors—anxiety and cognitive style.

According to "hypervigilance" theory (Eysenck, 1992), the most important cognitive characteristic of anxious people is "hypervigilance" or "a propensity to attend to any task-irrelevant stimuli which are presented". This characteristic is commonly known as "distractibility". As the attentional system of anxious people is "attuned" to the detection of threat, it should render such people vulnerable to the distracting influence of threat-related stimuli. But what theoretical mechanisms could account for this effect? According to Fox (1994), a deficit in "cognitive inhibition" may explain why anxious people tend to be more distractible than control subjects. To explain, "cognitive inhibition" refers to the suppression of distracting information. Briefly, some models of attention (e.g. Neill, 1977) propose that allocation of central resources may be achieved through selective inhibition of undesired channels rather than through the "opening up" of desired ones (as postulated by Broadbent, 1958). Evidence for cognitive inhibition has been gathered from research on "negative priming". In this paradigm, the processing of a target stimulus is usually inhibited if that stimulus (or something resembling it closely) had served as a distractor previously (Eysenck & Keane, 1995). More generally, this paradigm shows that responses to recently ignored stimuli are often slower and less accurate than are responses to novel stimuli (Fox, 1994). Unfortunately, "priming" techniques have not been used to date in sport psychology. They may be valuable, however, in exploring the type of controlled processing displayed by anxious athletes when threat-related stimulus material is presented to them (see Dalgleish, Cameron, Power, & Bond, 1995, for further details).

Distractibility could also be influenced by the characteristic manner in which people perceive things—their preferred "cognitive style". One of the most pervasive cognitive styles is that known as "field dependence-independence" (FDI; see Witkin, Oltman, Raskin, & Karp, 1971). Briefly, this construct refers to a continuum of analytical perceptual ability. At one end of this continuum, "field dependent" (FD) perceivers tend to rely greatly on the structure of the prevailing visual field. By contrast, at the opposite end of the spectrum, "field independent" (FI) perceivers are adept at distinguishing target items from the background contexts in which they occur. Field independence is usually measured by the Embedded Figures Test (Witkin, Oltman, Raskin, & Karp, 1971) which requires subjects to find "target" figures which are concealed within distracting, embedding backgrounds. Applying this construct to sport, it may be expected that FD athletes, who are influenced by contextual factors in perceptual tasks, should be more vulnerable to external distractions than their field-independent counterparts. As Abernethy (1993) indicates, the assumption is "that those individual who can ignore the irrelevant background information in order to focus only on the characteristics of the target item (classified as field-independent individuals) will also be better equipped to avoid distractions in natural tasks of the type that exist in sport" (p. 159). Unfortunately, this prediction has not yet been tested empirically on athletes. Therefore, an important issue for further research in this field is to explore the relationship between athletes' cognitive styles and their preferred strategies for dealing with distractions. An interesting hypothesis for this study would be that field-independent marathon runners should prefer to use "associative" concentration strategies in competition (see Chapter 5) whereas field-dependent counterparts may favour "dissociative" attentional techniques. Incidentally, it is noticeable that virtually no research has been conducted by sport psychologists on the influence of emotions other than anxiety on athletes' concentration skills. For example, how does *anger* affect people's ability to focus on, and perform, sport skills?

A final "new direction" for research in concentration concerns the measurement of individual differences in the attentional skills of athletes.

Improving measurement techniques

In Chapter 5, I considered three main approaches (i.e. psychophysiological, experimental and psychometric) to the measurement of attentional processes in athletes. These different assessment approaches are necessary simply because attention is a multi-dimensional construct with physiological, cognitive and behavioural referents (see Chapter 2). A crucial question facing future researchers on attention in sport concerns whether or not these measurement approaches could be combined in order to produce a suitable concentration test battery for athletes.

In this regard, perhaps the self-report paradigm could be augmented by experimental measures of attention. This amalgamation may be necessary because although the self-report approach has led to the development of such popular measures as the "Test of Attentional and Interpersonal Style" (TAIS; Nideffer, 1976a), it is afflicted by persistent conceptual and methodological difficulties (see Chapter 5 for details). For example, Summers, Miller, & Ford (1991) have criticised the TAIS on the grounds that it neglects "attentional flexibility" (or the capacity to switch concentration successfully), which is vitally important in most sports. I shall now consider how this capacity might be measured using laboratory techniques derived from experimental psychology.

The construct of "attentional flexibility" (see also Chapter 5) refers to the ability to switch the focus of one's attention rapidly and effectively between one source of information and another in accordance with sudden changes in circumstances (Keele & Hawkins, 1982). It is a highly valued skill among athletes because in sport, the attentional demands of dynamic sport situations often shift in dramatic and unpredictable ways. For example, a defender in soccer must learn to alternate attention rapidly between the variable positions of attacking players and an imaginary line joining fellow defenders on the pitch which marks the "offside" boundary. If the defender concentrates for too long on one or other of these sources of information, a costly error could result. This challenge of changing attention between cues available in different spatial locations is made more difficult by opponents who use "decoy" runs to disrupt the "offside trap". Not surprisingly, there is evidence that expert athletes display greater attentional flexibility than novices (Castiello & Umilta, 1988).

Because the cognitive processes underlying attentional flexibility are extremely fast, they are difficult, if not impossible, to assess using self-report measures. But they may be amenable to investigation through experimental methods like the spatial cueing task developed by Posner (1980). This task is designed to reveal the attentional costs and benefits associated with either knowing, or not knowing, in advance the likely location of an expected stimulus. Briefly, in this laboratory procedure, subjects are required to participate in a type of signal detection experiment in which they have to respond to targets presented on a computer screen. The target displays are preceded by cues. Each trial begins with the cue displaying an arrow pointing either to the left or right of a central fixation point. On most trials, the target is presented in a location which is compatible with the direction cued earlier. Less frequently, however, the target's position conflicts with the directional cue. Regardless of the congruence between the cue and the target location, the task for the subject is the same: They are required to press a response key as soon as the target is detected. In this task, therefore, people are required to perform rapid switches of attention in different timed situations.

As expected, results derived from Posner's (1980) task tend to show that response times are fastest on "valid" trials (where the perceiver is cued correctly about the likely location of the target) than on the less frequent, "invalid" trials (where an incongruence exists between the cue and the spatial location of the target). This rapid response pattern which occurs when people detect the target in the valid cued location may be called an "attentional benefit". Conversely, an "attentional cost" refers to a decrease in response speed which occurs at the invalidly cued spatial location. In summary, this laboratory task permits the study of the benefits and costs associated with rapidly-switched visual attentional processes.

Even a cursory analysis of this topic will show an interesting analogy between the mental demands of Posner's (1980) paradigm and those found in certain sport situations. For example in "adversarial" sporting contests, where opponents compete against each other directly (e.g. fencing, boxing), athletes are confronted with the problem of alternating attention between valid and spurious (i.e. deliberately misleading) anticipatory cues. For example, soccer players may lean their shoulders one way but then move quickly in the other direction as a ploy to disguise a "body swerve". Given the prevalence of such attempts to provide spurious cues to athletic opponents, it would be interesting to evaluate the extent to which people's performance on Posner's (1980) task predicts athletic success in sport. Unfortunately, few authors have grasped this challenge. An exception is a study which used Posner's task to explore expert-novice differences in sport. Specifically, these authors required expert and novice athletes to detect signals presented to them in one of four different locations on either side of a central fixation point. Results showed that little difference existed between the speed with which experts responded to cued and uncued locations. The authors interpreted these results to indicate that expert athletes have learned to be attentive to all signals in any uncertain environment. This conclusion seems rather surprising, however, given the "cognitive advantage" which experts enjoy over relative novices in most sport (see Chapter 1). Clearly, further research is required to replicate the findings of Nougier et al. (1991).

Another potentially fruitful new direction for research on the measurement of attentional skills may be provided by well-designed psychometric scales such as the "Cognitive Failures Questionnaire" (CFQ; Broadbent, Cooper, Fitzgerald, & Parkes, 1982). Briefly, the background to this test began with the observation that everyday life is replete with situations in which there is a disjunction between our intentions and our actions. This gap between what we intend to do and what we *actually* do is revealed by such cognitive anomalies as "action slips" (e.g. absent-minded behaviour) and failures of "prospective" memory (i.e. the system which reminds us to perform future actions). "Action slips" refer to situations in which we execute an inappropriate sequence of actions (the "wrong" plan) at the wrong time. For example, if we are preoccupied by task-irrelevant personal concerns, we may inadvertently put salt instead of sugar into our tea. Failure of prospective memory occurs when we fail to execute some intended plan (e.g. forgetting to make a telephone call). Both categories of unintentional behaviour may be classified as "cognitive failures" which have implications for attentional processes. Indeed, Reason & Mycielska (1982) claimed that these anomalies tend to occur in situations in which difficulties are encountered in distributing attention between two concurrent tasks. As a result, there is a "failure of focal attention to switch to the task in hand at the appropriate moment" (ibid.). This type of research raises at least two interesting questions. What theoretical mechanisms help to explain such problems in attentional distribution? Furthermore, could similar mechanisms account for the fact that experienced athletes may sometimes make elementary mistakes in competitive situations?

As with other lapses of attention, "cognitive failures" are attributable partly to "stimulus" factors (e.g. the degree of automaticity of the action involved) and partly to "internal" influences (e.g. self-generated distractions; see Chapter 4). Interestingly, a clue to the cause of cognitive failures emerges from the fact that most absent-minded behaviour and action slips occur in the performance of highly practised, well-learned skills (e.g. driving a car, making coffee). As we learned in Chapter 1, these skills are executed with minimal conscious monitoring by the performer and are believed to be represented in long-term memory as "production rules" (Anderson, 1983). Therefore, it seems likely that some defect in either the representation or the execution of these production rules may account for cognitive failures. For example, if two or more action sequences share certain a common behavioural element or path, then some "cross talk" may occur at the "junction" of the underlying production rules. In this case, the "wrong" behavioural track might be followed unwittingly. For example, a person may absent-mindedly enter their bedroom to change clothes but may undress and go to bed instead. Here, a failure to monitor the junction between two similar behavioural programmes (i.e. the "changing clothes" and the "undressing for bed" sequences) may have triggered an unfortunate "cross talk" between actions. The common element in this example is the "entering the bedroom" routine. By analogy, unintended "cross talk" between automated action sequences may occur in sport also. For example, during a tennis match in which there is no umpire, the fact that both balls are lying within the receiver's court may influence them to believe falsely that it is their turn to serve. Here, collecting the balls may trigger automatically a "my turn to serve" programme. Paradoxically, therefore, it seems that automatic sequences need to be monitored intermittently in order to produce desired behavioural effects as efficiently as possible. In summary, without occasional conscious monitoring, familiar action sequences may "switch tracks" and lead to subsequent deterioration of task performance.

Influenced by these ideas, Broadbent, Cooper, Fitzgerald, & Parkes (1982) developed the "Cognitive Failures Questionnaire" (CFQ) in an attempt to measure individual differences in people's susceptibility to everyday cognitive failures. In devising this instrument, they were motivated by the desire to examine how defective mental control mechanisms might affect strategic aspects of information processing. Briefly, their test contains 25 items which purport to measure individual differences in susceptibility to various anomalies in cognitive performance (e.g. item 1, "Do you read something and find you haven't been thinking about it and must read it again?"). In other words, it attempts to assess "a general liability to failure" (ibid.). More precisely, respondents are asked to provide estimates of the frequencies with which they have experienced each of 25 different types of performance breakdown or "cognitive failure" in the preceding six months. These items describe everyday cognitive failures in the areas of perception, memory and action. For each item, respondents must indicate the frequency with which they have made a designated mistake, using a 5 point scale ranging from "very often" to "never".

Available evidence suggests that a high score on the CFQ is associated with impaired cognitive performance in situations where people are faced with concurrent attentional demands. Interestingly, this finding appears to be analogous to results from the research literature on self-focused attention (Ingram, 1990). To explain, when task demands are high, and when people are anxious, self-focused attention tends to impair performance either by preventing sufficient attentional resources to be allocated to the task and/or by promoting an anxiety-induced withdrawal from it. These results have some relevance to "slips of action" (e.g. a mis-placed pass by an anxious soccer player) which often happen in sport settings. Therefore, it would be worthwhile either to validate the CFQ on athletes performing in competitive sport or to develop a sport-related version of this test. Specifically, we would expect that athletes who score highly on the CFQ would show weaknesses in their distribution of attention across concurrent tasks. Interestingly, some progress has been made in the assessment of the psychological correlates of attentional lapses in sport. For example, Bird & Horn (1990) found that cognitive anxiety in female softball players was, as expected, positively associated with frequency of "mental errors" (as assessed by coaches). In summary, the preceding discussion has shown that the measurement of attentional skills in athletes can be improved by exploring ideas borrowed from the work of such cognitive researchers as Posner (1980) and Broadbent, Cooper, Fitzgerald, & Parkes (1982).

SUMMARY

In this chapter, I tried to summarise the main theoretical and methodological benefits which arise from the study of concentration in sport performers. I also explored some potentially fruitful new directions for further research in this field. Before addressing these objectives, however, I indicated a major obstacle to research on concentration in sport performers. Briefly, this problem concerns the absence of a coherent theoretical paradigm which is necessary both to generate research and to integrate findings in this field. Although the information processing tradition of cognitive psychology can provide such a paradigm, there has been a marked reluctance among cognitive theorists to explore mental aspects of athletic performance. This reluctance was attributed mainly to the predominance of "disembodied" computational models in this field. Despite this problem, a number of benefits could be yielded by research collaboration between cognitive and sport psychologists. These benefits were outlined as follows.

To begin with, studies of concentration in athletes raise questions about the relationship between mental effort and physical action. For example, what types and amount of deliberate practice are required to enhance automaticity of performance of specific sport skills? Further, what instructional strategies tend to hasten this process? Such questions have been neglected to date due a lack of understanding about the behavioural functions of the attentional system. Secondly, the attempt to understand why athletes often experience disconcerting lapses of attention in competition challenges researchers to investigate the role played by "internal" distractors (e.g. thoughts and emotions) in skilled performance. These distractors have been typically overlooked by cognitive researchers due to the fact that they are not easily measured or manipulated objectively. However, it is encouraging to note that Wegner has devoted explicit attention to cognitive factors in his model of the "ironic" monitoring system alleged to underlie mental "wandering". A new direction in this field would be to test predictions derived from this model on competitive athletes. A third benefit of research on attention in athletes is that it can illuminate certain issues in the psychology of expertise. For example, does the "cognitive advantage" displayed by expert athletes over less proficient performers extend to attentional skills? This hypothesis seems plausible in view of the fact that experts in most cognitive domains tend to allocate their mental resources (including attention) more efficiently in comparison with relative novices. Another contribution yielded by the study of concentration in athletes is that it revives interest among cognitive researchers in the measurement of individual differences in attentional skills. Clearly, this topic has enormous practical significance for coaches and sport psychologists. To illustrate, programmes of talent-detection and psychological skills training could be improved considerably if they are based on a well-validated battery of concentration measures.

In the latter half of this chapter, I reviewed four potentially fruitful new directions in research on the concentration processes of athletes. These topics included "meta-attentional" processes (i.e. athletes' beliefs about, and strategic control over, their own concentration), affective influences on attention (e.g. the relationship between anxiety and concentration), the issue of attentional narrowing under perceived pressure, and the attempt to improve the measurement of concentration skills (e.g. by developing valid self-report measures of attentional lapses).

References

Abernethy, B. (1987). Selective attention in fast-ball sports, I: General principles. *Australian Journal of Science and Medicine in Sport, 19*, 3–6.

Abernethy, B. (1988). Visual search in sport and ergonomics: Its relationship to selective attention and performance expertise. *Human Performance, 1*, 205–235.

Abernethy, B. (1990). Expertise, visual search and information pick-up in squash. *Perception, 19*, 63–77.

Abernethy, B. (1991). Visual search strategies and decision-making in sport. *International Journal of Sport Psychology, 22*, 189–210.

Abernethy, B. (1993). Attention. In R.N. Singer, M. Murphey & L.K. Tennant (Eds.), *Handbook of Research in Sport Psychology* (pp. 127–170). New York: Macmillan.

Abernethy, B. (1994a). The nature of expertise in sport. In S. Serpa, J. Alves, V. Pataco & V. Ferreira (Eds.), *International perspectives on sport and exercise psychology* (pp. 57–68). Morgantown, WV: Fitness Information Technology.

Abernethy, B. (1994b). Introduction: Special issue on expert-novice differences in sport. *International Journal of Sport Psychology, 25*, 241–248.

Abernethy, B., Neal, R.J., & Koning, P. (1994). Visual-perceptual and cognitive differences between expert, intermediate and novice snooker players. *Applied Cognitive Psychology, 8*, 185–211.

Abernethy, B. & Russell, D.G. (1987). The relationship between expertise and search strategy in a racquet sport. *Human Movement Science, 6*, 283–319.

Acedevo, E.O., Dzewaltowski, D.A., Gill, D.F., & Noble, J.M. (1992). Cognitive orientations of ultra-marathoners. *The Sport Psychologist, 6*, 242–252.

263

Adair, T. (1994). Just William. *The Sunday Tribune, 28 August*, B1.

Adams, J.A. (1987). Historical review and appraisal of research on the learning, retention and transfer of human motor skills. *Psychological Bulletin, 101*, 41–74.

Adams, J.A. (1990). The changing face of motor learning. *Human Movement Science, 9*, 209–220.

Ainscoe, M. & Hardy, L. (1987). Cognitive warm-up in a cyclical gymnastics skill. *International Journal of Sport Psychology, 18*, 269–275.

Alain, C. & Sarrazin, C. (1990). Study of decision-making in squash competition: A computer simulation approach. *Canadian Journal of Sport Sciences, 15*, 193–200.

Albinson, J.G. & Bull, S.J. (1988). *A mental game plan*. Eastbourne, UK: Spodyn.

Albrecht, R.R. & Feltz, D.L. (1987). Generality and specificity of attention related to competitive anxiety and sport performance. *Journal of Sport Psychology, 9*, 231–248.

Allard, F. (1982). Cognition, expert performance and sport. In J.H. Salmela, J.T. Partington & T. Orlick (Eds.), *New paths of sport rearing and excellence* (pp. 42–51). Ottawa: Coaching Association of Canada.

Allard, F. & Burnett, N. (1985). Skill in sport. *Canadian Journal of Psychology, 39*, 294–312.

Allard, F., Graham, S., & Paarsalu, M.E. (1980). Perception in sport: Basketball. *Journal of Sport Psychology, 2*, 14–21.

Allard, F. & Starkes, J.L. (1991). Motor-skill experts in sports, dance and other domains. In K.A. Ericsson & J. Smith (Eds.), *Toward a general theory of expertise: prospects and limits* (pp. 126–152). Cambridge: Cambridge University Press.

Allport, A. (1989). Visual attention. In M. Posner (Ed.), *Foundations of cognitive science* (pp. 631–682). Cambridge, MA: MIT Press.

Allport, A. (1992). Attention and control: Have we been asking the wrong questions? A critical review of twenty-five years. In D.E. Meyer & S. Kornblum (Eds.), *Attention and performance, XIV: Synergies in experimental psychology, artificial intelligence, and cognitive neuroscience* (pp. 183–218). Cambridge, MA: MIT Press.

Allport, D.A., Antonis, B., & Reynolds, P. (1972). On the division of attention: A disproof of the single channel hypothesis. *Quarterly Journal of Experimental Psychology, 24*, 255–265.

Allport, F.H. (1924). *Social psychology*. Boston: Houghton Mifflin.

Anderson, J.R. (1983). Acquisition of cognitive skill. *Psychological Review, 89*, 369–406.

Anderson, J.R. (1995a). *Learning and memory*. New York: John Wiley.

Anderson, J.R. (1995b). *Cognitive psychology and its implications* (4th ed.) New York: W.H. Freeman.

Anderson, W.G. (1899). Studies in the effects of physical training. *American Physical Education Review, 4*, 265–278.

Annett, J. (1985). Motor learning: A review. In H. Heuer, U. Kleinbeck & K.H. Schmidt (Eds.), *Motor behaviour: programming, control and acquisition* (pp. 189–212). New York: Springer-Verlag.

Annett, J. (1991). Skill acquisition. In J.E. Morrison (Ed.), *Training for performance: principles of applied human learning* (pp. 13–51). Chichester: John Wiley.

Annett, J. (1992). *International Workshop on Imagery and Motor Processes: Proceedings of Conference*. Leicester: British Psychological Society.

Annett, J. (1995). Imagery and motor processes: Editorial. *British Journal of Psychology, 86*, 161–167.

Anshel, M.H (1989). Applied sport psychology. In W.L. Gregory & W.J. Burroughs (Eds.), *Introduction to Applied Psychology* (pp. 424–456). Glenview, I.L: Scott Foresman.

Anshel, M.H., & Wrisberg, C.A. (1993). Reducing warm-up decrement in the performance of the tennis serve. *Journal of Sport and Exercise Psychology, 15*, 290–303.

Anshel, M.H., & Wrisberg, C.A. (1988). The effect of arousal and focused attention on warm-up decrement. *Journal of Sport Behaviour, 11*, 18–31.

Anshel, M.H., Freedson, P., Hamill, J., Haywood, K., Horvat, M. & Plowman, S.A. (1991). *Dictionary of sport and exercise sciences*. Champaign, IL: Human Kinetics.

Anshel, M.H. (1995). Anxiety. In T. Morris & J. Summers (Eds.), *Sport psychology: theory, applications and issues* (pp. 29–62). Chichester: John Wiley.

Arthur, W., Jr., Strong, M.H., Jordan, J.A., Williamson, J.E., Shebilske, W.L., & Regian, J.W. (1995). Visual attention: Individual differences in training and predicting complex task performance. *Acta Psychologica, 88*, 3–23.

Arthur, W., Jr., & Doverspike, D. (1992). Locus of control and auditory selective attention as predictors of driving accident involvement: A comparative longitudinal investigation. *Journal of Safety Research, 23*, 73–80.

Atkinson, R.C. & Shiffrin, R.M. (1968). Human memory: A proposed system and its control processes. In K.W. Spence & J.T. Spence (Eds.), *The psychology of learning and motivation: Advances in research and theory*, vol. 2 (pp. 89–195). New York: Academic Press.

Austin, S. & Miller, L. (1992). An empirical study of the SyberVision golf videotape. *Perceptual and Motor Skills, 74*, 875–881.

Baars, B.J. (1986). *The cognitive revolution in psychology*. New York: Guilford Press.

Baddeley, A.D (1989). Cognitive psychology and cognitive science. In A.D. Baddeley & N.O. Bernsen (Eds.), *Cognitive psychology: Research directions in cognitive science (European perspectives, Vol. 1*, pp. 1–8). Hillsdale, NJ: Lawrence Erlbaum Associates Inc.

Baddeley, A.D. (1990). *Human memory: Theory and practice*. Hove: Lawrence Erlbaum Associates Ltd.

Baddeley, A.D. (1986). *Working memory*. Oxford: Oxford University Press.

Bahill, A.T. & La Ritz, T. (1984). Why can't batters keep their eyes on the ball? *American Scientist, 72*, 249–253.

Bain, A. (1868). *The senses and the intellect*. London: Longmans.

Baker, L. (1989). Metacognition, comprehension monitoring, and the adult reader. *Educational Psychology Review, 1*, 3–38.

Barber, P. (1988). *Applied cognitive psychology: An information-processing framework*. London: Methuen.

Bard, C. & Fleury, M. (1976). Analysis of visual search activity in sport problem situations. *Journal of Human Movement Studies, 3*, 214–222.

Bard, C., Fleury, M., Carriere, L., & Halle, M. (1980). Analysis of gymnastic judges' visual search. *Research Quarterly, 51*, 267–273.

Bard, C., Fleury, M., & Goulet, C. (1994). Relationship between perceptual strategies and response adequacy in sport situations. *International Journal of Sport Psychology, 25*, 266–281.

Barr, K.A., & Hall, C. (1992). The use of imagery by rowers. *International Journal of Sport Psychology, 23*, 243–261.

Bartlett, F.C. (1932). *Remembering: A case-study in experimental and social psychology*. Cambridge: Cambridge University Press.

Bartlett, F.C. (1947). The measurement of human skill. *British Medical Journal, June 14*, 835–838.

Bartlett, F.C. (1958). *Thinking: An experimental and social study*. London: Unwin University Books.

Bartlett, K. (1994). For many athletes, fear is the opponent to beat. *Providence Journal, 13 Feb*, 9–10.

Baumeister, R.F. & Showers, C.J. (1986). A review of paradoxical performance effect: Choking under pressure in sports and mental tests. *European Journal of Social Psychology, 16*, 361–383.

Becker had to struggle to survive. (1992, April 23). *The Irish Times*, p.14.

Becker's gesture upsets Bergstrom. (1994, June 30). *The Orlando Sentinel*, D-11.

Bedard, J. & Chi, M.T.H. (1992). Expertise. *Current Directions in Psychological Science, 1*, 135–139.

Bedon, B.G. & Howard, D.E. (1992). Memory for the frequency of occurrence of karate techniques: A comparison of experts and novices. *Bulletin of the Psychonomic Society, 30*, 117–119.

Benson, H., Beary, J.F., & Carol, M.P. (1974). The relaxation response. *Psychiatry, 37*, 37–46.

Berardi-Coletta, B., Buyer, L.S., Dominowski, R.L., & Rellinger, E.R. (1995). Metacognition and problem solving: A process-oriented approach. *Journal of Experimental Psychology: Learning, Memory and Cognition, 21*, 205–223.

Berlyne, D.E. (1960). *Conflict, arousal and curiosity*. London: McGraw-Hill.

Bernstein, D.A., Roy, E.J., Srull, T.K. & Wickens, C.D. (1994). *Psychology* (3rd ed.). Boston: Houghton Mifflin.

Bernstein, N.A. (1967). *The control and regulation of movements*. Oxford: Pergamon Press.

Berry, D.C. & Broadbent, D.E. (1984). On the relationship between task performance and associated verbalizable knowledge. *Quarterly Journal of Experimental Psychology, 36A*, 209–231.

Best, J.B. (1995). *Cognitive psychology* (4th ed.). St. Paul, MN: West.

Bird, A.M. & Horn, M.A. (1990). Cognitive anxiety and mental errors in sport. *Journal of Sport and Exercise Psychology, 12*, 217–222.

Bliss, C.B. (1892–1893). Investigations in reaction time and attention. *Studies from the Yale Psychological Laboratory, 1*, 1–55.

Bonanno, G.A. & Singer, J.L. (1993). Controlling one's stream of thought through perceptual and reflexive processing. In D.M. Wegner & J.W. Pennebaker (Eds.), *Handbook of mental control* (pp. 149–170). Englewood Cliffs, NJ: Prentice Hall.

Bond, J. & Sargent, G.I. (1995). Concentration skills in sport: An applied perspective. In T. Morris & J. Summers (Eds.), *Sport psychology: Theory, applications and issues* (pp. 386–419). Chichester: John Wiley.

Borgeaud, P. & Abernethy, B. (1987). Skilled perception in volleyball defence. *Journal of Sport Psychology, 9*, 400–406.

Botham, I. (1980). *Botham on cricket*. London: Cassell.

Boutcher, S.H. (1990). The role of performance routines in sport. In J.G. Jones & L. Hardy (Eds.), *Stress and performance in sport* (pp. 231–245). Chichester: John Wiley.

Boutcher, S.H. (1992). Attention and athletic performance: An integrated approach. In T. Horn (Ed.), *Advances in sport psychology* (pp. 251–265). Champaign, IL: Human Kinetics.

Boutcher, S.H. & Crews, D.J. (1987). The effect of a preshot routine on a well-learned skill. *International Journal of Sport Psychology, 18*, 30–39.

Boutcher, S.H. & Rotella, R.J. (1987). A psychological skills education programme for closed-skill performance enhancement. *The Sport Psychologist, 1*, 127–137.

Boutcher, S.H. & Zinsser, N. (1990). Cardiac deceleration of elite and beginning golfers during putting. *Journal of Sport and Exercise Psychology, 12*, 37–47.

Brady, F. (1995). Sport skill classification, gender and perceptual style. *Perceptual and Motor Skills, 81*, 611–620.

Brennan, J. (1992a). Italians seek ban on Irish. *The Evening Press, 18 May*, p. 21.

Brennan, J. (1992b). Evening race suits Sonia. *The Evening Press, 6 August*, p. 24.

Brennan, J. (1992c). Costello way below best. *The Evening Press, 31 July*, 28.

Brewer, B.W., Van Raalte, J.L. & Linder, D.E. (1992). *Attentional focus and endurance performance.* Unpublished manuscript, Springfield College, Massachusetts, Department of Psychology, Springfield, MA.

Brewer, B.W., Van Raalte, J.L., Linder, D.E., & Van Raalte, N.S. (1991). Peak performance and the perils of retrospective introspection. *Journal of Sport and Exercise Psychology, 8*, 227–238.

Brewin, C.R. (1988). *Cognitive foundations of clinical psychology*. Hove: Lawrence Erlbaum Associates Ltd.

Broadbent, D.E. (1958). *Perception and communication*. Oxford: Pergamon.

Broadbent, D.E. (1971). *Decision and stress*. London: Academic Press.

Broadbent, D.E. (1980). The minimization of models. In A.J. Chapman & D.M. Jones (Eds.), *Models of man* (pp. 113–128). Leicester: British Psychological Society.

Broadbent, D.E., Cooper, P.F., Fitzgerald, P., & Parkes, K.R. (1982). The Cognitive Failures Questionnaire (CFQ) and its correlates. *British Journal of Clinical Psychology, 21*, 1–16.

Brooks, L.J. (1968). Spatial and verbal components of interference between different pairs of tasks. *Canadian Journal of Psychology, 22*, 349–368.

Brown, L. (1993). *The New Shorter Oxford English Dictionary*. Oxford: Clarendon Press.

Browne, M.A. & Mahoney, M.J. (1984). Sport psychology. *Annual Review of Psychology, 35*, 605–625.

Buckolz, E., Prapavessis, H., & Fairs, J. (1988). Advance cues and their use in predicting tennis passing shots. *Canadian Journal of Sport Science, 13*, 20–30.

Budney, A.J., Murphy, S.M. & Woolfolk, R.L. (1994). Imagery and motor performance: What do we really know? In A.A. Sheikh & E.R. Korn (Eds.), *Imagery in sports and physical performance* (pp. 97–120). Amityville, NY: Baywood.

Budney, A.J. & Woolfolk, R.L. (1990). Using the wrong image: An exploration of the adverse effects of imagery on motor performance. *Journal of Mental Imagery, 14*, 75–86.

Bunker, L., Williams, J.M. & Zinsser, N. (1993). Cognitive techniques for improving performance and building confidence. In J.M. Williams (Ed.), *Applied sport psychology: Personal growth to peak performance* (pp. 225–242). Mountain View, CA: Mayfield Publishing Company.

Burke, K.L. (1992). Concentration. *Sport Psychology Training Bulletin, 4*, 1–8.

Burn, G. (1992). *Pocket money: Inside the world of professional snooker.* London: Heinemann.

Burton, D. (1992). The Jekyll/Hyde nature of goals: Reconceptualizing goal-setting in sport. In T.S. Horn (Ed.), *Advances in sport psychology* (2nd ed., pp. 267–297). Champaign, IL: Human Kinetics.

Carpenter, W.B. (1894). *Principles of mental physiology.* New York: Appleton-Century-Crofts.

Carr, T.H. (1992). Automaticity and cognitive economy: Is word recognition "automatic"? *American Journal of Psychology, 105*, 201–237.

Carver, C.S. & Scheier, M.F. (1990). Self-focus and self-attention. In M.W. Eysenck (Ed.), *The Blackwell Dictionary of Cognitive Psychology* (pp. 317–325). Oxford: Basil Blackwell.

Casey, G. & Moran, A. (1989). The computational metaphor and cognitive psychology. *Irish Journal of Psychology, 10*, 143–161.

Castiello, U. & Umilta, C. (1988). Temporal dimensions of mental effort in different sports. *International Journal of Sport Psychology, 19*, 199–210.

Castiello, U. & Umilta, C. (1992). Orienting of attention in volleyball players. *International Journal of Sport Psychology, 23*, 301–310.

Caudill, D. & Weinberg, R.S. (1983). The effects of varying the length of the psych-up interval on motor performance. *Journal of Sport Behaviour, 6*, 86–91.

Caudill, D., Weinberg, R.S., & Jackson, A. (1983). Psyching-up and track athletes: A preliminary investigation. *Journal of Sport Psychology, 5*, 231–235.

Cautela, J.R. (1993). Covert conditioning: Assumptions and procedures. In J.R. Cautela & A.J. Kearney (Eds.), *Covert conditioning casebook* (pp. 3–10). Monterey, CA: Brooks/Cole.

Cavanaugh, J. (1994). Raymond started thinking and started losing to Graf. *New York Times, 25 July*, c7.

Chadband, I. (1995). Who on earth can beat this man? *The Sunday Times, 30 July*, p. 12.

Charness, N. (1979). Components of skill in bridge. *Canadian Journal of Psychology, 33*, 1–16.

Chartrand, J.M., Jowdy, D.P., & Danish, S.J. (1992). The Psychological Skills Inventory for Sports: Psychometric characteristics and applied implications. *Journal of Sport and Exercise Psychology, 14*, 405–413.

Chase, W.G. & Simon, H.A. (1973). Perception in chess. *Cognitive Psychology, 4*, 55–81.

Chen, D. & Singer, R.N. (1992). Self-regulation and cognitive strategies in sport participation. *International Journal of Sport Psychology, 23,* 277–300.

Cherry, C. (1953). Some experiments on the recognition of speech with one and with two ears. *Journal of the Acoustical Society of America, 25,* 975–979.

Chi, M.T.H., Bassok, M., Lewis, M.W., Reimann, P., & Glaser, R. (1989). Self-explanations: How students study and use examples in learning to solve problems. *Cognitive Science, 13,* 145–182.

Chi, M.T.H., Glaser, R. & Rees, E. (1982). Expertise in problem solving. In R.J. Sternberg (Ed.), *Advances in the psychology of human intelligence,* Vol. 1. (pp. 7–75). Hillsdale, NJ: Lawrence Erlbaum Associates Inc.

Chomsky, N. (1959). Review of B.F. Skinner's "Verbal Behaviour". *Language, 35,* 26–58.

Cioffi, D. (1991). Beyond attentional strategies: A cognitive-perceptual model of somatic interpretation. *Psychological Bulletin, 109,* 25–41.

Cioffi, D. (1993). Sensate body, directive mind: Physical sensations and mental control. In D.M. Wegner & J.W. Pennebaker (Eds.), *Handbook of mental control* (pp. 410–442). Englewood Cliffs, NJ: Prentice Hall.

Clark, J.E. (1995). On becoming skilful: Patterns and constraints. *Research Quarterly for Exercise and Sport, 66,* 173–183.

Clark, L.V. (1960). Effect of mental practice on the development of a certain motor skill. *Research Quarterly, 31,* 560–569.

Claxton, G. (1980). Cognitive psychology: A suitable case for what sort of treatment? In G. Claxton (Ed.), *Cognitive psychology: New directions* (pp. 1–25). London: Routledge & Kegan Paul.

Clay, D. (1988). Golf's forgotten ritual. *Golf Monthly, August,* 116–118.

Clingman, J.M. & Hilliard, D.V. (1990). Race walkers quicken their step by tuning in, not stepping out. *The Sport Psychologist, 4,* 25–32.

Cohen, G., Kiss, G. & Le Voi, M. (1993). *Memory: Current issues* (2nd ed.) Buckingham: Open University Press.

Cohn, P.J. (1990). Preperformance routines in sport: Theoretical support and practical applications. *The Sport Psychologist, 4,* 301–312.

Cole's comments open the doors. (1993, December, 3). *The Evening Press,* p. 3.

Coles, M.G.H. (1972). Cardiac and respiratory activity during visual search. *Journal of Experimental Psychology, 96,* 371–379.

Coles, M.G.H. (1983). Situational determinants and psychological significance of heart rate changes. In A. Gale & J.A. Edwards (Eds.), *Physiological correlates of human behaviour, Volume 2: Attention and performance* (pp. 171–185). London: Academic Press.

Cooke, N. (1992). Modelling human expertise in expert systems. In R.R. Hoffman (Ed.), *The psychology of expertise: Cognitive research and empirical AI* (pp. 29–60). New York: Springer-Verlag.

Coon, D. (1994). *Essentials of psychology* (6th ed.) St. Paul, MN: West.

Cooney, A. (1995). Steve tops at mind games. *The Evening Press, 21 March,* p.24.

Corbin, C.B. (1972). Mental practice. In W.P. Morgan (Ed.), *Ergogenic aids and muscular performance* (pp. 93–118). San Diego, CA: Academic Press.

Cote, J., Salmela, J., & Papathanasopoulu, P.P. (1992). Effects of progressive exercise on attentional focus. *Perceptual and Motor Skills, 75,* 351–354.

Cote, J., Salmela, J., Trudel, P., Baria, A., & Russell, S. (1995). The coaching model: A grounded assessment of expert gymnastic coaches' knowledge. *Journal of Sport and Exercise Psychology, 17,* 1–17.

Courneya, K.S. & Carron, A.V. (1992). The home advantage in sport competitions: A literature review. *Journal of Sport and Exercise Psychology, 14*, 28–39.

Couture, R.T., Singh, M.L., Lee, W., Chahal, P., Wankel, L., Oseen, M., & Wheeler, G. (1994). The effect of mental training on the performance of military endurance tasks in the Canadian infantry. *International Journal of Sport Psychology, 25*, 144–157.

Cox, R.H. (1994). *Sport psychology: Concepts and applications*. Madison, WI: Brown & Benchmark.

Cox, R.H., Qiu, Y. & Liu, Z. (1993). Overview of sport psychology. In R.N. Singer, M. Murphey & L.K. Tennant (Eds.), *Handbook of research in sport psychology* (pp. 3–31). New York: Macmillan.

Cratty, B.J. (1983). *Psychology in contemporary sport*. Englewood Cliffs, NJ: Prentice-Hall.

Craver-Lemley, C. & Reeves, A. (1992). How imagery interferes with vision. *Psychological Review, 99*, 633–649.

Crews, D. & Landers, D.M. (1993). Electroencephalographic measures of attentional patterns prior to the golf putt. *Medicine and Science in Sports and Exercise, 25*, 116–126.

Crews, D.J. & Boutcher, S.H. (1986a). An observational behaviour analysis of ladies professional golf association tour players. *Journal of Sport Behaviour, 9*, 51–58.

Crews, D.J. & Boutcher, S.H. (1986b). Effects of structured preshot behaviours on beginning golf performance. *Perceptual and Motor Skills, 62*, 291–294.

Crews, D.J. (1993). Self-regulation strategies in sport and exercise. In R.N. Singer, M. Murphey & L.K. Tennant (Eds.), *Handbook of research in sport psychology* (pp. 557–568). New York: Macmillan.

Dalgleish, T., Cameron, C.M., Power, M.J., & Bond, A. (1995). The use of an emotional priming paradigm with clinically anxious subjects. *Cognitive Therapy and Research, 19*, 69–89.

Dalloway, M. (1992). *Visualization: The master skill in mental training*. Phoenix, AZ: Optimal Performance Institute.

Dalloway, M. (1993). *Concentration: Focus your mind, power your game*. Phoenix, AZ: Optimal Performance Institute.

Daniels, F.S., Wilkinson, M.O., Hatfield, B.D. & Lewis, D.A. (1981). *Synchrony of autonomic perception and physiological reactivity as related to performance accuracy*. Paper presented at a meeting of the North American Society for the Psychology of Sport and Physical Activity, Asilomar, 1981.

Darcy asks for whom the mobile phone rings. (1995, May 19). *The Irish Times*, p.17. David-Neel, A. (1967). *Magic and mystery in Tibet*. London: Souvenir Press.

Davids, K., Handford, C., & Williams, M. (1994). The natural physical alternative to cognitive theories of motor behaviour: An invitation for interdisciplinary research in sports science? *Journal of Sports Sciences, 12*, 495–528.

De Groot, A.D. (1965). *Thought and choice in chess*. The Hague: Mouton.

De Groot, A.D. (1966). Perception and memory versus thought: Some old ideas and some recent findings. In B. Kleinmuntz (Ed.), *Problem solving*. New York: John Wiley.

Deary, I.J. & Mitchell, H. (1989). Inspection time and high-speed ball games. *Perception, 18*, 789–792.

Decety, J. & Ingvar, D.H. (1990). Brain structures participating in mental simulation of motor behaviour: A neruopsychological interpretation. *Acta Psychologica, 73*, 13-34.

Decety, J., Jeannerod, M., Durozard, M., & Baverel, G. (1993). Central activation of autonomic effectors during mental simulation of motor actions. *Journal of Physiology, 461*, 549–563.

Decety, J. & Michel, F. (1989). Comparative analysis of actual and mental movement times in two graphic tasks. *Brain and Cognition, 11*, 87-97.

Deikman, A.J. (1963). Experimental meditation. *Journal of Nervous and mental Disease, 136*, 329–373.

Deikman, A.J. (1966). Deautomatization and the mystic experience. *Psychiatry, 29*, 324–338.

Denis, M. (1985). Visual imagery and the use of mental practice in the development of motor skills. *Canadian Journal of Applied Sport Sciences, 10*, 4s-16s.

Deshimaru, T. (1982). *The Zen way to the martial arts.* New York: Viking Penguin.

Deutsch, J.A., & Deutsch, D. (1963). Attention: Some theoretical considerations. *Psychological Review, 70*, 80-90.

Doust, D. (1995). South Africa's wild one set to become the new God of golf. *The Sunday Tribune, 1 Jan*, p. 7.

Driskell, J.E., Copper, C., & Moran, A. (1994). Does mental practice enhance performance? *Journal of Applied Psychology, 79*, 481–492.

Druckman, D. & Swets, J.A. (1988). *Enhancing human performance: Issues, theories and techniques.* Washington, DC: National Academy Press.

Duncker, K. (1945). On problem solving. *Psychological Monographs, 58:5* (whole no. 270).

Duval, S. & Wicklund, R.A. (1972). *A theory of objective self-awareness.* New York: Academic Press.

Dweck, C.A. (1992). The study of goals in psychology. *Psychological Science, 3*, 162–167.

Easterbrook, J.A. (1959). The effect of emotion on cue utilisation and the organisation of behaviour. *Psychological Review, 66*, 183–201.

Eccleston, C. (1995). Chronic pain and distraction: An experimental investigation into the role of sustained and shifting attention in the processing of chronic persistent pain. *Behaviour Research and Therapy, 33*, 391–405.

Edmondson, R. (1995). Staying ahead of the game. *The Irish Times, 13 November*, p. 8.

Eloi, S. & Denis, M. (1987). Imagerie et repetition mentale dans l'acquisition d'une habilite sportive. In A. Vom Hofe & R. Simmonet (Eds.), *Recherches en psychologie du sport* (pp. 45–53). Issey-les-Moulineaux: EAP.

Epstein, M.L. (1980). The relationship of mental imagery and mental rehearsal to performance of a motor task. *Journal of Sport Psychology, 2*, 211–220.

Ericsson, K.A. & Charness, N. (1994). Expert performance: Its structure and acquisition. *American Psychologist, 49*, 725–747.

Ericsson, K.A., Krampe, R.T., & Tesch-Romer, C. (1993). The role of deliberate practice in the acquisition of expert performance. *Psychological Review, 100*, 363–406.

Ericsson, K.A., & Lehmann, A.C. (1996). Expert and exceptional performance: Evidence of maximal adaptation to task constraints. *Annual Review of Psychology, 47*, 273-305.

Eriksen, B. & Eriksen, C.W (1974). Effects of noise letters upon the identification of target letters in a non search task. *Perception and Psychophysics, 16*, 143–149.

Estes, W.K. (1991). What is cognitive science? *Psychological Science, 5*, 282.

Etelapelto, A. (1993). Metacognition and the expertise of computer program comprehension. *Scandinavian Journal of Educational Research, 37*, 243–254.

Etzel, E.F. (1979). Validation of a conceptual model characterising attention among international rifle shooters. *Journal of Sport Psychology, 1*, 281–290.

Eysenck, M.W. (1988). Anxiety and attention. *Anxiety Research, 1*, 9–15.

Eysenck, M.W. (1990). *The Blackwell Dictionary of Cognitive Psychology*. Oxford: Blackwell.

Eysenck, M.W. (1992). *Anxiety: The cognitive perspective*. Hove: Lawrence Erlbaum Associates Ltd.

Eysenck, M.W. (1993). *Principles of cognitive psychology*. Hove: Lawrence Erlbaum Associates Ltd.

Eysenck, M.W. & Keane, M.T. (1990). *Cognitive psychology: A student's handbook*. Hove and London: Lawrence Erlbaum Associates Ltd.

Eysenck, M.W. & Keane, M.T. (1995). *Cognitive psychology: A student's handbook* (3rd ed.) Hove: Lawrence Erlbaum Associates Ltd.

Farah, M., Peronnet, F., Gonon, M.A., & Giard, M.H. (1988). Electrophysiological evidence for a shared representation medium for visual images and percepts . *Journal of Experimental Psychology: General, 117*, 248–257.

Fazey, J. & Hardy, L. (1988). *The inverted-U hypothesis: A catastrophe for sport psychology?* Leeds: British Association for Sport Sciences.

Feltz, D.L., & Reissinger, C.A. (1990). Effects of in vivo emotive imagery and performance feedback. *Journal of Sport and Exercise Psychology, 12*, 132–143.

Feltz, D.L. & Landers, D.M. (1983). The effects of mental practice on motor skill learning and performance: A meta-analysis. *Journal of Sport Psychology, 5*, 25–57.

Fenigstein, A., Scheier, M.F., & Buss, H. (1975). Public and private self-consciousness: Assessment and theory. *Journal of Consulting and Clinical Psychology, 43*, 522–527.

Fenz, W.D. (1975). Coping mechanisms and performance under stress. In D.M. Landers, D.V. Harris & R.W. Christina (Eds.), *Psychology of sport and motor behaviour, II* (pp. 3–23). University Park, PA: Pennsylvania State University.

Finke, R.A. (1979). The functional equivalence of mental images and errors of movement. *Cognitive Psychology, 11*, 235–264.

Finke, R.A. (1989). *Principles of mental imagery*. Cambridge, MA: MIT Press.

Fisk, A.D., Derrick, W.L., & Schneider, W. (1986–1987). A methodological assessment and evaluation of dual-task paradigms. *Current Psychology Research and Reviews, 5*, 315–327.

Fiske, S.T. & Emery, E.J. (1993). Lost mental control and exaggerated social control: Social-cognitive and psychoanalytic speculations. In *Handbook of mental control* (pp. 171–199). Englewood Cliffs, NJ: Prentice Hall.

Fitts, P. & Posner, M.I. (1967). *Human performance*. Monterey, CA: Brooks/Cole.

Flavell, J.H. (1979). Metacognition and cognitive monitoring. *American Psychologist, 34*, 906–911.

Flavell, J.H. & Wellman, H.M. (1977). Metamemory. In R.V. Kail, Jr. & J.W. Hagen (Eds.), *Perspectives on the development of memory and cognition* (pp. 3–34). Hillsdale, NJ: Lawrence Erlbaum Associates Inc.

Foley, M. & Hart, A. (1992). Expert-novice differences and knowledge elicitation. In R.R. Hoffman (Ed.), *The psychology of expertise: Cognitive research and empirical AI* (pp. 233–244). New York.: Springer-Verlag.

Fox, A. & Evans, R. (1979). *If I'm the better player, why can't I win?* Kentfield, CA: Adidas Tennis Camps.

Fox, E. (1994). *Trait anxiety, distractibility and cognitive inhibition.* Unpublished manuscript, University of Essex, Department of Psychology, Colchester, U.K.

Frith, D. (1977). *The fast men*. London: Corgi.

Gabriele, T.E., Hall, C.R., & Lee, T.D. (1989). Cognition in motor learning: Imagery effects on contextual interference. *Human Movement Science, 8*, 227–245.

Gagne, E.D., Yekovich, C.W. & Yekovich, F.R. (1993). *Cognitive psychology of school learning*. New York: Harper Collins.

Gardner, H. (1985). *The mind's new science*. New York: Basic Books.

Garfield, C.A. & Bennett, H.Z. (1984). *Peak performance: Mental training techniques of the world's greatest athletes*. Los Angeles: Tarcher.

Garland, D.J. & Barry, J.R. (1991). Cognitive advantage in sport: The nature of perceptual structures. *American Journal of Psychology, 104*, 211–228.

Garner, W.R. (1974). *The processing of information and structure*. Potomac, MD: Lawrence Erlbaum Associates.

Gauron, E. (1984). *Mental training for peak performance*. Lansing, NY: Sport Science Associates.

Gayton, W.F., Cielinski, K.L., Francis-Keniston, W.J., & Hearns, J.F. (1989). Effects of preshot routine on free-throw shooting. *Perceptual and Motor Skills, 68*, 317–318.

Gellatly, A. (1986). *The skilful mind: An introduction to cognitive psychology*. Buckingham: Open University Press.

Gibson, J.J. (1979). *The ecological approach to visual perception*. Boston: Houghton Mifflin.

Gill, D.L. & Strom, E.H. (1985). The effect of attentional focus on performance of an endurance task. *International Journal of Sport Psychology, 16*, 217–223.

Gilleece, D. (1991). It takes imagination to shoot low scores - Feherty. *The Irish Times, 23 March*, p. 14.

Gilleece, D. (1992). Golf's great gaffes. *The Irish Times, 14 December*, p. 6.

Gilleece, D. (1994). Histrionics of the hurricane not enough to put off either the referee or Doherty. *The Irish Times, 19 April*, p. 17.

Glaser, R. & Chi, M.T.H. (1988). Overview. In M.T.H. Chi, R. Glaser & M.J. Farr (Eds.), *The nature of expertise* (pp. xv-xxviii). Hillsdale, NJ: Lawrence Erlbaum Associates Inc.

Glencross, D.J. (1992). Human skills and motor learning: A critical review. *Sport Science Review, 1*, 65–78.

Glisky, M. & Williams, J.M. (1993). *Internal and external mental imagery perspectives and performance on two tasks.* Unpublished manuscript, University of Arizona, Dept. of Psychology, Tucson, AZ.

Golf. (1992, April 20). *The Irish Times*, p.18.

Gopher, D. (1992). The skill of attention control: Acquisition and execution of attention strategies. In D.E.. Meyer & S. Kornblum (Eds.), *Attention and performance, XIV: Synergies in experimental psychology, artificial intelligence, and cognitive neuroscience.* Cambridge, MA: MIT Press.

Gopher, D. & Kahneman, D. (1971). Individual differences in attention and the prediction of flight criteria. *Perceptual and Motor Skills, 33*, 1335–1342.

Gordon, S. (1990). A mental skills training programme for the Western Australia State Cricket Team. *The Sport Psychologist, 4*, 386–399.

Gould, D., Eklund, R., & Jackson, S. (1992a). 1988 US Olympic wrestling excellence, I: Mental preparation, precompetitive cognition and affect. *The Sport Psychologist, 6*, 358–382.

Gould, D., Eklund, R.C., & Jackson, S.A. (1992b). 1988 US Olympic wrestling excellence, II: Thoughts and affect occurring during competition. *The Sport Psychologist, 6*, 383–402.

Gould, D., Weinberg, R.S., & Jackson, A. (1980). Mental preparation strategies, cognitions and strength performance. *Journal of Sport Psychology, 2*, 329–339.

Gould, D., Finch, L.M., & Jackson, S.A. (1993). Coping strategies used by national champion figure-skaters. *Research Quarterly for Exercise and Sport, 64*, 453–468.

Gould, D., Hodge, K., Peterson, K., & Giannini, J. (1989). An exploratory examination of strategies used by elite coaches to enhance self-efficacy in athletes. *Journal of Sport and Exercise Psychology, 11*, 128–140.

Gould, D. & Krane, V. (1992). The arousal-athletic performance relationship: Current status and future directions. In T.S. Horn (Ed.), *Advances in sport psychology* (pp. 119–141). Champaign, IL: Human Kinetics.

Gould, D. & Udry, E. (1994). Psychological skills for enhancing performance: Arousal regulation strategies. *Medicine and Science in Sports and Exercise, 26*, 478–485.

Goulet, C., Bard, C., & Fleury, M. (1989). Expertise differences in preparing to return a tennis serve: A visual information processing approach. *Journal of Sport and Exercise Psychology, 11*, 382–398.

Goulet, C., Bard, C., & Fleury, M. (1992). Les exigences attentionelle de la preparation au retour de service au tennis. *Canadian Journal of Sport Sciences, 17*, 98–103.

Graydon, J. & Eysenck, M.W. (1989). Distraction and cognitive performance. *European Journal of Cognitive Psychology, 1*, 161–179.

Green, L.B. (1994). The use of imagery in the rehabilitation of injured athletes. In A.A. Sheikh & E.R. Korn (Eds.), *Imagery in sports and physical performance* (pp. 157–174). Amityville, NY: Baywood.

Groden, J., Cautela, J.R., Le Vaseur, P., Groden, G. & Bausman, M. (1991). *Imagery procedures for people with special needs.* Champaign, IL: Research Press.

Grouios, G. (1992). Mental practice: A review. *Journal of Sport Behaviour, 15*, 42–59.

Guerin, B. (1993). *Social facilitation.* Cambridge: Cambridge University Press.

Haberlandt, K. (1994). *Cognitive psychology*. Boston: Allyn and Bacon.

Hackfort, D. & Schwenkmezger, P. (1993). Anxiety. In R.N. Singer, M. Murphey & L.K. Tennant (Eds.), *Handbook of research in sport psychology* (pp. 328–364). New York: Macmillan.

Hale, B.D. (1994). Imagery perspectives and learning in sports performance. In A.A. Sheikh & E.R. Korn (Eds.), *Imagery in sports and physical performance* (pp. 75–96). Amityville, NY: Baywood.

Hall, C.R., Pongrac, J., & Buckolz, E. (1985). The measurement of imagery ability. *Human Movement Science, 4*, 107–118.

Hall, C.R., Schmidt, D., Durand, M.C. & Buckolz, E. (1994). Imagery and motor skills acquisition. In A.A. Sheikh & E.R. Korn (Eds.), *Imagery in sports and physical performance* (pp. 121–134). Amityville, NY: Baywood.

Hall, C.R., Bernoties, L., & Schmidt, D. (1995). Interference effects of mental imagery on a motor task. *British Journal of Psychology, 86*, 181–190.

Hall, C.R., Rodgers, W.M., & Barr, K.A. (1990). The use of imagery by athletes in selected sports. *The Sport Psychologist, 4*, 1–10.

Hall, E.G. & Hardy, C.J. (1991). Ready, aim, fire ... Relaxation strategies for enhancing pistol marksmanship. *Perceptual and Motor Skills, 72*, 775–786.

Hampson, P.J. (1989). Aspects of attention and cognitive science. *Irish Journal of Psychology, 10*, 261–275.

Hampson, P. J., & Morris, P. E. (1996). *Understanding cognition*. Oxford: Basil Blackwell.

Hanin, Y.L. (1980). A study of anxiety in sports. In W.F. Straub (Ed.), *Sport psychology: An analysis of athlete behaviour* (pp. 236–249). Ithaca, NY: Mouvement Publications.

Hanrahan, S. (1995). Attribution theory. In T. Morris & J. Summers (Eds.), *Sport psychology: Theory, applications and issues* (pp. 122–142). Brisbane: John Wiley.

Hardy, L. (1989). Sport psychology. In A.M. Colman & J.G. Beaumont (Eds.), *Psychology survey, Vol. 7* (pp. 211–231). Leicester: British Psychological Society.

Hardy, L. & Fazey, J. (1990). *Concentration training*. Leeds: National Coaching Foundation.

Hardy, L. & Jones, G. (1994). Current issues and future directions for performance-related research in sport psychology. *Journal of Sports Sciences, 12*, 61–92.

Hardy, L. & Nelson, D. (1988). Self-regulation in sport and work. *Ergonomics, 31*, 1573–1583.

Hardy, L. & Parfitt, G. (1991). A catastrophe model of anxiety and performance. *British Journal of Psychology, 82*, 163–168.

Harris, D.V. & Harris, B.L. (1984). *The athlete's guide to sport psychology: Mental skills for physical people*. New York: Leisure Press.

Harris, D.V. & Williams, J.M. (1993). Relaxation and energizing techniques for regulation of arousal. In J.M. Williams (Ed.), *Applied sport psychology: Personal growth to peak performance* (2nd ed., pp. 185–199). Mountain View, CA: Mayfield.

Harris, H. (1995). Kev calls for FA action over replays. *Daily Mirror, 30 October*, p.32.

Hartley, A. (1992). Attention. In F.I.M. Craik & T.A. Salthouse (Eds.), *Handbook of aging and cognition* (pp. 3–50). Hove: Lawrence Erlbaum Associates Ltd.

Harvey, N. (1988). The psychology of action: Current controversies. In G. Claxton (Ed.), *Growth points in cognition* (pp. 66–90). London: Routledge.

Hashman, J. (1982). *Winning badminton*. London: Hyperion Books.

Hatfield, B.D. & Landers, D.M. (1987). Psychophysiology in exercise and sport research: An overview. *Exercise and Sport Science Reviews, 15*, 351–388.

Hatfield, B.D., Landers, D.M., & Ray, W.J. (1984). Cognitive processes during self-paced motor performance: An electroencephalographic study of elite rifle shooters. *Journal of Sport Psychology, 6*, 42–59.

Hayes, J.R. (1985). Three problems in teaching general skills. In J. Segal, S. Chipman & R. Glaser (Eds.), *Thinking and learning skills, Vol. 2: Research and open questions* (pp. 391–406). Hillsdale, NJ: Lawrence Erlbaum Associates Inc.

Hayes, L. (1995). Collins produces a magical brew. *The Sunday Press, 26 March*, p. 38.

Head, H. (1920). *Studies in neurology, Vol. 2*. London: Oxford University Press.

Heaney, S. (1991). Markings. In *Seeing things*. Boston: Faber & Faber.

Hecker, J.E. & Kaczor, L.M. (1988). Application of imagery theory to sport psychology: Some preliminary findings. *Journal of Sport and Exercise Psychology, 10*, 363–373.

Helin, P., Sihvonen, R., & Hanninen, O. (1987). Timing of the triggering action of shooting in relation to the cardiac cycle. *British Journal of Sports Medicine, 21*, 33–36.

Hemery, D. (1988). *The pursuit of sporting excellence*. Champaign, IL: Human Kinetics.

Henderson, S.E. (1975). Predicting the accuracy of a throw without visual feedback. *Journal of Human Movement Studies, 1*, 183–189.

Hernandez-Peon, R. (1964). Psychiatric implications of neuropsychological research. *Bulletin of the Menninger Clinic, 28*, 165–188.

Herrigel, E. (1953). *Zen in the art of archery*. London: Routledge.

Heuer, H. (1989). A multiple representations approach to mental practice of motor skills. In B. Kirkcaldy (Ed.), *Normalities and abnormalities in human movement* (pp. 36–57). Basel: Karger.

Highlen, P.S. & Bennett, B.B. (1979). Psychological characteristics of successful and unsuccessful elite wrestlers: An exploratory study. *Journal of Sport Psychology, 1*, 123–137.

Highlen, P.S. & Bennett, B.B. (1983). Elite divers and wrestlers: A comparison between open- and closed-skill athletes. *Journal of Sport Psychology, 5*, 390–409.

Hilgard, E.R. (1980). The trilogy of mind: Cognition, affection and conation. *Journal of the History of the Behavioural Sciences, 16*, 107–117.

Hilgard, E.R. (1992). Divided consciousness and dissociation. *Consciousness and Cognition, 1*, 16–31.

Hinshaw, K. (1991–1992). The effects of mental practice on motor skill performance: Critical evaluation and meta-analysis. *Imagination, Cognition and Personality, 11*, 3–35.

Hird, J.S., Landers, D.M., Thomas, J.R., & Horan, J.J. (1991). Physical practice is superior to mental practice in enhancing cognitive and motor task performance. *Journal of Sport and Exercise Psychology, 13*, 281–293.

Hirst, W. (1986). The psychology of attention. In J. Le Doux & W. Hirst (Eds.), *Dialogues in cognitive neuroscience* (pp. 105–141). Cambridge: Cambridge University Press.

Hoberman, J. (1992). *Mortal engines: Human engineering and the transformation of sport.* New York: Free Press.

Hodgson, G. (1994). Hendry savours win as White reflects on another black day. *The Irish Times, 4 May,* p. 19.

Hoffman, R.R. & Deffenbacher, K.A. (1992). A brief history of applied cognitive psychology. *Applied Cognitive Psychology, 6,* 1–48.

Holyoak, K.J. & Spellman, B. (1993). Thinking. Annual Review of Psychology, 44, 265–315.

Horsley, C. (1989). Developing attentional skills for rowing. *Excel, 6,* 13–16.

Houlston, D.R. & Lowes, R. (1993). Anticipatory cue-utilization processes amongst expert and non-expert wicketkeepers in cricket. *International Journal of Sport Psychology, 24,* 59–73.

Howe, B.L., (1991). Imagery and sport performance. *Sports Medicine, 11,* 1–5.

Huey, E.G. (1968). *The psychology and pedagogy of reading.* Cambridge, MA: MIT Press.

Hull, C.L. (1943). *Principles of behaviour.* New York: Appleton-Century-Crofts.

Ingram, R.E. (1990). Self-focused attention in clinical disorders: Review and a conceptual model. *Psychological Bulletin, 107,* 156–176.

Irvine, D. (1994). Sampras makes everything click. *The Guardian, 29 January,* p. 15.

Isaac, A.R. (1992). Mental practice: Does it work in the field? *The Sport Psychologist, 6,* 192–198.

Isaac, A.R. & Marks, D.F. (1992). The theoretical basis of imagery and motor processes: Imagery and the planning of action. In J. Annett (Ed.), *Conference proceedings: International workshop on imagery and motor processes* (pp. 2–14). Leicester: British Psychological Society.

Isaacs, L.D. & Finch, A.E. (1983). Anticipatory timing of beginning and intermediate tennis players. *Perceptual and Motor Skills, 57,* 451–454.

Jackson, S.A. (1995). Factors influencing the occurrence of flow state in elite athletes. *Journal of Applied Sport Psychology, 7,* 138–166.

Jackson, S.A. & Roberts, G.C. (1992). Positive performance states of athletes: Toward a conceptual understanding peak performance. *The Sport Psychologist, 6,* 156–171.

Jacobson, E. (1932). Electrophysiology of mental activities. *American Journal of Psychology, 44,* 677–694.

Jacobson, E. (1938). *Progressive relaxation.* Chicago: University of Chicago Press.

Jahoda, G. (1969). *The psychology of superstition.* London: Allen Lane.

James, W. (1890). *Principles of psychology.* Holt, Rinehart & Winston, New York.

Janssen, J.J. & Sheikh, A.A. (1994). Enhancing athletic performance through imagery: An overview. In A.A. Sheikh & E.R. Korn (Eds.), *Imagery in sports and physical performance* (pp. 1–22). Amityville, NY: Baywood.

Jeannerod, M. (1994). The representing brain: Neural correlates of motor intention and imagery. *Behavioural and Brain Sciences, 17,* 187–245.

Johnson, M. (1995). Stubborn Atherton chisels out epic draw. *The Irish Times, 5 December,* p. 18.

Johnson, P. (1982). The functional equivalence of imagery and movement. *Quarterly Journal of Experimental Psychology, 34A,* 349–365.

Johnston, W.A. & Dark, V.J. (1986). Selective attention. *Annual Review of Psychology, 37*, 43–75.

Johnston-O'Connor, E.J. & Kirschenbaum, D.S. (1986). Something exceeds like success: Positive self-monitoring for unskilled golfers. *Cognitive Therapy and Research, 10*, 123–136.

Jones, G. (1995). Psychological preparation in racket sports. In T. Reilly, M. Hughes & A. Lees (Eds.), *Science and racket sports* (pp. 203–211). London: E. & F. N. Spon.

Jones, J.G. (1991). Recent developments and current issues in competitive state anxiety research. *The Psychologist, 4*, 152–155.

Jones, K. (1994). Foreman is again the man. *The Irish Times, 7 November*, p. 1.

Jonides, J. (1980). Towards a model of the mind's eye movements. *Canadian Journal of Psychology, 34*, 103–112.

Jowdy, D.P. & Harris, D.V. (1990). Muscular responses during mental imagery as a function of motor skill level. *Journal of Sport and Exercise Psychology, 12*, 191–201.

Judd, C.H. (1908). The relationship of special training and general intelligence. *Educational Review, 36*, 28–42.

Kahneman, D. (1973). *Attention and effort.* Englewood Cliffs, NJ: Prentice-Hall.

Kahneman, D. & Treisman, A.M. (1984). Changing views of attention and automaticity. In R. Parasuraman & D.R. Davies (Eds.), *Varieties of attention* (pp. 29–62). New York: Academic Press.

Kahney, H. (1993). *Problem solving: Current issues.* Buckingham: Open University Press.

Karoly, P. (1993). Mechanisms of self-regulation: A systems view. *Annual Review of Psychology, 44*, 23–52.

Kavanagh, D. (1987). Mood, persistence and success. *Australian Journal of Psychology, 39*, 307–318.

Keele, S.W. & Hawkins, H.L. (1982). Explorations of individual differences relevant to high level skill. *Journal of Motor Behaviour, 14*, 3–23.

Kelly, G.A. (1955). *The psychology of personal constructs.* New York: Norton.

Kelso, J.A.S. (1995). *Dynamic patterns: The self-organisation of brain and behaviour.* Cambridge, MA: MIT Press.

Kerr, J.H. & Cox, T. (1991). Arousal and individual differences in sport. *Personality and Individual Differences, 12*, 1075–1085.

Kimble, G.A. & Perlmutter, L.C. (1970). The problem of volition. *Psychological Review, 77*, 361–384.

Kimiecik, J.C. & Stein, G.L. (1992). Examining flow experiences in sport contexts: Conceptual and methodological concerns. *Journal of Applied Sport Psychology, 4*, 144–160.

Kinchla, R.A. (1992). Attention. *Annual Review of Psychology, 43*, 711–742.

Kirschenbaum, D.S. (1984). Self-regulation and sport psychology: Nurturing an emergent symbiosis. *Journal of Sport Psychology, 6*, 159–183.

Kirschenbaum, D.S. & Bale, R.M. (1984). Cognitive-behavioural skills in golf. In R.M. Suinn (Ed.), *Psychology of sports: Methods and application* (pp. 334–343). Minneapolis, MN: Burgess.

Kirschenbaum, D.S. & Wittrock, D.A. (1984). Cognitive-behavioural interventions in sport: A self-regulatory perspective. In J.M. Silva & R.S. Weinberg (Eds.), *Psychological foundations of sport* (pp. 81–98). Champaign, IL: Human Kinetics.

Kjellberg, A. (1990). Subjective, behavioural and psychophysiological effects of noise. *Scandinavian Journal of Work, Environment and Health, 16*, 29–38.

Klatzky, R.L. (1984). *Memory and awareness.* San Francisco: W.H. Freeman.

Klein, G.A. (1992). Using knowledge engineering to preserve corporate memory. In R.R. Hoffman (Ed.), *The psychology of expertise: Cognitive research and empirical AI* (pp. 170–190). New York: Springer-Verlag.

Klinger, E., Barta, S.G., & Glas, R.A. (1981). Thought content and gap time in basketball. *Cognitive Therapy and Research, 5*, 109–114.

Kohl, R.M. & Roenker, D.L. (1980). Bilateral transfer as a function of mental imagery. *Journal of Motor Behaviour, 12*, 197–206.

Kohl, R.M., Roenker, D.L., & Turner, P.E. (1985). Clarification of competent imagery as a prerequisite for effective skill imagery. *International Journal of Sport Psychology, 16*, 37–45.

Konttinen, N. & Lyytinen, N. (1992). Physiology of preparation: Brain slow waves, heart rate and respiration preceding triggering in rifle shooting. *International Journal of Sport Psychology, 23*, 110–117.

Konttinen, N., Lyytinen, N., & Konttinen, R. (1995). Brain slow potential reflecting successful shooting performance. *Research Quarterly for Exercise and Sport, 66*, 64–72.

Korean shooter reveals secrets. (1992, July 30). *The Irish Times*, p. 14.

Korn, E.R. (1994). Mental imagery in enhancing performance: Theory and practical exercises. In A.A. Sheikh & E.R. Korn (Eds.), *Imagery in sports and physical performance* (pp. 201–230). Amityville, NY: Baywood.

Kosslyn, S.M. (1994). *Image and brain: The resolution of the imagery debate.* Cambridge, MA: MIT Press.

Kosslyn, S.M. & Koenig, O. (1992). *Wet mind: The new cognitive neuroscience.* New York: Free Press.

Kosslyn, S.M., Seger, C., Pani, J.R., & Hillger, L.A. (1990). When is imagery used in everyday life? A diary study. *Journal of Mental Imagery, 14*, 131–152.

Kozar, B., Whitfield, K.E., Lord, R.H., & Mechikoff, R.A. (1993). Timeouts before free throws: Do the statistics support the strategy? *Perceptual and Motor Skills, 76*, 47–50.

Kremer, J. & Scully, D. (1994). *Psychology in sport.* London: Taylor & Francis.

Kyllo, L.B. & Landers, D.M. (1995). Goal setting in sport and exercise: A research synthesis to resolve the controversy. *Journal of Sport and Exercise Psychology, 17*, 117–137.

LaBerge, D. (1973). Attention and the measurement of perceptual learning. *Memory and Cognition, 1*, 268–276.

Lacey, J.I. (1967). Somatic response patterning and stress: Some revision of activation theory. In M.H. Appley & R. Trumbull (Eds.), *Psychological stress: Issues in research* (pp. 170–179). New York: Appleton-Century-Crofts.

Lachman, R., Lachman, J.C.L. & Butterfield, E.C. (1979). *Cognitive psychology and information processing.* Hillsdale, NJ: Lawrence Erlbaum Associates Inc.

Lahey, B.B. (1992). *Psychology: An introduction* (4th ed.). Dubuque, IA: W.C. Brown.

Laidlaw, R. (1993). Faldo is learning to relax. *The Evening Press, 8 May*, p. 16.

Landers, D.M. (1982). Arousal attention and skilled performance: Further considerations. *Quest, 33,* 271–283.

Landers, D.M. (1983). Whatever happened to theory-testing in sport psychology? *Journal of Sport Psychology, 5,* 135–151.

Landers, D.M. & Boutcher, S.H. (1993). Arousal-performance relationships. In J.M. Williams (Ed.), *Applied sport psychology: Personal growth to peak performance* (2nd ed., pp. 163–184). Palo Alto, CA: Mayfield.

Landers, D.M., Boutcher, S.H., & Wang, M.Q. (1986). A psychobiological study of archery performance. *Research Quarterly for Exercise and Sport, 57,* 236–244.

Landers, D.M., Christina, R., Hatfield, B.D., Daniels, F., & Doyle, L. (1980). Moving competitive shooting into the scientist's lab. *American Rifleman, 128,* 36–37.

Landers, D.M., Furst, D.M. & Daniels, F.S. (1981, May). *Anxiety / attention and ability level in open and closed shooting activities.* Paper presented at a meeting of the North American Society for the Psychology of Sport and Physical Activity, Asilomar.

Landers, D.M., Han, M., Salazar, W., Petruzzello, S.J., Kubitz, K.A., & Gannon, T.L. (1994). Effects of learning on electroencephaolgraphic and electrocardiographic patterns in novice archers. *International Journal of Sport Psychology, 25,* 313-330.

Landers, D.M., Petruzzello, S.J., Salazar, W., Crews, D., Kubitz, K.A., Gannon, T.L., & Han, M. (1991). The influence of electrocortical biofeedback on performance in pre-elite archers. *Medicine and Science in Sports and Exercise, 23,* 123–129.

Landers, D.M., Qi, W.M., & Courtet, P. (1985). Peripheral narrowing among experienced and inexperienced rifle-shooters under low- and high-stress conditions. *Research Quarterly for Exercise and Sport, 56,* 122–130.

Lansdowne is the only real one left. (1993, March 22). *The Evening Press,* p. 19.

Lashley, K.S. (1915). The acquisition of skill in archery. *Carnegie Institutions Publications, 7,* 107–128.

Lee, C. (1990). Psyching up for a muscular endurance task: Effects of image content on performance and mood state. *Journal of Sport and Exercise Psychology, 12,* 66–73.

Lee, D.N. (1976). A theory of visual control of braking based on information about time-to-collision. *Perception, 5,* 437–459.

Lee, D.N., Lishman, J.R., & Thomson, J.A. (1982). Regulation of gait in long jumping. *Journal of Experimental Psychology: Human Perception and Performance, 8,* 448–459.

Lee, D.N. & Reddish, P.E. (1981). Plummeting gannets: A paradigm of ecological optics. *Nature, 293,* 293–294.

Lee, T.D. & Magill, R.A. (1983). The locus of contextual interference in motor-skill acquisition. *Journal of Experimental Psychology: Learning, Memory and Cognition, 9,* 730–746.

Leith, L.M. (1988). Choking in sports: Are we our own worst enemies? *International Journal of Sport Psychology, 19,* 59–64.

Lejeune, M., Decker, C., & Sanchez, X. (1994). Mental rehearsal in table tennis performance. *Perceptual and Motor Skills, 79,* 627–641.

Lesser, M. & Murphy, S.M. (1988, August). *The Psychological Skills Inventory for Sports (PSIS): Normative and reliability data.* Paper presented at the annual meeting of the American Psychological Association, Atlanta.

Line, L. (1978). Hadlee - the cat with the snarl of a tiger. *Daily Express, 9 June,*

Lobmeyer, D.L. & Wasserman, E.A. (1986). Preliminaries to free throw shooting: Superstitious behaviour? *Journal of Sport Behaviour, 9,* 70–78.

Locke, E.A. & Latham, G.P. (1985). The application of goal setting to sports. *Journal of Sport Psychology, 7,* 205–222.

Loehr, J.E. (1986). *Mental toughness training for sports: Achieving athletic excellence.* New York: The Stephen Greene Press.

Loehr, J.E. (1989). Mental training for tennis. In J.L. Groppel, J.E. Loehr, D.S. Melville & A.M. Quinn (Eds.), *Science of coaching tennis* (pp. 251–264). Champaign, IL: Leisure Press.

Logan, G.D. (1988). Toward an instance theory of automatisation. *Psychological Review, 95,* 492–527.

Logan, G.D. (1995). Linguistic and conceptual control of visual spatial attention. *Cognitive Psychology, 28,* 103–174.

Lohman, D. (1989). Human intelligence: An introduction to advances in theory and research. *Review of Educational Research, 59,* 333–373.

Lovie, S. (1983). Attention and behaviourism - fact and fiction. *British Journal of Psychology, 74,* 301–310.

Lovejoy, J. (1995). England's striking success. *The Sunday Times, 3 December,* p. 19.

Luria, A.R. (1961). *The role of speech in the regulation of normal and abnormal behaviour.* New York: Liveright.

Mackay, D.G. (1981). The problem of rehearsal or mental practice. *Journal of Motor Behaviour, 13,* 274–285.

Mackey, L. (1994). Looking after number 1. *The Sunday Press, 2 October,* p. 38.

Mackworth, N.H. (1976). Ways of recording line of sight. In R.A. Monty & J.W. Senders (Eds.), *Eye movements and psychological processes* (pp. 173–178). Hillsdale, NJ: Lawrence Erlbaum Associates Inc.

Mahoney, M.J. & Avener, M. (1977). Psychology of the elite athlete: An exploratory study. *Cognitive Therapy and Research, 1,* 135–141.

Mahoney, M.J., Gabriel, T.J., & Perkins, T.S. (1987). Psychological skills and exceptional athletic performance. *The Sport Psychologist, 1,* 181–199.

Mahoney, M.J. (1989). Sport psychology. In I.S. Cohen (Ed.), *The G. Stanley Hall lecture series, Vol. 9* (pp. 97–134). Washington, DC: American Psychological Association.

Marquie, J.M. & Baracat, B. (1992). Task complexity effects, attentional cost and strategies in young and older adults. *Cahiers de Psychologie Cognitive, 12,* 333–362.

Martens, R. (1987). *Coaches guide to sport psychology.* Champaign, IL: Human Kinetics.

Martin, K.A. & Hall, C.R. (1995). Using mental imagery to enhance intrinsic motivation. *Journal of Sport and Exercise Psychology, 17,* 54–69.

Masson, M.E.J. (1990). Cognitive theories of skill acquisition. *Human Movement Science, 9,* 221–239.

Masters, K.S. (1992). Hypnotic susceptibility, cognitive dissociation and runner's high in a sample of marathon runners. *American Journal of Clinical Hypnosis, 34,* 193–201.

Masters, K.S. & Lambert, M.J. (1989). The relations between cognitive coping strategies, reasons for running, injury and performance of marathon runners. *Journal of Sport and Exercise Psychology, 11,* 161–170.

Masters, R.S.W. (1992). Knowledge, "knerves" and know-how: The role of explicit versus implicit knowledge in the breakdown of complex motor skill under pressure. *British Journal of Psychology, 83*, 343–358.

Mathews, A. (1993). Biases in processing emotional stimuli. *The Psychologist, 6*, 493–499.

Matlin, M.W. (1994). *Cognition* (3rd ed.). Orlando, FL: Harcourt Brace Jovanovich.

Maxeiner, J. (1987). Concentration and distribution of attention in sport. *International Journal of Sport Psychology, 18*, 247–255.

Maxwell, B. (1994). Why talking trash is so popular. *Gainesville Sun, 19 June*, 2g.

McCaffrey, N. & Orlick, T. (1989). Mental factors related to excellence among top professional golfers. *International Journal of Sport Psychology, 20*, 256–278.

McCaul, K. & Malott, J.M. (1984). Distractions and coping with pain. *Psychological Bulletin, 95*, 516–533.

McClelland, J.L., Rumelhart, D.E. & The PDP Research Group, (1986). *Parallel distributed processing: Vol. 2, Psychological and biological models.* Cambridge, MA: MIT Press.

McCrone, J. (1993). Shots faster than the speed of thought. *The Independent on Sunday*, 27 June, p. 71.

McCullagh, P., Weiss, M.R. & Ross, D. (1989). Modelling considerations in motor skill acquisition and performance: An integrated approach. In K.B. Pandolf (Ed.), *Exercise and sport sciences reviews* (pp. 475–513). Baltimore: Williams & Wilkins.

McEnroe blames lack of concentration. (1991, May 28). *The Irish Times*, p.17.

McIlvanney, H. (1993). Mouths that menace sportsmanship. *The Observer, 4 July*, p. 42.

McKenzie, A.D. & Howe, B.L. (1991). The effect of imagery on tackling performance in rugby. *Journal of Human Movement Studies, 20*, 163–176.

McLean, N.J. & Richardson, A. (1994). The role of imagery in perfecting already learned physical skills. In A.A. Sheikh & E.R. Korn (Eds.), *Imagery in sports and physical performance* (pp. 59–74). Amityville, NY: Baywood.

McLean, N.J. (1986). Cognitive processes and sport performance. *Behaviour Change, 3*, 112–119.

McLeod, P. (1977). A dual-task response modality effect: Support for multiprocessor models of attention. *Quarterly Journal of Experimental Psychology, 29*, 651–667.

McLeod, P. (1987). Visual reaction time and high-speed ball-games. *Perception, 16*, 49–59.

McLeod, P. & Jenkins, S. (1991). Timing, accuracy and decision-time in high-speed ball games. *International Journal of Sport Psychology, 22*, 279–295.

McNally, R.J. (1995). Automaticity and the anxiety disorders. *Behaviour Research and Therapy, 33*, 747–754.

McPherson, S.L. (1993). The influence of player experience on problem solving during batting preparation for baseball. *Journal of Sport and Exercise Psychology, 15*, 304–325.

McPherson, S.L. & Thomas, J.R. (1989). Relation of knowledge and performance in boys' tennis: Age and expertise. *Journal of Experimental Child Psychology, 48*, 190–211.

McShane, J., Dockerell, J., & Wells, A. (1992). Psychology and cognitive science. *The Psychologist, 5*, 252–255.

Meichenbaum, D. (1977). *Cognitive behaviour modification*. New York: Plenum Press.

Merrill, S. (1981). How to beat the wall. *Runner, 3*, 42–46.

Mestre, D.R. & Pailhous, J. (1991). Expertise in sports as a perceptivo-motor skill. *International Journal of Sport Psychology, 22*, 211–216.

Meyers, A.W. & Schleser, R.A. (1980). A cognitive behavioural intervention for improving basketball performance. *Journal of Sport Psychology, 2*, 69–73.

Meyers, A.W., Schleser, R., & Okwumabua, T.M. (1982). A cognitive behavioural intervention for improving basketball performance. *Research Quarterly for Exercise and Sport, 53*, 344–347.

Meyers, A.W., Schleser, R., Cooke, C.J., & Cuvillier, C. (1979). Cognitive contributions to the development of gymnastic skills. *Cognitive Therapy and Research, 3*, 75–85.

Miller, E. (1994). Optimal sports performance imagery. In A.A. Sheikh & E.R. Korn (Eds.), *Imagery in sports and physical performance* (pp. 175–182). Amityville, NY: Baywood.

Miller, P.H. & Bigi, L. (1979). The development of children's understanding of attention. *Merrill-Palmer Quarterly, 25*, 235–250.

Miller, S. & Ittyerah, M. (1991). Movement imagery in young and congenitally blind children: mental practice without visuo-spatial information. *International Journal of Behavioural Development, 15*, 125–146.

Mineka, S. & Sutton, S.K. (1992). Cognitive biases and emotional disorders. *Psychological Science, 3*, 65–69.

Molander, B. & Backman, L. (1989). Age differences in heart rate patterns during concentration in a precision sport: Implications for attentional training. *Journal of Gerontology: Psychological Sciences, 44*, 80–87.

Moore, W.E. & Stevenson, J.R. (1994). Training a pre-shot routine for golf. *Applied Research in Coaching and Athletics Annual, March*, 161–167.

Moran, A. (1993). Conceptual and methodological issues in the measurement of mental imagery skills in athletes. *Journal of Sport Behaviour, 16*, 156–170.

Moran, A. (1994a). Coping with pressure: Some lessons from sport psychology. In C. Keane (Ed.), *Nervous breakdown* (pp. 195–209). Cork: RTE/Mercier Press.

Moran, A. (1994b). Mental rehearsal in sport: From practice to theory. *Journal of Sport and Exercise Psychology, 16*, s91(abstract).

Moran, A. (1994c). The psychology of concentration in tennis. *Coaches and Coaching, 15*, 3–5.

Moran, A. (1995). How effective are psychological techniques used to enhance performance in tennis? The views of some international tennis coaches. In T. Reilly, M. Hughes & A. Lees (Eds.), *Science and racket sports* (pp. 221–225). London: E. & F.N. Spon.

Moray, N. (1969). *Attention: Selective processes in vision and hearing*. London: Hutchinson Educational.

Morgan, W.P. (1978). The mind of the marathoner. *Psychology Today, April*, 38–40, 43, 45–46, 49.

Morgan, W.P., Horstman, D.H., Cymerman, A., & Stikes, J. (1983). Facilitation of physical performance by means of a cognitive strategy. *Cognitive Therapy and Research, 7*, 251–264.

Morgan, W.P., O'Connor, P.J., Ellickson, K.A., & Bradley, P.W. (1988). Personality structure, mood states and performance in elite male distance runners. *International Journal of Sport Psychology, 19*, 247–263.

Morgan, W.P. & Pollock, M.L. (1977). Psychologic characterisation of the elite distance runner. *Annals of the New York Academy of Sciences, 301*, 382–403.

Morris, A. & Burwitz, L. (1989). Anticipation and movement strategies in elite soccer goalkeepers at penalty kicks. *British Journal of Sport Sciences, 7*, 79–80.

Morris, T. & Summers, J. (1995). Future directions in sport and exercise psychology. In T. Morris & J. Summers (Eds.), *Sport psychology: Theory, applications and issues* (pp. 592–604). Brisbane: John Wiley.

Mumford, M.J. & Hall, C.R. (1985). The effects of internal and external imagery on performing figures in figure skating. *Canadian Journal of Applied Sport Science, 10*, 171–177.

Murphy, S.M. (1990). Models of imagery in sport psychology: A review. *Journal of Mental Imagery, 14*, 153–172.

Murphy, S.M. (1994). Imagery interventions in sport. *Medicine and Science in Sports and Exercise, 26*, 486–494.

Murphy, S.M. & Jowdy, D.P. (1992). Imagery and mental practice. In T. Horn (Ed.), *Advances in sport psychology* (pp. 221–250). Champaign, IL: Human Kinetics,

Murphy, S.M., Jowdy, D.P. & Durtschi, S.K. (1989). *Report on the United States Olympic Committee survey on imagery use in sport: 1989*. Unpublished manuscript, United States Olympic Committee Training Centre, Colorado Springs, CO.

Nacson, J. & Schmidt, R.A. (1971). The activity-set hypothesis for warm-up decrement. *Journal of Motor Behaviour, 3*, 1–5.

Navon, D. & Gopher, D. (1979). On the economy of the human processing system. *Psychological Review, 86*, 214–255.

Neill, W.T. (1977). Inhibitory and facilitatory processes in selective attention. *Journal of Experimental Psychology: Human Perception and Performance, 3*, 444–450.

Neiss, R. (1988). Reconceptualizing arousal: Psychobiological states in motor performance. *Psychological Bulletin, 103*, 345–366.

Neiss, R. (1990). Reconceptualizing relaxation treatments: Psychobiological states in sport. *Clinical Psychology Review, 8*, 139–159.

Neisser, U. (1967). *Cognitive psychology*. New York: Appleton-Century-Crofts.

Neisser, U. (1976). *Cognition and reality*. San Francisco: W.H. Freeman.

Nelson, D. & Hardy, L. (1990). The development of an empirically validated tool for measuring psychological skills in sport. *Journal of Sport Sciences, 8*, 71.

Nelson, D. & Hardy, L. (1992). *The development and validation of the Sport Psychological Skills Inventory*. Unpublished manuscript, University of Wales, Dept of Health and Human Performance, Bangor, Wales.

Nelson, J.E., Duncan, C.P., & Kiecker, P.L. (1993). Toward an understanding of the distraction construct in marketing. *Journal of Business Research, 26*, 201–221.

Newell, A. & Simon, H.A. (1972). *Human problem solving.* Englewood Cliffs, NJ: Prentice-Hall.

Nicklaus, J. (1974). *Golf my way.* New York: Heinemann.

Nideffer, R.M. (1976a). Test of Attentional and Interpersonal Style. *Journal of Personality and Social Psychology, 34,* 394–404.

Nideffer, R.M. (1976b). *The inner athlete: Mind plus muscle for winning.* New York: Thomas Crowell.

Nideffer, R.M. (1980). The role of attention in optimal athletic performance. In P. Klavora & J. Daniel (Eds.), *Coach, athlete and the sport psychologist* (pp. 92–112). Toronto: University of Toronto.

Nideffer, R.M. (1985). *Athletes' guide to mental training.* Champaign, IL: Human Kinetics.

Nideffer, R.M. (1986). Concentration and attention control training. In J. Williams (Ed.), *Applied sport psychology* (pp. 257–269). Palo Alto, CA: Mayfield.

Nideffer, R.M. (1987). Issues in the use of psychological tests in applied settings. *The Sport Psychologist, 1,* 18–28.

Nideffer, R.M. (1990). Use of the Test of Attentional and Interpersonal Style (TAIS) in sport. *The Sport Psychologist, 4,* 285–300.

Nideffer, R.M. (1992). *Psyched to win.* Champaign, IL: Leisure Press.

Nideffer, R.M. (1993a). Attention control training. In R.N. Singer, M. Murphey & L.K. Tennant (Eds.), *Handbook of research in sport psychology* (pp. 542–556). New York: Macmillan.

Nideffer, R.M. (1993b). Concentration and attention control training. In J.M. Williams (Ed.), *Applied sport psychology: From personal growth to peak performance* 2nd ed. (pp. 243–261). Mountain View, CA: Mayfield.

Nigro, G. (1983). *Improvement in skill through observation and mental practice.* Unpublished doctoral dissertation, Cornell University.

Nisbett, R.E. & Wilson, T.D. (1977). Telling more than we can know: Verbal reports on mental processes. *Psychological Review, 84,* 231–259.

Norman, D.A. (1968). Toward a theory of memory and attention. *Psychological Review, 75,* 522–536.

Norman, D.A. (1980). Twelve issues for cognitive science. *Cognitive Science, 4,* 1–32.

Norman, D.A. (1982). *Learning and memory.* San Francisco: W.H. Freeman.

Nougier, V., Stein, J.F., & Bonnel, A.M. (1991). Information processing in sport and orienting of attention'. *International Journal of Sport Psychology, 22,* 307–327.

O'Keeffe, J. (1993). Mind games are crucial. *The Irish Times, 8 May,* p. 17.

Ogles, B.M., Hoeffel, T.D., Lynn, S.J., Marsden, K.A., & Masters, K.S. (1993–1994). Runners' cognitive strategies and motivations: Absorption, fantasy style and dissociative experiences. *Imagination, Cognition and Personality, 14,* 163–174.

Okwumabua, T.M., Meyers, A.W., Schlesser, R., & Cooke, C.J. (1983). Cognitive strategies and running performance. *Cognitive Therapy and Research, 7,* 363–370.

Onestak, D.M. (1991). The effects of progressive relaxation, mental practice and hypnosis on athletic performance: A review. *Journal of Sport Behaviour, 14,* 247–282.

Orlick, T. (1990). *In pursuit of excellence.* Champaign, IL: Leisure Press.

Orlick, T. & Partington, J. (1988). Mental links to excellence. *The Sport Psychologist, 2*, 105–130.

Osherson, D.N. & Lasnik, H. (1990). *An invitation to cognitive science, Volume 1*. Cambridge, MA: MIT Press.

Paas, F.G.W., Van Meerienboer, J.J.G., & Adam, J.J. (1994). Measurement of cognitive load in instructional research. *Perceptual and Motor Skills, 79*, 419–430.

Padgett, V.R. & Hill, A.K. (1989). Maximizing athletic performance in endurance events: A comparison of cognitive strategies. *Journal of Applied Social Psychology, 19*, 331–340.

Paivio, A. (1985). Cognitive and motivational functions of imagery in human performance. *Canadian Journal of Applied Sport Science, 10*, 22S-28S.

Palmer, C., & van de Sande, C. (1995). Range of planning in music performance. *Journal of Experimental Psychology: Human Perception and Performance, 21*, 947–962.

Palmer, S.L. (1992). A comparison of mental practice techniques as applied to the developing competitive figure skater. *The Sport Psychologist, 6*, 148–155.

Parasuraman, R. (1984). Sustained attention in detection and discrimination. In R. Parasuraman & D.R. Davies (Eds.), *Varieties of attention* (pp. 243–271). New York: Academic Press.

Pargman, D. (1993). Individual differences: Cognitive and perceptual styles. In R.N. Singer, M. Murphey & L.K. Tennant (Eds.), *Handbook of sport psychology* (pp. 379–401). New York: Macmillan.

Parker, H. (1981). Visual detection and perception in netball. In I.M. Cockerill & W.W. Mac Gillivary (Eds.), *Vision and sport* (pp. 42–53). London: Stanley Thornes.

Pashler, H. (1994). Dual-task interference in simple tasks: Data and theory. *Psychological Bulletin, 116*, 220–244.

Patmore, A. (1986). *Sportsmen under stress*. London: Stanley Paul.

Pelton, T. (1983). The shootists. *Science 83, 4*, 84–86.

Pennebaker, J.W. (1982). *The psychology of physical symptoms*. New York: Springer-Verlag.

Pennebaker, J.W. & Lightner, J.M. (1980). Competition of internal and external information in an exercise setting. *Journal of Personality and Social Psychology, 39*, 165–174.

People's favourite departs as Navratilova bows out. (1993, September 7). *The Irish Times*, p. 14.

Perry, C. & Morris, T. (1995). Mental imagery in sport. In T. Morris & J. Summers (Eds.), *Sport psychology: Theory, applications and issues* (pp. 339–385). Chichester: John Wiley.

Perry, A.R. & Laurie, C.A. (1993). Sustained attention and the type A behaviour pattern: The effects of daydreaming on performance. *Journal of General Psychology, 119*, 217–222.

Petrakis, E. (1987). Analysis of visual search patterns of dance teachers. *Journal of Teaching in Physical Education, 6*, 145–156.

Petruzzello, S.J., Landers, D.M., & Salazar, W. (1991). Biofeedback and sport/exercise performance: Applications and limitations. *Behaviour Therapy, 22*, 379–392.

Philips, H.C. (1988). *The psychological management of chronic pain: A treatment manual*. New York: Springer-Verlag.

Phillips, W.A. & Christie, D.F.M. (1977). Interference with visualization. *Quarterly Journal of Experimental Psychology, 29*, 637–650.

Polich, J., & Kok, A. (1995). Cognitive and biological determinants of P300: An integrative review. *Biological Psychology, 41*, 103–146.

Pope, K.S. (1978). How gender, solitude and posture influence the stream of consciousness. In K.S. Pope & J.L. Singer (Eds.), *The stream of consciousness: Scientific investigations into the flow of human experience* (pp. 259–300). New York: Plenum Press.

Posner, M.I. (1980). Orienting of attention. *Quarterly Journal of Experimental Psychology, 32*, 3–25.Posner, M.I. & Boies, S.J. (1971). Components of attention. *Psychological Review, 78*, 391–408.

Posner, M.I. & Boies, S.J. (1971). Components of attention. *Psychological Review, 78*, 391-408

Posner, M.I. & Carr, T.H. (1992). Lexical access and the brain: Anatomical constraints on cognitive models of word recognition. *American Journal of Psychology, 105*, 1–26.

Posner, M.I. & Petersen, S.E. (1990). The attention system and the human brain. *Annual Review of Neuroscience, 13*, 25–42.

Posner, M.I. & Rothbart, M.K. (1992). Attentional mechanisms and conscious experience. In A.D. Milner & M.D. Rugg (Eds.), *The neuropsychology of consciousness* (pp. 91–111). London: Academic Press.

Potter, S. (1947). *The theory and practice of gamesmanship*. Harmondsworth, Middlesex: Penguin.

Privette, G. (1981). The phenomenology of peak performance in sport. *International Journal of Sport Psychology, 12*, 51–60.

Quinlan, P.T. (1991). *Connectionism and psychology: A psychological perspective on new connectionist research*. Hemel Hempstead: Harvester Wheatsheaf.

Radford, P. (1992). Seles takes title in marathon. *The Sunday Tribune, 7 June*, A20.

Ravizza, K. (1989). Applying sports psychology. In J. Kremer & W. Crawford (Eds.), *The psychology of sport: Theory and practice* (pp. 5–15). Leicester: Northern Ireland Branch of British Psychological Society.

Ray, W.J. & Cole, H.W. (1985). EEG alpha activity reflects attentional demands, and beta activity reflects emotional and cognitive processes. *Science, 228*, 750–752.

Reason, J. & Mycielska, K. (1982). *Absent-minded? The psychology of mental lapses and everyday errors*. Englewood Cliffs, NJ: Prentice-Hall.

Reddy, P. (1991). *Attention and skills learning*. Leicester: British Psychological Society.

Reed, E.S. (1982). An outline of a theory of action systems. *Journal of Motor Behaviour, 14*, 98–134.

Reed, E.S. (1988). Applying the theory of action systems to the study of motor skills. In O.G. Meijer & K. Roth (Eds.), *Complex movement behaviour: The motor-action controversy* (pp. 45–86). Amsterdam: North-Holland.

Reed, E.S., Montgomery, M., Palmer, C., & Pittenger, J. (1995). Method for studying the invariant knowledge structure of action: Conceptual organisation of an everyday action. *American Journal of Psychology, 108*, 37–65.

Reed, S.K. (1996). Cognition: Theory and application (4th ed.). Pacific Grove, CA: Brooks/Cole.

Regan, E.C. & Franklin, J.P. (1994). *A summary of mental practice research, November 1993–March 1994, Working Paper 4/94.* Unpublished manuscript, Army Personnel Research Establishment, Ministry of Defence, Farnborough, Hampshire.

Regnier, G., Salmela, J. & Russell, S.J. (1993). Talent detection and development in sport. In R.N. Singer, M. Murphey & L.K. Tennant (Eds.), *Handbook of research in sport psychology* (pp. 290–313). New York: Macmillan.

Reisberg, D. & McLean, J. (1985). Meta-attention: Do we know when we are being distracted? *The Journal of General Psychology, 112,* 291–306.

Reynolds, R.I. (1982). Search heuristics of chess players of different calibres. *American Journal of Psychology, 95,* 383–392.

Richardson, P.A. (1967a). Mental practice: A review and discussion, Part II. *Research Quarterly, 38,* 263–273.

Richardson, P.A. (1967b). Mental practice: A review and discussion, Part I. *Research Quarterly, 38,* 95–107.

Ripoll, H. (1989). Uncertainty and visual strategies in table-tennis. *Perceptual and Motor Skills, 68,* 507–512.

Ripoll, H. (1991). Foreword. *International Journal of Sport Psychology, 22,* 187–188.

Ripoll, H. & Fleurance, P. (1988). What does keeping one's eye on the ball mean? *Ergonomics, 31,* 1647–1654.

Rishe, H.L., Krenz, E.W., McQueen, C. & Krenz, V.D. (1994). Optimal arousal, stress and imagery. In A.A. Sheikh & E.R. Korn (Eds.), *Imagery in sports and physical performance* (pp. 135–146). Amityville, NY: Baywood.

Roberts, J. (1992a). The Courier machine steamrolls Korda. *The Irish Times, 8 June,* p. 4.

Roberts, J. (1992b). Stich ends Connors' antics. *The Irish Times, 28 May,* p. 15.

Roberts, J. (1992c). Seles too good for Capriati. *The Irish Times, 3 June,* p. 17.

Roberts, J. (1993a). Bailey within an ace of making Britain's day. *The Independent, 25 June,* p. 38.

Roberts, J. (1993b). Struggling Lendl loses control and crashes out in Monte Carlo. *The Irish Times, 23 April,* p. 15.

Roberts, J. (1994). Sampras leaves Melbourne with his sights set firmly on Paris. *The Irish Times, 31 January,* p. 5.

Roche, P. (1995). Second gold medal for Smith. *The Irish Times, 28 August,* p. 1.

Rodgers, W.M., Hall, C., & Buckolz, E. (1991). The effect of an imagery programme on imagery ability, imagery use and figure skating performance. *Journal of Applied Sport Psychology, 3,* 109–125.

Roland, P.E., Skinhoj, E., Lassen, N.A., & Larsen, B. (1980). Different cortical areas in man in organisation of voluntary movements in extrapersonal space. *Journal of Neurophysiology, 43,* 137–150.

Rose, D.J. & Christina, R.W. (1990). Attention demands of precision pistol-shooting as a function of skill level. *Research Quarterly for Exercise and Sport, 61,* 111–113.

Ross, S.L. (1985). The effectiveness of mental practice in improving the performance of college trombonists. *Journal of Research in Music Education, 33,* 221–230.

Rotella, R.J., Gansneder, B., Ojala, D., & Billing, J. (1980). Cognitions and coping strategies of elite skiers: An exploratory study of young developing athletes. *Journal of Sport Psychology, 4,* 350–354.

Rotella, R.J. & Lerner, J.D. (1993). Responding to competitive pressure. In R.N. Singer, M. Murphey & L.K. Tennant (Eds.), *Handbook of research in sport psychology* (pp. 528–541). New York: Macmillan.

Rugg, M.D. & Coles, M.G.H. (1995). *Electrophysiology of mind: Event-related brain potentials and cognition.* Oxford: Oxford University Press.

Rumelhart, D.E., McClelland, J.L. & The PDP Research Group, (1986). *Parallel distributed processing: Vol. 1, Foundations.* Cambridge, MA: MIT Press.

Rumelhart, D.E. & Norman, D.A. (1983). Representation in memory. In R. Atkinson, R.J. Herrnstein, B. Lindzey & R.D. Luce (Eds.), *Handbook of experimental psychology.* Chichester: John Wiley.

Rumelhart, D.E. & Todd, P.M. (1993). Learning and connectionist representations. In D.E. Meyer & S. Kornblum (Eds.), *Attention and performance, XIV: Synergies in experimental psychology, artificial intelligence and cognitive neuroscience* (pp. 3–30). Cambridge, MA: MIT Press.

Rushall, B.S. (1989). Sport psychology: The key to sporting excellence. *International Journal of Sport Psychology, 20*, 165–190.

Rushall, B.S., Hall, M., & Rushall, A. (1988). Effects of three types of thought content instructions on skiing performance. *The Sport Psychologist, 2*, 283–297.

Russell, S.J. & Salmela, J.H. (1992). Quantifying expert athlete knowledge. *Journal of Applied Sport Psychology, 4*, 10–26.

Ryan, E.D. & Simons, J. (1981). Cognitive demand, imagery and frequency of mental rehearsal as factors influencing acquisition of motor skills. *Journal of Sport Psychology, 3*, 35–45.

Sachs, M.L. (1991). Reading list in applied sport psychology: Psychological skills training. *The Sport Psychologist, 5*, 88–91.

Sachs, M.L. (1984). The mind of the runner: Cognitive strategies used during running. In M.L. Sachs & G.W. Buffone (Eds.), *Running as therapy: An integrated approach* (pp. 288–303). Lincoln: University of Nebraska Press.

Sackett, R.S. (1934). The influence of symbolic rehearsal upon the retention of a maze habit. *Journal of General Psychology, 10*, 376–395.

Salazar, W., Landers, D.M., Petruzzello, S.J., Crews, D.J., Kubitz, K.A., & Han, M. (1990). Hemispheric asymmetry, cardiac response and performance in elite archers. *Research Quarterly for Exercise and Sport, 61*, 351–359.

Salthouse, T.A. (1991). Expertise as the circumvention of human processing limitations. In K.A. Ericsson & J. Smith (Eds.), *Toward a general theory of expertise: Prospects and limits* (pp. 286–300). Cambridge: Cambridge University Press.

Sampras back on winning track. (1994, November 14). *The Irish Times*, p. 4.

Samuels, M. & Samuels, N. (1975). *Seeing with the mind's eye.* New York: Random House.

Savelsbergh, G.J.P. & Bootsma, R.J. (1994). Perception-action coupling in hitting and catching. *International Journal of Sport Psychology, 25*, 331–343.

Schedlowski, M. & Tewes, U. (1992). Physiological arousal and perception of bodily state during parachute jumping. *Psychophysiology, 29*, 95–103.

Schill, T., Monroe, S., Evans, R., & Ramanaiah, N. (1978). The effects of self-verbalization on performance: A test of the rational-emotive position. *Psychotherapy: Theory, Research and Practice, 15*, 2–7.

Schmid, A. & Peper, E. (1993). Training strategies for concentration. In J.M. Williams (Ed.), *Applied sport psychology: Personal growth to peak performance* 2nd ed. (pp. 262–273). Mountain View, CA: Mayfield.

Schmidt, R.A. (1987). The acquisition of skill: Some modifications to the perception-action relationship through practice. In H. Heuer & A.F. Sanders (Eds.), *Perspectives on perception and action* (pp. 77–103). Hove: Lawrence Erlbaum Associates Ltd.

Schmidt, R.A. (1975). A schema theory of discrete motor skill learning. *Psychological Review, 82*, 225–260.

Schmidt, R.A. (1988). *Motor control and learning: A behavioural emphasis.* Champaign, IL: Human Kinetics.

Schneider, W., Dumais, S.T. & Shiffrin, R.M. (1984). Automatic and control processing and attention. In R. Parasuraman & D.R. Davies (Eds.), *Varieties of attention* (pp. 1–27). New York: Academic Press.

Schomer, H.H. (1986). Mental strategies and the perception of effort of marathon runners. *International Journal of Sport Psychology, 17*, 41–59.

Schomer, H.H. (1987). Mental strategy training programme for marathon runners. *International Journal of Sport Psychology, 18*, 133–151.

Schwenkmezger, P. & Laux, L. (1986). Trait anxiety, worry and emotionality in athletic competition. In C.D. Spielberger & R. Diaz-Guerrero (Eds.), *Cross-cultural anxiety, Vol. 3* (pp. 65–77). Washington, DC: Hemisphere.

See, J.E., Howe, S.R., Warm, J.S., & Dember, W.N. (1995). Meta-analysis of the sensitivity decrement in vigilance. *Psychological Bulletin, 117*, 230–249.

Seibert, P.S. & Ellis, H.C. (1991). Irrelevant thoughts, emotional, mood states and cognitive task performance. *Memory and Cognition, 19*, 507–513.

Seiderman, A. & Schneider, S. (1985). *The athletic eye: Improved sport performance through visual training.* New York: Hearst Books.

Seiler, R. (1992). Performance enhancement–A psychological approach. *Sport Science Review, 1*, 29–45.

Shalvey, J. (1995). Order of the boot. *The Irish Times,* 17 May, pp. 24–25.

Shannon, C.E. & Weaver, W. (1949). *The Mathematical Theory of Communication.* Urbana, Champaign: University of Illinois Press.

Shaw, W.A. (1938). The distribution of muscular action potentials during imaging. *Psychological Record, 2*, 195–216.

Shaw, W.A. (1940). The relation of muscular action potentials to imagined weight lifting. *Archives of Psychology, 35*, 5–50.

Shea, J.B. & Morgan, R.L. (1979). Contextual interference effects on the acquisition, retention, and transfer of a motor skill. *Journal of Experimental Psychology: Human Learning and Memory, 5*, 179–187.

Sheedy, A. (1971). The optimal limits of concentration time relative to success in basketball free-shooting. *International Journal of Sport Psychology, 2*, 21–32.

Shelton, T.O. & Mahoney, M.J. (1978). The content and effects of "psyching up" strategies in weight lifters. *Cognitive Therapy and Research, 2*, 275–284.

Shepard, R.N. & Metzler, J. (1971). Mental rotation of three-dimensional objects. *Science, 171*, 701–703.

Shiffrin, R.M. & Schneider, W. (1977). Controlled and automatic human information processing, II: Perceptual learning, automatic attending and a general theory. *Psychological Review, 84*, 127–190.

Shock wins for Italians. (1992, May 7), *The Irish Times*, p. 17.

Silva, J.M. & Applebaum, M.I. (1989). Association-dissociation patterns of United States Olympic marathon trial contestants. *Cognitive Therapy and Research, 13*, 185–192.

Simon, H.A. (1992). What is an "explanation" of behaviour? *Psychological Science, 3*, 150–161.

Simon, H.A. (1995). The information-processing theory of mind. *American Psychologist, 50*, 507–508.

Simon, H.A. & Gilmartin, K.A. (1973). A simulation of memory for chess positions. *Cognitive Psychology, 5*, 29–46.

Singer, R.N. (1992). What in the world is happening in sport psychology? *Journal of Applied Sport Psychology, 4*, 63–76.

Singer, R.N., Cauraugh, J.H., Tennant, L.K., Murphey, M., Chen, D., & Lidor, R. (1991). Attention and distractors: Considerations for enhancing sport performance. *International Journal of Sport Psychology, 22*, 95–114.

Skelton, J.M. & Eriksen, C.W. (1976). Spatial characteristics of selective attention in letter matching. *Bulletin of the Psychonomic Society, 7*, 136–138.

Smith, D. (1987). Conditions that facilitate the development of sport imagery training. *The Sport Psychologist, 1*, 237–247.

Smith, R.E., Smoll, F.L., & Schutz, R.W. (1990). Measurement and correlates of sport-specific cognitive and somatic trait anxiety: The Sport Anxiety Scale. *Anxiety Research, 2*, 263–280.

Smyth, M.M., Collins, A.F., Morris, P.E. & Levy, P. (1994). *Cognition in action (2nd ed.)*. Hove: Lawrence Erlbaum Associates Ltd.

Smyth, M.M. & Pendleton, L.R. (1994). Memory for movement in professional ballet dancers. *International Journal of Sport Psychology, 25*, 282–294.

Soloway, E., Adelson, B. & Ehrlich, K. (1988). Knowledge and processes in the comprehension of computer programs. In M. Chi, R. Glaser & M.J. Farr (Eds.), *The nature of expertise* (pp. 129–152). Hillsdale, NJ: Lawrence Erlbaum Associates Inc.

Solso, R.L. (1995). *Cognitive psychology* (4th ed.). Boston: Allyn & Bacon.

Spelke, E., Hirst, W., & Neisser, U. (1976). Skills of divided attention. *Cognition, 4*, 215–230.

Starkes, J.L. & Allard, F. (1993). *Cognitive issues in motor control*. Amsterdam: North-Holland.

Starkes, J.L., Allard, F., Lindley, S., & O'Reilly, K. (1994). Abilities and skill in basketball. *International Journal of Sport Psychology, 25*, 249–265.

Starkes, J.L. & Deakin, J. (1984). Perception in sport: A cognitive approach to skilled performance. In W.F. Straub & J.M. Williams (Eds.), *Cognitive sport psychology* (pp. 115–128). New York: Sport Science Associates.

Stauth, C. (1992). *The golden boys: The unauthorized inside look at the US Olympic basketball team*. New York: Pocket Books.

Steptoe, A. & Fidler, H. (1987). Stage fright in orchestral musicians: A study of cognitive and behavioural strategies in performance anxiety. *British Journal of Psychology, 78*, 241–249.

Steptoe, A., Malik, F., Pay, C., Pearson, P., Price, C., & Win, Z. (1995). The impact of stage fright on student actors. *British Journal of Psychology, 86*, 27–39.

Straub, W.F. (1978). *An analysis of athlete behaviour*. New York: Mouvement Publications.

Stroop, J.R. (1935). Studies of interference in serial verbal reactions. *Journal of Experimental Psychology, 18*, 643–662.

Stylish O'Brien overwhelms Hendry. (1994, March 25). *The Irish Times*, p. 16.

Suinn, R.M. (1972). Behaviour rehearsal training for ski racers. *Behaviour Therapy, 3*, 210–221.

Suinn, R.M. (1993). Imagery. In R.M. Singer, M. Murphey & L.K. Tennant (Eds.), *Handbook of research in sport psychology* (pp. 492–510). New York: Macmillan.

Suinn, R.M. (1994). Visualization in sports. In A.A. Sheikh & E.R. Korn (Eds.), *Imagery in sports and physical performance* (pp. 23–42). Amityville, NY Baywood.

Suls, J. & Fletcher, B. (1985). The relative efficacy of avoidant and nonavoidant coping strategies: A meta-analysis. *Health Psychology, 4*, 249–288.

Summers, J.J., Miller, K., & Ford, S.K. (1991). Attentional style and basketball performance. *Journal of Sport and Exercise Psychology, 8*, 239–253.

Summers, J.J. & Ford, S. (1995). Attention in sport. In T. Morris & J. Summers (Eds.), *Sport psychology: Theory, applications and issues* (pp. 63–89). Chichester: John Wiley.

Summers, J.J., Sargent, G.I., Levey, A.J., & Murray, K.D. (1982). Middle-aged, non-elite marathon runners: A profile. *Perceptual and Motor Skills, 54*, 963–969.

Summers, J.J. & Ford, S.K. (1990). The Test of Attentional and Interpersonal Style: An evaluation. *International Journal of Sport Psychology, 21*, 102–111.

Summers, J.J., Miller, K., & Ford, S. (1991). Attentional style and basketball performance. *Journal of Sport and Exercise Psychology, 13*, 239–253.

Surburg, P.R. (1989). Application of imagery techniques to special populations. *Adapted Physical Activity Quarterly, 6*, 328–337.

Swift, E.J. (1910). Relearning a skilful act: An experimental study of neuromuscular memory. *Psychological Bulletin, 7*, 17–19.

Syer, J. (1986). *Team spirit: The elusive experience*. London: Simon & Schuster.

Syer, J. & Connolly, C. (1987). *Sporting body, sporting mind: An athlete's guide to mental training* London: Sports Pages.

Taylor, J. (1993). *The mental edge for competitive tennis: The winning mind set*. Aurora, CO: Alpine Taylor Consulting.

Tenenbaum, G. & Bar-Eli, M. (1993). Decision-making in sport: A cognitive perspective. In R.N. Singer, M. Murphey & L.K. Tennant (Eds.), *Handbook of research in sport psychology* (pp. 171–192). New York: Macmillan.

Thelen, E. (1995). Motor development: A new synthesis. *American Psychologist, 50*, 79–95.

They all agree: It was one of the great test innings. (1995, December 5). *The Guardian*, p. 25.

Thomas, K.T. & Thomas, J.R. (1994). Developing expertise in sport: The relation of knowledge and performance. *International Journal of Sport Psychology, 25*, 295–312.

Thornley, G. (1992a). Capriati stretches Sabatini in late-night thriller. *The Irish Times, 1 July*, p. 17.

Thornley, G. (1992b). Irish lay foundations for comprehensive win. *The Irish Times, 18 July*, p. 13.

Thornley, G. (1993). Graf profits as Novotna loses her nerve. *The Irish Times,* *5 July,* p. 6.

Thornton, B. (1994). Clark blows a fuse. *The Star, 1 April,* p. 55.

Titchener, E.B. (1908). *Lectures on the elementary psychology of feeling and attention.* New York: Macmillan.

Tolman, E.C. (1932). *Purposive behaviour in animals and men.* New York: Appleton-Century-Crofts.

Townsend, A. (1995). Some fatherly advice for young Jason. *The Sunday Independent, 3 September,* p. 26.

Treisman, A.M. (1964). Verbal cues, language and meaning in selective attention. *American Journal of Psychology, 77,* 206–219.

Treisman, A.M., Vieria, A., & Hayes, A. (1992). Automaticity and preattentive processing. *American Journal of Psychology, 105,* 341–362.

Treisman, A.M. (1960). Contextual cues in selective listening. *Quarterly Journal of Experimental Psychology, 12,* 242–248.

Triplett, N. (1898). The dynamogenic factors in pacemaking and competition. *American Journal of Psychology, 9,* 507–533.

Turner, R.G. & Gilliland, L. (1977). Comparison of self-report and performance measures of attention. *Perceptual and Motor Skills, 45,* 409–410.

Turvey, M.T. (1994). From Borelli (1680) and Bell (1826) to the dynamics of action and perception. *Journal of Sport and Exercise Psychology, 16,* 128–157.

Turvey, M.T. & Kugler, P.N. (1984). An ecological approach to perception and action. In H.T.A. Whiting (Ed.), *Human actions: Bernstein reassessed* (pp. 373–412). Amsterdam: North-Holland.

Turvey, M.T. (1990). Coordination. *American Psychologist, 45,* 938–953.

Ungerleider, S. & Golding, J.M. (1991). Mental practice among Olympic athletes. *Perceptual and Motor Skills, 72,* 1007–1017.

United States Olympic Committee (1994). *Staying focused at the Olympic Games.* Colorado Springs, CO: United States Olympic Committee.

Vallacher, R.R. (1993). Mental calibration: Forging a working relationship between mind and action. In D.M. Wegner & J.W. Pennebaker (Eds.), *Handbook of mental control* (pp. 443–472). Englewood Cliffs, NJ: Prentice-Hall.

Vallerand, R.J. (1983). Attention and decision-making: A test of the predictive validity of the Test of Attentional and Interpersonal Style (TAIS) in a sport setting. *Journal of Sport Psychology, 5,* 449–459.

Van der Heijden, A.H.C. (1992). *Selective attention in vision.* London: Routledge.

Van Esbeck, E. (1995). Ireland lose concentration in second half. *The Irish Times, 21 January,* p. 18.

Van Gyn, G.H., Wenger, H.A., & Gaul, C.A. (1990). Imagery as a method of enhancing transfer from training to performance. *Journal of Sport and Exercise Psychology, 12,* 366–375.

Van Raalte, J.L., Brewer, B.W., Rivera, P.M., & Petitpas, A.J. (1994). The relationship between self-talk and performance of competitive junior tennis players. *NASPSPA Conference Abstracts, 16 Supplement,* S118 (abstract).

Van Schoyck, S.R. & Grasha, A.F. (1981). Attentional style variations and athletic ability: The advantage of a sport-specific test. *Journal of Sport Psychology, 3,* 149–165.

Vealey, R.S. (1994). Current status and prominent issues in sport psychology interventions. *Medicine and Science in Sports and Exercise, 26,* 495–502.

Vealey, R.S. & Walter, S.M. (1993). Imagery training for performance enhancement and personal development. In J.M. Williams (Ed.), *Applied sport psychology: Personal growth to peak performance* (2nd ed., pp. 200–224). Mountain View, CA: Mayfield.

Vealey, R.S. & Walter, S.M. (1994). On target with mental skills: An interview with Darrell Pace. *The Sport Psychologist, 8*, 428–441.

Viviani, P. (1992). Strategies for understanding movement. In D.E. Meyer & S. Kornblum (Eds.), *Attention and performance, XIV: Synergies in experimental psychology, artificial intelligence, and cognitive neuroscience* (pp. 851–860). Cambridge, MA: MIT Press.

Volkov finds Muster and weather too hot. (1994, January 24). *The Evening Press*, p. 24.

Wachtel, P. (1967). Conceptions of broad and narrow ability. *Psychological Bulletin, 68*, 417–429.

Wang, M.Q. & Landers, D.M. (1986). Cardiac response and hemispheric differentiation during archery performance: A psychophysiological investigation. *Psychophysiology, 23*, 469 (abstract).

Washburn, M.F. (1916). *Movement and mental imagery.* Boston: Houghton Mifflin.

Watson, J.B. (1913). Psychology as the behaviourist views it. *Psychological Review, 20*, 158–177.

Watson, L. (1973). *Supernature.* London: Hodder and Stoughton.

Webster, R. (1984). *Winning ways.* Sydney: Fontana.

Webster, W. & Smith, A. (1984). *Clinical hypnosis.* New York: Lippincott.

Wechsler, D. (1955). *Manual for the Wechsler Adult Intelligence Scale.* San Antonio: The Psychological Corporation.

Wegner, D.M. (1992). You can't always think what you want: Problems in the suppression of unwanted thoughts. *Advances in Experimental Social Psychology, 25*, 193–225.

Wegner, D.M. (1994). Ironic processes of mental control. *Psychological Review, 101*, 34–52.

Wegner, D.M. & Pennebaker, J.W. (1993). *Handbook of mental control.* Englewood Cliffs, NJ: Prentice Hall.

Wegner, D.M., Schneider, D.J., Carter, S.R., III., & White, T.L. (1987). Paradoxical effects of thought suppression. *Journal of Personality and Social Psychology, 53*, 5–13.

Weinberg, R.S., Stitcher, T., & Richardson, P. (1994). Effects of a seasonal goal-setting programme on lacrosse performance. *The Sport Psychologist, 8*, 166–175.

Weinberg, R.S. (1982). The relationship between mental preparation strategies and motor performance: A review and critique. *Quest, 33*, 195–213.

Weinberg, R.S. (1988). *The mental advantage: Developing your psychological skills in tennis.* Champaign, IL: Leisure Press.

Weinberg, R.S. (1989). Anxiety, arousal and performance: Theory, research and applications. In D. Hackfort & C.D. Spielberger (Eds.), *Anxiety in sports: An international perspective* (pp. 95–115). New York: Hemisphere.

Weinberg, R.S., Bruya, L., Garland, H., & Jackson, A. (1990). Effects of goal difficulty and positive reinforcement on endurance performance. *Journal of Sport and Exercise Psychology, 12*, 144–156.

Weinberg, R.S. & Richardson, P.A. (1990). *The psychology of officiating.* Champaign, IL: Human Kinetics.

Weinberg, R.S., & Gould, D. (1995). *Foundations of sport and exercise psychology*. Champaign, IL: Human Kinetics.

Weinberg, R.S. (1992). Goal-setting and motor performance: A review and critique. In G.C. Roberts (Ed.), *Motivation in sport and exercise* (pp. 177–198). Champaign, IL: Human Kinetics.

Welford, A.T. & Bourne, L.E. (1976). *Skilled performance*. Glenview, IL: Scott Foresman.

Wellman, H.M. (1985). The origin of metacognition. In D.L. Forrest-Pressley, G.E. McKinnon & T.G. Waller (Eds.), *Cognition, metacognition and performance* (pp. 1–31). New York: Academic Press.

Weltman, G. & Egstrom, G. (1966). Perceptual narrowing in novice divers. *Human Factors, 8*, 499–506.

Whelan, J.P., Epkins, C., & Meyers, A.W. (1990). Arousal interventions for athletic performance: Influence of mental preparation and competitive experience. *Anxiety Research, 2*, 293–307.

Whelan, J.P., Mahoney, M., & Meyers, A.W. (1991). Performance enhancement in sport: A cognitive behavioural domain. *Behaviour Therapy, 22*, 307–327.

White, A. & Hardy, L. (1995). Use of different imagery perspectives on the learning and performance of different motor skills. *British Journal of Psychology, 86*, 169–180.

White, J. (1988). *Jimmy White's snooker masterclass*. London: Queen Anne Press.

White, S.A. (1993). The relationship between psychological skills, experience and practice commitment among collegiate male and female skiers. *The Sport Psychologist, 7*, 49–57.

Whiting, H.T.A. (1978). Input and perceptual processes in sports skills. In D.J. Glencross (Ed.), *Psychology and sport* (pp. 22–47). Sydney: McGraw-Hill.

Whiting, H.T.A. (1979). Subjective probability in sport. In G.C. Roberts & K.M. Newell (Eds.), *Psychology of motor behaviour and sport* (pp. 3–25). Champaign, IL: Human Kinetics.

Wickens, C.D. (1984). Processing resources in attention. In R. Parasuraman & D.R. Davies (Eds.), *Varieties of attention* (pp. 63–102). New York: Academic Press.

Wiggins, D.K. (1984). The history of sport psychology in North America. In J.M. Silva & R.S. Weinberg (Eds.), *Psychological foundations of sport* (pp. 9–22). Champaign, IL: Human Kinetics.

Wilkes, R.L. & Summers, J.J. (1984). Cognitions, mediating variables and strength performance. *Journal of Sport Psychology, 6*, 351–359.

Williams, A.M., Davids, K., Burwitz, L., & Williams, J. (1992). Perception and action in sport. *Journal of Human Movement Studies, 22*, 147–204.

Williams, J.M. (1986). Psychological characteristics of peak performance. In J.M. Williams (Ed.), *Applied sport psychology: Personal growth to peak performance* (pp. 123–132). Palo Alto, CA: Mayfield.

Williams, J.M. & Roepke, N. (1993). Psychology of injury and injury rehabilitation. In R.N. Singer, M. Murphey & L.K. Tennant (Eds.), *Handbook of research in sport psychology* 38th ed. (pp. 815–839). New York: Macmillan.

Williams, J.M. & Straub, W.F. (1993). Sport psychology: Past, present, future. In J.M. Williams (Ed.), *Applied sport psychology: Personal growth to peak performance* (2nd ed., pp. 1–10). Mountain View, CA: Mayfield Publishing Company.

Williams, R. (1992). Tearing up the track. *The Independent on Sunday (Sport)*, *15 November*, 27–28.

Wilson, V., Ainsworth, M., & Bird, E. (1985). Assessment of attentional abilities in male volleyball players. *International Journal of Sport Psychology*, *16*, 296–306.

Wine, J. (1971). Test anxiety and direction of attention. *Psychological Bulletin*, *76*, 92–104.

Winter, G. & Martin, C. (1991). *Sport 'psych' for tennis*. Adelaide: South Australia Sports Institute.

Witkin, H.A., Oltman, P.K., Raskin, E. & Karp, S.A. (1971). *Manual for Embedded Figures Test, Children's Embedded Figures Test and Group Embedded Figures Test*. Palo Alto, CA: Consulting Psychologists' Press.

Wolpe, J. (1958). *Psychotherapy by reciprocal inhibition*. Stanford, CA: Stanford University Press.

Wood, G. (1983). *Cognitive psychology: A skills approach*. Monterey, CA: Brooks/Cole.

Woolfolk, R.L., Parrish, M.W., & Murphy, S.M. (1985). The effects of positive and negative imagery on motor skill performance. *Cognitive Therapy and Research*, *9*, 335–341.

Wright, C.E. (1990). Controlling a sequential motor activity. In D.N. Osherson, S.M. Kosslyn & J.M. Hollerbach (Eds.), *Visual cognition and action, Vol. 2* (pp. 285–316). Cambridge, MA: MIT Press.

Wrisberg, C.A. & Pein, R.L. (1992). The preshot interval and free throw accuracy: An exploratory investigation. *The Sport Psychologist*, *6*, 14–23.

Wundt, W. (1907). Outlines of psychology (7th ed., C.h. Judd, Trans.). Leipzig: Engleman (Original work published 1896).

Yandell, J. (1990). *Visual tennis: Mental imagery and the quest for the winning edge*. New York: Doubleday.

Yerkes, R.M. & Dodson, J.D. (1908). The relationship of strength of stimulus to rapidity of habit formation. *Journal of Comparative Neurology and Psychology*, *18*, 459–482.

Zaichkowsky, L. & Fuchs, C. (1988). Biofeedback applications in exercise and athletic performance. *Exercise and Sport Science Reviews*, *16*, 381–421.

Zaichkowsky, L. & Takenaka, K. (1993). Optimizing arousal levels. In R.N. Singer, M. Murphey & L.K. Tennant (Eds.), *Handbook of research in sport psychology* (pp. 511–527). New York: Macmillan.

Zani, A. & Rossi, B. (1991). Cognitive psychophysiology as an interface between cognitive and sport psychology. *International Journal of Sport Psychology*, *22*, 376–398.

Zimbardo, P. (1992). *Psychology and life* (13the ed.). New York: Harper Collins.

Zukier, H. & Hagen, J.W. (1978). The development of selective attention under distracting conditions. *Child Development*, *49*, 870–873.

Author index

Abernethy, B. 4–5, 13, 24–26,
  32, 38, 57, 60, 69, 72, 77–78,
  80, 82–91, 94–95, 110–111,
  135, 140, 148, 236, 249, 256
Acedevo, E.O. 150, 154
Adair, T. 118
Adam, J.J. 70
Adams, J.A. 6, 15, 211, 217, 224
Adelson, B. 21
Ainscoe, M. 226
Ainsworth, M. 146
Alain, C. 82
Albinson, J.G. 170–171, 189, 193
Albrecht, R.R. 144, 148
Allard, F. 12–14, 23, 25–26, 38,
  83, 86, 94–96, 176
Allport, A. 43, 53, 57, 108, 237
Allport, D.A. 55–56
Allport, F.H. 108
Anderson, J.R. 6, 14–19, 24, 26,
  35, 37, 57, 59, 96, 104, 180,
  260
Anderson, W.G. 204

Annett, J. 58, 202, 211–212, 221
Anshel, M.H. 123, 127, 173, 178
  184–185, 226, 242
Antonis, B. 55–56
Applebaum, M.I. 156
Arthur, W. 47, 60, 240
Atkinson, R.C. 46
Austin, S. 221
Avener, M. 75, 169, 183, 215, 219

Baars, B.J. 27
Backman, L. 137
Baddeley, A.D. 11, 48, 241
Bahill, A.T. 78, 81
Bain, A. 15
Baker, L. 249
Bale, R.M. 147–148
Bar-Eli, M. 5
Baracat, B. 49
Barber, P. 10, 236
Bard, C. 50, 82, 85, 111
Baria, A. 34

Barr, K.A. 202, 210–211
Barry, J.R. 5, 23–24, 26, 95
Barta, S.G. 77, 122, 241
Bartlett, F.C. 14–16, 35, 78, 81, 170, 228
Bartlett, K. 208
Bassok, M. 248
Baumeister, R.F. 93, 126, 129–130
Bausman, M. 217
Baverel, G. 218
Beary, J.F. 191
Bedard, J. 22, 33, 85
Bedon, B.G. 25
Bennett, B.B. 75, 196
Bennett, H.Z. 73
Benson, H. 191
Berardi-Coletta, B. 240
Berlyne, D.E. 118
Bernoties, L. 224
Bernstein, D.A. 41
Bernstein, N.A. 28–30
Berry, D.C. 14, 75
Best, J.B. 9, 39–41, 45, 104
Bigi, L. 246
Billing, J. 195–196
Bird, E. 146
Bliss, C.B. 117
Boies, S.J. 39, 49
Bonanno, G.A. 127
Bond, A. 253, 256
Bond, J. 70, 123, 133, 143–145, 150, 170, 172–173, 203
Bonnel, A.M. 259
Bootsma, R.J. 28
Borgeaud, P. 26
Botham, I. 70, 103, 244
Bourne, L.E. 14
Boutcher, S.H. 76–77, 92, 123, 136–139, 142, 170–171, 176–179, 181, 184, 235
Bradley, P.W. 154
Brady, F. 134

Brennan, J. 116, 125, 129
Brewer, B.W. 68, 73, 75, 136, 155-157, 196–197, 212, 216
Brewin, C.R. 173
Broadbent, D.E. 14, 43–45, 47–48, 53–54, 63, 75, 86, 113, 238, 256, 259–261
Brooks, L.J. 223
Brown, L. 103
Browne, M.A. 75
Bruya, L. 174
Buckolz, E. 81, 208, 214, 216
Budney, A.J. 209, 211, 213, 217, 221, 224–225
Bull, S.J. 170–171, 189, 193
Bunker, L. 194
Burke, K.L. 170–171
Burn, G. 101, 125
Burnett, N. 13–14, 83, 86, 176
Burton, D. 174
Burwitz, L. 27, 83, 96
Buss, H. 129
Butterfield, E.C. 6, 8, 43, 238
Buyer, L.S. 240

Cameron, C.M. 253, 256
Carol, M.P. 191
Carpenter, W.B. 204, 219
Carr, T.H. 51, 59
Carriere, L. 82
Carron, A.V. 119
Carter, S.R. 209, 215
Carver, C.S. 122
Casey, G. 7, 8, 20, 237
Castiello, U. 49, 62, 70, 86, 89–90, 149, 258
Caudill, D. 193
Cauraugh, J.H. 34, 72, 168, 172, 198
Cautela, J.R. 206, 217
Cavanaugh, J. 101
Chadband, I. 5

Chahal, P. 156

Charness, N. 16, 19, 21–22, 33, 80, 81, 94, 239

Chartrand, J.M. 159, 160

Chase, W.G. 18, 21, 24–25, 94, 95

Chen, D. 34, 72, 168, 172, 198, 244

Cherry, C. 45, 47

Chi, M.T.H. 21–22, 33, 85, 248

Chomsky, N. 8

Christie, D.F.M. 223

Christina, R.W. 77, 89, 94, 137

Cielinski, K.L. 177

Cioffi, D. 108–109, 254

Clark, J.E. 6, 27–28, 96

Clark, L.V. 215

Claxton, G. 7

Clay, D. 176

Clingman, J.M. 157–158

Cohen, G. 245

Cohn, P.J. 177–178, 180

Cole, H.W. 110

Coles, M.G.H. 136–137, 140

Collins, A.F. 237

Connolly, C. 229

Cooke, C.J. 155, 195, 204

Cooke, N. 21

Coon, D. 182

Cooney, A. 114

Cooper, P.F. 259–261

Copper, C. 202–203, 212–213, 215, 220

Corbin, C.B. 214, 219

Cote, J. 34, 149

Courneya, K.S. 119

Courtet, P. 140–141

Couture, R.T. 156

Cox, R.H. 12, 67, 69, 82, 92, 150, 230

Cox, T. 76

Cratty, B.J. 149

Craver-Lemley, C. 223

Crews, D.J. 70, 135–136, 138, 176, 178–180, 184, 192

Cuvillier, C. 195, 204

Cymerman, A. 109

Dalgleish, T. 253, 256

Dalloway, M. 122, 170–172, 196, 204, 209, 229

Daniels, F.S. 138, 146–148, 240

Danish, S.J. 159–160

Dark, V.J. 109, 277

David-Neel, A. 153

Davids, K. 23, 26–27, 31, 96, 207

De Groot, A.D. 21

Deakin, J. 23

Deary, I.J. 80

Decety, J. 203–204, 218, 223, 241

Decker, C. 212

Deffenbacher, K.A. 236

Deikman, A.J. 118, 190

Dember, W.N. 109

Denis, M. 207, 227

Derrick, W.L. 50, 90–91

Deshimaru, T. 111, 167

Dockerell, J. 8

Dodson, J.D. 185

Dominowski, R.L. 240

Doust, D. 182

Doverspike, D. 60

Doyle, L. 138

Driskell, J.E. 202–203, 212–213, 215, 220

Druckman, D. 192, 212

Dumais, S.T. 57–59

Duncan, C.P. 103

Duncker, K. 11

Durand, M.C. 214

Durozard, M. 218

Durtschi, S.K. 210

Duval, S. 110

Dweck, C.A. 174

Dzewaltowski, D.A. 150, 154

Easterbrook, J.A. 77, 92–93, 113, 140, 188, 254
Eccleston, C. 108, 109
Edmondson, R. 208
Egstrom, G. 141
Ehrlich, K. 21
Eklund, R.C. 74–75, 104, 128, 179–180
Ellickson, K.A. 154
Ellis, H.C. 108, 122
Eloi, S. 227
Emery, E.J. 107–108
Epkins, C. 184, 194
Epstein, M.L. 220
Ericsson, K.A. 16, 19, 21–22, 33, 40, 80–81, 94, 207, 227, 237, 239, 242
Eriksen, B. 119
Eriksen, C.W. 41, 119
Estes, W.K. 7
Etelapelto, A. 248
Etzel, E.F. 71, 147
Evans, R. 114, 196
Eysenck, M.W. 7–10, 15, 32, 39, 41–42, 45–46, 55, 60, 105–106, 108, 110, 116, 128, 130, 136, 187, 189–170, 227, 236, 240–241, 246, 248, 250–252, 254, 255–256

Fairs, J. 81
Farah, M. 222
Fazey, J. 168, 170–171, 187
Feltz, D.L. 144, 148, 205, 211, 213–214, 219, 223, 225–226
Fenigstein, A. 129
Fenz, W.D. 122, 138
Fidler, H. 128
Finch, A.E. 81, 84
Finch, L.M. 76, 211
Finke, R.A. 203, 206, 223
Fisk, A.D. 50, 90–91

Fiske, S.T. 107–108
Fitts, P. 61, 117, 178, 224
Fitzgerald, P. 259–261
Flavell, J.H. 244–246
Fletcher, B. 109
Fleurance, P. 79, 90
Fleury, M. 50, 82, 85, 111
Foley, M. 21
Ford, S.K. 28, 40, 45, 60, 68–70, 83–84, 135, 139, 147–148, 257
Fox, A. 114
Fox, E. 255–256
Francis-Keniston, W.J. 177
Franklin, J.P. 212
Freedson, P. 184
Frith, D. 115, 273
Fuchs, C. 192
Furst, D.M. 146–148

Gabriel, T.J. 76, 134, 158–159, 169
Gabriele, T.E. 19
Gagne, E.D. 96, 240
Gannon, T.L. 70, 136, 192
Gansneder, B. 195–196
Gardner, H. 8
Garfield, C.A. 73
Garland, D.J. 5, 23–24, 26, 95
Garland, H. 174
Garner, W.R. 52
Gaul, C.A. 223, 225
Gauron, E. 71, 186
Gayton, W.F. 177
Gellatly, A. 6
Giannini, J. 196
Giard, M.H. 222
Gibson, J.J. 28
Gill, D.F. 150, 154
Gill, D.L. 155
Gilleece, D. 112, 114, 202
Gilliland, L. 147
Gilmartin, K.A. 24

Glas, R.A. 77, 122, 241
Glaser, R. 21, 248
Glencross, D.J. 31, 61
Glisky, M. 220
Golding, J.M. 208, 210
Gonon, M.A. 222
Gopher, D. 49, 56, 60–62, 170
Gordon, S. 69
Gould, D. 71, 74–76, 104,
    127–128, 169–171, 175, 177,
    179–180, 183–185, 187–188,
    193–196, 211
Goulet, C. 50, 85, 111
Graham, S. 23, 26, 95
Grasha, A.F. 148
Graydon, J. 108
Green, L.B. 194
Groden, G. 217
Groden, J. 217
Grouios, G. 213
Guerin, B. 12

Haberlandt, K. 9, 11, 51, 58–59,
    104, 140
Hackfort, D. 190–191
Hagen, J.W. 107
Hale, B.D. 211, 225
Hall, C.R. 19, 202, 206, 208,
    210–211, 214, 216, 220, 224
Hall, E.G. 190–191, 212
Hall, M. 196
Halle, M. 82
Hamill, J. 184
Hampson, P.J. 5, 46, 52, 58, 104,
    236
Han, M. 70, 135–136, 192
Handford, C. 23, 26–27, 31, 207
Hanin, Y.L. 185
Hanninen, O. 137
Hanrahan, S. 5
Hardy, C.J. 190–191, 212
Hardy, L. 77, 134, 148, 158,

160–161, 168, 170–171, 185,
    187–188, 195, 198, 219, 226
Harris, B.L. 170–171
Harris, D.V. 170–171, 187, 190,
    193, 215–217, 220–221
Harris, H. 120
Hart, A. 21
Hartley, A. 56, 110
Harvey, N. 30
Hashman, J. 72
Hatfield, B.D. 134–135, 138,
    180, 240
Hawkins, H.L. 257
Hayes, A. 59
Hayes, J.R. 18, 21
Hayes, L. 114
Haywood, K. 184
Head, H. 16
Heaney, S. 201, 203
Hearns, J.F. 177
Hecker, J.E. 226
Helin, P. 137
Hemery, D. 210
Henderson, S.E. 213
Hernandez-Peon, R. 42
Herrigel, E. 41, 106, 190
Heuer, H. 32, 207
Highlen, P.S. 75, 196
Hilgard, E.R. 6, 42
Hill, A.K. 155, 157
Hillger, L.A. 207
Hilliard, D.V. 157–158
Hinshaw, K. 208, 213–214, 216
Hird, J.S. 206, 214, 218
Hirst, W. 52, 54–56, 58, 60–61
Hoberman, J. 12
Hodge, K. 196
Hodgson, G. 127
Hoeffel, T.D. 155
Hoffman, R.R. 236
Holyoak, K.J. 10–11
Horan, J.J. 206, 214, 218
Horn, M.A. 261, 266

Horsley, C. 144
Horstman, D.H. 109, 283
Horvat, M. 184
Houlston, D.R. 79, 81
Howard, D.E. 25
Howe, B.L. 212–213, 220
Howe, S.R. 109
Huey, E.G. 59
Hull, C.L. 185

Ingram, R.E. 128–129, 239, 261
Ingvar, D.H. 204, 240
Irvine, D. 111
Isaac, A.R. 204–205, 215, 217, 222
Isaacs, L.D. 81, 84
Ittyerah, M. 212

Jackson, A. 174, 193
Jackson, S. 74, 128, 179–180
Jackson, S.A. 73–76, 104, 122, 128, 175–176, 179–180, 211
Jacobson, E. 183, 189, 204, 218, 219
Jahoda, G. 182
James, W. 7, 32, 37, 39, 41–42, 55, 57, 103, 105, 110, 167, 204, 237
Janssen, J.J. 208, 209, 226
Jeannerod, M. 174, 208, 218, 222
Jenkins, S. 79
Johnson, M. 69
Johnson, P. 221, 224
Johnston-O'Connor, E.J. 196
Johnston, W.A. 109, 277
Jones, G. 168–169, 188, 195
Jones, J.G. 184, 186
Jones, K. 102
Jonides, J. 41
Jordan, J.A. 47, 60, 240
Jowdy, D.P. 159–160, 204, 210,

213, 215–217, 220–222, 224
Judd, C.H. 12

Kaczor, L.M. 226
Kahneman, D. 45, 47–48, 50, 53–54, 56, 59–61, 63, 187
Kahney, H. 18
Karoly, P. 4
Karp, S.A. 256
Kavanagh, D. 205
Keane, M.T. 8, 10, 15, 32, 39, 41, 45–46, 55, 60, 105, 116, 136, 228, 236, 240–241, 246, 250, 256
Keele, S.W. 257
Kelly, G.A. 33
Kelso, J.A.S. 28
Kerr, J.H. 76
Kiecker, P.L. 103
Kimble, G.A. 129
Kimiecik, J.C. 74
Kinchla, R.A. 53
Kirschenbaum, D.S. 3, 147–148, 196, 245
Kiss, G. 245
Kjellberg, A. 110
Klatzky, R.L. 118
Klein, G.A. 20
Klinger, E. 77, 122, 240
Koenig, O. 39, 120, 216, 223
Kohl, R.M. 218, 223
Kok, A. 140
Koning, P. 13, 24–25, 86
Konttinen, N. 134, 137
Konttinen, R. 134
Korn, E.R. 204, 211
Kosslyn, S.M. 39, 52, 120, 207, 216, 223
Kozar, B. 124, 126
Krampe, R.T. 19, 33, 40, 207, 227, 237, 242
Krane, V. 183–185

Kremer, J. 13, 34, 77, 175, 188, 193
Krenz, E.W. 211–212
Krenz, V.D. 211–212
Kubitz, K.A. 70, 135–136, 192
Kugler, P.N. 26
Kyllo, L.B. 174

La Ritz, T. 78, 81
LaBerge, D. 59
Lacey, J.I. 110, 137–139
Lachman, J.C.L. 6, 8, 43, 238
Lachman, R. 6, 8, 43, 238
Lahey, B.B. 182
Laidlaw, R. 209
Lambert, M.J. 154–155, 235
Landers, D.M. 67, 70, 77, 123, 134–141, 146–148, 150, 174, 180, 184, 191–192, 205–206, 213–214, 218–219, 223, 225–226
Larsen, B. 223
Lashley, K.S. 12
Lasnik, H. 8
Lassen, N.A. 223
Latham, G.P. 174–175
Laurie, C.A. 71
Laux, L. 122
Le Vaseur, P. 217
Le Voi, M. 245
Lee, C. 198, 226
Lee, D.N. 28, 30
Lee, T.D. 19
Lee, W. 156
Leith, L.M. 126
Lejeune, M. 212
Lerner, J.D. 128
Lesser, M. 160
Levey, A.J. 154, 157
Levy, P. 237
Lewis, D.A. 240
Lewis, M.W. 248

Lidor, R. 34, 72, 168, 172, 198
Lightner, J.M. 104, 108, 157
Linder, D.E. 68, 73, 75, 136, 155–157, 212, 216
Lindley, S. 23
Line, L. 115
Lishman, J.R. 30
Liu, Z. 12
Lobmeyer, D.L. 180
Locke, E.A. 174–175
Loehr, J.E. 5, 122, 127, 170, 172, 186
Logan, G.D. 54, 58–59, 228, 229
Lohman, D. 11
Lord, R.H. 124, 126
Lovejoy, J. 67
Lovie, S. 44
Lowes, R. 79, 81
Luria, A.R. 197
Lynn, S.J. 155
Lyytinen, N. 134, 137

Mackay, D.G. 214
Mackey, L. 5
Mackworth, N.H. 84
Magill, R.A. 19
Mahoney, M.J. 74–76, 134, 158–160, 169, 183, 186, 193, 215, 219
Malik, F. 128
Malott, J.M. 109
Marks, D.F. 204
Marquie, J.M. 49
Marsden, K.A. 155
Martens, R. 168, 186
Martin, C. 72, 168, 170, 175, 186, 206, 229
Martin, K.A. 206, 281
Masson, M.E.J. 15, 20
Masters, K.S. 126, 129,,153–155, 235
Masters, R.S.W. 126, 281

Mathews, A. 7, 250, 252–253, 255
Matlin, M.W. 6, 8, 39, 41, 104, 125, 202, 223, 236, 244, 246
Maxeiner, J. 77
Maxwell, B. 116
McCaffrey, N. 74, 104, 120, 211
McCaul, K. 109
McClelland, J.L. 10
McCrone, J. 80
McCullagh, P. 27
McIlvanney, H. 115
McKenzie, A.D. 212
McLean, J. 147, 149, 243, 247
McLean, N.J. 13, 195, 202, 204, 206–207, 210, 212–215, 221–222, 225
McLeod, P. 57, 79, 80, 81
McNally, R.J. 250
McPherson, S.L. 23, 249
McQueen, C. 211–212
McShane, J. 8
Mechikoff, R.A. 124, 126
Meichenbaum, D. 195, 196
Merrill, S. 152
Mestre, D.R. 83
Metzler, J. 205, 223, 239
Meyers, A.W. 155, 184, 186, 194–195, 204, 211, 230
Michel, F. 203–204, 223
Miller, E. 204
Miller, K. 69, 147–148, 257
Miller, L. 221
Miller, P.H. 246
Miller, S. 212
Mineka, S. 252
Mitchell, H. 80
Molander, B. 137
Monroe, S. 196
Montgomery, M. 14, 37
Moore, W.E. 177
Moran, A. 7, 8, 20, 76, 127, 170, 202–203, 205, 210, 212–213, 215–216, 220, 237
Moray, N. 45
Morgan, R.L. 11, 19
Morgan, W.P. 76–77, 109, 149, 151–158, 240
Morris, A. 83
Morris, P.E. 5, 46, 52, 104, 236–237
Morris, T. 176, 202, 207, 213, 225, 230, 235, 238
Mumford, M.J. 220
Murphey, M. 34, 72, 168, 172, 198
Murphy, S.M. 5, 160, 204, 209–211, 213, 216–222, 224–225
Murray, K.D. 154, 157
Mycielska, K. 116, 118, 259

Nacson, J. 226, 228
Navon, D. 56, 60
Neal, R.J. 13, 24–25, 86
Neill, W.T. 256
Neiss, R. 186, 189
Neisser, U. 7, 8, 12, 20, 46, 54, 58, 60, 205
Nelson, D. 77, 134, 158, 160–161, 185, 198
Nelson, J.E. 103
Newell, A. 11, 24
Nicklaus, J. 124, 167, 170
Nideffer, R.M. 72, 116, 121, 133–134, 142–150, 161–162, 170, 188–189, 194, 198, 256
Nigro, G. 206
Nisbett, R.E. 75, 141–142
Noble, J.M. 150, 154
Norman, D.A. 15, 54, 117, 237
Nougier, V. 259

O'Connor, P.J. 154

O'Keeffe, J. 125
O'Reilly, K. 23
Ogles, B.M. 155
Ojala, D. 195–196
Okwumabua, T.M. 155, 230
Oltman, P.K. 256
Onestak, D.M. 190, 213
Orlick, T. 41, 72, 74, 103–104,
    118, 120, 168–173, 189, 201,
    210–211, 213, 229
Oseen, M. 156
Osherson, D.N. 8

Paarsalu, M.E. 23, 26, 95
Paas, F.G.W. 70
Padgett, V.R. 155, 157
Pailhous, J. 83
Paivio, A. 206
Palmer, C. 13–14, 37
Palmer, S.L. 222
Pani, J.R. 207
Papathanasopoulu, P.P. 149
Parasuraman, R. 40, 44
Parfitt, G. 187
Pargman, D. 151
Parker, H. 88
Parkes, K.R. 259–261
Parrish, M.W. 209
Partington, J. 74, 169, 210
Pashler, H. 47, 49, 58, 72
Patmore, A. 116
Pay, C. 128
Pearson, P. 128
Pein, R.L. 179
Pelton, T. 138
Pendleton, L.R. 5
Pennebaker, J.W. 4, 104, 108,
    157, 208
Peper, E. 71, 170–172, 190
Perkins, T.S. 76, 134, 158–159,
    169
Perlmutter, L.C. 129

Peronnet, F. 222
Perry, A.R. 71
Perry, C. 176, 202, 207, 213,
    225, 230
Petersen, S.E. 40, 51, 52
Peterson, K. 196
Petitpas, A.J. 196–197
Petrakis, E. 86
Petruzzello, S.J. 70, 135–136,
    191, 192
Philips, H.C. 42
Phillips, W.A. 223
Pittenger, J. 14, 37
Plowman, S.A. 184
Polich, J. 140
Pollock, M.L. 76, 77, 149,
    151–158, 240
Pongrac, J. 216
Pope, K.S. 106, 281
Posner, M.I. 39–40, 45, 49,
    51–52, 61, 117, 178, 224,
    258–259, 261
Potter, S. 74, 113, 115–116
Power, M.J. 253, 256
Prapavessis, H. 81
Price, C. 128
Privette, G. 73

Qi, W.M. 140–141
Qiu, Y. 12
Quinlan, P.T. 11

Radford, P. 104
Ramanaiah, N. 196
Raskin, E. 256
Ravizza, K. 184, 189
Ray, W.J. 110, 135
Reason, J. 116, 118, 259
Reddish, P.E. 30
Reddy, P. 44, 187
Reed, E.S. 14, 28, 37, 93

Rees, E. 21, 248
Reeves, A. 223
Regan, E.C. 212
Regian, J.W. 47, 60, 240
Regnier, G. 94
Reimann, P. 248
Reisberg, D. 147, 149, 243, 247
Reissinger, C.A. 211
Rellinger, E.R. 240
Reynolds, P. 55–56
Reynolds, R.I. 21, 287
Richardson, A. 202–207, 210,
    212–215, 221–222, 225
Richardson, P.A. 82, 175
Ripoll, H. 5, 79, 84, 90
Rishe, H.L. 211–212
Rivera, P.M. 196–197
Roberts, G.C. 175–176
Roberts, J. 114, 119–121, 123,
    126
Roche, P. 67
Rodgers, W.M. 202, 208, 210–211
Roenker, D.L. 218, 223
Roepke, N. 195
Roland, P.E. 223
Rose, D.J. 77, 89, 94
Ross, D. 27
Ross, S.L. 212
Rossi, B. 13, 140
Rotella, R.J. 128, 171, 178,
    195–196
Rothbart, M.K. 51–52
Roy, E.J. 41
Rugg, M.D. 140
Rumelhart, D.E. 10–11, 15
Rushall, A. 196
Rushall, B.S. 195–196
Russell, D.G. 25, 83–84
Russell, S.J. 33–34, 94
Ryan, E.D. 214

Sachs, M.L. 153, 156, 168

Sackett, R.S. 218, 221, 224
Salazar, W. 70, 134, 136, 191,
    192
Salmela, J. 33–34, 94, 149
Salthouse, T.A. 21, 38
Samuels, M. 191
Samuels, N. 191
Sanchez, X. 212
Sargent, G.I. 70, 123, 133,
    143–145, 150, 154, 157, 170,
    172–173, 203
Sarrazin, C. 82
Savelsbergh, G.J.P. 28
Schedlowski, M. 152
Scheier, M.F. 122, 129
Schill, T. 196
Schleser, R.A. 155, 195, 204,
    211, 230
Schmid, A. 71, 170–172, 190
Schmidt, D. 214, 224
Schmidt, R.A. 14–17, 34–35,
    59, 118, 180, 214, 222,
    226–228
Schneider, D.J. 209, 215
Schneider, S. 79
Schneider, W. 50, 57–59, 90–91,
    108, 228
Schomer, H.H. 152, 154, 157,
    241
Schutz, R.W. 251–252
Schwenkmezger, P. 122, 190–191
Scully, D. 13, 34, 77, 175, 188,
    193
See, J.E. 109
Seger, C. 207
Seibert, P.S. 108, 122
Seiderman, A. 79
Seiler, R. 168
Shalvey, J. 179
Shannon, C.E. 8
Shaw, W.A. 218, 220
Shea, J.B. 11, 19
Shebilske, W.L. 47, 60, 240

Sheedy, A. 77
Sheikh, A.A. 208–209, 226
Shelton, T.O. 193
Shepard, R.N. 205, 223, 239
Shiffrin, R.M. 46, 57–59, 90,
    108, 228
Showers, C.J. 94, 126, 129–130
Sihvonen, R. 137
Silva, J.M. 156
Simon, H.A. 7, 11, 18, 21,
    24–25, 38, 94–95, 228
Simons, J. 214
Singer, J.L. 127
Singer, R.N. 13, 34, 72, 168,
    172, 198, 244
Singh, M.L. 156
Skelton, J.M. 41
Skinhoj, E. 223
Smith, A. 153
Smith, D. 220
Smith, R.E. 251–252
Smoll, F.L. 251–252
Smyth, M.M. 5, 237
Soloway, E. 21
Solso, R.L. 9, 41
Spelke, E. 58
Spellman, B. 10–11
Srull, T.K. 41
Starkes, J.L. 12, 23, 25–26, 38,
    94–96
Stauth, C. 184, 201
Stein, G.L. 74
Stein, J.F. 259
Steptoe, A. 128
Stevenson, J.R. 177
Stikes, J. 109
Stitcher, T. 175
Straub, W.F. 3–5, 12–13
Strom, E.H. 155
Strong, M.H. 47, 60, 240
Stroop, J.R. 253
Suinn, R.M. 191, 203, 207,
    219–220, 227

Suls, J. 109
Summers, J. 28, 40, 45, 60,
    68–70, 83–84, 135, 139, 235,
    238
Summers, J.J. 28, 40, 45, 60,
    68–70, 83–84, 135, 139,
    147–148, 154, 157, 194,
    226, 235, 238, 257
Surburg, P.R. 212
Sutton, S.K. 252
Swets, J.A. 192, 212
Swift, E.J. 12
Syer, J. 114, 129, 229

Takenaka, K. 184, 188,
    190–191, 193
Taylor, J. 229
Tenenbaum, G. 5
Tennant, L.K. 34, 72, 168, 172,
    198
Tesch-Romer, C. 19, 33, 40, 207,
    227, 237, 242
Tewes, U. 152
The PDP Research Group 10
Thelen, E. 28
Thomas, J.R. 21–23, 33, 206,
    214, 217, 238, 249
Thomas, K.T. 21–22, 33, 238
Thomson, J.A. 30
Thornley, G. 111, 121, 126–
    127
Thornton, B. 120
Titchener, E.B. 43
Todd, P.M. 10–11
Tolman, E.C. 174
Townsend, A. 104
Treisman, A.M. 48, 53, 59
Triplett, N. 12
Trudel, P. 34
Turner, P.E. 223
Turner, R.G. 147
Turvey, M.T. 26, 28–31

Udry, E. 177, 183, 185, 187–188
Umilta, C. 49, 62, 70, 86, 89–90,
    149, 258
Ungerleider, S. 208, 210

Vallacher, R.R. 116–118, 129
Vallerand, R.J. 148–149
van de Sande, C. 13
Van der Heijden, A.H.C. 42
Van Esbeck, E. 101
Van Gyn, G.H. 223, 225
Van Meerienboer, J.J.G. 70
Van Raalte, J.L. 68, 73, 75, 136,
    155–157, 196–197, 212, 216
Van Raalte, N.S. 68, 73, 75, 136,
    212, 216
Van Schoyck, S.R. 148
Vealey, R.S. 167–168, 172, 176,
    184, 194, 204, 211, 218, 221,
    229
Vieria, A. 59
Viviani, P. 31–32

Wachtel, P. 47, 110, 141, 143
Walter, S.M. 167, 172, 176, 184,
    194, 204, 211, 218, 221, 229
Wang, M.Q. 123, 137
Wankel, L. 156
Warm, J.S. 109
Washburn, M.F. 204, 219
Wasserman, E.A. 180
Watson, J.B. 44, 205–206
Watson, L. 153
Weaver, W. 8
Webster, R. 93
Webster, W. 153
Wechsler, D. 147
Wegner, D.M. 4, 105–107, 117,
    131, 208–209, 215, 238, 248
Weinberg, R.S. 71–72, 82,
    125–127, 168–171, 174–175,

177, 183, 193–195, 215, 222,
    229, 230
Weiss, M.R. 27
Welford, A.T. 14
Wellman, H.M. 245–246, 248
Wells, A. 8
Weltman, G. 141
Wenger, H.A. 223, 225
Wheeler, G. 156
Whelan, J.P. 184, 186, 194
White, A. 219
White, J. 172
White, S.A. 160
White, T.L. 209, 215
Whitfield, K.E. 124, 126
Whiting, H.T.A. 96–97
Wickens, C.D. 41, 48–49, 56
Wicklund, R.A. 110
Wiggins, D.K. 204
Wilkes, R.L. 194, 226
Wilkinson, M.O. 240
Williams, A.M. 27, 96
Williams, J.M. 12–13, 27, 73,
    96, 187, 190, 193–195, 220
Williams, M. 23, 26, 27, 31,
    207
Williams, R. 74
Williamson, J.E. 47, 60, 240
Wilson, T.D. 75, 141–142
Wilson, V. 146
Win, Z. 128
Wine, J. 129
Winter, G. 72, 168, 170, 175,
    186, 229
Witkin, H.A. 256
Wittrock, D.A. 196, 245
Wolpe, J. 211
Wood, G. 6
Woolfolk, R. 209
Woolfolk, R.L. 209, 211, 213,
    217, 221, 224–225
Wright, C.E. 15
Wrisberg, C.A. 178–179, 226

Yandell, J. 92, 121, 221
Yekovich, C.W. 96, 240
Yekovich, F.R. 96, 240
Yerkes, R.M. 185

Zaichkowsky, L. 184, 188,
    190–193
Zani, A. 13, 140
Zimbardo, P. 43, 53
Zinsser, N. 137–139, 179, 194
Zukier, H. 107

Subject index

Absent-mindedness 259-60
Action slips 259-60, 261
Adversity training 172-3
Alertness 39, 40, 63
  and attention 69, 70, 183
  physiology of 50-2
  "psych up/down" techniques
    183-4
American football 71, 95, 172
  arousal enhancement 193
Anticipation 80-2, 83
Anxiety 83, 106, 107, 144-5
  see also Worry
  and attentional narrowing 93,
    133, 254-7
  "Choking" under pressure 126-30
  effect on concentration 242-3,
    248, 250-4, 255
  effect on memory 255
  "hypervigilance" theory 254-6
Archery 12, 34, 87, 123, 134-5, 143
  attentional style in 143
  and concentration exercises
    172
  and heart rate 136-7, 136-9
  pre-performance routines 176,
    177, 180, 183-4

Arousal xii, 77, 78, 93-4, 113, 140-1,
    147, 162
  and attention 187
  control 173-4, 183-94
  definition 184-5
  enhancement 192-3
  and mental practice 226
  multi-dimensional nature of
    186-7
  reduction 188-92
  in sport performance 184-7
Association/dissociation
  in marathon running 151-8,
    255-6
  research 155-7, 157-8
Associationism
  and motor skills 15
Associative concentration strategies
  134
Athletes
  attentional processes 65, 98-9
  cognitive processes 94-7
  profiles of successful 75-6
  selective attention in 67
  thoughts and images 13
  views on concentration 67-8,
    71-3, 98

Attention xi, 1, 5, 6, 9, 17, 98
  see also Concentration;
    Distractions
  and arousal 187
  capacity models 54-7
  characteristics 37-63
  divided 46, 48-50, 63, 71-2, 77,
    86-91
  and expertise 80-2
  flexible 42, 71, 149-50, 156
  history of research 43-6
  individual differences 60-2, 240-1
  "internal" determinants 238-9
  lapses in 101-31, 238-9
  measuring 65, 133-63, 257-61
  and mental practice 225-9
  meta-attention 99, 105, 149, 233,
    243-9
  metaphors 41-2
  "narrowing" under pressure 92-4
  nature 39-43
  physiology 50-2
  and practice 57-60, 61
  psychology 1, 7
  psychophysiological correlates
    133
  selective 46-8, 63, 70, 71, 77-80,
    82, 91-2
  as a skill 57-60, 61, 91, 92, 98-9
  in sport 34
  strategies 76-7
  theories 45-6, 52-7, 63
  types of 46-52
Attentional flexibility 42, 71, 149-50,
    156, 163, 257-8
  in soccer 257-8
Attentional Focusing Questionnaire
    157-8
Attentional processes x, 65, 98-9,
    133-63, 142, 147, 149
  in marathon runners 150-8
Attentional style 142-50
Attribution 5
Australian Institute for Sport 145
Automaticity 58-60, 87-8, 118, 129,
    237
  in sport 4, 59, 88, 179, 227-9
Badminton 83-4, 126
Ball games
  catching 28, 88
  fast 28, 78-9, 98

throwing 12, 17, 79
Bangor Sport Psychological Skills
    Inventory 160-1, 163
Baseball 78, 79, 123
  expert/novice differences 249
Basketball 26, 49, 95, 143, 174
  anxiety 92-3
  attentional style in 143, 144
  distractions 115-6, 124
  eye-movements 85
  pre-performance routines 177,
    179, 184
  "thought sampling" 241
Behaviourist approach 8, 13, 14, 15,
    24, 44, 238
Biofeedback 136, 138
  training 191-2
Bowling 34, 134
  pre-performance routines 178
Boxing 102
  gamesmanship in 114, 121
Brain states 133-6
Breath control 184, 188-9, 189,
    192
Broadbent's theory of attention 86,
    113
Capacity model 54-7
Cardiac acceleration/deceleration
    110, 136-9, 161-2
Catastrophe model 187
Chess 18, 21, 24, 94, 95
"Choking" under pressure 126-30,
    131, 236
  in snooker 127
  in tennis 127
Co-ordination 29-30
  of skilled behaviour 63
Cognition 8-9
  and action 32
  behavioural consequences 8
  connectionist approach 31
  definition 6-7
  meta-cognition 33, 244-9
  in sport 32-4, 37
  symbolic approach 10, 31, 36
Cognitive advantage 38
Cognitive Failures Questionnaire
    259-61
Cognitive Interference
    Questionnaire 122
Cognitive performance 9-10

Cognitive processes 1, 7, 8, 46, 94, 151, 248-9
Cognitive psychology
    in sport 12, 32-4
Cognitive style 256-7
Cognitive theories 4, 6, 7-8, 27, 28, 29, 218-9
Communication theory 8
Compliments 114-5
Computational approach 237
Computer model of mind 45
Conation, definition 6
Concentration
    see also Attention; Distractions
    exercises xii, 171-3
    flexibility 42
    importance in sport 65, 72, 97
    lapses 101-31, 238-9
    long-term in cricket 69-70
    and mental practice 202-3
    nature ix, 39, 70-2
    practical principles 242-3
    practice 42
    processes 63
    psychometric tests 134
    research 68-99, 77-8, 91-2, 133-63
    skills x, xi, 39, 98, 133-4, 142, 168, 198-9, 236
    and sport performance 134, 147
    techniques 165-200
    views of athletes 67-8, 72-3
    views of sport psychologists 71-3
Connectionism 8, 10-11, 20, 27, 31
    see also Neural network; Parallel distributed processing
Contextual interference 11
Control, loss of 4
Controlled processes 59
Cricket 16, 68, 69-70, 83-4, 98
    distractions 103, 115
    expert/novice differences 80-1
    selective attention 79-80
Cue utilisation theory 77, 78-9, 82, 83-4
Cue-words xii, 172-3, 193, 194-7
Cues 25, 26, 73, 92, 93, 98
    and anxiety 128, 252
    misleading 258-9
    task-relevant 89, 94, 121, 129, 178
Cycling 12, 33-34, 116

arousal enhancement 193
Decision-making 5, 82, 84, 96, 99
    in cycling 34
    expert/novice differences 96
    and heart rate 137
    in squash 82
    in tennis 33, 82
Direct perception theory 27-32, 36
    see also Natural physical theory
Discipline, mental 4
Discus throwing 182
Dissociative concentration strategies 134
Distractibility 75-6, 233, 247
Distraction, defined 103-5
Distraction control 246
Distractions 1, 41-2, 101-31, 136
    see also Attention; Concentration
    anxiety 83, 93, 106, 107, 126-30, 144-5
    auditory 112-3
    compliments 114-5
    in cricket 103
    effects on performance 102, 108
    external 71, 75-6, 82, 103-4, 109-21
    fatigue 33, 107, 125-6
    in golf 104
    and injury 123
    internal 4, 46, 71, 75-6, 103-5, 109-10, 121-31
    intimidation 115-6
    noise 83, 103, 110-3
    pain 107, 108-9
    regrets 123
    "screening out" 77
    in soccer 104
    stress 107
    in tennis 73, 104, 107, 111, 119-20
    visual 110, 119-21
Divided attention 46, 48-50, 63, 71-2, 77, 86-91
    in athletes 86-7
    in basketball 86
    and dual-task paradigm 91
    in tennis 50
Diving 116, 120
    attentional style in 144
    and mental practice 208
Drive theory 185
Drugs 5, 125

Dual-task paradigm 86-91, 94, 98,
    133, 140-1, 162
Electroencephalogram (EEG) 133,
    134-6, 161-2
Emotion
    effect on performance x, 3-4, 92,
        99, 106, 250-4
    neglect of 7, 34
Endurance events 109
Endurance march 156-7
Energy
    in "flow states" 74-5
Event-related cortical potentials
    (ERP) 134-5, 140
Evoked potentials 134-5, 140
Expert/novice differences 5, 18, 22,
    38, 67, 98
    see also Expertise
    attention 91-2, 95, 262
    in basketball 26
    in cricket 80-1
    in decision-making 96
    eye-movements 84-6
    information processing 80
    in karate 25
    in parachute jumping 122
    in pistol shooting 89
    in snooker 25
    in spatial cueing tasks 259
    in tennis 23-4, 78-9, 80-2
    in volleyball 26, 86
Expertise 20-27, 239-40
    see also Expert/novice differences
    athletic xi, 1, 19, 21-2, 25, 26, 34,
        38
    and attention 80-2, 92, 95-7
    and eye-movements 84-6
    "hardware/"software" 20, 80-1,
        91-2, 94
External distractions 71, 75-6, 82,
    103-4, 109-21
Eye-movements 84-6, 97
Fatigue 33, 150-1
    effect on concentration 107,
        125-6, 248
Fear
    of danger 122
    of failure 106, 126, 128, 130
Field independence 256
Figure skating 27
    see also Skating

focusing strategies 76
Filter models of attention 52-4, 86
Fitness
    and concentration 72
"Flow states" 65, 73-5, 136, 179
Focusing skills see Attention
Football
    American 71, 95, 172
    Australian Rules 93, 123
    Gaelic 125
    rugby 101, 112
    soccer 4, 5, 67, 73, 83-4, 104, 115,
        120, 123, 143, 257-8
"Fortune telling" 123-4
Gamesmanship 110, 113-8, 131
    in boxing 114
    in tennis 113-4
Gestalt 11
Goal-setting xii, 35, 174-6
Goals 14
    performance 28, 175-6
    result 175-6
Golf 27, 34, 70, 73, 74, 143
    attentional style 143
    distractions 104, 112-3, 120, 123,
        124-5
    and heart rate 137, 138-9
    mental imagery 211
    pre-performance routines 176,
        177, 178, 179
Grunting 111-2
Gymnastics 34, 59, 75, 82, 143
    attentional style 143
    self-talk 194
"Haka" dance 193
Heart rate 133, 134-9
    acceleration 137, 184
    deceleration 136-9
    and information processing 137
    measures 136-9, 161-2
High-jumping 118-9
    and mental practice 208
Hockey 124
Hurdle running 89
    arousal enhancement 193
Imagery rehearsal see Mental
    practice
Importance in sport, concentration
    65, 72
Information processing 1, 6-7, 11-14,
    80, 90, 97

expert/novice differences 80, 97
and heart rate 137
nature of 28-9, 30
research 45
symbolic approach 8-9, 10, 19,
    27, 35, 96
theories 28
Intelligence 7-8
Intentional monitoring system 106-7
Internal distractions 4, 46, 71, 75-6,
    103-5, 109-10, 121-31
Intimidation 115-6
Introspection 141-2
Inverted-U hypothesis 185-7
Ironic monitoring system 106-7, 248,
    262
Jogging 108
    see also Marathon Running;
        Running
Karate 25
Kinaesthetic feedback 213-4, 218,
    219, 220, 228
Knowledge
    connectionist theory 11
    declarative 97
    episodic 9, 97
    expert 21, 22
    and expert-novice differences
        94-7
    and practice 228-9
    procedural 9, 97
    semantic 9, 97
    strategic 97
    symbolic theory 11
Long-jumping 30, 192
"Lung-gom" 152-3
Marathon running xi, 71, 109, 149
    see also Jogging; Running
    arousal enhancement 192
    association/dissociation 151-8,
        255-6
    attentional processes in 150-8,
        162
    focusing strategy 76
    monotony 151, 152
    pain 152
    "wall" experience 152, 156
Martial arts 111-2
Meditation 190-1
    Trancendental 190-1
    Zen 188, 190-1

Memory 5, 9, 17, 46, 244-5
    procedural 24
    and sport skills 13, 19, 25-6, 95
    working 24, 78, 93
Mental chronometry 9
Mental control 4, 35
Mental effort 70-1
    and physical action 237-8, 262
Mental imagery 5, 8, 13, 35, 177, 202
    see also Mental practice
    in basketball 230
    in cricket 225
    in golf 211
    in gymnastics 226
    negative 208-9, 215
    positive 208-9
    in squash 211
    in tennis 222, 225-6, 229
Mental organisation 9
Mental practice 165-6, 191, 201-32
    see also Mental imagery
    and arousal 226
    and attention 225-9
    cognitive theories 218-9, 221-5, 231
    as concentration technique
        202-3, 229-30
    definition 203-4, 231
    effect on performance 206, 206-7,
        209, 212-7, 230-1
    empirical research 230
    history of research 204-6
    and motivation 206
    neuromuscular theories 218-21
    physiological theories 219-21
    and strategic planning 222
    theories 217-25
Mental skills training 4-5, 156-7,
    168-200, 244
Meta-attention 99, 105, 149, 233,
    243-9, 262
Meta-cognition 33, 244-9
Mind, tendency to wander 85-6, 102,
    105-7, 131, 157-8, 248
Monotony, in marathon running 151
Motivation 7, 34, 185
    and concentration 72, 126
    inadequate 124-5, 131
    and mental practice 206, 245
Motor program 16, 180
Motor racing 74
Muscle memory 218

Music 13, 32
    distractions in 117-8
    divided attention in 55, 56, 58
Narrow attentional focus 77, 92-4,
    131, 133, 141, 162
Natural physical theory 27-32, 207
    see also Direct perception theory
Netball 88
Neural network 10
    see also Connectionism; Parallel
        distributed processing
Neuromuscular theories 218-21
Nideffer's theory of attentional
    styles 142-50, 162
    assumptions 143-5
Noise 83, 103, 110-3, 131
Occlusion paradigm 83-4, 85, 97, 98
Olympic Games 74, 104-5, 125,
    135-6, 169
Pain 107, 108-9, 150-1, 152-3, 156
Parachute jumping
    expert/novice differences in 122
Parallel distributed processing 10
    see also Connectionism; Neural
        network
"Paralysis-by-analysis" 114-5, 179
Pattern recognition 18
Peak performance 73-5, 98, 169
Perception 5, 99
Perception-action link 83
Performance 22
    enhancement 12
    mental factors ix-xii, 3-36
    in sport 22
Physiological changes
    EEG activity 135-6
    heart rate 40, 110, 136-9
    nausea 128
Pistol shooting 89-91, 134-6
    see also Rifle shooting; Shooting
    expert-novice difference 89, 98
    and heart rate 136-7
Playing conditions 110, 118-9
Practice 14, 27
    and attention 42, 57-60
    deliberate 18-19, 40, 237-8
    mental xii, 1, 13, 34, 35
Pre-performance routines xii, 173,
    176-83
    efficacy 179-81
    nature and functions 177-9

and superstitions 181-3
Pressure 124-5, 126, 131
Procedural knowledge 17
Processing systems 9, 79, 131
Production systems 14, 17, 27, 35,
    37-8
Progressive muscular relaxation 189
"Psych out" 114
Psychological Skills Inventories
    158-161, 163
Psychological Skills Inventory for
    Sports (PSIS) 159-60, 163
Psychological skills training xii,
    168-200
Psychophysiological measurement
    techniques 134-9, 134-40
    electroencephalogram 134-6
    heart rate 134-9
Race-walking, internal/external
    focus 158
Racquet sports 68, 83, 92
    see also Squash; Tennis
Refereeing 82
Regrets 123
Relaxation 69, 184, 188-9, 189, 230
    muscular 189-90, 192
Research
    absence of theory 235-6, 261
    benefits 236-43
    concentration 68-99, 77-8, 91-2,
        133-63
    mental practice 204-6
    new directions 243-61
    "thought sampling" 241
Result-consciousness 122, 181
Rifle shooting 34, 94, 135-8, 146, 172
    see also Pistol shooting; Shooting
    and heart rate 136-8
    pre-performance routines 180
Rowing
    attentional style in 144
Rugby 101, 112
    pre-performance routines 176,
        179
Running 89, 108, 125
    see also Jogging; Marathon
        running
Schema/Schemata 13-20, 27, 28, 35,
    95, 180, 228
Schemata, definitions 15-16
Scuba diving 141

Selective attention 46-8, 63, 70, 71, 77-80, 82
  in fast-ball sports 78-9
  implications for coaching 92
  as a skill 91-2
Self-consciousness 41, 115, 116-7, 122, 127, 129, 181
Self-hypnosis 153
Self-regulation 3, 4
Self-report procedures 141-2, 149
Self-talk
  effect on performance 196-7, 210
  instructional 174, 177, 194-6, 197
  negative 181, 195, 196, 197
  positive 195, 196-7
Serial processing 10
Shooting
  see also Pistol shooting; Rifle shooting
  attentional style in 144
Shot-putter 128-9
Skating
  see also Figure skating
  attentional style in 144
Skiing, and mental practice 207
Skill 72
  cognitive 17, 26, 29
  and concentration 72
  goal-directed 14, 35, 61
  instruction and performance 97
  learning xi, 11, 14, 17, 19, 27, 28, 31, 36, 88
  and memory 13, 16-17
  motor 17
  and problem solving 14, 35, 61
  representation 1, 15, 16-17, 35
  sequence 18
  talent/practice controversy 32-3
Snooker 25, 74, 101, 107, 125, 127
Soccer 4, 5, 67, 73, 83-4, 143
  attentional flexibility 257-8
  attentional style 143
  distractions 104, 115, 120, 123
Social factors 12, 34
Softball 87, 261
Spatial cueing tasks 258
  expert/novice differences 259
Sport Anxiety Scale 252
Sport performers see Athletes
Sport psychologists
  views on concentration 71-3

Sport psychology
  and competition 12
Spotlight metaphor of attention 41-2, 91, 127-8
Sprinting 5
  arousal enhancement 193
Squash 25, 76, 83-4, 98
  decision-making 82
  expert/novice differences 76
  eye-movements 85
  focusing strategies 76
  mental imagery 211
"Stage fright" 128
Strategic planning 222
  and mental practice 222
Stress 107, 150, 162
Superstitions 181-3
Swimming 67, 146
  instructional self-talk 194
Symbolic representation 8-9, 11
Table-tennis 28, 29, 79
  eye-movements 84, 90
TAIS 133-4, 142-50, 162
  Conceptual and methodological issues 148-50, 257
  Sport-specific versions 148
Tennis 18, 38, 83-4
  anxiety 126-7
  attentional style 144
  co-ordination 29
  concentration 3-4, 72, 101, 102
  cues 25
  decision-making 22, 33
  distractions 73, 104, 107, 111, 116, 118, 119, 120-1, 123, 125, 126-7
  divided attention 50, 89-90
  dual-task paradigm 89-90
  expert/novice differences 23-4, 78-9, 80-2, 249
  gamesmanship 113-4, 115, 116
  knowledge-base 97
  mental imagery 222, 225-6, 229
  motivation 125
  pre-performance routines 176
  schema/schemata 15, 16
  selective attention 78-9
Test of Attentional and Interpersonal Style see TAIS

Tests
    physiological 151
    psychometric 151
    ratings of perceived exertion 151
Training 14
United States Olympic Committee,
    102, 293
Visualisation *see* Mental imagery;
    Mental practice
Volleyball 49, 62, 86, 89, 92, 146
    dual-task paradigm 90
    expert/novice differences 86
    eye-movements 86
Weather 110, 118-9, 131, 156
Wechsler Adult Intelligence Scale
    147
Weight lifting
    arousal enhancement 193
    pre-performance routines 177
Winning 12, 35
Worry 73, 93, 106, 122, 124, 128,
    130, 250-2
    see also Anxiety
Wrestling 75, 75-6, 104-5, 128, 129
    pre-performance routines 179,
    180, 183
Yerkes-Dodson law 185-7
"Zone of optimal functioning" 185